Pearce. 1991.

# BLUE AND SCARLET

## BY THE SAME AUTHOR

Published by The Sportsman's Press
*Lionel Edwards: Master of the Sporting Scene* (1986)
*The World of Polo: Past and Present* (1986)
*A Concise Guide to Hunting* (1988)
*Millais: Three Generations in Nature, Art and Sport* (1988)
*A Concise Guide to Polo* (1989)
*Collecting Sporting Art* (Editor: 1988)
*Horse and Carriage: The Pageant of Hyde Park* (1990)

\* \* \* \*

*The Book of Foxhunting* (Batsford, 1977)
*Victorian and Edwardian Field Sports from
Old Photographs* (Batsford, 1978)
*Captain-General and Rebel Chief: The Life of James,
Duke of Monmouth* (Allen & Unwin, 1979)
*British and Irish Hunts and Huntsmen* 2 Vols (Batsford 1982)
*Sefton: The Story of a Cavalry Horse* (Souvenir, 1983)
*British and Irish Hunts and Huntsmen* Vol 3 (Batsford, 1986)

\* \* \* \*

*The World's Greatest Horse Stories* (Editor: Paddington, 1979)
*The World's Greatest Dog Stories* (Editor: Century Hutchinson, 1985)
*Gannet: The Story of a Terrier* (fiction: Ashford, 1990)

# AN AUTOBIOGRAPHY

# JNP WATSON

° THE °
SPORTSMAN'S
PRESS
*LONDON*

Published by The Sportsman's Press 1990

*To Lavinia with Love*

British Library Cataloguing in Publication Data

Watson, J. N. P. (John N. P.)
  Blue and scarlet: an autobiography.
  1. Sports. Reporting. Watson, J. N. P. (John N. P.)
  I. Title
  070.449796092

  ISBN 0–948253–42–8


Photoset and printed by
Redwood Press Limited, Melksham, Wiltshire

# Contents

Acknowledgments                                          6

List of illustrations                                    7

1  'Thirties Boyhood                                     9

2  Wartime Eton                                         18

3  Virginia and Westphalia                              30

4  The King's Cavalry                                   39

5  Against Two Colonels                                 60

6  Soldiering in the 'Sixties                           81

7  *Country Life*, Club Life and Wild Life             100

8  From the Hunting Field                              115
   *Dashing Midlands*                                  118
   *Proud South*                                       134
   *Golden North*                                      151
   *Merry Beaglers*                                    161
   *Buoyant Ireland*                                   172
   *Scarlet Coats Abroad*                              180

9  To the Polo Ground                                  208

10  Sussex Then and Now                                214

Index                                                  224

# *Acknowledgments*

My thanks are due to the Editor of *Country Life* for allowing me to quote from articles I contributed to the magazine between 1965 and 1989.

Many of the photographs come from my personal archives and it is not possible to trace all the photographers. I am grateful to Michael Chevis for copying some of the more precious originals, and for taking the recent photograph at Pannett's Shipley. I would also like to thank the following for permission to reproduce their photographs: Freudy Photos (Mrs John Hannum); John F. Hughes (Glamorgan, 1981); David A. Guiver (Triathlon); Bob Langrish (France, 1988); Jim Meads (Sinnington, 1971; Mrs Mollie Gregson; Ben Hardaway); Mike Roberts (polo); Mary Tarry (Waterford, 1983).

# List of Illustrations

*Facing page 32*

My mother.
My father.
JW in 1936.
1938: with 'Mr Smith'.

*Facing page 33*

Eton: heading for the Division Room.
Michael, Fourth of June 1942.
M'Tutor (Dick Routh) taking private study.

*Facing page 48*

Shooting VIII, 1944.
Lavinia as a debutante.
Moray playing the part of Bohun in Shaw's *You Never Can Tell*, 1966.

*Facing page 49*

Queen's Birthday Parade, Nicosia, Cyprus, 1957: leading my squadron past the saluting base.
Suez 1956.
Famagusta, Cyprus, 1958. Officers and senior NCOs of A Squadron of the Blues.

*Facing page 80*

Cyprus 1958: anti-terrorist strategem – donkey patrol for cooperation with armoured cars.
The officers of the Guards Independent Parachute Company assembled to mark my relinquishing command, 1961.
The Guards Parachute Company dressed for 'keeping the ground' at the Queen's Birthday Parade, 1960.

*Facing page 81*

Gibraltar, 1962: British and Spanish staffs during a visit to the Governor by the Governor of Algeciras province.
Rabat, 1962: changing ponies during a polo match against the Royal Moroccan Army.
Herford, Westphalia, 1964: greeting NCOs of Denmark's Jutland Dragoons during their visit to the Blues.

*Facing page 96*

Ronda, Spain, 1965: with Alastair Boyd at the start of one of our Andalusian rides.
1967: A Sovereign's Escort commander.

*Facing page 97*

The four joint-Masters posing on my Sinnington day in 1971.
1974: with Lavinia at Pannett's Shipley.
1971: Lavinia with the Radnor and West.

*Facing page 128*

December 1977: over a Galway Blazers' Wall.
November 1978: with the Cottesmore.
The Eton College Beagles, 1973.

*Facing page 129*

Tyrone and Caroline Waterford with their son, James, on my day with the
    Waterford foxhounds in 1983.
February 1981: Anthony and Fiona Martyn of the Glamorgan.

*Facing page 144*

Mrs Mollie Gregson, the Grand Old Lady of the Crawley and Horsham.
Derek Gardiner, huntsman to the Goathland at a meet in the 1986–7 season.

*Facing page 145*

Mrs John Hannum, Master of Mr Stewart's Cheshire, over a typical American
    stake-and-rail, 1974.
Ben Hardaway, Master and huntsman of the Midland since 1950.

*Facing page 176*

1988: receiving a warm French greeting.
At the start of the *curée* which concluded my day with the Rallye Vouzeron.

*Facing page 177*

A moment during the 1988 Pony Club polo championships.
England versus USA, Smith's Lawn, 1988.

*Facing page 192*

Competing with the *Country Life* Triathlon team.
Receiving my Churchill Fellowship award from Lord Tonypandy.

*Facing page 193*

Talking to the Prince of Wales with Lavinia.
1989: At Home.

# 1

# *'Thirties Boyhood*

My father who was the god of my childhood, was killed by a German shell in May 1940, leading his company of soldiers along the road to Dunkirk. And, as he was then still under forty, he was essentially a man of no other era than the 1920s and '30s. Being a foxhunter, fly fisherman, game shot and deer-stalker and having a fairly broad and active interest in the Turf, he was what was then regarded as an 'all-round sportsman'. He was, incidentally, a first-class tennis player, a scratch golfer and (at Charterhouse and Christ Church, Oxford) a prominent cricketer. But he would have classed those recreations firmly in the category of games, not sport. If someone had enquired of him, between the months of October and March, whether he had been 'enjoying good sport' he would have had no hesitation in replying in the context of the hunting season. Had he the same question put to him during the summer months he would have replied in terms of his fishing. He drove a bus during the 1926 General Strike (which he described as 'good sport'!).

If he were to return to life today to be told that I am one of *The Times* sporting correspondents – I cover the polo for the paper – he would correct me: 'You mean, don't you, that you're a *games* correspondent?' But if I then mentioned to him that, for over twenty years, I have been a sporting writer – i.e. the regular contributor of hunting articles to *Country Life* – he'd have agreed: 'that indeed makes you a *sporting* correspondent of the first order!'

The distinction carried subtle social overtones as well as its traditional significance. Games were either associated with schools and universities in both their recreational syllabi and their competitive motivation or, beyond the academic world, were tainted with professionalism, whereas the country sports – shooting, fishing, hunting, coursing and falconry – were more or less private matters. Racing, structured as it was into an exclusive hierarchy of stewards and owners, trainers, handicappers and starters, jockeys and other salary earners, was a sport that was a law unto itself. Other equestrian activities, such as hunter trials and showjumping, were sports (though the days of showjumping as a 'gentleman's sport' are long over), but polo was a game, along with tennis, golf and cricket. Some people made money out of those diversions. As for football and hockey, well . . .

The pursuits of hunting live quarries with hounds, which in many circles today are looked upon as crimes, or at best scarcely tolerated 'blood sports', still received such wide approval in my father's day that the opposition camp was a tiny minority. A high proportion of Britain's leading and most

respected families set an example by their indulgence in those sports, which
are steeped in the heritage of the British countryside. Attitudes changed
with the post-war social revolution; at the same time townsfolk, becoming
increasingly jealous of 'the countryman's privileged position', began to find
fault with his way of life. The anti field sports movement has never been
based exclusively on an animal welfare concern. Far from it.

A childhood memory from about 1934, still vividly recalled, is that of
unwrapping, in our Chelsea home, a birthday present consisting of a set of
brightly painted lead figures representing a huntsman, whipper-in and
half-a-dozen foxhounds, turning them over in a state of profound enchant-
ment, parading them with great care on the floor and hearing my father say
to my mother, 'just look at John's face, we've got a budding *sportsman* here!'
But it was not so much the vision of an impending chase that caught my
imagination as the sheer pageantry of the scarlet-coated men on their sparkling bay horses and the gaiety of the tricolour hounds.

I fantasised endlessly through my collection of model exotic animals,
completed with palm trees, oases and jungle scrub. I imagined our Siamese
cats as Bagheera and Shere Khan and myself as Mowgli, sharing their lives.
Kipling's *Jungle Books* were among the first I ever read. Lying in a London
hospital in 1936, recovering from the removal of tonsils and adenoids, I
received a visit, amid an aura of rarefied furs, painted fingernails and scent,
from a friend of my mother's, Angela Selby Lowndes, who spotted those
treasured volumes on my bedside table along with two or three others by the
same author. She told me she was 'a personal friend of dear Rudyard . . . and
how would you like it, John, if I got him to autograph them?' She whisked
them away, returning a couple of days later with the books unsigned, and
informing me that the great man had just died. I still have the books.

Animal suffering of any kind, or death – from a slight lameness or sore to
subjects of cruelty, from euthanasia to victims of traffic accidents – touched
me deeply. When our fat and dreamy cook, Lottie, upset boiling fat from a
frying-pan on the head of our cat, Mr Smith (our Chelsea house was in Smith
Street), soon reducing the dainty triangle of its chocolate-coloured ear to a
hairless stub of gristle, and rendering the sky-blue eye on that side of its
head to be tear-filled ever after, I lay for hours against the poor whining
creature's side in consolation.

Down with measles in my prep school's attic sick room one evening in
1936, I was reading Percy Fitzpatrick's bull-terrier story, *Jock of the Bushveldt*,
with those wonderful little drawings on every page by Edmund Caldwell,
when the matron came in to say 'lights out!' The curtains were drawn wide,
and a little later I was awoken by a sudden fierce gold and orange-red glow in
the sky. I went to the window to investigate; the heavens seemed to be
ablaze, though I could not understand why. The light was enough to read
by, and my only thought was what a wonderful opportunity it presented for
continuing *Jock* from a perch at the window. Anyone who knows that story
well must remember the opening words of the last chapter, describing the
tragic circumstances of the gallent dog's death: 'And Jock? I never saw my
dog again . . .' I wept so bitterly throughout it and lay awake for such sad

hours afterwards thinking about it that the matron must have noticed by red and swollen eyes when she came in cheerfully in the morning with this breezy enquiry: 'Well, I hope you weren't awake all night watching the Crystal Palace burn down?'

My parents referred to our little home near Petworth, in Sussex, as the weekend cottage, but it was where we spent nearly all our school holidays during the 1930s and, being in quite a remote spot, it was a delightful haven after school and in contrast to London. My father, who had a broad knowledge of wild life, encouraged my brothers and me to learn the names of the mammals, birds, trees and flowers, and taught us a great respect for Mother Nature. Pheasant copse, right next to the house, was the first favourite haunt, while Mens Wood, a little under a mile away, was sheer magic.

My mother came from Norfolk and most summer holidays we stayed a week or so at Blakeney on the county's north coast and messed about in boats or hid up with my father in the sand-dunes to watch the waders feeding, or on the marshes to see the wildfowl coming in to roost.

Notwithstanding all his reverence for nature my father taught us that it was good form, good sport and a useful exercise, too, to shoot verminous creatures along with game mammals and birds. He produced an exciting box of tricks, a toy that propelled cardboard pheasants, grouse and partridges, by means of elastic. The set included a pop gun with which we practised our childish marksmanship on the flicking paper targets. He presented me with a .410 bolt-action shotgun for my ninth birthday. The quarries then were rabbits, grey squirrels, pigeons, jays, crows and magpies. He taught me how to stalk rabbits and how to camouflage myself in a pigeon hide, but my favourite sport was grey squirrel shooting for which an old keeper called Brooker was my mentor. Now, far from being tempted to shoot a squirrel, I sink for a second in gloom every time I see the flattened body of one that has fallen victim to a motorist. Today, indeed, it saddens me to think of any creature bursting with joy, revelling in life one moment, eclipsed the next. My attitude was entirely different half a century ago. Squirrels have a crafty way of freezing high on a tree trunk or branch on the side that is blind to the shooter, and twisting, hide-and-seek fashion, around it, as the shooter circles. It was my delight as a boy to follow their arboreal ballet, their extraordinary branch-to-branch acrobatics until they froze on their chosen bark, and I crept this way and that until a breeze flaunted their give-away tails and I found the target. Brooker, the old keeper, taught me much, though having a strong Sussex brogue he was rather difficult to understand. One of the sadnesses, I think, of modern Britain is the vanishing of the county dialects.

So far as the ethics of squirrel shooting was concerned my conscience was salved not only by the fact that these American intruders had driven the pretty indigenous red squirrels from their rightful habitats but also because the greys were classified then, as they still are, as vermin on account of the damage they caused to trees. The Ministry of Agriculture offered a shilling for every grey squirrel tail turned in, and, during the war, there were other spin-offs. Colonel and Mrs Maitland, proprietors of a Petworth restaurant –

which traded under the charming name of the Four and Twenty Blackbirds (he was the waiter, she the cook) – bought the carcases in those meat-rationing days for what they called 'game pie'. (Squirrel, I thought, was meatier and richer than rabbit, sweeter than lamb). Anyhow, that was another 1s 6d per squirrel, and for a time I was getting 6d for each pelt, the fur helping the war effort, so far as I remember, in the capacity of felt for aircraft seats. That three shillings per squirrel mostly went into the .410 cartridge fund.

To return to the 1930s, Chelsea was an uncrowded village and the shops in King's Road, though delightful to me, were terribly drab I suppose compared with that thoroughfare's boutique-and-bistro image today. There was little movement in our Smith Street – a car or a taxi every now and then, an occasional scarlet-coated figure from the Royal Hospital, a scruffy cyclist in a black beret with a big bunch of onions for sale athwart his shoulder, a guardsman from Chelsea barracks, perhaps, residents taking their dogs for a run in Burton Court, an artist or an actor once in a while. None of the hectic bustle, a ghost of the traffic hum, of today. Talking of actors, Robert Newton occupied one of the flats in the new block at the end of the street, as my brother Moray and I remember well, because we were woken late one night by the sound of him chasing his wife down the middle of the street, hurling abuse and a variety of kitchen utensils at her back. We craned out of the window roaring with laughter.

My father was a director of the shipbroking firm of Galbraith Pembroke, which was founded by my great-grandfather, Edward Pembroke and which became part of the Baltic Exchange. About the period 1933–35 my father was in the habit, whilst driving to his West End office, in South Molton Street, of dropping Moray and me off at Mr Gibbs's pre-preparatory school at the Sloane Square end of Sloane Street. And that reminds me of another chase. The school uniform was topped by a rather floppy crimson cloth cap. As my class were being escorted in a crocodile towards Knightsbridge one morning a loony-looking man snatched my cap from my head and made off with it in the direction of Pavilion Road, then headed left towards Cadogan Gardens. Giving chase (in contradiction to a shouted order not to do so by the teacher-in-charge) I caught up with the felon close to Peter Jones department store where a bobby, sizing up the situation, saw the cap given back to me. Though a very small incident in retrospect, it did give much cause for speculation among my fellow seven-year-olds. 'Coo, surprising you didn't trip up . . . was he put in prison? . . . Golly, did he have a pistol?'

Up in Brompton Road lay the magical world of Harrods, a relatively quiet, uncrowded place in those days with the unforgettable aromatic blend of sawdust and spices and rarefied meats in its food shop and of leather and polish in its great hall where the bank was – replete with sofas, and where my sybarite mother seemed to meet elegant friends at every visit. One day Moray and I couldn't believe our luck when we were advised to take along our autograph books, because Sabu, the Indian boy actor, a hero of ours, was signing upstairs in the bookshop.

Then there were my father's offices in South Molton street with their beautifully fashioned model steamers. There was tea at the Conservative Club with my grandfather, Arthur Watson (a director during the early war years of Christie's). And there was the International Sportsmen's Club, in Upper Grosvenor Street, London's first mixed club, of which my mother was one of the first members. The image of its immaculate, obsequious hall porter still lingers on the senses and so do the Turkish cigarette fumes, the Chanel No. 5, the richly hanging curtains, the heavenly odours of the dining room, and downstairs the chlorinated, echoing swimming pool with its burly instructor who taught us the breaststroke with a rod from which hung a rope and a sling to catch us by the armpits.

The club backed onto Grosvenor House, from near the top of which, in a luxurious apartment taken by my parents' friends, Eddie and Stella Nissen, we witnessed the Coronation of George VI and Queen Elizabeth, mainly through periscopes, bought at Hamleys, I think, because we were frightened of falling out of the window.

My father was not very happy in his role as a businessman, but, on his own admission, he loved every minute of his time as a territorial soldier. He held a commission in the Middlesex Yeomanry (Duke of Cambridge's Own Hussars). The regiment was based on the Duke of York's headquarters in Chelsea, where I had my first riding lessons. I can almost re-live in my mind's eye, days spent at the Yeomens' annual summer camp with its spick tent lines and troop drills, its showjumping, tentpegging and sword, lance and revolver competitions. I can still all but smell the odour of the August grass mingled with that of sunburned canvas and guy-ropes, and hear the regimental bandsmen with their stirring tunes, drowning the sleepy insect hum; the orderly officer, on his inspection round, Sam Browne belt glistening; and the whinnying from the horse-lines, glossy-coated chestnuts and bays, swishing tails and snorting heads; and the khaki puttees-and-serge stable guards' oaths when a nag lashed out at its neighbour, or bit at its neighbour's neck for trying to steal from its hay-net.

I can envisage, as though it were yesterday, the officers' mess marquee laid out for luncheon, the sparkling white tablecloths heavy with silver trophies and flowers and wine glasses, and my father and his friends, booted and spurred, hot from the morning's equestrian activities, taking out their trim cigarette cases from tunic pockets, and calling to smartly uniformed waiters for ale or gin. And Moray and I gazing spellbound. My father's brother-officers came often to our Smith Street house. I remember George Sale and Patrick Doyle, Reggie Malden and Douglas Baird-Murray (rather a rake, the last-named, my mother said).

Our diminutive Sussex home was a remote and tranquil enclave set in the great Leconfield estate, which the third Baron Leconfield, Lord-Lieutenant of Sussex - 'old Lordy' as he was affectionately known by the locals - ruled with a strict, if benevolent, dictatorship from his seventeenth century palace, Petworth House, famous particularly for Grinling Gibbons and Turner in the rooms, and for fallow deer and black sheep in the high-walled Capability Brown park. Much of the estate was geared to the interest of his hunt, 'Lord Leconfield's hounds', one of the last private packs in Britain, to which my parents subscribed. The priority Lordy gave to his venery was evident from the smart chestnut gates, giving access to every enclosure (he hated jumping), and the well-kept rides with which all the woodlands were liberally intersected.

The attitude of the followers was rather different from that which prevails today. The horse was merely a vehicle, if a deeply respected one, from which to witness hounds working (whereas now most people seem to regard hunting as an excuse for galloping their horses over other people's land, with the hounds as nothing more than a means to that end). Children had to be impeccably behaved or they were not welcome again (Lordy made that quite plain). They were carefully instructed in hunt etiquette and dress, and were expected to have imbibed a broad knowledge of the sport (from parents and Pony Club) before attending their first meet. They were taught to pay their respects to the Master, the hunt secretary and the huntsman (to each the subtly different honour due to his station); they were made aware that the hounds were the most important feature in the scene; and that it was a child's duty to dismount from his, or her, pony to assist if a member of the hunt staff had difficulty in opening a gate or encountered any such problem for that matter.

I believe that the child of those days received a much sounder grounding in equitation than is now the case. Whereas nowadays young people appear to hold on by their ankles and lower legs (with their knees loose) we were taught to grip with our thighs to the extent that 'a half-crown cannot be squeezed between the knees and the saddle'. Our lower legs were relaxed – only to be brought into action as aids. Balance, control and unified movement were thus much more effective and considerably kinder to the pony. I have the impression, too, that the young rider of today is heavier handed. He or she seems to be too often working on the pony's mouth, whereas we were taught the importance of light hands and maintaining gentle contact by flexy wrists and fingers that firmly controlled yet moved in sympathetic harmony with the pony. Much more emphasis was put on grooming up to a quarter of a century ago, and considerably more time spent on it.

When competition riding began to take pride of place on the young equestrian schedule after the war the old veneration for the hunting-field began to wane. The hunting-field seemed to become, for many, nothing better than a practice arena for the showring. (I remember standing with Colonel Guy Cubitt, the founder of the Pony Club, in the Surrey Union kennels a few weeks before he died in the 1970s, to hear him complain bitterly, 'I didn't start the Pony Club so that children could learn devil-take-the-hindmost go-getting first-past-the-post selfish competition at Wembley and the White City; I started it in order that they could be taught good manners in the hunting-field. The old obedience seems to have vanished for ever . . .') But the 1930s were still days of obedience and woe betide anyone who disobeyed Lordy, a stickler for conventional behaviour.

He was not one for letting people off with a caution, either. I remember him taking a man to court for shooting a fox running in front of the Leconfield hounds. The man was fined five guineas. I suppose the magistrates were much too frightened to suggest that the offender had, technically, committed no crime. I think the only person who wasn't even a little bit afraid of him was his wife, Violet. He was a portly, fiery man of small stature, while she was a tall, willowy, daunting, eccentric and very energetic woman. Stories about them abounded. I recall my parents returning from a party at Petworth House – given by Violet Leconfield to celebrate her husband's birthday – and regaling us with their description of the *pièce de résistance* of her entertainment, a surprise for Lordy, which ended in tears. She organised a moonlight parade in the park, of shepherds and sheep, ploughmen, cattle and horses, all whitewashed from head to foot. Lordy was so enraged at the sight of his men and beasts being treated thus that he promptly closed the party and sent everyone home.

He was no less angry when, having cancelled an important meet of his hounds, in mourning I believe for a neighbouring landowner, he heard that his wife had boxed her horse over for a day with the adjacent Crawley and Horsham hunt. In the event she was quite badly injured that day; he called that poetic justice. In the late 1930s she started calling herself Violette, instead of Violet. A neighbour, Eddy Winterton, told my mother that when he received a luncheon invitation signed 'Violette', he replied, 'Non, Edouard'. 'Violette' finished her days in a mental home.

Come the winter of 1940–41 the Leconfield hounds were piloted, close to Petworth, across a football field while a match was in progress, and the scent was thus foiled. Reaching the touchline a furious Lordy raised himself in his stirrup-irons, addressing the players with a full-throated, well modulated demand of 'Haven't you people got anything better to do in w-a-r-t-i-m-e?'

Having no children Charles and Violet Leconfield adopted a boy and a girl, Elizabeth and Peter Wyndham. Unfortunately, both their lives were sadly marred. Peter Wyndham was, like me, rather wild and irresponsible. He and I committed a terrible crime in the spring of 1942. We each took a rowing boat out on the big lake in Petworth Park, moored at one or other of its several islands, searched for moorhens' eggs; and, having found two or three clutches each pushed onto the water again and enjoyed a naval battle with them, bombarding one another with eggs until we ran out of them. Lordy, discovering the felony, reprimanded Peter in conservationist terms, complaining that he liked to see plenty of moorhens on the lake and that 'now I shall be deprived of that pleasure'. When he told my mother she only remarked that it was a sin to waste such valuable protein in times of dire food shortage. For whatever reason I realized that it was certainly a sin. The Leconfields who were close friends of my parents, were very kind and comforting to my mother after my father was killed.

Just before the war the Middlesex Yeomanry were converted to signals, or 'lines of communication' as the branch was then known. Not liking the prospect of that my father transferred to the Royal Sussex, to the 4th (Territorial) Battalion, which had just come under command of that great soldier, Lashmir (Bolo) Whistler, who after the war, would become a full general. Early in December 1939, the battalion was posted to Dorset, poised to join the British Expeditionary Force in France. It camped in the grounds of

Cerne Abbey, the home of the Digby family, who were magnificent hosts. My parents took a house in the village of Long Burton, a few miles south of Sherborne, from which they did not fail to hunt with the Blackmore Vale hounds on Saturdays. I believe my father was invited regularly to shoot, too, yet his company complained that he 'trained them off their feet six days a week'. So not much dust can have settled on him.

My most vivid memory of that sojourn was the Dinky toy set my parents gave me for Christmas. A present obviously chosen with care by my father, it comprised an entire infantry company, complete with machine gunners, mortar men, medical orderlies and dispatch riders. After lunch on Boxing Day I crept into the sitting-room to find him and two of his fellow company commanders, Christopher Nix and Bernard Norfolk, kneeling on the carpet, bottoms in the air, each with one of my toy soldiers in his hand, debating the logic of a certain deployment. When later I found my father standing alone at the box where the toys were kept, and then with intense care and study positioning them on the floor, in different battle, or line of march, for-mations, I did not need to be further persuaded that they were bought more for his benefit than mine.

The battalion's departure on the first leg of its journey to France and the front line was heralded by an emotive concert, or revue, at which my parents, my brothers and I sat alongside the Whistler family in the front row, reeling with laughter at the comedians and joining in the choruses with gusto. There can scarcely have been more tears flowing at a rendering of 'Auld Lang Syne' than were seen that evening. Next afternoon – headed by the regimental band, playing 'Sussex by the Sea' – the battalion marched to Sherborne station. Moray and I swung our arms at our father's side for the first few hundred yards, with the possibility of never seeing him again not entering our heads for a moment. But from May 1940 for me life was never quite the same again. His black-and-tan bull terrier bitch, Judy, was the creature I felt closest to for the remainder of that year. It was as though she was a little corner of him still living.

In the 1960s my mother received a small packet bearing a government stamp. With mystified fingers she cut the string and opened a box containing a strange assortment: a gold wrist watch with a crocodile strap, three receipts from Harrods, two very faded Paisley silk handkerchiefs, a cigarette case and a letter addressed to her, bearing the date 18 May 1940, but never posted.

The career of that collection was rather bizarre. While my father's retreat-ing company rested at a Belgian roadside, he walked accompanied by his sergeant-major to a farm shed, there protected from the wind and noise of battle, to study his maps. In those moments the shed received a direct hit from a German shell. And when the soldiers of Sussex marched on without their commander, the farmer, whose building it was, salvaged the few surviving articles from my father's shattered body and hid them in his house. Then the Hun dominated the land. Five years later Belgium was liberated, by which time the items were in the care of the farmer's widow. Feeling some compunction she discussed the problem with a neighbour.

*Peut-etre la famille du soldat aimerait avoir ces choses? . . . Mais Oui!* She sent them to the British embassy in Brussels who passed them onto the Ministry of Defence. My mother having changed her name twice since the war, several years elapsed before the authorities were able to trace her. Moray wears the wristwatch to this day.

I have few classroom memories from the Surrey prep school at which I boarded between the autumn of 1935 and the summer of 1940 except those of inky fingers and bent Relief nibs: of having my hair pulled long and painfully for not paying attention, and being rapped over the knuckles with a thick white pencil for recording the wrong answers in my exercise book; and long draughty prison-like hours of prep. What I recall more vividly is a heavy tuckbox that smelt of Brighton rock and bullseyes that stuck to its wooden sides, mingled with the odours of cricket bat oil, a catapult's rubber sling and oranges, all of which got mixed up with sets of cigarette cards and my much loved little 'Observer's' handbooks on animals, birds, butterflies and wild flowers. I recall in sharp outline the dining hall with the roll of scholarship awards engraved on an oak board; asking the headmaster if I might have a piece from the knuckle when he carved a leg of mutton; the day which was fishcakes day because those golden potato and tinned-salmon spheres comprised the most delicious breakfasts of the week; and cricket and football teas with cream buns and marzipan cake and watercress sandwiches when an opposing team came to play. I remember the scanty red triangular slips, fastened with white tapes, which we wore for swimming; the little boarded garden plots each of us were allotted; the melancholy of 'Nunc Dimittis' at the close of evening chapel; inter-gang warfare, with fir cones as ammunition, in the adjacent conifer wood; the awesomeness of those pipe-smoking leather-patch masters; and Moray screaming in the night with earache.

# 2

# _Wartime Eton_

A resolution was taken in 1940 to close down the Eton College Hunt but fortunately for me, among forty or fifty other regular followers, that did not happen. Bob Manners, who took over the Mastership from Hugh Arbuthnot in the winter half (when I was a new boy) appealed to the headmaster, Claude Elliott, to reverse the decision on the grounds of the great popularity of hunting at the school, and Elliott relented. He told Manners that, provided the hunt had the support of the farmers and kept a reasonably low profile, the pack could be maintained with a view to two meets a week (three after Christmas). Manners carried the horn that winter, with Julian Mond (afterwards Melchett), Bill Birch Reynardson and Bob Chaworth Musters turning hounds to him. Though I refer to them in that familiar Christian-name way I would not have dreamed of addressing them other than by their surnames, if I dared speak to them at all, which would only have been conceivable if they accosted me first. For I was just a few months past the age of thirteen, while they were in their last Eton year.

It was clear to me that, when Manners and company dressed up in their lint-white breeches and stocks, their brown velvet coats and hunt caps and black stockings they thought themselves to be the most important people in the school. (The hunt motto, _Floreant Canes Etonenses_ surely sounded sweeter in their ears than the school motto, _Floreat Etona?_) I suppose I looked upon them as being of demigod status just as they doubtless regarded the former Masters whose names were inscribed on the board in the kennels on the Datchet road as demigods. From the 1930s that roll was composed almost entirely of young men whose names were to ring loud in the world of venery: Gerald Gundry, Charles Wood (Halifax), Hugh Percy (Northumberland), R. E. Wallace, Bill Brownlow and Hugh Arbuthnot. It was apparent that every boy who rose to the Mastership of the Eton Beagles came from a distinguished hunting family.

Anyhow I was one of several Lower Boys whose principal motive for hunting – far from aspiring to carry a whip, let alone to the Mastership – was for the excuse it offered to escape the immediate vicinity of the school. The joy of running over pastures, ploughs and heaths as distant as Winkfield Row, Hawthorn Hill, Stoke Poges and the far side of Windsor racecourse (and even quite close places like Dorney and Datchet) with the sound of hound music and the horn in front, gave a wonderful sense of freedom. The only pity was that, as Lower Boys, the demands put upon us for football practice and other forms of recreation were so heavy, we could only hunt at the most once a week. But why should I be possessed of this imperative to escape the school environment, why the need for this venatic solace? In a word because I found the place claustrophobically terrifying.

On principle every Eton boy had his own room. M'Tutor's (my house) however, contained two large rooms reserved for brothers. During my first half one of these was shared by the Pilkingtons, Robert and George, and the other by my brother, Michael, and me. Michael was a precocious, academically bright sixteen-year-old with any amount of youthful *savoir faire*, who, since 1937, had been enjoying a thoroughly successful Eton career based on a room of his own. Nor did he fail to show how much he resented having to share with a younger brother whose untidiness constantly spilled over into his personal space. There was little in the way of harmony in that freezing cold room.

I arrived from a casual easy-going grey-flannel prep school – too easy-going by far – of a mere fifty boys of which I had been listed at the top. I could not have been confronted with a more alarming contrast than that which faced me, aged thirteen, among nearly a thousand Etonians. Waking on my first morning – to 'it's six-forty-five, Mr Watson minor, Sir, time to be up' from the crone who was the passage boy's maid – and reviewing my new uniform arrayed on the bedside chair, I felt again the daunting weight of unwished-for privilege being thrust at me, privilege for which an awesome return was expected. Nor did that intuition deceive. First there was the white shirt and studs; then there were the black pinstripe trousers, the black tie and the deep starched Eton collar, the black braided waistcoat and the Eton jacket, the collar of which had to be got, by hook or by crook, beneath the deep starched one which had been securely fastened to the impossible studs; and the new uncomfortable shoes, nicely polished by the 'boys' man'. To cap all that was the black silk top hat which must be fondly brushed and carefully handled. The sartorial battle over I was set to sally forth on the first academic marathon.

Having secured the half-dozen prescribed text books and stationery under my elbows I proceeded to the cloisters in school yard to look up my division list and thus my division room. (I ought to have done that and discovered the whereabouts of the classroom the previous afternoon.) Following a long and hectic search for my name I was already late for my lesson, which was Latin construe. Elbows clinging to the books, top hat pressed on ears, I headed into the street at the double. It was raining and although I had a brand-new umbrella there was no free hand to unfurl it. Except for one other boy – like me bewildered, late, running – I was alone, my footsteps resounding as I dropped books, recovered them and dropped them again in my panic. Meanwhile I forgot the name of the schoolroom for which I was destined, though I remembered the beak I was up to. I knocked on a weighty, heavily studded door. 'Please, Sir, is this Mr —'s division?' A cold glowering face turned on me. 'What's your name, boy?' 'Watson minor, Sir'. 'A-a-h, *degoutante personage!*' (for it was Mr Fortescue, the dreaded French master, bony, iron-grey Fortescue, of the razor sharp invective, the lashing tongue, the trenchant jibes). 'Mr — is in Number Three New

Schools. You'll be in trouble, won't you, Watson minor . . .' New Schools, now which are they? I wondered as I closed the door on the faces of twenty tittering boys' faces. (This experience, which was repeated nearly every day of my first week, became a subject of my nightmares for years afterwards.)

There were not only fresh academic subjects to absorb, Greek, trigonometry, Byzantine history and chemistry, for example, but we new boys were required, within a fortnight of arriving, to learn the whereabouts and names of all the twenty-six boys' houses and the locations of the squash courts, the fives courts, the gymnasium, the numerous playing fields, and the book shops; the house-colour combinations, who was keeper of this and captain of that and the various housemasters' initials. We looked forward to the 'colour test' with particular foreboding.

Then I had to know my place in Lower Chapel, which required daily attendance and twice on Sundays, matins and evensong. (At least I knew I wouldn't be in the Lower Chapel choir. Having lamentably failed the Precentor's singing test my place was far from it.) Waiting for the hour of chapel, boys thronged round a little old man with watery eyes and a walrus moustache, called Joby, who sold sweets from a basket trolley. He knew just where most Lower Boys were to be found at any given moment of the day and had an astonishing memory for the faces and names of those who owed him money. He enjoyed a roaring trade.

Despite being deeply unhappy I believe I only cried once in public during my first half and that was during the singing in Lower Chapel of 'Valiant Hearts' on Remembrance Sunday, when I was confronted by a most vivid and poignant image of my father. (It annoyed me, in the 1980s, when the pacifist clerics had the hymn removed from their Remembrance Day services. When I asked our priest why it was no longer sung he replied evasively 'I've never heard of it'. (Of course he had!) The local vicar was more open. He told me that the Anglicans had dropped it because '. . . it glorifies war. Also the words are blasphemous: *O Valiant Hearts who to your Glory came*. They came to no glory, only Christ did that.' When the hymn was sung, after a lapse of some years, at the 1988 Cenotaph parade, the radio and television announcers made a point of explaining that this was 'at the special request of the Duke of Edinburgh'. In 1989, its music was played on that occasion but the words not uttered. But I was delighted to see, during BBC Television's *Songs of Praise* which took place the same evening in the Guards Chapel that my friend Simon Cooper – Major-General commanding the Household Division – made a point of asking for 'Valiant Hearts' for the service.)

My father's death had a profound effect on me. He had been worth working for, worth getting good school reports for. I needed someone who would, like him, appreciate my doing well. My mother, who was not very interested in intellectual matters, didn't seem to mind much what happened at Eton, provided that she was one of the women most admired on our great holiday of the summer half, the Fourth of June. So I drifted through my first four or five halfs with my head in the clouds. It was the only escapism except perhaps, beagling, available.

M'Tutor (in plain English my housemaster) was that fine historian, Mr C. R. N. Routh, who had been with my father at Christ Church where he was, incidentally, president of the Oxford Union. He was an historian of prodigious learning and also a Shakespearean scholar. I suppose I hoped he would assume the role of surrogate father, instead of which I found him frighteningly remote and, not unnaturally, disdainful of untidy and inattentive boys like me, of which there were a good deal too many in his house for his liking.

The most benign character of those first few weeks was the vice-Provost, Henry Marten (Quickswood was Provost). It was Marten's custom to invite every new boy to breakfast in his fine old rooms by Lupton's Tower; we regarded our host as if he had just stepped down from Olympus, and we trod the carpet towards his sideboard as though on sacred ground. A car arrived for him from Windsor two or three times a week to convey him to the Castle for the lessons in constitutional history he gave Princess Elizabeth and Princess Margaret Rose.

Eton discipline was generally in the hands of the boys, in those of 'Pop', the Eton Society, the (unofficial) school prefects, but much more powerfully and directly in the hands of the house captains and the members of the house libraries, who were in effect the house monitors. In my first half Routh's house captain was a tyrant whose answer to every crime, and most peccadilloes, too, was the cane. He was universally feared and hated by the Lower Boys. He was obliged to seek M'Tutor's permission to beat a boy, but that consent, so far as we could tell, was never refused The ritual appeared to continue night after night, shortly following the hour at which boys were confined to their rooms.

*Footsteps are heard down the passage – as a dog can distinguish between different familiar human footsteps we began to recognise those of each library member – and, almost certain it is my turn, my heart misses a beat as I anticipate the turning of the doorknob. The library member to whom the task of messenger has been deputed ignores my brother (diligent at his desk) and gazes severely at me. 'You are wanted immediately; go and wait outside the library door'. The house captain's strength is a byword; there is numb terror in my heart. Two contemporaries are there in front of me, Norman ('Snoopy') Lonsdale and Michael Hughes-Hallett. We make frightened faces at one another. Each is called in his turn. I hear the hectoring, followed by the strokes. I am summoned. I face the all-powerful one, sitting on the 'bumrack' before the Library fire, the cane held across his thighs, the merciless expression behind his spectacles. His lecture is over quickly, I am instructed to bend my head under the lip of the table . . .*

I was beaten eight times during my first two years at Routh's, each with six, seven or eight strokes according to the severity of the crime. For example I was given six for leaving some books on a forbidden spot called 'the slab' in the boys' entrance to the house, and eight for being caught out of bounds – in the back streets of Slough, on the way to a cinema in the company of a future Master of the Quorn foxhounds, David Keith. (Our gas masks secreted under a grassy bank, dressed in what we thought was the unmistakable guise of town boys, we strode confidently along the back streets towards the Odeon Cinema as we had done several times before. But a sharp-eyed beak, Nigel Wykes, driving his car two hundred yards away, spotted us unhesitatingly as Eton boys up to no good.)

I believe there is only one of Routh's inmates in my time who was beaten more often than me, and that was Richard Beaumont, now chairman of Purdeys, the gunmakers. (He had it in for that house captain ever after. 'If I saw the swine turning the corner towards us now I'd go straight up and kick him very hard in the balls,' said Richard to me as we were walking down St James's Street recently.) The other primitive ritual was cold baths; I was lucky; no more than a dozen of those were ordered for me. (But that was enough to make me paranoid about freezing water ever after.)

Indolent boys like me lived in constant fear, too, of the different forms of classroom chastisement. Bad work was 'ripped' or 'torn over'. Bad behaviour, or inept oral response, was rewarded with a 'ticket'. Rips and tickets – with which my first Eton year was trailled, as pieces of paper trail a paperchase – must be returned to the master concerned, initialled by M'Tutor. (Some boys forged his initials; I lacked the courage.) A heinous classroom offence was punished with a white ticket, which had to be taken to the supreme authority over Lower Boys, the benevolent Mr A. E. Conybeare, the Lower Master. In my second half I was awarded a 'Georgic' which involved copying out 500 lines of Virgil. For mathematics, the subject at which I was least adept, I was up to bald, scarlet-faced, heavy Mr 'Nobby' Huson, who had a particular admiration for brother Michael (a born mathematician). My first fortnightly order card, or report, contained only two words: 'Unlike Mike'. The second was adorned with only one. It said 'Miker'. Nobby Huson was famous for what he called his 'love taps', which entailed a couple of books, of encyclopaedic proportions, being brought down very heavily on the offender's head. The concussion effects left me, on each occasion, in a foggy daze for the rest of the lesson. To complete my first half I failed in 'Trials' (end of term exams). There followed a period of a sense of utter failure in everything.

New boys started fagging after a couple of weeks. My first fagmaster was a fair-minded fellow called Andrew Burnaby-Atkins. I was responsible for tidying his room, finding out what he required for tea every day, procuring it and preparing it (always being very careful not to burn his toast or overcook his egg). But there was more to fagging than that. Any member of the Library could send a Lower Boy on an errand, such as fetching his slippers, or taking a message to a friend in another house. For this purpose the senior one stood outside the Library, or in the doorway of his own room and shouted 'Bo-o-oy!', lungs at full stretch, at which we all rushed down the passages and up the stairs as fast as our little legs could carry us, the last to arrive being the one to whom the task was given. (And woe betide the boy who hid in his room at hearing the command.) I was, briefly, the Library fag, my job being to keep that room in good shape and in particular getting the *Tatlers*, *Fields* and *Country Lifes* back into their correct piles. My memory of the role is mingled with four songs pouring from the gramophone: Fred Astaire with 'Cheek to Cheek', Noel Coward singing 'I'll see you again', 'Wild Thyme' from Gertrude Lawrence and 'Dusty Shoes' by the deep-throated Hutch (this last being the only Library ditty tolerated by M'Tutor).

Air raids were on the increase from the end of 1940 through 1941, nearly always at night; and our evening study or sleep was frequently interrupted by the wailing sirens. On a wet evening during my first half, one of Goering's planes, being chased from Windsor Castle by anti-aircraft guns, released, in retreat, a couple of bombs on Eton. One landed on Upper School, the oldest and largest of the division rooms, which flanked School Yard – and the other on the home of Doctor Ley, the music master and his wife, who fortunately, were out to dinner. Their house stood opposite Mr Routh's, the Timbralls; and, in particular, directly opposite the room occupied by Michael and me. M'Tutor entered the room to find us in the prescribed position, flat on our faces, hands behind our heads, in a sea of broken glass, to which was glued the precautionary anti-splinter netting. 'Get up,' he ordered, 'collect your respirators, gum boots and blankets and go straight to the shelter!'

I don't remember how often the sirens beckoned us to that shelter carved underground beside M'Tutor's garden wall. But I do know that, despite the discomfort of the unyielding wooden bunks and the dampness, it was all rather fun, for those alarming nights were mitigated by sandwiches, cocoa, camaraderie, gossip and song.

One night a boy called McCreery occupying a bunk next to me related his father's entire military career for my edification. What he did not know then was that in 1944 General McCreery was to be Montgomery's successor in command of the Eighth Army. What I could not possibly conceive was that Michael McCreery would become secretary of the British Communist Party not long after leaving Oxford. He seemed such a conventional boy. He was murdered in his twenties. A memorable air-raid shelter tradition was the comic repertoire of duets sung by Eddie Boyle (that Billy Bunter figure who was to become an MP within ten years of leaving Eton and a cabinet minister within twenty), and George Douglas-Home (the youngest of the celebrated brothers, who would be killed with the RAF in 1943). Their signature refrain was 'Miss Otis Regrets', which never failed to have the shelter shaking with gales of laughter. There was even disappointment when the 'all clear' sounded.

The name Douglas-Home recalls another scene. One of the great ruses at M'Tutors was to convice Miss Joan Owen, M'Dame (the equivalent of a house matron) that one's body was short of vitamins and iron. Boys who were short of vitamins and iron, she thought, required Radio Malt, and Radio Malt to small boys, in those wartime food-rationing days, was like nectar to the gods. (Dried (powdered) potato and egg were the two most memorable items at boys' meals.) One's Radio Malt jar resided in her cupboard, labelled with one's name, the ration being as much of the sticky brown-gold substance as you could wind once onto a dessertspoon every day after lunch. With this treat often went a recitation by M'Dame from a witty little ABC of people, written by George Douglas-Home's brother, William, the playwright, who left Routh's house in, I suppose, about 1930. Unconsciously adding to the comedy Miss Owen, a straight-backed middle-aged spinster, invariably held her hand to her throat, as though checking a tiresome cough and spoke in a strident monotone. Fifty years having swept by I only remember a single verse. It is from the alphabet's letter D:

> *The debutante has always been,*
> *Described as sweet and seventeen*
> *By gossip writers who delight*
> *In writing something rather trite . . .*

Thanks to Michael's urgent plea, in 1941, to M'Tutor, for a room of his own I was allotted one, too, a tiny but treasured sanctuary, complete with a bureau (known as a burry and comprising bookcase, drawers and desk), an ottoman box for clothes and bric-a-brac, a small sock (food) cupboard nailed to the wall, a table and a bed that, for daytime purposes, swung up against the wall. I broke the monotony of the walls with Lionel Edwards and Peter Scott prints. The room, overlooking the field known as 'Sixpenny' was once occupied by the travel writer, Peter Fleming, to which his name, carved in the stone window-frame, bore witness.

I returned from Sussex for the summer half of that year with ugly scars on my upper lip and chin from going straight over the handlebars of my bicycle onto the tarmac a mile on the east side of Petworth. (I was enjoying a race against Moray when the front mudguard came loose and clamped on the tyre. Petrol rationing being what it was at least fifteen minutes passed before a kind motorist drew up to take me home. I spent a week in hospital.) I also returned to Routh's house with, in my pocket, a baby squirrel that had fallen from its nest. I called it Cyril. I kept it fed it and exercised it in my room, undetected, for three weeks. Then the boy's maid responsible for the passage off which the room lay, discovered it and went shrieking to M'Dame who told M'Tutor, and I expected to be summarily expelled. Mr Routh, however, proved the soul of kindness on that occasion. He had a special cage constructed for Cyril in his summer-house, which I could see from my window. I wished I could not see it. To my dismay Cyril spent his entire waking life describing, pathetically, the same small circle on the wire mesh, and died within another week. The pathos was not unlike that Jock of the Bushveldt experience on the Crystal Palace night five years before, but far, far worse, of course. It was all a great mistake.

It was my first summer half; I was a 'wet bob' and I enjoyed the river, particularly when in command of my own whiff in which I could scull up and down the Thames at will and loiter under the willows on the Windsor side, hoping for the sound of galloping hooves on the racecourse. On the occasions of the half's two or three whole holidays we were permitted to row our slim boats up to Boveney Lock, and, having negotiated that, scull on to the river island of Queen's Eyot, with its exciting summer-house, the only place at which a Lower Boy might indulge in a pint of beer or cider (but only one); and, with that on board, make the five-mile return journey – to Rafts, the home of the boats, by Windsor bridge, where Alf, the head boatman presided – happily intoxicated.

We answered 'absence' (roll call) on Queen's Eyot, the man who took the names being an eccentric mathematics beak with a gaunt face and curly white hair called Hope-Jones. Close to the landing-stage grew a large bed of stinging-nettles, into which Hope-Jones hurled the oars of any boy failing to comply with his regulations for disembarkation. Having left Nobby Huson's division, I was up to Hope-Jones that year. He was also Eton's wartime salvage officer, and delighted in telling us boys of his success in recovering scrap metal. An example: 'Yesterday I salvaged from the river Jordan (a stream running through the playing fields) three alumin-i-um buckets, one bi-cycle, two dust-bins and one perambu-la-tor . . .' He was used to a variety of plays on his name. We were about to earn a 'run' – which meant deserting our division room if a beak was more than fifteen minutes late – when a boy spotted him coming. 'It's no good, Hojo's arrived!' Mr Hope-Jones overheard him and, while we all scrambled, disappointed, to our desks, he proceeded sedately to his dais with a loud and familiar declamation: 'My name is neither Hope-Jiggers, Hope-Jaggers nor Hope-Joggers. Nor is it Hojo. It is *H-o-p-e-J-o-nes!*'

Back to the river – to a terrible little drama about the time of my fourteenth birthday. I was being tried out as cox to the house four. Burnaby-Atkins, the coach, was bicycling along the towpath with a megaphone. The boat cut the river at a spanking pace. Clutching the rudder-strings I inclined my torso between my knees, as Mr Routh's representative oarsmen heaved against the Thames, sitting upright as they feathered and down again as their oars penetrated the water. All went well until a Windsor family, father, mother and three large children, swung across our bows. 'Stop the boat, Watson!' yelled Burnaby-Atkins. 'Hey, stop rowing, everyone!' I screamed. The crew took absolutely no notice. My dazed mind fumbled for the right words ('easy oar – stop her all!' if I remember rightly) but did not find them. Our bows, travelling at a terrific pace now, carved into the gig with explosive splintering. The family were all in the water, their pleasure boat sinking. From the waves a furious red face, topped over the skull by a white handkerchief tied at the four corners, hurled abuse at Mr Routh's oarsmen. Burnaby-Atkins hurled even stronger abuse at me. So much for my career as a cox.

In 1942 I was positioned bow in the house bumping four, the aim of which was to race against the stopwatch, catch up and bump the stern of the boat in front and so work one's way up the Head of the River challenge. Being just superior to the two ahead, and with our cox, Bill Warre, timing his rudder-work nicely we scored a couple of bumps. But that was our limit, despite the fact that we were gifted with the guidance of one of the best oar coaches of his day. This was Bill's great-uncle, Edmond ('Bear') Warre, the friend of such literary luminaries as Belloc, Baring, Kipling and Chesterton. Square-jawed, blue-eyed, white-moustachioed and wrapped in the pink of a Leander scarf, Bear looked just the part as he pedalled down the towpath, growling at us through his megaphone.

Things were soon to be looking up. Advancing to 1943 and having –

through the house bumping fours and the sculling races – made some progress as an oarsman, I was awarded my 'Boats' which, though no great accomplishment, meant I could perform in an eight in the Procession of Boats on the Fourth of June, transfer from the whiff to a rigger with a sliding seat, wear a zephyr with magenta stripes and a cap to match, and discard the scug cap (for those who had won no sporting distinction). On sultry summer afternoons one sometimes wandered up to Ward's Mead (Cuckoo Weir for Lower Boys) for a swim, and once, for a bet, I swam from there to Boveney Lock and back. I had my house colours now, a cap, a twelve feet long woollen scarf and stockings, all in black-and-white hoops or stripes; those were for prominence at Eton football, the field game. There were other versions of football, soccer and rugby in the spring half; and there was the esoteric and muddy wall game, a duel of attrition. But the field game, with its 'rouges' and 'bullys' and 'cornering' and 'sneaking' was the great winter contest that all had a go at, and nearly all enjoyed. I played squash and fives, ran up front in the school steeplechase and practised with a .22 rifle in the miniature range, but had to wait another year to find my place in the Shooting Eight.

There was less time for beagling, but I do have an amusing memory from December 1943 when Michael Holland-Hibbert, I think, was carrying the horn. Teddy Gwynne and I were hurrying back across Agar's Plough to be in time for lock-up, following an afternoon's hunting from a meet at Stoke Place, the home of 'Wombat' Howard-Vyse (who I would know later as Colonel of the Blues). We were accosted by a couple of sightseeing GIs, one tall, languid, bespectacled, the other squat and perky (it was just two years after the Pearl Harbour attack). 'Can you guys tell us,' the short one asked, 'just where the Battle of Waterloo was won?' When we retailed that one to M'Tutor the great historian fairly doubled with mirth.

Teddy Gwynne was my mess-mate, along with Archie Kidston. That is to say, pooling our resources, we clubbed together for tea, which was the exciting meal of the day considering it was composed – apart from the house ration of bread, margarine and tea – of crumpets, sardines, eggs, tinned pork and beans and a variety of other good things of our choosing, bought from Rowland's or Jack's sock shop by the five courts, and cooked on the gas ring at the end of the passage. The three of us occupied rooms on the senior top passage now, the scene of that sweaty, riotous evening diversion, passage football, which we always joined in – rather than endure the noise from our inky desks. (Alas, Teddy was to die in his forties and Archie in his fifties.)

What did Eton boys most despise in other boys? Perhaps it could best be summed up in the word 'side'. While modest pride was permitted, any obvious conceit or showing off was regarded as vulgar, ungentlemanly and highly unattractive. To say of another 'he's a good man, he has no side' was to endow a golden accolade.

With school certificate behind me I was a history specialist and Routh was now my classical – as well as my house – tutor. For history I was also up to a stimulating beak called Geoffrey Agnew (later chairman of the Bond Street art dealers of that name). There was more time to spare for the drawing schools, a favourite haunt of mine, where Mr Wilfrid Blunt reigned, in tandem with Mr Menzies Jones, the pottery expert. Receiving much encouragement from Mr Blunt, I enjoyed the gratification of seeing my naive efforts hung in the school exhibitions on the Fourth of June and St Andrew's day in 1943 and 1944. Dick Routh presided over the preparation for our confirmation and first communion at this time. (At a dinner at White's Club in 1977 – for some twenty Old Etonians born in 1927 – I asked Archie Kidston if he recalled anything at all about our confirmation classes. 'Oh yes,' he replied, without hesitation, 'masturbation. Don't you remember Routh telling us that Legge Lambert expelled any boy he caught doing that? But that although he, Routh, would never go to those lengths, would we please refrain from it . . .?')

My brother Moray, arriving in 1941, became Watson minimus, but when Michael left to join the 60th Rifles in 1942, I was 'major' and Moray 'minor'. Eton was then, as it remains, renowned for its many extra-mural interests and, in particular, for its various societies. I was a member of the Natural History society, the only recollection of which I have is of bird-watching on the nearby Sewage Farm. Moray, who was to become one of the most distinguished actors of his generation, attempted, unavailingly, to start a dramatic society. His classical tutor took the proposal enthusiastically to the headmaster, Claud Elliott. But Elliott, who was rather a stick-in-the-mud about such things, turned down the suggestion.

For Geoffrey Agnew, being an Eton master was a 'reserved occupation'. He was exempted for the Armed Services on medical grounds. But that did not prevent him holding the post of a company commander in the Officers Training Corps, my company commander. When I first joined the Corps a boy called Althorp (who would one day lead the Princess of Wales up the aisle to her wedding) was the senior cadet officer. We wore the school's unique and stylish rust-coloured uniform (or mulberry as it was called) with tunic, breeches, puttees, shirts, ties and caps all of that hue. But the war soon reduced us to khaki battledress, clipped uncomfortably at the neck, gaitered constrictingly at the ankles and topped by a khaki fore-and-aft. Rather a come-down. We marched through Windsor to so-called 'field days' in the Great Park. If we were riflemen we fired blank cartridges at one another; if bren gunners we waved red flags, denoting automatic fire; or, if two-inch mortarmen, green flags. Our haversack rations, usually composed of musty pork pies or thick white bread sandwiches filled with thin spreads of fish paste or mousetrap cheese, mostly finished by being broken up and used as missiles in battles that had nothing to do with the field days in question. In 1945 I was also in the Eton branch of the Home Guard, which superfluous employment was to earn me the Defence Medal.

All through the war real soldiers who had been Eton boys only months before, returned dressed as officers, the interim in the ranks being very short in those days. Ninety per cent were in the army, and ninety per cent of those guardsmen, riflemen (Greenjackets) or cavalrymen. The comments on some of their brother-officers was sometimes naively amusing, especially on those

*Died May 12, 2017 aged 88*

who had been at schools other than Eton, which was to say schools of which they had probably had no previous acquaintance ('The products of the catholic schools, especially Downside and Ampleforth are most like us . . . They're really quite nice,' a Scots Guards ensign observed, returning to M'Tutors a few months after the Normandy landings. 'The Harrow ones are as hearty as one always imagined,' a 10th Hussar told us, 'and Winchester very intense.')

I remember a boy in M'Tutor's asking Routh why nearly all his boys went into 'those sort of regiments' and not the various corps or the county regiments, and Routh replying crisply that 'the best must go to the best'. By the same token, I suppose, that the Eton housemasters vied with one another to secure the 'best' boys for their respective houses, so the regiments, in their officer recruiting endeavours, competed for the 'best' young men, which generally meant the most personable and socially acceptable rather than the most intelligent. Routh persuaded me to go for the Rifle Brigade in which he himself had served during the First World War. When I was sixteen the two Colonels Commandant of that regiment interviewed me in his study and I was 'accepted'.

When boys with whom one had been acquainted as seniors in 1942–43 returned uniformed from Normandy, Italy or Burma in 1944–45 – to visit brothers, other younger relations, friends or tutors – often with a limb missing or even as passengers in wheelchairs, it brought home to one the terrific tempo of the war. And, of course, many did not return at all. There were moving, sad yet uplifting, evening services in College Chapel, Intercessions, at which we prayed for Old Etonians at the front and for the souls of those who were killed in action. Sometimes quite long lists of names were read out.

My mother who had been war-working as a driver with the Americans, had taken up with a swashbuckling cavalry colonel called John L. Hornor Junior. From 1943 nearly all her Eton visits were in company with this extrovert little product of West Point, who was then busy organising General Patton's Commissariat. His staff car and driver pulling up outside M'Tutor's caused quite a stir among our friends.

He found some holiday work for Moray and me. For reasons best known to the United States army, its senior officers were allotted large crates of citrus and other fruit, which arrived at the London wharfs, after running the gauntlet of the U-boats. Moray and I, each being allotted a car with a British girl driver (wearing an American uniform) were given the unusual task of collecting these crates and delivering them to the officers concerned. Jack Hornor insisted on us being smartly dressed in London suits and polished shoes, and the cynical smiles on the faces of the dockers, as we searched the wharfs for the offices concerned, told us how out of place we must have looked there. One of my crates was for General Eisenhower (in Grosvenor Square) who was very pleasant. My regret was that his orderly signed for them, rather than the great man himself. Had it been Ike's signature I would have kept and treasured the top copy and handed in the counterfoil.

Before the war was over my mother married Hornor and he was posted to

Washington. He was also a joint-Master of the Old Dominion hounds in Virginia and she was in good time for the start of the 1945–46 season. The end of 1946 saw Moray and me hunting there, too.

I was as profoundly sorry, in 1945, to be leaving Eton forever as I had been enthusiastic to leave it for my first Christmas holidays from there in 1940. Comparing the school as it was then with what it was to become, I doubt whether I or a great many of my friends would find a place there had we been born a generation later. In our day Winchester was the school with the name for academic elitism; now Eton is on a par. 'The headmastership of Eton,' wrote Robert Birley's biographer, 'is the peak of school teaching.' Birley, who had been an assistant master there in the 1920s, having finished his job as educational adviser in post-war Germany, succeeded Elliott in 1949. He did away with the lowest strata, Third Form and Lower Fourth, thus setting a new threshold of entry, and Old Etonians with dim sons who could not pass the common entrance were among the first to denigrate him as 'Red Robert', the man who was out to 'alter the old social image of the school'. 'O' and 'A' Levels being introduced in 1951 did away with school certificate and Eton's exclusive Grand July exam, and boys were obliged to work much harder. Birley inculcated a fresh respect for scholarship. In our day most boys looked up to the captain of the cricket eleven and the Boats, the president of Pop and the keeper of the Field, as the primary heroes; by the end of the 1950s the winners of such accolades as the Newcastle scholarship or the Rosebery history prize, who might in the old days have been looked down upon by many as mere 'saps', were now widely esteemed. It was the same with the Collegers, or King's Scholars; their nickname of Tugs was no longer spoken so much in a tone of disdain. Money was in new hands and, while the school fees rose, entry has been open from Birley's day onward, to an increasingly wider spectrum of society. The criterion of money and social position gave way to that of money and brains. While Birley was also careful to preserve the old Eton traditions, all the changes he introduced proved entirely right. Since his day fagging and corporal punishment have more or less disappeared too.

I wonder, however, whether his successors, Messrs Chevenix Trench and McCrum, didn't turn the academic pressure a twist too far – at the expense of sports, games and other extra-mural activities? When I ran with the beagles, along with my wife, Lavinia, in March 1973, I was surprised to hear nearly all the boys complain that they had very little time for games, let alone following the school hounds. They were much too busy, they insisted, studying for their 'O's and 'A's. They didn't feel they were getting nearly enough exercise and recreation. Nevertheless a great many hunting men and women have been seeing their sons progress from casual Lower Boy followers to Masters of the ECH. A Manners and a Birch Renyardson, sons of boys who were, as I mentioned, respectively Master and whipper-in during my first half, were wearing the famous brown velvet on my *Country Life* day, thirty-three years later.

# 3

# _Virginia and Westphalia_

The Rifle Brigade – not being born until just after the eighteenth century had turned the corner into the nineteenth – was the ninety-fifth regiment to join the infantry of the line, hence its first name, the 95th Rifles. Both the 95th and its sister regiment, the 60th, wore bottle green uniforms, vividly contrasting themselves with the run-of-the-mill infantry, the 'red coats'. The 95th's march, 'I'm 95', was put into lyrics, of which this is one of its verses:

> _Though dark be our dress, and sombre our braid,_
> _The deeds of the Corps are not hid in the shade_
> _I'm thankful I've chosen the soldiering trade,_
> _And glad I belong to the Rifle Brigade._

Originally the 60th and the 95th, 'the Greenjackets', were the only regiments to be armed with the then recently invented rifle. Following their gallantly executed performances as skirmishers, flank guards and snipers during the Peninsular and Waterloo campaigns, both were taken out of the line, the 60th being re-designated the King's Royal Rifle Corps (though still propularly known as 'the 60th') and the 95th as the Rifle Brigade. Nor were they ever to lose their reputations as _corps d'élites_.

They seemed to me, when I joined them in 1945, to take a pride in being as different as could be from the Foot Guards – no polishing of brass, no stiff, sedate marching, no sloping arms, no ramrod postures, no stamping, none of the pomp and circumstance of the Brigade style. We wore black buttons on our battle dress blouses and dubbin on our boots, and marched at a terrific pace, carrying our rifles at 'the trail'. Those rifles had to be treated like adored sons; the faintest hair on the bolt, or a scarcely detectable smudge in the barrel landed many a rifleman on a charge. The only item that was polished was the revered white-metal cap badge, a Maltese cross topped by a crown and surrounded by a wreath festooned with the regiment's principal battle honours. Marksmanship, speed, agility and readiness were the watchwords in training.

We enlisted at the Rifle Depot, Winchester. Our recruit squad was composed half of working-class boys destined to see out their National Service (or War Emergency Service as it was till termed) in the ranks, and half of public schoolboys being groomed for commissions. It did not take long for those of us in the latter category to get over the embarrassment of having our la-di-da voices and mannerisms interminably imitated and our legs forever pulled in other ways, too, with caustic Cockney humour by the other faction (the Greenjackets largely recuited from London). And, while our respective backgrounds kept us, in essence, poles apart, the mutual suspicion and mistrust with which relationships in the two halves of the barrack room began, soon developed into quite a comradely dialogue, mostly marked by a warm exchange of teasing banter.

Following our month's basic training at Winchester we were posted to the Rifle Brigade's training battalion at Ranby Camp in Nottinghamshire. My most vivid recall from those weeks was the day of the first post-war general election when dressed in our denim fatigues, we listened to the results on the Nissen hut wireless, 'interior economy' (that is to say weapon and kit cleaning and maintenance) being on the training programme . . .

*The sergeant enters, checking up on us. A rifleman is cleaning his mess tins. 'Oo's yer best friend lad? . . . Yer rifle is, ain't it?' says the sergeant, picking up the man's weapon. 'Now leave yer mess tins and get on with this lot . . .' I am cleaning my rifle bolt with a rag. The sergeant takes an oily toothbrush from the jumble on my bunk. "Ere, you want to use this on the bolt, Rifleman Watson, you can't get into the crevices with a cloth, you can't . . .' After a few more bouts of terse advice and admonition he leaves the Nissen hut to sighs of relief all round, and someone turns up the croaky radio:*

*'Here are some more Election results . . . Labour . . . Labour . . . Labour landslide.' Alvar Liddell's silky voice.*

*'You wouldn't know about unemployment, would you?' Big Rifleman Allen, his mind reacting to the wireless, flings the query from his battle-dress trousers whose creases are receiving attention on the ironing-board. (His rifle is done; its working parts wrapped in a protective duster). '. . . but the voters know all about it this time, mate; no Tory wool over their eyes.'*

*'Ask your dad!' advises one of the others, and his mates triumphing in the political kill, all laugh with the mockery of serfs who have broken their bonds to achieve equality.*

*'I know exactly what'll happen when a Labour government's in,' objects Rifleman Micky Butterwick, one of our faction, self-assured son of an Eton housemaster. 'They'll make a hash of the economy, my dear fellow. That tax-the-rich and spread-the-wealth business just doesn't work in practice, y'know. Simply renders the whole nation poor. You wait.' Butterwick breathes fastidiously on his rifle butt and, smiling his patronising smile, applies a yellow duster with elegant fingers.*

*"Ere, listen to that Butterwick, 'e's got lip!"*

*'Ow, Butterwick, you try telling that to my dad, what was on the dole. You never bin on the dole 'av yer?' Rifleman Allen approaches Butterwick's bunk threateningly.*

*'Just you wait and see, my dear fellow.' Butterwick peers at Allen, dabs Allen's nose with the duster, then turns his attention to Alvar Lidell's voice: 'Woodford, Essex. Conservative majority . . . Mr Churchill retains his seat.'*

*'Reduced majority' notes John Hoskyns, a clever Wykhamist, who one day would be director-general of the Institute of Directors (and whose father, incidentally, was killed in 1940, commanding a Rifle Brigade battalion at Calais.) 'Ungrateful country, kicking poor old Winston out of office after he won the war for us.'*

*'Yeah, 'e's not so fit to win the peace though, 'Oskyns mate' put in Rifleman Cadlow, 'what does 'e know about the workers?*

*'Just wait till you go on leave, 'Oskyns, cry on your mum's shoulder, tell 'ow she brought you up to be a fat industrialist, only you can't be now 'cos Labour's in. Tell 'er it ain't fair!'*

More caustic mirth from those destined to serve out their conscription in the ranks; resignation from those soon to be officers.

Pre-OCTU at Wrotham Camp, in Kent, was followed by cadetship at Eaton Hall, in Cheshire, then Sandhurst. But that was still only the wartime Sandhurst. After commissioning we were informed that Sandhurst would soon be on the old pre-war footing again. How would we like to be in the first intake? Well, having spent a year striving to earn the stars now on our shoulders, we all turned down the proferred honour. I was posted as a platoon commander to the Greenjackets Training Battalion at Barton Stacey. Meanwhile my mother had been successfully conspiring with 'Jumbo' Wilson – a former Rifle Brigade officer who ended the war a field-marshal, and was then Chief of the British Military Mission in Washington – to get Moray, a rifleman in the 60th, and me on leave to Virginia. ✺

We landed at Halifax from the troopship Samaria and took the train to Washington, via Montreal, where we stayed overnight. Our stepfather, Jack Hornor, had just relinquished command of the Remount Depot at Front Royal, Virginia, and was now a student at the Defence College in Washington. He was also a joint-Master of the Old Dominion hounds and managed, throughout the 1946–47 season, to continue putting in two days foxhunting a week.

All I can remember of our Viginian sojourn was the hunting and all that surrounded it. You never knew whether hounds would find, in any particular covert, the indigenous grey fox, or the red whose ancestors had been imported by British sportsmen in the eighteenth century (or perhaps earlier). But you soon became aware of which scent they were on from the way they ran. While a red would lead them as straight as in Europe, the smaller grey circled like a hare. The Virginian countryside was then characterized by the zigzag chestnut 'snake-rail' fences, which obliged followers to turn at the last moment if they were to put their horses at right-angles to the obstacles. Every one took their own line within reason (but since then, disease having killed off the chestnuts, the timber has been replaced by wire, the jumping is over 'chicken-coops' and riders are requested to follow the field Master). The Old Dominion also contained regions of stone-wall country. The *Baily's* of the day recommended 'a well-bred horse that is an exceptional jumper'.

Jumbo Wilson and his wife, Hester, who were generous in many ways to my mother and Hornor, were often invited to stay. The field-marshal was always provided with a horse (though weighing some eighteen stone, he was a difficult man to mount). Hester, who was a keen ornithologist (and looked rather bird-like) went bird-watching rather than hunting. The ADC was a young Welsh Guards officer, with a DSO and an MC to his name, called John Miller (he became Crown Equerry after leaving the army in the '60s). At first sight the American foxhunters were not impressed by John's wartime gallantry awards (which they reckoned 'had just come up in routine

My mother.

My father.

JW in 1936.

1938: with 'Mr Smith'.

Michael, Fourth of June 1942.

Eton: heading for the Division Room.

M'Tutor (Dick Routh) taking private study.

with the rations'), and were embarrassed by his somewhat chinless appearance, his stoop, his limp handshake and evasive eyes. They could not tally all that with a man who scarcely knew the meaning of fear. But when they saw him put his horse (on each visit an unfamiliar horse) at obstacles few of them would dare challenge – and bravely clear them – they changed their minds about Miller.

American entertainment – following close on the heels of our wartime fare (Britain was still on ration books) – left Moray and me, innocent teenagers, bewitched; in particular by the banquets known as hunt breakfasts, to which everyone repaired the moment they turned their horses in. You were not given a choice of pre-prandial drinks as you entered the hall of one of the great white Colonial houses concerned, but were faced by a negro butler with a dazzling tray of 'old-fashioneds', that homely euphemism for neat bourbon on the rocks, disguised at the bottom by a twist of lemon peel and a sugar lump soaked in angostura. Amid the Southern splendour of the big rooms, the tables groaned with as great a variety of food as my brother and I had ever seen. Hunts vied with one another as to which could parade the grandest swank. When an Old Dominion hostess put her coloured footmen in tail coats of the hunt livery, a Warrenton *grande dame* upstaged her the following week, dressing hers in eighteenth-century costume complete with periwigs.

One of the foxhunters' after-dark entertainments was raccoon hunting, a diversion that Moray and I, not approving, never joined in. Out they would go, men and women, of a winter night, usually well tanked up with bourbon, equipped with their coon rifle, coon hounds and coon flashlamps, to track the innocent raccoons to treetops, from which they shot them down by torchlight. (I regret to say the coon is still cruelly persecuted in the States.)

Just after Christmas I went down with jaundice and lay for a few days in the Walter Reed hospital in Washington. The doctor prescribed a month's sick leave but as I felt in the prime of health by early in the New Year, I spent most of January hunting with the various Virginia packs, the Blue Ridge, Piedmont, Warrenton, Orange County and Rappahannock, as well as the Old Dominion, to which I whipped for three weeks, a marvellous experience.

Meanwhile the less fortunate Moray was sailing home to complete his army training before the New Year began. Hornor's debonair joint-Master, Al Hinckley, who had ended the war a colonel in the Army Air Force was a member of the New York Stock Exchange, and was planning a week working on Wall Street later in the month. 'How would you like to join me at the Waldorf Astoria?' he invited. 'I could show you every corner of the city in six days.'

Al and I began our journey by calling in on a drinks party given by the motor tycoon, Walter P. Chrysler, whom he described to me as 'the most unpopular man in Virginia.' Chrysler, having been socially cold-shouldered by the establishment Virginia families and ostracised by all the hunts, revenged himself by buying up a long broad stretch of land across the middle of the Old Dominion country and converting it into a massive turkey farm with a chain-link wire perimeter. 'Then why are we drinking with him?' I asked Al. 'Keep him sweet' came the reply, 'we don't want him extending that turkey farm.'

Sterling Larrabee, stocky, hard-riding, big-game hunting, leg-pulling pre-war Master of the Old Dominion was already full of old-fashioneds when he escorted us to the party. He had a habit if fixing his eye on some object or other and ridiculing it for the entertainment of all present. As he entered the Chryslers' mansion a bear rug adorning the hall took his fancy, the taxidermist head of which carried a lolling tongue with a ga-ga expression. 'Hold it!' cried old Larrabee, keeping back the other guests with outstretched arms as he tiptoed around the black fur, gazing intently at it. 'Why, it's so square,' he said to me, 'so *square*. I guess its father must have been a jeep!' Humourless Chrysler, taking all this as a personal insult, told Larrabee to shut up. They met each other eye to eye and very nearly came to blows. The house being then devoid of a party atmosphere, Al and I drove to Washington whence we emplaned for New York.

Al Hinckley, handsomely bronzed and blue-eyed with a steel-grey crew cut, not only viewed his chances with girls very optimistically but appeared to know most of the New York belles, too. Air hostesses and hotel receptionists as well as dinner hostesses, floor-show girls along with debutantes, wherever we went would throw their arms round him. 'Why, it's A-a-l . . . Hi, Al! . . . Where you been since the fall Al?' It soon dawned on me that I was a mere decoy, my invitation being the excuse offered to his charming wife Steady (short for Steadman) for the unavoidable necessity of visiting all the New York nightspots. Al was a man whose greatest pleasure, apparently, apart from foxhunting, was to be surrounded by glamorous women. With admirable dedication and systematic patience he would sit on the end of his bed in the Waldorf Astoria telephoning them by the dozen. He had this young Englishman with him, he explained, to whom he wanted to show the bright lights and beautiful girls of New York. It would be just great if Betty or Carmen or Lana or Marylou or whoever could join us at the El Morocco, the Manhattan or the Diamond Horseshoe. And there, sure enough when the floor show opened, would be four or five young women greeting us, dolled up to the nines and none of them in the least put out by the presence of their rivals. I was enraptured by the floor shows, some of which were on ice, others with jungle, desert or nautical settings. They, like the gracious living of Virginia, brought home to me how little America had been affected by the war. Although we rarely returned to the hotel before three o'clock in the morning, Al was invariably up early and hailing a taxi for Wall Street, whereas I slept till lunchtime.

He was insistent from the beginning that I should wear uniform in public places. The reason he gave was that it was only thus that the waiters could be persuaded that I was not underage for alcoholic drinks. (I was a young-looking nineteen), though I suspect that it was more to impress his New York friends that he was doing a special service for Anglo-American relations. Dressed as a subaltern in the Rifle Brigade I endured several embarrassing encounters. That winter of 1947–48, the coldest in Europe for many years, the King and Queen sailed off on their South African tour. This was a good cue for a Waldorf cloakroom attendant uncertain as to the benefits of constitutional monarchy. 'You British?' he demanded. 'Well, your King and Queen should sure be ashamed of themselves basking in the sun while their subjects freeze . . .' Britain was having a good deal of trouble in Palestine at the time, and as I walked Fifth Avenue every eye of the city's considerable Jewish population seemed to be on me. A small crowd collected as, twice, I was confronted with 'how dare you wear that uniform in the USA, you who persecute our people . . .' So (*pace* Al Hinckley) I donned only civilian clothes until I disembarked from the *Queen Elizabeth* a month later and unpacked at the Greenjackets Training Battalion at Barton Stacey.

That summer I was posted to the Rifle Brigade's second battalion, which was stationed in one of Hitler's spacious barracks some thirty kilometres from Hamburg, near the village of Buxtehude. The Rifle Brigade had spent the war as motorized infantry, in support of tanks; our fighting vehicles at Buxtehude were armoured half-tracks. Enormously proud of their record of battle efficiency and their unique Greenjackets style in everything, the officers, warrant officers and sergeants viewed their work with intense professionalism. Three out of four of the battalion's majors, then in their twenties – Tom Acton, Hew Butler and Dick Worsley – were to become generals during the 1960s.

Here is a dialogue I remember (from the morning it occurred) between Dick Worsley (afterwards General Sir Richard) and an intelligent, if rather laid-back subaltern called Michael Barthorp who had arrived at the battalion the previous day. Worsley, while inspecting Barthorp's platoon next morning, peppered him with a burst of questions, such as 'how many married men have you got?' ('I don't know' shrugged Barthorp.) 'Has Jones been promoted to corporal yet?' ('I don't know'). 'Are any of your two-inch mortars in for repair?' ('I don't know'). 'Have you any men reporting sick?' ('I don't know'). 'How many on leave?' ('I haven't the least idea'). At last the exasperated Worsley called Barthorp away from the lined-up soldiers to the relative privacy of the balcony outside their room. 'How is it you know nothing about your platoon?' he enquired angrily. 'I only arrived yesterday,' the unrepentant Barthorp objected. 'Well now, let me tell you this,' retorted Worsley jabbing at the offending junior's chin with his silver-headed regimental cane. 'In my company it's the subalterns' business to find out everything they can about their men before they even meet their platoon sergeants . . . Now go to work!' he added dismissing the perplexed Barthorp, who subsequently transferred to the Northamptonshire Regiment. Michael told me only the other day that when he arrived at the Staff College some ten years later who should he find as one of his instructors but the same martinet!

The Commanding Officer, less quintessential Rifle Brigade, was cast in a more benign mould. Victor Turner, kind and delightful, if very highly principled, had, five years earlier, won the Victoria Cross, not only directing, but loading and firing too, the anti-tank guns of the battalion he

commanded during some of the most crucial moments of the battle of El
Alamein. The famous crimson decoration heading the war medals on his
battle dress, was complemented by a hole in his forehead, the width of a
penny, suffered in the same action. Essentially a countryman, Colonel Vic
was a person of simple tastes, the chief of which was a yen for game
shooting. During the autumn of 1947 he would take me and others, who had
brought guns to Germany, for weekend flighting on the North sea coast,
expeditions which we looked forward to with the greatest relish, albeit we
often lay drenched to the skin in the sand-dunes for hours on end without
firing a shot. He told me that his only consideration in choosing a suitable
place to retire to would be whether the shooting opportunities were promis-
ing. (On leaving the regiment Vic Turner joined the Royal Bodyguard of the
Yeomen of the Guard.)

The incessant training – fieldcraft, platoon tactics, company tactics, night
patrols, firing on the range, first aid, route marches, deployment of battle
vehicles, road blocks, etc – was occasionally broken up by a most unpleasant
task. East of Hamburg lay a number of 'displaced persons' camps, occupied
by refugees from the Baltic states, and administered by the Red Cross. For
health reasons the inmates were not permitted to keep livestock. My battalion was given the task, from time to time, of supporting the Control
Commission (CCG) in searching the premises for domestic animals. The
displaced persons showed a quite remarkable facility for acquiring chickens,
ducks, rabbits and piglets and for secreting them under the floorboards of
their huts the moment the authorities appeared on the scene, though a
frantic squawking, whining or quacking usually gave the game away. The
DPs lived in the utmost squalor and the stench was appalling. More than
one rifleman was obliged to go behind a hut to be physically sick. I came
closest to that on seeing a couple of emaciated Latvian women eating large
crusts of bread, covered in flies, quite unperturbed by the fact that they were
eating the flies, too.

The battalion was allotted two horses for recreational purposes and I
believe there were only two of us who availed ourselves of their backs. The
mare proved a good jumper and, with the enthusiastic help of the German
groom and to the patronising amusement of my brother-officers, I entered
her for several of the army gymkhanas.

In accordance with current plans to cut the British army down to peacetime proportions the Rifle Brigade was to be reduced to one battalion, and
pending this, I, along with a number of other non-regulars, were dispatched
on extra-regimental duty. I served for a few weeks on the headquarters of
the 7th Armoured Division. Subsequently, as an intelligence officer in Hamburg, I exchanged the desert rat emblem on my arm for one of white crossed
keys on a black background.

This job gave me a closer feel of the pulse of post-war Germany. More than
half Hamburg had been flattened by the Allied air forces, the Allied governments had confiscated a large proportion of the country's industrial resources and presented them to nations that had been occupied and pillaged
by the German army; the economy was ruined and the people still at

starvation level. Their bodies were emaciated, their skin wore a yellowy-grey pallor, they smelt of rancid sauerkraut and home-made tobacco while most of their talk was of the black market and of where ever the nearest commodities could be obtained. The starkly-painted prostitutes parading themselves for hire in the shop windows of the Reeperbahn looked a little healthier than the majority of their compatriots. They did well from the black market. I found myself comparing all this with the life I had shared with the Virginian foxhunters a year before.

As intelligence officer, my responsibilities were largely involved with refugee control and black market surveillance, making contact with former German officers and informing my superiors how they and their confederates were spending their time, in particular whether in political intrigue. For these purposes I enjoyed the luxurious advantage of a self-drive Volkswagen. Through friendships forged with two girls called Rosa von Richthofen (a niece of the First World War flying ace) and Hedda von Bülow, both of whom had an excellent command of English, I tracked down an old friend of my parents, Miles Reincke, who had been well-known in pre-war European society and a member of the German polo team. In 1945 he had returned from the Russian front with a leg missing. He had been nearer to death from freezing, he told me, than from loss of blood as he lay wounded in the snow at Stalingrad.

I used to take bottles of brandy, tins of coffee and numerous packets of cigarettes to Miles's dingy little flat, for much of which, I hope, he secured large sums of money on the black market. He would then pull aside the curtains of his larder, a diminutive corner cupboard, containing perhaps a couple of slices of stale ersatz bread and a few shrivelled apples, and, from the back of it, extract a bottle of Moselle and a couple of wine glasses for us. He was very sad to hear of the death of my father at the hands of German gunners in 1940. When I questioned him about the activities of his friends he always shrugged and said they were much too busy keeping body and soul together and the cold weather out to involve themselves in neo-Nazi plotting, or any political concerns for that matter. (In the mid–1950s I was to hear that Miles had re-built his old business, was a leading figure in German social life again and chairman of the revived Hamburg polo club.)

Although the era of non-fraternization in the Army of the Rhine had been relaxed to the extent that we were permitted to communicate with Germans on their own ground, it was still strictly against regulations to invite them into any British premises. I transgressed that law on several occasions and was eventually found out. Several of the great hotels and *schlösser* in North Rhine-Westphalia had been converted into officers' clubs. Those in Hamburg were the Atlantic and the Vier Jahreszeiten. Entry required the wearing of uniform while guests were requested to sign their names and give their addresses in a closely supervised visitors' book in the hall. An amusing friend of mine from the Black Watch, Michael Telfer-Smollett, and I dined Hedda von Bülow and Rosa von Richthofen, at the Vier Jahreszeiten, they having entered false English names in the visitors' book. Michael a tall, languid officer, was dressed in his regimental tartan trews and short cutaway blue jacket, I in my Rifle Brigade bottle-green; so our party may have stood out somewhat in the crowd.

We had just ordered coffee when Hedda whose looks Michael described as 'a sort of teutonic version of Deborah Kerr' and who had been complaining that the British had 'americanized' the Vier Jahrzeiten – interrupted herself suddenly with 'there's a nasty man sitting over there, staring at us!' Rosa added: 'Yes, and obviously discussing us with his companion. I think we had better leave.' One of the men, looking agitated, advanced on our table, whereupon the girls spirited themselves out of the dining room as fast as finches when a hawk hovers. 'Were those German girls?' the man demanded, producing a Control Commission police warrant. We saw his confederate move briskly towards the entrance. It looked as though Hedda and Rosa would be intercepted.

'They were German' we admitted. Hamburg's Provost Marshal was dining at the Club; we were informed he wanted to see us; we were then told that Hedda and Rosa were being interviewed by the Military Police. Why had we brought them there? Why had we allowed them to sign false names in the book . . .?

Michael returned to his battalion to be duly reprimanded by his commanding officer (who was Bernard Fergusson, of Chindit fame) while I was deprived of my appointment in Hamburg and returned to Buxtehude to face the wrath of Vic Turner – if wrath was the right word, for his reproaches were of the mildest brand. Yet of all men he was the least that any soldier would have wished to displease.

I decided the time had come for me to go to University. I wrote to Dick Routh, who penned a letter of recommendation to the Master of University College, Oxford, who invited me for an interview. I spent half an hour in the company of that friendly man. He suggested I should go up the following term with a view to reading politics, philosophy and economics. 'Must it be PPE, sir?' I protested. 'I had in mind history or literature.' He explained that PPE was the best grounding for a business career and 'presumably,' he added, 'if you have no specialist professional ambitions, you will be heading for a business career? It was what Dick Routh suggested . . . Well I look forward to seeing you next term.' But I did not go. The thought of spending the rest of my life in city offices and on commuter trains pursuing a profession for which I accurately sensed I possessed no natural gift, depressed me. The solution to the dilemma seemed to be to stay in the army for the time being.

It was through meeting two old school friends, both of whom were serving in the Royal Horse Guards (Blues) that first steered me towards that regiment. I discovered that their commanding officer was Walter Sale, the brother of George, my father's Colonel in the Middlesex Yeomanry. My mother, who had known him in pre-war days, wrote him a letter saying she hoped he would consider me for a place in his regiment, while Vic Turner also composed a most generous introductory note, containing no reference to my recent disgrace in Hamburg.

# 4

# *The King's Cavalry*

Notwithstanding the prowess won by the British cavalry regiments with tanks and armoured cars throughout Hitler's conflict, they still hankered to some extent after their old glory, the military eliteness of lancers, hussars and dragoons, once endowed by horses. For long after the war it remained their nostalgic regret that the smell and spirit of the troop stables had given way forever to that of the armoured vehicle hangar; that the dashing uniforms, topped by plumed helmet, busby and feathered lancer cap, had been replaced irrevocably by tank suit, denim overall and beret; that sabre, lance and revolver had to be put aside in favour of the turret howitzer and machine gun; that, from now on, the ugly roar of engines, rather than the thrilling hoofbeat and bugle call of cavalry *en masse*, would be the theme tune of their field days.

This yearning, this reluctance to break with the past, though not generally admitted by those concerned, was manifest in the Rhine Army – for at least the first decade after the war, and to a lesser degree for much longer – in the military race meetings and regimental horse shows; the eager return to the polo field and the hunting field; the lavish and self-indulgent parading of mess silver and paintings, nearly all of it redolent of the old horse cavalry; the dressing up in regimental striped overalls and spurs or boots and breeches; the insistence on continuing to refer to their combat squadrons and troops as 'sabre' squadrons and troops; the carrying – and intermittent slapping of the legs with – riding whips on vehicle maintenance parades; and, above all by the contempt in which officers who did not ride were held by those who did. The regiments of the cavalry of the line (which comprised those not in the Household Cavalry), had nearly all been mechanized long before the war and were by then to be found in the Army List under the heading Royal Armoured Corps along with the Royal Tank Regiment. So there was less excuse for them, if excuses were needed, in all those pretensions than for my regiment, the Royal Horse Guards (the Blues), who shared the prestige of Household Cavalry with the Life Guards, each manning since 1945 a horsed squadron in London to fulfil the daily mounting of the Queen's Life Guard and many other ceremonial duties.

Up to 1939 the Blues who then listed fewer than twenty officers, were always stationed in England, alternating with the Life Guards between London and Windsor. Until that date the officers were recruited (mostly) from Eton, (mostly) from renowned landowning families, (mostly) with regimental family connections, and (entirely) from young men with very substantial private incomes – a *sine qua non*, considering they were expected to join in the continuous sporting and social round, not to mention maintaining from their own pockets extensive wardrobes of uniforms and stores of saddlery. While the Household Cavalry led the league in this requirement of financial resources, the line cavalry, Foot Guards and Greenjackets and several others, too – in none of which was it possible to subsist pre-war on army pay – all stated their thresholds for officers in regard to capital outlay and income.

Here is General Horrocks, who had the Household Cavalry in his Corps in 1944–45:

> My first introduction to the Household Cavalry came in 1936–37 when I was Brigade Major of the 5th Infantry Brigade . . . I am afraid that we who considered ourselves to be professional soldiers were inclined to regard their officers as picturesque amateurs, who, after a short period in the army would normally depart to look after some vast family estate which they had inherited . . . On one particular occasion an astonished umpire saw a large Rolls Royce with headlights blazing, nosing its way up a very rough track to the 'front line'. The uniformed chauffeur, on being asked what he was doing replied haughtily that 'he was taking up his Lordship's breakfast' and proceeded to do just that despite the umpire's protestations . . . But I have often felt that it was 'his Lordship's breakfast' frame of mind which made the Household Cavalry so successful in battle . . .

In 1939 the Life Guards and Blues had joined forces to form the 1st Household Cavalry Regiment. As such they sailed with their horses to the Middle East in 1941, but converted to the combustion engine within a year. Meanwhile, in 1940, a 2nd Household Cavalry Regiment was put together, this one being destined to win its laurels in 1944–45 as the armoured reconnaissance element of the Guards Armoured Division. The complement of both officers and 'other ranks' in the Household Cavalry was, of course, more than doubled during that time. Nor when peace came, and the Life Guards and Blues were again separated, was there any great reduction in the strengths, since both regiments had, as I say, a horsed squadron as well as a full armoured car regiment to maintain.

In 1948, when I reached them, the Blues armoured car regiment deployed a headquarters squadron and three 'sabre' squadrons, each of the latter having seven troops, five composed of two Daimler armoured cars (with two-pounder turret guns) and two Daimler Scout cars (with machine guns), one with two vehicles of heavy guns and one of motorised foot soldiers. Since other ranks in the Household Cavalry had to be over 5 ft 9½ ins they were apt to stand out when in company with men from the line regiments. Another distinction was the fact that they wore cavalry caps instead of berets, except when on training or maintaining their vehicles; and the shoulder-points of their battle dress were emblazoned with the words 'Royal Horse Guards', red on blue. The warrant officers (corporal-majors, not sergeant-majors) had all been pre-war regulars and had mostly kept the unmistakable loose-limbed air of confidence and superiority so readily acquired by horse soldiers. And the new young corporals-of-horse (not sergeants) emulated them. The tall and languid, yet upright and soldierly style of our men, struck looks of wonder into the Americans when we shared manoeuvres with them in Bavaria.

Despite the greatly increased strength of officers since pre-war days, the regiment still made every effort to attract young bucks of the old stamp, even those completing their compulsory eighteen months' service as cornets (second-lieutenants). But there was a small element, too, generally in the rank of captain, who had joined during the war, none of whom would have dreamed of applying for a commission in a smart cavalry regiment in the 1930s or before. These officers, the last of whom did not shuffle off the regimental coil until the late 1950s, were disparagingly nicknamed, for their predilection for things mechanical, as 'sprockets' by the others, many of whom quite literally regarded them as a species apart.

Although less than a decade had passed since the sublime 1930s and there lurked this undercurrent of distaste for mechanization, all ranks, at least all the regulars, were enormously proud of the regiment's war record, and there was a great determination to uphold standards. As was natural for a regiment with a unique and traditional ceremonial role this was reflected in shop window spit-and-polish smartness; but it was demonstrated, too, in the rivalry between the squadrons as to who should lead in terms of fighting efficiency. This aspiration was hindered, however, as it was throughout the British army, by National Service, the fact that a continuous turnover of recruits – including young officers – had to be trained all through their two years' service. There was relatively little field training in those days (as compared with the Rhine Army of today), the regiment being all too busy instructing conscripts as gunners, radio operators, drivers and riflemen. We were largely involved in border patrols, that is to say keeping a presence along the Iron Curtain and reporting East German troop and police movement, which was quite a tense role in the years 1948–49 when the Berlin airlift was on.

Sport was enormously encouraged. For the troopers that meant football, basket ball, boxing and hockey; for the officers skiing (in the Hartz mountains) and game shooting (since we belonged to the army of occupation we could shoot anywhere we liked, in season, beyond the barrack gates); and racing, hunting and other equestrian activities (though not polo, which had yet to be organized in the Rhine Army). There were factions. The *haute école* clique was led by Lawrence Rook (who went on to find a place in the British Olympic equestrian team at Helsinki) and Mark Darley (who, in 1953 won the Badminton three-day event on his horse Emily Little, which was descended from the Darley Arabian imported by Mark's ancestor early in the eighteenth century).

Then there were the regimental hounds to which I helped to whip in. They were hunted by my squadron leader, Max Gordon, (one day to be Master and huntsman of Yorkshire's Badsworth foxhounds) and mainly comprised of drafts from Dumfriesshire's black-and-tans, provided by Rupert Buchanan-Jardine, who was then joint-Master with his father of that hunt, having recently retired from the Blues. He had been a hero of the 2nd

Household Cavalry Regiment. The Blues' hounds were supervised by a National Service officer, David Holman, who, in the 1950s, was to become a joint-Master of the Ashford Valley, and, notoriously, of his own private pack in Kent (which was made famous in a Giles cartoon as the 'pirate pack', after Holman was prompted to disband it). The quarry was supposed to be the hare, but it more often tended to be the roe deer, which led the hounds for miles through the great Westphalian forests, obliging us to spend many a winter's twilight attempting to call them back. Mounts were no problem since the regiment was allotted a number of troop horses with which to introduce volunteers for the mounted squadron to the rigours of riding school.

David Smiley, the regimental second-in-command, a man covered in glory from operations with special forces in Yugoslavia during the war, was in charge of the racing stables. He, Tom Coombs, Richard Sale and I were the jockeys. (Sale, son of Walter Sale, the commanding officer, deeply embarrassed his father on one occasion by guiding his scout car over the border, being imprisoned by the East Germans, and only achieving release by the direct intervention of Rhine Army's supremo). Julian Berry, another squadron leader, who was in time to be a great Turfite and owner of racehorses in England, was a significant power in our racing club, the Severn Club (so called after the first horse we stabled).

The two racecourses, at Hanover and Dortmund, were run with all the brisk efficiency, and most of the elegance, of Sandown and Cheltenham, under the stewardship of such well-known pre-war figures of the turf as Peter Payne-Gallwey, commander of the 11th Hussars, and Peter Grant-Lawson, a Grand National rider of the 1930s, who took over command of the Blues from Walter Sale towards the end of 1948. We rode on the flat and we rode over hurdles and steeplechase courses and there was a great deal of vying between the cavalry regiments as to who could produce the most successful horses and jockeys. It was the same with all equestrian and other sporting events; though the generals may have judged between regiments in terms of their military efficiency, the regiments themselves were more inclined to rate each other according to their sporting prowess and social elan.

Indiscreet drinking and horseplay were rife among the young officers. Evening outings generally took the form of dining riotously at one of Rhine Army's officers' clubs. Nearly all the German places were still out of bounds, hence the notorious 'Königen Bar affair' in which half-a-dozen of us were involved. Headed by Max Gordon, my (28-year-old) squadron leader, our party included the regimental quartermaster, Charles Firth, a splendid square-jawed giant of a veteran, with the most impressive iron-grey moustache. Having dined rather too well at the officers' club in Hanover, we decided to take a look at some of the illicit native night spots. The one which (most ominously) we alighted upon was the Königen Bar.

We were, as usual in uniform, box-collared blue 'patrols', and, although we vaguely sensed the atmosphere of uneasiness and hostility our entry aroused we did not know the place was an habitual haunt of the clandestine neo-Nazi youth movement. The place was upstairs at the end of a corridor divided by several pairs of swing doors. We took a table and ordered drinks. And I believe our visit would have passed without undue drama had not our quartermaster, who was very drunk, entertained himself by taking over different instruments of the band (and playing them atrociously) and making advances on a young German's girl-friend. Feeling the anger arising all around us we made a move to depart. But the Königen habitues were not prepared to let us off lightly.

As we made our way towards the door a large number of them intervened, suddenly appearing armed with knives, knuckle dusters, chair legs, bicycle chains and coshes. There was a scuffle in the doorway and, although we managed to get out of the first entrance, several of the youths manoeuvred behind us. A running fight down the passage and through the windowed swing doors ensued, with much broken glass flying. The battle continued at closer quarters on the street, and but for the arrival of mobile patrols of both German police and British military police, the violence was by then so intense that the fracas could easily have ended in one or more deaths. As it was, our adversaries were rounded up and arrested while we were taken, bleeding and bruised, to the military hospital.

The Germans were charged in their courts, convicted and punished. Then our turn came. The old quartermaster was court-martialled, but acquitted owing largely to the skill of his advocate, Arthur Collins, a wartime Blue, who was flown out to defend him. Max Gordon, being the senior officer present at the incident received a severe reprimand, a fact officially registered in his documents for the remainder of his career (although the stigma did not prevent him being promoted, in due course, to lieutenant-colonel). The rest of us, all subalterns, were sent to face General Arkwright, the commander of 7th Armoured Division, who brusquely admonished us. Whether it was to relieve the regiment of my wild presence, or because of my preoccupation with horses I don't know – probably a combination of both considerations – I was posted later in the month to the mounted squadron in London.

In the old Victorian Knightsbridge Barracks (or Hyde Park Barracks to give the Household Cavalry's London home its more formal name) the Life Guards squadron occupied the Hyde Park Corner end and the Blues the Kensington end, both with their horses stabled at ground level and their troop rooms above them. There were three troops to each squadron, each troop comprising about twenty-five men and twenty horses. The horses were bought principally from dealers in Ireland and Yorkshire. But, in those days, there was also quite a large contingent of Dutch, a present from Queen Wilhelmina to the King. In general those were ugly and somewhat intractable and troop leaders thought up every excuse to rid their stables of Dutch horses.

The troopers lived in primitive conditions in that old barracks. The troop rooms were damp and draughty, and their lockers, coupled with the small bedspace each was allotted, were really quite inadequate to both contain and keep clean their myriad items of uniform, some of which they often had to spend four hours and more polishing for the next day's parade. Although I took command of a troop, on arrival, I had no part in ceremonial duties pending my completion of riding school. Troopers went through a course of twenty weeks in riding school, but since it was assumed that officers posted to the barracks for the first time were already fairly experienced horsemen they were placed in a ride that was perhaps a third or half way through the course.

We started in khaki, then progressed by degrees to wear a state sword, then a helmet, then jackboots (the long black ceremonial boots, winged across the thigh) and cuirasses. We walked, trotted, cantered, jumped brush fences and, in the park, went through the mounted drill movements by the hour. *Quickest and best, mount!* the 'rough riding' instructor's voice echoed in the high-ceilinged tan-floored, wooden-walled school. *Adjust your reins! . . . Ride, draw swo-rds! From the right form single file, walk march! At the board, leading file to the left! . . . At the quarter marker, right incline! Ride, quit and cross your stirrups! From the left tell off by sections! Flanks of sections prove! Number one section at the half marker right turn! Turn and change! . . . Lower leg back, Mr Watson, sir, sit up sir!* (Instructors felt licenced to be as abrasive and abrupt as they liked to young officers, provided they slipped in 'sir' with every injunction). *Ride, near fore leading, canter . . . Ride trot, ride walk . . . Ride, return swords . . . Make much of your horses!* And so on.

In the afternoons, with the same progression to get accustomed to the various items of full dress uniform the ride spent forty-five minutes or so in the barrack yard on dismounted sword drill under the supervision of a corporal-of-horse. *Draw swords! Slope swords! Carry swords! By the left, quick march! Form sections! (Carry your sword blade upright, Mr Watson, sir!) Form half-sections, head left whe-el! . . .* At last there was a universal cadence, a concordant cavalry rhythm, every soldier at one with his horse, or nearly so, a centaur-like accomplishment, and my ride was duly paraded in full dress and put through its paces in Rotten Row under the hawk eye of the commanding officer, Colonel Henry Abel Smith (later Governor of Queensland), accompanied by his equitation officer, David Westmorland (since 1978 Master of the Horse to the Queen) and two squadron leaders, 'G' Gerard Leigh, of the Life Guards and Valerian Douro (since Wellington) of the Blues. From that winter day of 1949 I was a fully fledged 'Knightsbridge officer', qualified to take my place on the Queen's Birthday Parade, on escorts, at the Garter ceremony and at the head of the Queen's Life Guard.

Long and close familiarity with Household Cavalry escorts has never bred the least blaséness in my eyes or heart. The sights and sounds of the bobbing heads and clattering feet of the horses, the tossing red, or white, plumes of their riders, the jingle of bit, bridle and bright chain, the dazzle of sword and cuirass, all in one disciplined trotting momentum, excites me as much now as it did forty years ago.

The Life Guards and Blues alternated daily, mounting guard at Whitehall, finding 'short' guards, under a corporal-of-horse, when the King and Queen were out of London, or 'long' guards – with a make-up of an officer, corporal-major (carrying the regimental standard) and one or two other personnel – when the monarch and his consort were staying at the palace.

*It is 10.15 am. You are the officer of the King's Life Guard for the first time. You climb the mounting-block at the entrance to the officer's house, swing your leg astride your black charger, take your helmet from your soldier-servant, curl the polished bridoon over the second finger of your gauntlet, and the bit rein over the index finger and third finger, take your sword from your groom, and – rehearsing your sequence of commands like a schoolboy his Latin construe – ride to the barrack yard, positioning yourself in front of the guard. You salute the adjutant, the man in charge of the ceremony. Meanwhile you notice that one or two brother-officers are hanging around – as they were wont to do when a subaltern mounts guard for the first time – because if they can catch him out for inaccuracy or orders or drill movements it will be 'drinks all round'.*

*There was a policeman to see the Guard over Hyde Park Corner, but he was scarcely necessary, there being about seventy-five per cent less traffic than that to which we are now accustomed, and proceeding more slowly, too. People looked less anxious, less intense, and most pedestrians stopped with a fond smile to watch us pass. It was a gentler, more elegant, less impatient, more courteous London. I shout an Eyes right! at Buckingham Palace and an Eyes left! at Marlborough House. (On nearly every occasion old Queen Mary could be seen standing in her window, her hand raised to acknowledge the salute. Princess Margaret's name was linked with that of Sunny Blandford, another subaltern at the barracks in my time. The tabloids had it that the Princess always stood in a window of Buckingham Palace to receive Blandford's salute, but he denied it.)*

*The 'old guard' in their scarlet tunics and white-plumed helmets turn out in Horse Guards forecourt; the clock above Horse Guards arch strikes eleven; the new guard, in their dark blue tunics and red-plumed helmets, swing into line to face them; the ritual of guard changing ensues; the Blues' sentries take over from the Life Guards, the Blues horses occupy the vacated stalls, and the men change for stables parade. So it went on, day in and day out, as it still goes on today.*

The quarter of the officer of the King's Life Guard was on ground level at that time, with a nicely decorated little sitting room and bedroom. (Now it overlooks Whitehall from the upper level.) He faced the choice of having plates of the men's meals brought to him, or of sending his soldier-servant out to buy some dainties of his own choosing. One day, in the process of guard changing I spotted Humphrey Bogart and Lauren Bacall in the crowd of spectators and invited them to have lunch with me, which they did. They spent the entire meal bombarding me with questions about the Household Cavalry, based on a rather uninformative pamphlet they had bought. When were the Life Guards formed? By Charles II at the Restoration. When did the Royal Horse Guards, Blues, become Household Cavalry, Mr Watson? After the Battle of Waterloo. Who are the Gold Sticks in Waiting? The honorary colonels of the two regiments. Who is the Silver Stick? The officer commanding, or his deputy. What exactly are you guarding here? Well, technically the Monarchs. The entrance here is the traditional gateway to Royal London. Do King George and Queen Elizabeth often come and lunch with you? No . . .

Bogart asked the questions, Bacall took down the answers with a very chic little notebook and pencil. I escorted them round the stables. Why are the horses black? Because in the days when horses went to war, black was considered the most awe-inspiring, warlike colour. Why is the trumpeter's horse grey? Because he is the officer's signaller, and in field deployment, if he stood out from the colour of his horse, you'd know where the officer was, too. What's this story we've been hearing about the horse with the green tail? Well, I replied, in the late 1930s some non-commissioned officers of the guard took a fancy to a couple of girls standing in the forecourt. Would you care to come in and see a very special horse of ours, they suggested. It has a green tail? The girls were duped, the NCOs were court martialled. I leave the rest to your imagination . . . Bacall's little pencil worked vigorously in the chic notebook.

The officer could, if he chose, temporarily hand over his command after seven o'clock in the evening in order to dine with the officers of the King's Guard at St James's Palace, at whose elegant table a permanent place was reserved for him on the guard commander's right. If the Foot Guards commander had a special guest he was obliged to ask the Household Cavalryman if he would mind giving up his privileged place; and that could be refused, although of course it never was. I look back on those evenings with many fond memories, though one of them was marred by an unfortunate incident on the journey home.

The Horse Guards gates were locked at night and the sentries were under strict instructions not to let anyone in who did not know the password, including all members of the guard; and they took a special delight in keeping the officer out if he had forgotten it (especially if the officer in question happened to have 'taken his name' earlier in the day for idle turnout, or whatever). The telephone exchange of London District headquarters being then installed in the room next to the gate, I tapped on the window. It was manned (womanned?) by the ATS (now the WRAC). They opened it and let me in, cloak, helmet and all. However, the officious woman officer in charge contacted the London District duty officer (that night a Major Wigram, of the Grenadiers), and told him that I had 'terrified her girls'. Wigram reported my indiscreet conduct to Colonel Ferris St George (the Life Guardsman who had recently taken over from Henry Abel Smith as commander of the Household Cavalry), and I was awarded a week's 'extra orderly officers'.

The orderly officer's duties included visiting the men's dining hall at meal-times and enquiring whether they were satisfied with their food; inspecting the barrack guard; doing an evening round of all the stable, and checking the stable guards, with the duty corporal-of-horse; and generally being on call. He rode at the head of what was known as the watering order, the early morning exercise party for all horses not otherwise being used that day, that is to say all those not on King's Guard, riding school or special duties, such as, in the summer, the musical ride. The orderly officer led this detachment for an hour through the streets of London in any direction he wished. It was a great excuse for steering through streets where girl-friends lived and those might, if he was lucky – being forewarned by the clip-clop trot on the tarmac – throw open their windows, in, say, Kensington or Chelsea, and wave and blow kisses – usually to the great amusement of the troopers. His other principal duty, on the occasions when there was a 'short guard' at Whitehall, was to dress up in a frock coat and ride down to inspect the sentries and the rest of the guard at four o'clock.

Talking of girls in Kensington there was a house (I think in Elvaston Place) run by a Mrs Fetherstonhaugh (popularly known as 'Ma Feathers'). She kept a number of girls who she described as 'very well-to-do, but impecunious'. One wag made up a little verse about her. 'Oh dear Mrs Fetherstonhaugh, I can't go on any more; I'm covered in sweat and I haven't come yet; and what's more its a quarter past four!' She did good business with unmarried officers from the barracks, which reminds me of an amusing incident. One of the Blues' troop leaders was seen limping in the squadron yard one morning, and afterwards tenderly massaging his foot in the ante-room of the officers house. 'What's wrong, David?' we asked. 'Well, I was at Ma Feathers last night,' he replied sheepishly. 'Got your foot bitten?' we wanted to know. 'Well, I was on the floor, you see, and my toe was caught on the bars of one of her blasted electric fires.' It did not deter him. Ma Feathers was a much more civilized place than the notorious Bag O'Nails.

The Blues' honorary Colonel (Gold Stick) at that time was Field-Marshal Lord Birdwood. He was also president of one or two organizations and it sometimes fell to Blues subalterns to take a staff car to the old man's grace-and-favour residence at Hampton Court, escort him to meetings and generally act as his temporary ADC. Being in a state of advanced senility Birdwood not only suffered severe memory loss, but his sense of time and event went seriously awry. One day, passing our Victorian walls at Knightsbridge, he remarked to me that he was 'so glad the builders have got your barracks completed at last'. On another occasion he enquired whether I knew 'who would take over as commander-in-chief from the Duke of Cambridge?' I am fond of the story emanating from the 1920s when Birdwood went to inspect one of the regiments that had been under him when he commanded the Australian and New Zealand Corps during the First World War. When he appeared on parade topped by his plumed general's hat, one young Aussie officer whispered to his neighbour 'Who is this guy?' And, when informed, wanted to know why the general didn't 'wear his tail feathers in his bottom like any other bloody *bird would*?'

Ordinary days began with a stables parade and, after breakfast, officers exercised their chargers for an hour, individually, in the park. (One day Gilbert Harding was at the head of a queue of impatient motorists held up by a regimental policeman while a pink-faced subaltern sauntered his charger across the road to Rotten Row, lifting a nonchalant finger in response to the soldier's stiff salute. And a day or two later one of the tabloids published Harding's furious comment '. . . the London traffic held up by a toffee-nosed puppy'.) Hyde Park was the only place where officers were to be seen by the public in khaki. Yet there was a civilian uniform, too, for every occasion. In London, during the daylight hours, you would not wish to be observed outside barracks without a well-cut dark suit, stiff white collar, bowler hat and furled umbrella. A country suit and soft hat was right for the races, while for dinner or theatre parties, black tie was more or less the rule. Most of us attended the four days of Royal Ascot.

White tie and tails were the habitual dress for dances, and between May and September you often wore them three or more times a week. In those days party goers could walk the streets of Mayfair or Piccadilly in full evening dress without anyone looking twice at them – not that there were many people out after the shops were closed to notice them.

The young of today would also scarcely believe how few vehicles there were on the London streets. One evening, after driving away from Buck's Club, my car was winged by another, so slightly, it seemed, that I drove on not giving the matter another thought. A month or so later, however, I was summoned to appear before the Bow Street magistrates. There I found an old school friend, amiable George Leeds (then serving with the Grenadiers at Wellington Barracks) sitting glumly in the waiting-room. 'Hullo George, what brings you here?' I asked him. (If you can imagine a high-colour edition of the Prince Regent, embellished by a spruce tawny moustache, you've got a good idea of George's face.) 'Some bloody fool collided with me in Bond Street last month,' he growled. I gave him a double take. 'What a co-incidence,' I said, 'some bloody fool who bumped me in Bond Street last month is prosecuting.' I don't know which of us was the more embarrassed as we faced one another in court. Anyhow, to his indignation the case was dismissed as 'frivolous'.

Young men must have been at a premium to strike the balance at debutante dances and other parties around 1950, because those shelves above the fireplaces in our draughty rooms in the officers' house were thronged with invitation cards during the season. Dance invitations usually included one for a preliminary dinner party; and, in return for the evening's hospitality, most girls expected to be taken on after to a night club. That dark and musty little room in Leicester Square, the '400', with its subdued red-shaded table lights, soft foxtrot band and diminutive dance floor, prompting cheek-to-cheek, was perhaps the favourite. Members could keep bottles of gin and whisky there, labelled with their names, and (distrusting who? – fellow-members or the staff?) made a habit of marking the level with their girl-friend's lipstick at the end of each visit. The Orchid Room and the Milroy were on a par with the 400 – white tie, or black, obligatory there, too – while the most entertaining restaurants, in my opinion, were the Mirabelle, Quaglino's and the Café de Paris. The annual Queen Charlotte's ball was an extraordinary occasion. I can now, forty years later, vividly recall images of those debutantes in their white dresses, each descending the stairs on the announcement of their names, as horses might be brought forward at a market. Among the prettiest and most enchanting in those two early London years of mine were Davina Merry, Sally Ann Vivian, Jacqueline (Jacques) Floor, Davina Portman and Caroline Thynne.

Davina Portman was the niece of a Life Guards colonel called Peter Williams, the provost marshal at London District, who occupied a married quarter in the barracks and on whom she was usually billeted during the

Shooting VIII, 1944: Front row (*left to right*) Jeremy Porter, Sandy Stirling, Christopher Curtis (captain), James Bruce, Dickie Birch Reynardson. Back row (*left to right*) David Bagnall, myself, Staff Serjeant Butcher (manager), Alan Ranken. The members are wearing the then recently adopted uniform of the College Officers Cadet Corps.

COUNTRY LIFE

Vol. CII No. 2641            AUGUST 29, 1947

MISS LAVINIA FRENCH

Miss Lavinia French is the daughter of the late the Honourable Bertram French and of the Honourable Mrs. Bertram French, and a grand-daughter of the 4th Baron de Freyne.

Lavinia as a debutante.

Moray playing the part of Bohun in Shaw's *You Never Can Tell* at the Haymarket Theatre in 1966.

Queen's Birthday Parade, Nicosia, Cyprus, 1957: leading my squadron past the saluting base; Field Marshal Sir John Harding is taking the salute.

(*left*) Suez 1956.

(*below*) Famagusta, Cyprus, 1958. Officers and senior NCOs of A Squadron of the Blues. Front row (*left to right*) Corporal-Major King, Ailwyn Broughton, Stephen Fox-Strangways (murdered by EOKA 1958), Squadron Corporal-Major Ford, JW, Patrick Beresford, David Blake, James Wilson, Corporal-Major Biles. Standing behind me is Mark Birdwood.

season. One night Michael Naylor-Leyland (who followed Westmorland as equitation officer) took the beautiful Davina home from a night club, but did not see her into the flat. She had lost her key and, unable to raise her uncle and aunt, got into a panic and began searching for Naylor-Leyland whose room was alongside the rest of us bachelors at the other end of the officers' house. On the way she knocked loudly on the door of the commanding officer, Colonel St George, who was immediately aroused. She then groped her way down our dimly-lit passages, and becoming more and more frightened and frustrated, she began screaming 'Michael! Michael!' as she hammered on all our doors. By this time scarlet-faced, white moustachioed Ferris St George was up and about, and so were we subalterns, and to our great amusement, as, pyjama-ed, we poked our heads from our doorways, we saw that he wore an old-fashioned nightshirt accompanied by a nightcap, complete with pompom finial, and carried a bedside candle. And never in the rest of my life have I witnessed quite such an evocative Dickensian scene as that of him sternly leading Davina, in her long white dress, by the arm back down the passage, observed by grinning heads in half-a-dozen doorways. (Three years later Michael Naylor-Leyland married the previously mentioned Jacques Floor.) &

In terms of the attitudes of the rich and privileged, 1950 was closer, in many ways, to 1930 than it was to 1960. People with very marked social advantages, those of the 'upper rank' seemed to take the view that although there was a socialist government, its greatly reduced majority in 1950 heralded a return to the good old days; that although taxation was heavier than ever and domestic servants were becoming increasingly difficult to find, they were gratified to observe that those who owned the land of Britain in the 1930s were the same people who owned it in 1950, which is to say themselves, while the poor were still the poor and 'knew their place', (though they were not quite as 'suitably deferential' as fifteen years before), Britain's traditionally privileged people still scarcely recognized the fact that the war had caused an irrevocable social revolution. Perhaps they were burying their heads in the sand in fear that a breakdown of the class hierarchy would result in anarchy. Anyhow they appeared to be saying with one voice: 'Five whole years have gone by since peace was declared; it is high time we not only picked up the threads of 1939 but worked them into the old pattern . . .' I noticed this nowhere more forcibly than in the hunting-field.

In the winter months Melton Mowbray was the Knightsbridge officer's home from home. There resided the army remount depot where freshly-bought army horses (for the King's Troop of the Horse Gunners and still, in a small way, for the Army Service Corps and the Military Police, as well as the Household Cavalry) arrived to be broken by the Royal Army Veterinary Corps. Since the ceremonial season ended for us early in November (with the Sovereign's Escort required for the State Opening of Parliament), and did not commence again until the following May (when rehearsals began for Trooping the Colour) there were horses to spare for recreational purposes during the winter months. Foxhunting was considered to be an activity of great moral and physical benefit to both young officers and young horses.

Straight after Parliament was opened those of us who yearned for the Shires dispatched what were euphemistically known as our 'second chargers' – the boldest and safest cross-country performers in our troops – to be stabled at the Remount Depot.

My second charger during the 1950–51 season was called Merlin, the most willing, gallant and lovable horse I ever rode. I discovered black Merlin's potential at Stoney Castle camp, in Surrey, to which open space each autumn the squadrons rode in turn at the crack of dawn and stayed under canvas for a fortnight, to practise on the rifle ranges, and to put in some cross-country riding and map reading exercises, and generally to give everyone and the horses a break from the London routine. When Merlin and I won the hunter trial and showjumping competitions I said to myself 'this horse is for the hunting-field next season'.

As often as duty allowed, having booked rooms at the George or the Bell, we would take the train to Melton and put in days with the Belvoir, the Cottesmore or the Quorn, many of whose meets were in easy hacking distance of the town. It was all wonderfully cheap. We paid for the additional forage required to keep horses in hunting condition, otherwise the stabling was free. The regiments paid lump-sum subscriptions and, as service officers, our 'cap' was a small fraction of the standard rates. If our second chargers were lamed, or otherwise laid up, we simply sent for another, or made use of the pool of Household Brigade Saddle Club horses, which were there for our use as well as for sporting Foot Guards officers. During the 1950–51 season I kept two troop horses at Melton and with the use of another from the Saddle Club would often put in as many as four or five consecutive days' hunting a week.

Leicestershire, the birthplace of modern foxhunting, Rutland and the Grantham side of Lincolnshire were ninety-five per cent grass in those days and nearly all the wire was taken down for the start of the season, so that followers could take their own line *ad lib*. To the newcomer the leading subscribers seemed awesomely grand. There were considerably more men wearing scarlet swallow-tails and champagne-topped boots than are seen nowadays, and nearly all the older women and quite a lot of the younger ones, too, rode sidesaddle, all impeccably turned out. Several of the men wore skin-tight leather breeches and white leather gloves and carried white whips, and I remember one follower, a General Fanshawe, a regular visitor to the Quorn from the Pytchley, was in a positive cloud of white dust at the meets, his whites were so heavily pipe-clayed. Now, flickering across my mind's eye, is a picture of one of those glittering meets with, in the foreground, three *grandes dames de la vénérie* called Cantrell-Hubbersty, a Quorn joint-Master, Everard and Earle, their impeccably made-up mouths conversing from behind fishnet veils, stretched on the expensive anchors of their chins and top hats.

Most of these Meltonians – each provided with two or three of the best hunters that money could buy – devoted their entire winters to the sport. Those whose principal homes were outside the Shires kept hunting boxes within them. The great houses – such as Baggrave, Lowesby, Quenby, and

Ragdale – of those who lived permanently in the country were synonymous with their own names. There were far fewer visitors then than there are now and among the subscribers everyone knew everyone else. As for the tenant farmers, in their black coats and velvet caps, they kept at a respectful distance, to one side, at the meets. *Nouveaux riches* were regarded with the gravest suspicion. A newcomer, such as I, was scrutinized from head to foot to ascertain that he was not committing some dreadful solecism, scrutinized usually with looks of open-mouthed incredulity as if to ask 'well what sort of intruder is *this*?' Was the angle of your top hat reasonable? Was your saddlery correct? Were the cut of your coat and breeches and boots up to standard? Was your stock (or rather, in the Shires, hunting tie) properly tied? Was your horse's mane well plaited? They might then remark to themselves that from the look of your horse it lacked breeding, until their eyes travelled to its forefeet of which one foot was branded with the letters RHG and on the other with a regimental number. 'Ah, Household Cavalry,' they would mutter with a shrewd inclination of the head. But the aura of hauteur was warmly blended with generosity and kindness. One was soon absorbed.

An amateur, Cyril Heber Percy, hunted the Cottesmore hounds, while professionals – respectively George Tonge and George Barker, carried the horn to the Belvoir and the Quorn. As for sport I seem to remember that Barker just had the edge, but that may have been owing to slightly better country and more enterprising foxes. With Barker hunting them the Quorn hounds always seemed to be speaking, we always galloping. Those were still the days of bullfinch and cut-and-laid fences, features now virtually extinct. Being very young and foolhardy we put our horses at anything, stiles, park railings, gates and yawning ditches. We cared little about the hounds' activities in those days; speed and derring-do were the things. We considered it *noblesse oblige* to be in front.

One morning towards the end of the 1949–50 season when three of us, Bobby Dolbey, Ben Wilson (now Nunburnholme) and I were due to ride off from the Melton Stables to a Kirby Gate meet together, Wilson, who had been orderly officer in London and was due to catch the milk train, did not turn up. So Dolbey and I proceeded to the meet without him. As Barker's melodious voice said *try- hy – hy -rit – push – 'im – up – then* at the first draw, Gartree, and we relished the Leicestershire air, Ben Wilson came cantering along and explained. He had been kept up most of the night on account of a raid on the barracks by a composite party of police special investigation branch and the military police. It transpired that a large number of Household Cavalrymen, from the rank of trooper up to corporal-major, had been involved with a close-knit ring of homosexuals, against whom the police were looking for evidence, and all the lights of the barracks were ablaze while the men 'stood to their beds' and had their lockers searched. None of them, I believe, confessed to being of similar proclivities as their murky patrons, but all admitted that, on their extremely meagre pay, they could not resist the offers of very tantalizing rewards for performing such painless, if bizarre, acts as walking round a London flat dressed in nothing but helmet and jackboots, or even accompanying their patrons on Continental week-ends. And who could really blame them? A day or two later Colonel St George summonded the entire regiment into the riding school for a moral lecture. I did not hear it: officers were excused.

I remember Ferris St George joking in the mess one day around that time about a dialogue with the Commandant of Sandhurst, who was then Gen-eral David Dawnay. St George visited the Academy to enquire how the two or three potential officers for the Household Cavalry were getting on. 'Well, we're rather concerned for young Ronald Ferguson,' Dawnay told him. 'He's very weak on the academic side. You do know, don't you, that he was superannuated from Eton?' St George gave the commandant a double take. 'I don't see anything wrong with that,' he retorted. 'So was I'.

I must confess one didn't need to be 'very strong on the academic side' to get by as a troop leader in the mounted squadrons. Nor, for that matter, have great energy. As there were six of us (three Life Guards, three Blues) orderly officer didn't come round, all things being equal, more than once a week at the most, or whole weekends one in six; and as the two squadron captains were also on the King's Life Guard roll (and it was only an officer's command if the Monarch was in London) that was even more infrequent. The ordinary routine on other days, after exercising one's charger in Hyde Park, consisted of morning stables from eleven o'clock until the horses were fed and watered at twelve-thirty; and evening stables from four-thirty until five-thirty, the early part of the afternoon being spent by the troopers in the cleaning of equipment, and the officers doing as they pleased. Nor was reveille stables, a 7 am parade, obligatory for officers. Really the most ar-duous part of serving as a subaltern at Hyde Park barracks, once riding school was behind one, in those days was having to change into this or that different order of dress, military or civilian, so many times a day! But none of that is to say that one was idle. One was responsible for the deployment, welfare and general supervision of some thirty NCOs and troopers and twenty-five horses, and every horse, as well as every man possessed a different character and temperament, different talents and limitations. As with any other command there was no success without devotion.

With the ceremonial surrounding the Festival of Britain, which was opened by the King, and a State Visit from the King and Queen of Denmark, along with all our perennial occasions, the summer of 1951 was a relatively busy one. It was my last as a troop leader, and I'm afraid it was a little blemished through my getting into another scrape. The wildest and most unpredictable of my brother-officers, Robin Keith (who had also been in M'Tutors), informed me late one evening that the 'Skylon' irritated him so much that he intended to cut it down. (Those old enough to have known the London horizon in 1951 will recall a tall metal erection, the symbol of the Festival, on the Embankment). I fondly imagined that I had succeeded in dismissing the idea from Keith's head by derision until he re-appeared fifteen minutes later announcing that his car was waiting outside with an axe in the boot, and why didn't I string along and watch the fun?

Thinking I might be able to prevent him making a fool of himself I accompanied him. My entreaties – which included a warning that his axe, however sharp, was unlikely to make much impact on steel – were of no avail. Parking his car on the bridge alongside the Skylon he took out the axe and started through the turnstile entry to the enclosure. A policeman was on the spot straight away and, between us, he and I relieved Keith of the axe and got him back in the car. The bobby accepted the explanation that my companion suffered from 'turns' and was not quite himself that evening. (No breathalyser in those days!) Driving back Keith then took an excited interest in a demonstration of searchlights making their ballet in the night sky. He insisted on discovering where they were sited as he wanted, he said, 'to play with them'. The good-humoured team manning one of them allowed him to do just that for a minute or so, and he got away with it, too. Unfortunately, however, the night's tragi-comedy was not quite over. There was an unpleasant fracas in the region of Hyde Park Corner on our way back. Keith behaved arrogantly and noisily, and although he again avoided the punitive arm of the law, there was a complaint from another quarter, and both our names were reported to Colonel St George next morning.

We were bitingly excoriated, and confined to barracks for a fortnight. And thereby hangs another tale. Shortly afterwards my (new) squadron leader, Mick Dillon, attended a dance (for the coming out of Mary Lou Hennessy, now de Zulueta) at which he was convinced he saw me. As I discovered – from a couple of subalterns who were at the same party – the person he imagined to be me was in fact my brother, Moray, to whom I am supposed to bear a striking resemblance. When Dillon started upbraiding me in the morning, and I interrupted to suggest the truth of the matter, he replied 'That's about the most flimsy and unlikely story I've ever heard. Just make sure you don't leave barracks again until your time of confinement's up!'

The moment Keith's 'time' was up he was posted to Germany, his regiment, the Life Guards, having exchanged places with the Blues who were by then at Windsor. He was a person with a wonderful wit and gift for mimicry and an accomplished amateur jockey. But he would punish himself and he was destined to die in his thirties, an alcoholic, when living in Andorra.

I was dispatched to the newly-formed armoured car training regiment near Carlisle, where the Household Cavalry were represented on an equal footing with the then other experts in that arm, including the Royal Dragoons, King's Dragoon Guards, 11th and 15th/19th Hussars and the 16th/5th Lancers. Having an infantry background and a Hythe small arms course behind me I was put in charge of the assault troopers wing. At first I looked upon this posting as a bleak exile, a feeling compounded on arrival at finding that the camp was entirely hutted and not very close to civilization.

As things turned out I spent a very happy two years in Cumberland. The commanding officer was a most stimulating man called Jamie Crawford, a Carabinier, formerly of the Central India Horse, whose attitude was – in common with many veterans of the late British *Raj* – that cavalry officers should spend at least half their week involved in some sporting activity or other, preferably one of the field sports. Any daylight leisure time not spent on sport was known in his vocabulary as 'poodle-faking'. He discovered the best means to acquire flighting on the Solway estuary; he made it his business to get to know most of the local landowners with pheasant shoots and grouse moors and persuaded them that his sporting officers would be ideal candidates if those hosts were short of guns; he encouraged the formation of a regimental pack of beagles, the Hadrian, of which I became joint-Master and huntsman; and he persuaded the Household Cavalry to send up a couple of good troop horses with which their officer representatives might hunt. Jamie and I and one or two others hacked regularly to meets of the Cumberland Farmers' hounds, or boxed up to the Dumfriesshire. We also made intermittent Saturday excursions to Northumberland, to the Tynedale and to Co Durham where the Zetland hounds were showing exceptional sport under the guidance of Captain Colin MacAndrew. In addition to all that shooting and hunting I had a point-to-point horse, which for the two seasons concerned I rode in the Cumberland members' race and at the various adjacent hunt meetings.

The Cumberland were then under the Mastership of George Fairbairn and the author-foxhunter, D. W. E. Brock, a delightful sportsman, who died a tragic death during my Carlisle time. Officially declared bankrupt and very deeply in debt, in 1952 he put a gun to his head in the garden of the bed-and-breakfast place at which he was staying, leaving his terrier whining over his dead body.

Rupert Buchanan-Jardine, who had retired from the Blues three years before, was in the process of taking over the horn of his family pack, the Dumfriesshire, from his father, Jock, when I started hunting with them in the autumn of 1951. Jock Buchanan-Jardine was a large man with a powerful personality to go with the heavy frame; he sported mutton chop whiskers, had a roguish sense of humour and, from Castle Milk, ruled his great estate in unique style. He had made a lifelong study of genetics and bred successful hybrids in any field he chose, from harriers to Highland cattle, from goats to fighting cocks. His book *Hounds of the World* remains a classic.

What he is best remembered for is the foundation of the black-and-tan Dumfriesshire pack, which he began to create in 1921 (at the age of twenty-one). I quote from my *British and Irish Hunts and Huntsmen* (Vol I): '... He wanted a pack of pure black-and-tans, possessing a better cry and nose and greater speed than the average English foxhound. He achieved this firstly by putting selected bitches to a field trial champion bloodhound called Ledburn Boswell. Sir John described a grandson of these experiments, Harlequin, a quarter bloodhound, as the best hound in the field that he ever saw. He also acquired a hound of Gascon breeding called Triomphe, and the foundation of his pack was the result of crossing Triomphe with Harlequin's sisters. He then brought in other black-and-tan influences, such as the Brecon Whipcord and Croome Clansman. In seventeen or eighteen years of selective breeding the white was eliminated. What emerged was a pure black-and-tan with a tremendous shoulder and depth through the heart, great long-distance speed, a bloodhound's nose and a golden voice once heard never forgotten – a perfect match for this steep country and its outsize foxes ...'

Rupert, who completed the Cirencester course after leaving the army, was running the Castle Milk estate by the time I arrived on the scene. Having hunted his own foot pack as a boy he was well qualified to take on the Dumfriesshire, too. Jock was keen for him to do so, but was, at the same time, reluctant to let his precious hounds ultimately out of his own control. The result was, in the 1951–52 season, that both men carried horns, and if Jock thought that Rupert had made a wrong decision, one heard huntsmen's voices and horn *twangs* from different directions, witnessed the pack divide and tempers growing high on both sides. These disputes normally ended with an exasperated Jock turning his horse for home, angrily muttering 'I've got a much better covert draw on my sideboard!' and the perplexed hounds probably doing nothing for Rupert for the rest of the day. (I sampled Jock's sideboard on several occasions and can vouch that it was well worth going home early for.) But even on a poor scenting day the Dumfriesshire black-and-tans were normally a joy to watch and listen to. They were capable, unlike any other hounds I have watched, of casting thoroughly over the whole extent of two fields at a time and breasting four-foot walls and fences without so much as touching the tops. The deep melody of their cry was, and is, positively thrilling.

Another colourful character was Bay de Courcy Parry ('Dalesman' of *Horse and Hound*), who was at that time hunting a fell pack in Cumberland. Although he only came out with the Hadrian on two or three occasions when I was hunting hounds, on those brief afternoons I learned much from him about the antics and wiles of the hare, about scent, about the recognition of a heel-line, about hunting upwind and downwind, about the deployment and posting of whips, and, above all, about patience and the avoidance of lifting hounds.

The Bishop of Carlisle who was a keen follower of our regimental beagles when I carried the horn, once asked me if I could arrange for him to have a day with the famous Dalesman. When I telephoned de Courcy Parry, although he consented he did so in rather dubious tones. I duly accompanied the Bishop to the meet. He wore his habitually neat hunting garb, a well-pressed knickerbocker suit, brogues and deerstalker, whereas de Courcy Parry looked, as usual, as though the clothes were about to fall off his back. By nature a warm, generous good-humoured man, on this occasion Dalesman was none of those things. 'Oh, you're the local bishop, are you?' he exclaimed looking the poor man up and down. 'Well, if you want to know, I'm the bloody Pope!' I never did discover the reason for this rude outburst. The bishop, however, took it in very good heart, telling me that it added to his 'rich image of the man'. As the day wore on de Courcy Parry made up for his discourtesy by giving the bishop a friendly discourse on the nature of hunting on the fells.

A marvellous sporting interlude during the period 1950–53 was an annual invitation from my old Rhine Army hunting friend, David Holman, whose parents' Scottish property was on the Argyllshire coast. For ten days or so each autumn David invited a party, girls included, to Shielbridge where we enjoyed an exhilarating programme of stalking, salmon fishing, lobster potting, mackerel fishing and grouse shooting. And for me the meat of those creatures, cooked the same day, has never tasted so good before or since.

As an instructor at the Household Cavalry Training Cadre at Windsor, in 1953 and 1954, I had the honour of training the team that won the Household Brigade Young Soldiers' competition in both years, the only occasions in which the Household Cavalry ever carried it off. This was an inter-regimental contest, conducted on a platoon basis with a continuum of tests of turn-out, forced march discipline and elaborate trials of marksmanship from distances of 400 yards down to 100. For those Household Cavalrymen, mostly conscripts, to have beaten the five regiments of Foot Guards at their own game, two years running, was a cherished achievement.

The all-rounder concept of that five-in-one sport, the Pentathlon, which was born in Greece over two-and-a-half thousand years ago, appealed strongly to me. The modern Pentathlon – first staged as an Olympic sport for the 1912 Olympiad at Stockholm – consists of the following five tests: fencing, with an epée, against every other competitor; shooting twenty rounds 'snap' with a pistol, at thirty yards range; and – against the clock – running two-and-a-half miles across country, swimming 330 yards, and riding over a rugged one-and-a-half mile course, containing sixteen obstacles. In 1954 Richard Abel Smith and I started up Pentathlon in the Household Cavalry and supervised the training of two teams, led by ourselves, for the British Championships. The great fun we enjoyed in this involvement culminated in our swimming, running and fencing at Aldershot, riding at Tweseldown and shooting at Bisley against seventy other competitors and with far greater success than we dared hope for. In particular our Lance-Corporals Hudson and Walker came respectively first and second in the swimming, Hudson beating the record time. The beauty of the Pentathlon lies in the fact that, because you may shine, say at three events and be relatively inept at two, knowing that everyone else is probably in the same position, there is a much greater incentive to improve your poor subjects than if you were to attempt them in isolation.

My dialogue with the Foot Guards was soon to be strengthened. In 1955 it was decided that the Guards Independent Parachute Company, the pathfinder unit of the Parachute Brigade, which until then had been recruited entirely from the Foot Guards, should now – particularly bearing in mind the armoured car soldier's superior training in radio and things mechanical – include an element from the Household Cavalry. Accordingly volunteers were invited to step forward. An officer (which was me), two corporals-of-horse and two or three troopers proposed their names, and were duly nominated for different courses. David Smiley, a wartime Special Forces hero, then commanding the Blues, told us that, in his opinion, the company was 'the small corps d'elite of the whole army'.

The first hurdle to be endured was ten unpleasant days' trial with 'P' Company at the Airborne Forces Depot at Aldershot. From dawn until dusk, with very few breaks, we battled over daunting varieties of obstacle course, jumped at various angles from the high boards of swimming pools, did knees-bends, press-ups, and wooden horse exercises till we were blue in the face; boxed one another until liberally sprinkled in blood; carried telegraph poles up hills until blind with sweat and fatigue; and double-marched many gruelling miles, making a chorus of ape-like battle noises as we did so – all to prove that we were 'para material', as they described the requirement. There was a seventy per cent failure rate. Being passed, after that bizarre experience, into the tender care of the Royal Air Force parachute school at their base at Abingdon, we were more or less ready and happy to jump out of anything they liked, with or without a 'chute.

The initial couple of weeks there were spent learning to roll like india-rubber balls on coconut-hair mats; practising aircraft drills and landings from fire-escape contraptions; and learning how to work a parachute and how to fit and release the weapon and equipment container, with which we jumped, strapped to our legs. Then came two tummy-sinking descents from a basket suspended from a balloon 800 feet up, followed by six from aircraft, Hastings C119s and Vickers Valettas, (three without, and two with, weapon containers), one being at night.

*You sit in your two rows against the fuselage, facing one another, a throb under the heaviness of every chinstrapped helmet, butterflies in every stomach, until, in hectic, staccato tones, you are told to stand up, face out towards the open door.* 'Prepare for action! Tell off for equipment check! Action Stations! Red on, prepare to jump! Green on, go! ... go! ... go!' *With a mighty rush you are flung into the slipstream, your canopy develops, you are suspended, a Lilliputian figure dangling below a white puff in the sky; you snatch at the latch and two hooks that hold the hundred-pound weight of your weapon and equipment container to your right leg; it is now carried on the end of a rope thirty feet below you; your hands fly up to the rigging lines; you steer; the container meets the ground with a thud; and you roll over on the turf like a ju-jitsuist.*

At the end of the Abingdon month we paraded to receive our 'wings' from the station commander and went our separate ways, I to the Guards Company at Pirbright Camp, Surrey, where I exchanged my Blues cap for a red beret adorned with the Parachute Regiment winged badge, backed, in our case, in silk with a Household Brigade blue-red-blue flash. The words Parachute Regiment also appeared on the shoulders of my battle dress in place of Royal Horse Guards. The three battalions of the Parachute Regiment – the Red Devils – all under command of 16 Parachute Brigade and immensely proud of recent battle honours, such as Arnhem and Bruneval, regarded themselves as the number one crack force of the British Army. In those days they were all seconded from the infantry regiments. The Parachute Brigade also had a number of supporting units under command, gunners, sappers, signals, ordnance, catering, electrical and mechanical engineers, army service corps, and so on.

Our diminutive, but carefully selected, Guards Company was composed of a major, four captains, and about 120 non-commissioned officers, guardsmen and troopers. Our three combatant sub-units were called 'sticks', a stick being the component of an aircraft group of paratroopers. The company's principal role in the airborne assault was to lay out the dropping zones for parachute task forces. This we did by means of radar with, by day, white cloth panels, and, by night, flares. We might also be required to form small *coup de main* patrols.

We were in the same camp as the Guards Training Battalion and shared their mess, a situation which gave me a better understanding of the character of the Foot Guards. Pride, discipline, conformity, high courage, dedication, obedience and panache, those were the hallmarks of 'the Brigade'. Most people knew of the valour, discipline and stirring initiative of the Guards at war and of their dashing presence in peacetime; few were aware of the mainspring that rendered them rather different from other regiments and corps. (I write of them in the past tense as their character may have changed a little since the 1950s.) The men who guided their destiny went by the premiss that judicious, traditional officer recruiting was the key to the maintenance of standards and the smooth running of the five regiments. What the colonels were looking for were young officers of similar background, the same cast of mind and the same rarefied education. Otherwise there could be no true harmonizing with the 'team'. While the criteria applied to much the same extent in other elitist regiments the Brigade of Guards were more rigid in their insistence upon social, as well as military, conformity. (Being, as a Household Cavalryman, in the Household Brigade, but not in the Brigade of Guards, I was in a favourable position to judge.)

An example of an officer misfit was pointed out to me in the Guards Training Battalion. I can best sum up this National Service ensign's failure to conform by saying that he offended against several of the upper-class norms of behaviour and offended some of the shibboleths listed by Nancy Mitford. His brother-officers knew from their first glance at his civilian clothes that, according to their standards, he was not quite 'right'. He took a dubious girl-friend to a regimental ball, and while his brother-officers raced or shot or fished or sailed, or attended smart dinner or cocktail parties, he spent the weekend in Brighton with the dubious girl-friend. Neither his seniors nor his contemporaries were positively unkind to him; they largely ignored him (which was almost as hurtful). Their main concern was this: 'how on earth did the fellow slip through the net? What on earth did 'they' think 'they' were doing letting him in? Preposterous . . .' But that ensign was the rare exception to prove the rule.

It was partly through this social rigidity and exclusivity (requiring a pattern of behaviour off parade as well as on) in the commissioned ranks that the special relationship between them and the NCOs and guardsmen worked. The other ranks knew by instinct whether one of their officers was 'right' or not; and, by paradox, despite the wide social gulf, the bond between the officers and the other ranks was as close as in any other branch of the army. The important thing was that the system worked beautifully.

That intolerance was not really the image presented to the visitor; which on the contrary was one of nonchalance, an insouciance as if they were saying to him 'whatever we do, we do it with ease and with a charming smile'. In peace or war imperturbable gallantry was the thing, something reflected in the remark supposed to have been made by a Guards officer who was asked what it was like 'over there' on his return from Dunkirk. ('My dear' – he is reputed to have said, as though having just left an overcrowded cocktail party – 'the *noise* and the *people* . . .')

Although the Foot Guards tribal image stems first and foremost from their strict officer orthodoxy (and they constitute, arguably, the most tribal military organization in the world) my brother-officers in the Guards Parachute Company, being veteran captains who took the Brigade conventions entirely for granted, were concerned with seeking military adventure more than anything else.

In the summer of 1956, as a member of the Household Brigade Shooting Eight, I was involved in competitions on the ranges at Bisley when Sergeant Smurthwaite, of the Coldstream Guards, another member of the company in that team, came across with the news that, along with other units of the Parachute Brigade, we had just been placed on short notice standby to fly to Cyprus. The 1st and 3rd battalions of the Parachute Regiment had already been on the island some months, as a contingency against the increasingly explosive situation in the Middle East.

The last British combatant troops left the Suez Canal zone that March. Cyprus was then the closest British base to Jordan, to whose aid we were committed to go if she was attacked, the potential aggressor being Israel, which, incidentally, had invaded Gaza in February. Jordan, probably prompted by Colonel Nasser of Egypt, had declined to join the Baghdad Pact, an association which Britain joined in April 1955. The Levantine powder keg grew closer to explosion in the summer of 1956, first with King Hussein's dismissal of Glubb Pasha and other British officers of the Arab Legion, and then with Nasser's nationalization of the Suez Canal, following the withdrawal of the American and British undertaking to finance the building of the Aswan High Dam. Meanwhile, Cyprus had been in a state of emergency for nearly a year, owing to the EOKA campaign. My parent regiment, the Blues, took over their armoured cars there in an anit-terrorist role in 1955.

The Guards Parachute Company flew out that June with the Parachute Regiment's second battalion, the headquarters of 16 Parachute Brigade and various supporting units. My only regret at the posting was having to give up Sebastian, my beloved Jack Russell. I asked the vet to find a suitable home for him, and Sebastian went to a 'little old lady'. Months later, when I was on operations against Colonel Grivas's henchmen in the Troodos mountains, I received a coloured photograph from his new owner, of Sebastian looking grossly overweight, sitting on a plush velvet cushion; poor Sebastian, who, with me, never had less than two hours scamper a day, whose youthful ecstasy had been to chase rabbits and squirrels to his heart's content around the Pirbright woods. Now that close and intuitive bond between owner and dog was broken, as it has been broken – by death, loss or force of circumstances – a thousand times a day world-wide over many thousands of years.

# 5

# *Against Two Colonels*

Imagine a force of fifteen paratroopers trudging the hot deserted rock-and-thyme strewn Troodos mountains of Cyprus, their shirts and the rims of their red berets white with sweat, white from the salt pills which the medical officer distributed to compensate for that which they lost through liberal and continuous perspiration during the hours of daylight. These men had the task of patrolling a defined area, half-a-dozen ordnance map squares of the mountain range's daunting undulations, ravines and escarpments, searching for EOKA terrorists who were known to lurk somewhere in the mighty massif. But the paratroopers – having recently arrived in the island and by no means acclimatized to the heat of 100° fahrenheit – led by me, proceeded from one of Troodos' rare water springs to another (I having carefully marked off the tiny pale-blue dots on my map), for their water bottles (two per man) required refilling some three times a day.

When the sun went down the temperature dropped sharply, pullovers were donned, a little fire was lit and ration tins opened; and when the stars twinkled with all their Mediterranean brilliance blankets and groundsheets were unrolled from packs and wrapped round aching bodies, from which only the berets and the boots were removed. At intervals in the deathly silence of the night each guardsman was woken, bleary eyed, for his sentry stint. Sometimes four or five of us would set an ambush on a pathway. But nothing ever happened. Each morning the men were lined up and stood to attention by Sergeant O'Leary, of the Irish Guards, for my inspection of themselves and their weapons. After breakfast we trudged on again, not without vigilance, on our first three hours trek of the day – to the next water-hole. In the areas of the adjacent map squares the other two patrols of the Guards Company, and, beyond them, those of the Parachute Regiments' second battalion, were engaged on the same sweltering business.

My patrol stayed out perhaps three or four days and nights in a row before returning for a rest day at the company base. And then out again. This could not be a very effective way of bringing the terrorist organization to heel, but it was an excellent means of learning to come to terms with the relatively harsh climate and the operational living conditions. From their well-concealed hides the EOKA guerillas probably watched our ponderous and somewhat aimless movements, just as Colonel Grivas had looked down from his Pindus hide, first upon the German comings and goings and then those of the Greek Communists, a dozen years and more before.

It was not easy for us to envisage those stark open heights as they looked in the spring, an all-enveloping treasury of wild flowers, including several rare orchids; or to imagine the foothills studded with almond, apricot and citrus blossom; or to see, in our mind's eye the mountains in winter, draped in snow (with, before the emergency, many of their slopes dotted with skiers). But even in high blistering summer the Troodos range with its nakedness, broken here and there by solitary olive and carob trees and stands of pine, boasts a singular beauty.

Those mountains, the geographical backbone of Cyprus, measure perhaps twenty miles by eight, in an island that is 140 miles long and, at its broadest, sixty wide. The whole comprises 3,584 square miles. Its resident population was made up of about 78 per cent Greek Cypriot, 18 per cent Turkish, and the remainder British, Jewish, Armenian and others. The Greek Cypriot nationalists aspired to throw off the British yoke and achieve 'Enosis', or 'union with Mother Greece'. How plausible was that dream? The seed of the island's Greek heritage was planted around 1400 BC when Mycenean traders began to colonize it. Then the conquerers came in their succeeding waves: the Romans followed the Phoenicians, the Mohammedans followed the Romans, the Crusaders followed the Arabs, and the Lusignans followed the Crusaders, until, in the sixteenth century, came the Turks to stay for more than 300 years. The Turkish coast lies only forty miles to the north. But owing to immigration from the Greek Cypriots' motherland and a higher indigenous birth rate, the Greek element of the population grew largest.

In 1878 Disraeli forced the Sultan of Turkey, then in imminent danger from Russia, to relinquish the administration of Cyprus to Britain. At the outbreak of the First World War Turkey ceded the island to Britain. Thus, by the time Colonel George Grivas set up his revolutionary network in 1954, the British had run the place for seventy-six years and held full sovereignty for forty. Among many benefits endowed by Britain were the improvements to the roads and ports, the introduction of electricity and piped water to the villages, the riddance of the malaria scourge and the opening up of trade and tourism. But there was no university and practically no cultural assets, other than the rich historical heritage. The police force was pitifully small. The Greek Cypriots harboured no hatred for their Anglo-Saxon rulers until the mid-1950s; there was even affection. The problem was simply that British colonial rule conflicted with the ages-old desire for Enosis.

Colonel Grivas, the founder and leader of EOKA – *Ethniki Organosis Kypriou Agoniston* (the National Organization of Cypriot Fighters) – was born in 1898 in the village of Trikomo, near Famagusta, the son of a prosperous cereal merchant. His distinguished career in the Greek army finished with some very successful experience as a guerilla leader, both against the Germans and during the Greek civil war that followed their retreat. It was in 1948 that, in collusion with the Greek government he began plotting the overthrow of the British in Cyprus. During the early 1950s he paid several preparatory visits to the island, organising the smuggling in of arms, ammunition and stores, recruiting and instructing terrorist group leaders, and finally setting up his headquarters in the Troodos in 1954. His pseudonym,

Dhigenis, was borrowed from the legendary twelfth century defender of the Byzantine empire against the Moslem invader. Combining guerilla know-how, cunning, ruthlessness, high courage and tenacity of purpose with unshakable integrity (he was ever a man of his word), Grivas possessed all the qualities of a good rebel chief. Yet he was no political animal.

At the outset he won the approval and support (albeit often circumspect) of one who was every inch a political animal, Archbishop Makarios, the spiritual head of the Greek Cypriots, the Ethnarch. Makarios, whose benign and kindly smile belied a mercurially devious mind, emerged from the humblest beginnings, his father being a shepherd. The Archbishop climbed to the top of his career ladder via entrance to the priesthood, through Kykko monastery, and scholarships to Boston and Athens. He and Grivas, between them, converted Enosis from a dream into a campaign for self-determination. (Many who discussed with the two men their patriotic aspirations were given the distinct impression that their interpretation of Enosis was in fact a state of Greece's union with Cyprus rather than vice versa. They seriously imagined that Nicosia could be the ruling capital.) During the period 1954–55, by sabotage, ambush, assassination, incitation to riot and the distribution of revolutionary leaflets, the ex-Greek colonel reduced Cyprus to a state of fear and turmoil, prompting the governor and commander-in-chief, Field Marshal Sir John Harding, to announce a state of emergency.

Retiring from the ultimate military appointment of Chief of the Imperial General Staff in 1955 Harding (another self-made man) had planned to farm in the West Country when Eden persuaded him to take on the prickly governorship of Cyprus. Recognizing Makarios as the evil genius behind the revolutionary movement, Harding had the Archbishop, together with the Bishop of Kyrenia, transported to the Seychelles. That action was more than vindicated the following spring when diaries, kept by Grivas and secreted in a number of glass jars, were discovered by the security forces. They revealed the Ethnarch to be deeply involved in EOKA's plans or, as Harding put it, 'up to his neck in terrorism'.

John Harding, a monumental administrator and leader of men, was, I think the kindest and most attractive of all our post-war generals. He appeared to possess almost infinite wisdom, moral strength and charm, while his wife, Mary, combined a warm heart with a wonderful sense of humour. The Blues who, under command of Valerian Douro, had arrived in the island about the same time as the Field-Marshal, enjoyed a special relationship with him, partly forged through the provision of his praetorian guard, his armoured car escort troop, and an ADC. (The escort troop commander, Charles Worthington, incidentally, kept a yacht, *Fieldfare*, in Kyrenia harbour. It was blown up by EOKA in the summer of '56.) The bond grew closer in 1957 when Harding succeeded Lord Athlone as Colonel of the Life Guards and thus Gold Stick. Thereafter, as Household Cavalrymen, we were to address him not as field marshal but by the 'family' sobriquet of colonel.

Both Harding and Grivas suffered from misconceptions – Harding internal, Grivas internal and external – regarding the Cyprus problem. Harding and the British hierarchy in Cyprus in general grossly under-estimated the support for Enosis, which was closer to ninety per cent of the Greek Cypriot population than the colonial estimate of five per cent. He and they did not seem to appreciate that a continuously repressive regime of house searchings and road blocks, interrogations and internment, curfews, collective fines and the brusque quelling of street demonstrations with batons and tear gas – not to mention the hangings – was bound to render almost the whole Greek Cypriot population pro-EOKA before long. Brilliant as the field marshal and his director of operations, Joe Kendrew (a quadruple DSO), undoubtedly were as conventional soldiers, neither, I think pos-sessed a true counter-insurgency mentality. They went in more for sat-urating suspect areas with troops, instead of co-ordinating specific clandestine operations on the basis of positive information (although, by the end of 1956, the military intelligence system greatly improved).

As for Grivas (Dhigenis) he wore Enosis blinkers. He more or less ignored the influence of the Turkish minority who were entirely unwilling to accept union with Greece. The Turks had no quarrel with the British; but if Cyprus was to throw off the British yoke then, said the Turks, it must be divided into Greek and Turkish zones. 'Partition and only partition!' became their cry. Grivas underestimated, too, the voice of the Greek Cypriot Communist party, AKEL, who wanted not Enosis but full independence, with a Russian affiliation.

There were other impediments scarcely recognized by the gallant Dhige-nis. One was that Britain, having just lost her Suez garrison, was unlikely to relinquish her well established strategic bases in Cyprus. Nor would she welcome the prospect of Greece, about the least politically stable of the NATO allies, gaining total sovereignty of the island; nor wish to see that nation permanently at loggerheads with a fellow NATO member, namely Turkey. Whatever the outcome, the Turkish Cypriots must be sure of real safeguards. In the eyes of Grivas the overwhelming priority of Enosis outshone all those considerations; and, as we were to see for ourselves, he contrived to persuade the Greek Cypriot population as a whole of that goal's preeminence. The Radcliffe Report of 1956 recommended self-government for Cyprus, suggesting safeguards for the rights of both the Greek and Turkish communities, but satisfying neither.

In August the Guards Parachute Company pitched their 160-pound tents alongside the Blues in Camp Elizabeth, near the capital, Nicosia. The Suez crisis took priority now, and putting internal security to one side for the moment we were in our conventional paratroopers' role again, practising aircraft drills, parachute landings and deployment from dropping zones, battle formations and field-firing exercises somewhere on that flat baking-hot land that radiates from Nicosia, the Mesaorian plain, barren except for its carpets of asphodel lilies. Occasionally our noses were returned to the EOKA scent again; and, on most such occasions, we were subjected to canards and false trails or, at best, wild conjecture as to terrorist movement. But sometimes intelligence was sound, and when that was so the Paras made good use of it. For we had in Tubby Butler, our perky, animal-alert, decisive Brigade commander, in Bala Bredin, 2 Para's commanding officer and in our own company commander, Kemmis Buckley, three crafty sleuth hounds, as they demonstrated on Operation Sparrowhawk.

Sparrowhawk followed tip-offs from reliable sources indicating the whereabouts of gangs in the Kyrenia mountains. EOKA's ears being everywhere, Butler and Bredin planned the operation with the utmost secrecy. The soldiers were told they were to proceed on another field-firing exercise, and indeed we bivouacked on the firing range before being driven to our first close-cordon positions east of Kyrenia in the dead of night. The gangs were not alerted, surprise was complete and we captured six wanted men along with two large arms caches. A couple of nights later we moved west of the town to the sprawling white citrus-grove village of Lapithos, where a large variety of bomb-making equipment was unearthed. John Harding flew up in a helicopter to congratulate all concerned.

Notwithstanding the island's tragic situation, one always sensed the haunting beauty of Cyprus and her romantic history. St Hilarion, built by the Crusaders and dominating the Kyrenia pass like a massive eagle's eyrie, was a fairy-tale castle albeit a ruin; Bellapais, renowned for its Gothic monastery and Tree of Idleness was another magic corner, and so were each of the riotous gardens of Kyrenia, backed by rustling palm fronds and banana leaves, with the purple mountains for their backcloth. Then there were the picturesque villagers – the older ones – in their heavy knee-boots and tucked-in trousers, voluminously baggy and rusty black; their women in black skirts and white headdresses; the shepherds playing their heavenly flutes in the moonlight; and the donkey and camel trains plodding over the fennel- and thyme-scented plains, oblivious of the emergency. And how can one ever forget those hours spent swimming in the limpid coastal shallows, or lying on the golden sands, baking as brown as the natives, surveying the silver sparkle on the sea that stretched north to nearby Anatolia; or those off-duty evenings talking far into the night, sipping ouzo or retsina in mountain cafes; or dining on the balcony of Kyrenia's Harbour Club, where the landlords, Roy and Judy Findlay, entertained us with piano-and-duet Jack and Daphne Barker or Noel Coward ditties. But (with the sole exception of our immersions in the Mediterranean) we were never without loaded nine-millimetre automatics tied to our waists, even at the journalist-gossipy Tyrolean Bar of the Ledra Palace Hotel or on the dance floor of that dark Nicosia restaurant, Quaglino's. (Captain John Stacpoole of the Parachute Regiment's Second Battalion was a particular friend of mine. He and I spent long evenings on moth-infested, vine-entangled terraces sipping ouzo or Keo wines discussing books and military gossip and life and putting the world to rights. Though he had been decorated during the Korean war – with the Duke of Wellington's Regiment – had been an exceptionally young adjutant of his battalion and could look forward to a rosy military future, he chose to leave the army some five years later and join the Benedictine Order at Ampleforth.)

The smell of war was in the air, sometimes pungent, sometimes faint.

Moshe Dayan's forces were poised to drive deep into Sinai, while sabres were sharpened and rattled in France and Britain. Plans were afoot to retrieve the Canal. The 1st and 3rd battalions of the Parachute Regiment had just returned from England, where they had undergone parachute refresher courses. French paratroopers, very professional, mostly veterans of the Indo-Chinese and Algerian wars, were now on the island and a visit to their camp convinced us straight away how much better armed and equipped they were than ourselves. Decisions were reversed as soon as they were made, and we began to doubt the mission to topple Colonel Nasser would ever materialize. At times we were led to believe that a political solution would be found. Even at the end of October our minds were still closely fixed on EOKA. We had been switched to Operation Foxhunter on the daunting heights of Paphos forest, where it seemed we had another three mountain gangs trapped in their fastnesses – when orders were abruptly issued to return to Nicosia and standby for Suez.

As late as the beginning of November, two or three of us in the Guards Parachute Company were among those dancing at Government House, dancing to a new rhythm, Rock 'n Roll, the Field Marshal's ADC, Darel Carey, having bought the first of the records the moment it was out. John and Mary Harding, diminutive figures upwards of sixty years of age, soon picked up the two-beat step and had everyone onto the floor wriggling and rollicking to the blare of this latest jazz. Next morning we put away our white dinner jackets and donned camouflage combat smocks and the encumbrance of battle-order webbing, which was to be our only dress for the next fortnight.

Murray de Klee, number one stick commander, a tough, leathery Scots Guardsman who never wasted words, and a French linguist to boot, was informed that, with eight guardsmen and a small sapper party he would be jumping with the French airborne forces, whose objectives were in and around Port Fouad. De Klee's little detachment flew off with the Nordatlas aircraft of Le Deuxième Regiment Parachutiste Coloniaux on 5 November. On the same day 3 Para emplaned for their target, Gamil airfield, while 2 Para, with the Guards company under command, embarked in the van of the main invasion fleet at Famagusta. Operation Musketeer was on the march.

There was little room either on deck or below, either in the spaces reserved for the officers or those of the other ranks. You had to keep a close eye on your weapon, pack, ammunition pouches and marked map lest your neighbour inadvertently picked them up and wandered with them to the other side of the craft. Sleep was almost impossible, talk mostly nervous and confused speculation. One moment we were told the aim was to intervene in the Israeli-Egyptian fight, divide the protagonists and send them home, although it seemed fairly certain that the Allies had been in deep collusion with the Israelis from the beginning. We knew the Anglo-French air forces had spent six days putting their Egyptian counterparts and Nasser's airfields out of action. We knew of another reason for that, another reason to prove

British collusion with Israel. We had promised Ben Gurion we would make it impossible for Nasser to bomb Israel. The guardsmen and troopers were of a more enquiring mind, more independent thinkers, in the mid-1950s than when I first joined the army. 'That there Mr Selwyn Lloyd, the Foreign Secretary, I read he don't go along with this invasion, sir,' a corporal said to me on the boat. 'If he thinks its wrong why does he support Mr Eden? . . .' But, of course, right or wrong, that corporal, along with the whole company was delighted to be in this fiasco for the dust-up. After all this was just the sort of thing they'd partly joined for. But what next?

Would we advance all the way to Cape Suez, sieze the Canal from end to end? It was what the French understood to be the plan; but unfortunately sick Anthony Eden rather than fit clear-headed Guy Mollet was at the helm of ultimate decision making, while in the top echelons of the military hierarchy the French commanders were, in every case, subordinate to the British. All through 5 November, until darkness fell, we could see the distant grey hulks of the American 6th Fleet on our flank, shadowing our progress, ready to stop us in our tracks if Eisenhower ordered it. The United States and the other Western powers were incensed, too, that, because of our action they were deprived of a stick with which to beat Russia for sending tanks into Budapest, and mercilessly suppressing the Hungarian uprising only four days before.

Also, behind us on the Mediterranean skyline we saw another fleet, a more motley one, the Anglo-French main force from Malta and Algiers. Would they really land, too, we wondered? Dawn on 6 November found us anchored a few miles off Port Said. In all directions the sea was studded with transport vessels of evey sort and description. Early in the afternoon we moved in towards the harbour. Someone had a service radio set tuned into the BBC. Eden's voice came across. We were not at war with Egypt, he told us, our object was simply to stop the fighting betweeen Israel and Egypt. The French and British governments had issued an ultimatum; it had not been obeyed. We were only striking military targets . . . Even as he spoke great palls of black smoke arose from the town, fighter-bombers swooped over its centre while machine-gun fire rattled from the same direction. We saw the sterns or bows of Nasser's sunk block ships grimly jutting from the water like dead marine monsters across the mouth of the Canal. Over to the right were the marine commandos' assault craft and, straight ahead on the quayside in the shadow of de Lesseps' statue where we were about to disembark, General Stockwell, the Land Forces commander, and his staff stood to greet us. It was like the setting for a war opera; we felt very forcibly in those moments that the collective mind of the whole civilized world was centred upon us and the conflagration of Port Said, the larger part of that collective mind in strong disapproval.

While the orders for disembarkation were given, our company piper, Edwards, of the Irish Guards, received another from Kemmis Buckley: 'Play some rousing tunes!' And as he did so, sounding buoyantly, though thinly, through the noises of war, he was cheered not only by the men in our craft, but by all those in the neighbouring boats, too. Heading in battle formation through the town we were met – bizarre circumstance – by a couple of dirty-postcard vendors who seriously imagined that the grim-faced guardsmen, loaded weapons at the ready, might stop to buy their murky wares. We moved into a concentration area, a block of flats, awaiting the order to advance. Our vehicles (champs) came up at dusk, but it was night before our little convoy led the task force south. We were met here and there by small groups of Egyptians loosing off wild bursts from their machine-guns and by riflemen firing indiscriminately from high windows, but we reached the outskirts of the town unscathed. The sky was still bright red with firelight.

At the north end of the Treaty road, which runs parallel with the Sweetwater canal, we made contact with elements of the French Parachute force and got into positions of all-round defence while awaiting the arrival of 2 Para and their supporting squadron of the 6th Royal Tank Regiment, who were to take over the lead. There I remember a French officer enquiring why on earth we didn't make a dash for Quantara; it was 'so close and practically undefended'. Why not indeed? Why not go the whole hog, for that matter and drive to Port Suez? But, under political constraint, we advanced slowly.

A spare radio set tuned into the BBC gave us the first indication that a cease-fire was imminent, but we passed three villages, Ras-el-Ish, El Tina and El Cap before the official order was given by our brigadier, Tubby Butler. He was furious. We were pretty angry, too. If it had been right to invade, we reasoned, then it must have been right to capture the Canal from end to end. Certainly we sensed the explanation given for the cease-fire – the cessation of hostilities between Israel and Egypt – to be specious. Murray de Klee and his eight guardsmen rejoined us at Ras-el-Ish. The French were to award Murray the *Croix de Guerre*.

We were two miles south of El Cap, four from Quantara. We were told to entrench ourselves in the narrow stretch of muddy sand that separated the Treaty road from the Sweetwater canal. This we proceeded to do under the stars, while Egyptian rifle bullets, coming from their outpost positions north of Quantara, whizzed overhead to hurry us in the job. No cease-fire order was yet forthcoming from Colonel Nasser. When dawn broke we set the sights of our rifles high and, picking out far-off clumps of cover that we supposed were enemy infantry positions, we fired back until ordered to stop. We looked at one another and laughed. The effect of digging slit trenches in that foul-smelling mud and then dozing off in them had rendered us grey phantoms.

My stick sergeant, O'Leary, with whom I shared a trench, asked me if I could arrange for him to see the Catholic padre. 'I want to make the confession, sorr,' he added. There was no cause to ask him why. He was a man who only had to see liquor to find the temptation of having a share of it nigh irresistible. In his corner of that Port Said block of flats he had discovered a bottle of whisky and had taken a swig from it, the length of which would have made most men sick. Though I did not see the act I had smelt it on him as had all the other men in the stick. Drinking spirits whilst on duty and on active service, too, not to mention petty looting was a grave military sin; he might have been in deep water. He was a fine soldier, whom the guardsmen held in much affection. Drink had already marred his record; he had been twice reduced from sergeant to guardsman and up to sergeant again. This time I judged the matter best left between him and his Maker. As we enjoyed the prospect of several days in our stinking trenches and the cease-fire was effective on both sides, all sorts of welfare items were brought forward, including the Catholic padre. O'Leary had no wish for the matter to be in confidence. He wanted everyone to know how ashamed he was. I moved to another trench while he made his confession. He was a true Catholic; I knew his contrition was heartfelt.

On the third day we were withdrawn the two miles to the outskirts of the fishing village of El Cap, where the peasantry, the grimy *felaheen*, went about their slow, crude business, to all appearances unconscious of the war, and where we dug fresh trenches in the wet putty-coloured sand and tried in vain to sweep the flies from our faces. There had been a United Nations resolution for the withdrawal of 'shock troops' from Egypt. After another forty-eight hours, the 29th Infantry Brigade took over from 2 Para and the Guards Company, so we retired to Port Said where a luxury liner, *New Australia*, was berthed, waiting to return us to Cyprus. The combination of shower baths, soft bunks, deep-pile carpet and interminable choices of well-cooked food made a sharp contrast with the hospitality of El Cap; and, as we steered for Limassol, the guardsmen were almost pinching themselves to be sure it was not a dream. Yet the whole Egyptian episode could have been a dream, a dream ingredients of which Lewis Carroll might have made good use.

The company went straight back to their alternative business of hunting EOKA. In December and January, in the snow-clad mountains, they helped break the back of the organization as a guerilla force. The captured Grivas diaries told the Field Marshal and his army a great deal more about the rebel organization and how the mind of its leader, Dhigenis, worked. Operation Black Mak put more than thirty hard-core terrorists behind bars, while the much vaunted group leader, Markos Drakos, was shot dead in a gun battle. The heyday of Colonel Grivas's mountain gangs was over. He himself lay safely hidden in a Limassol house however, and, through his clever courier system, kept in efficient and commanding touch with his elaborate network of subordinate leaders throughout the Greek Cypriot towns and villages of the island.

Meanwhile my two years as a parachute captain were up and I was due to take command of an armoured reconnaissance squadron of the Blues. Promotion to major at the age of twenty-nine carried on one's personal documents the significant letter T for 'temporary' in front of it, substantive rank not being due until the ripe old age of thirty-four. Although the five-year gap seemed, in exuberant youth, a yawning span, I was advised to start preparing for my promotion exam well in advance, since the knowledge required would be quite a marathon to imbibe in the throes of active service. There was a practical tactics test to be passed, along with seven written papers, for four of which one sat three hours apiece and the other three for two hours each.

There was 'Administration and Morale', 'Tactics A' (army organization), 'Tactics B' (conventional warfare), 'Tactics C' (Duties in Aid of the Civil Power, or Internal Security) and 'Military Law'. Then there were 'Current Affairs', the half-dozen questions on which might include anything from world economics to the oil crisis, or trade union power to the role of the United States in central America. And lastly there was 'Military History', which involved the detailed study of five campaigns or series of campaigns. In my year those were Marlborough on the Danube, the American Civil War and three campaigns from the Second World War – Burma, Italy and North-west Europe. By the time I left Cyprus, I am thankful to say, that exam was far behind me. But I was to serve another two years on the island, both of them as colourful and dramatic, in their way, as the first.

In the summer of 1957 my squadron was detached from the regiment to Famagusta and attached to 51 Brigade. Each of our five officer-led reconnaissance troops was composed of three Ferret scout cars and one Daimler armoured car including a total of twelve men. We also had three sections of assault troopers, conveyed in armoured personnel carriers, and an intelligence staff consisting of an officer, a corporal-of-horse and (for most of the time) an attached police interpreter. For the last eighteen months of the emergency the squadron was the mobile combat force of eastern Cyprus, covering an area of some 1,200 square miles. The foot soldiers garrisoning the same stretch were the 1st Battalion of the Royal Ulster Rifles and two artillery units, the 25th and 29th Field Regiments deprived of their guns and operating as infantry.

A road-block incident on 22 October 1957 illustrates very well the sort of small success we regularly enjoyed during those exhilarating months. The Greek Cypriot population were to be celebrating Oxi day within the next five days, Oxi being 29 October, (the date, in 1941, on which Greece gallantly refused Mussolini's surrender terms). We knew that Grivas would be intent upon widespread rioting and that his secret instructions for the day must now be filtering through his courier system. I duly dispatched a number of road block parties. One of my troop leaders, Ian Pilkington, set up his block between two villages south of Famagusta.

Trooper Murray ('Ruby' to his mates), a 19-year-old scout car driver, was not missing a movement as he watched a party of school children being summoned from the bus which was taking them home. Trooper Murray saw two boys hastily stuffing something down the back lining of their bus seat. He duly informed his troop leader, who had the two boys placed under separate guard while the other children were searched. Trooper Murray then went straight to the suspicious place and pulled out seven small paper packets bound with sellotape. Each contained a copy of Colonel Grivas's island-wide orders for rebellious activity on Oxi day. Those were the only copies in the whole island found by the Security Forces. Entirely owing to the alertness of that one soldier, therefore, realistic preventive measures were taken throughout Cyprus on 29 October. Always acting on information we maintained a relentless pressure.

Corporal-of-Horse Godfrey-Cass with his detective mentality and great zest for terrorist hunting, became a key figure in the squadron. Here are some random early quotes by Godfrey-Cass taken from my Famagusta journal. 'I spotted a youth in a coffee shop showing more than usual consternation. I ordered two of my men to cover the other occupants while I searched him. Secreted in the lining of his breast pocket was a general order from Pavlakkis (the EOKA leader for Famagusta) . . .' Again: 'I searched a church club in Patriki. On one of the occupants I found a document relating to the EOKA traitors' list. I arrested him.' And again: '. . . I had this very suspicious house surrounded and found on a certain Christos Lambris a list of vehicle numbers which proved to be those of police special branch cars earmarked for destruction.' Early in 1958 I appointed Godfrey-Cass squadron Intelligence Corporal-of-Horse and he proved himself admirably cut out for the job.

Patrick Beresford, the squadron second-in-command, was of similar genius. He had won the Sword of Honour of Sandhurst and was a soldier of singular accomplishment; he revelled in the counter-insurgency role. One of his first trials of patient vigilance, leading a small scout car patrol, resulted in his cornering a car, the occupants of which were Pavlikkis' two principal couriers, Kristofides and Iouliano. Those two confessed so much under interrogation that they gave the Security Forces the first clear picture of how EOKA operated in the Famagusta area. I believe Patrick to have been convinced that, if he had been lent two or three of the best men in the squadron for a month and was given a free hand, he could have winkled Grivas out of his hide with his hands up and brought the whole EOKA card house tumbling down. (He ended his regular military career with the Guards Parachute Company, and then joined the Territorial SAS. After that he was a very prominent figure in the Anglo-Irish bloodstock world, spent some time as personal bodyguard to Sheik Yemani, and became *chief d'equipe* of the British eventing team. He has also enjoyed a brilliant life as an all-round horseman.)

In October 1957 Field Marshal Harding handed over the Governorship of the island to Sir Hugh Foot, a former colonial secretary to Cyprus. Foot began a propaganda tour projecting himself as the harbinger of sweet reasonableness, shaking everyone's hands, lighting 'candles for peace' in the Orthodox churches and releasing a hundred EOKA detainees. Like Harding he kept reminding the world of the need of strong safeguards for the Turkish minority. Grivas wrote in his memoirs that 'Macmillan sent Selwyn Lloyd, his Foreign Secretary, to Turkey and Greece, hawking a plan for self-government, which was designed to encourage the Turks in their demands for partition . . . I saw little hope of any useful political developments and I wrote to Makarios that, since America was under the influence of Britain and Turkey, while Greece, with her dollar policy, was at Washington's mercy, the time had come to break new ground . . . If my suggestions are not adopted [Grivas told Makarios] then I must part company with the

Greek government and launch an intensive campaign to let the Greek people know what is being done in their name.'[1]

Hugh Foot had sent word to Grivas asking for a truce in the winter of 1957–58, and there was indeed a lull in the conflict just then. But, in February, the EOKA leader, frustrated at the lack of progress on the political front, put out a leaflet from his Limassol hideout warning the new Governor that 'the credit of time you asked for has run out and so has my patience. The fight must go on, because there is no other way to deal with Britain's uncompromising attitude.'[2] While strengthening the village EOKA 'cells' throughout the island he issued an edict to the effect that Greek Cypriot minds must be concentrated on the struggle and that there must be 'no gambling, alcohol drinking or frivolity' until it was successfully concluded. Shops were not to display British advertisements, let alone sell British goods. The Mukhtars (village heads) were to relinquish their seals of office. As the Mayor of Nicosia declared: 'Now we are all EOKA'.

The Security Forces launched a fresh offensive and the police special branch gained a new name for ruthlessness. Grivas now labelled the Governor 'Foot the Deceiver' and wrote to him that 'you bear the whole responsibility for the shameful, medieval methods used by the torturers of the intelligence services'.[3] A week later 'the Famagusta Execution Squad', as Grivas called it, murdered William Dear, the most successful of the interrogaters, through whose hands most of the suspects, captured by my squadron, passed. Alexander Constantinou, one of the gunmen concerned, died in an explosion in his Troodos retreat a week or so later. His funeral cortège was feted in every village through which it passed on the way for the burial service in his native Famagusta. The squadron was allotted the task of intercepting the cortège outside Nicosia, removing all hangers-on, except family mourners, forming a close escort and rushing the cars to Famagusta before dark. Wreaths, garlands, whole barrelfuls of flowers were showered on the car bearing the coffin, while men, women and children knelt and lowered their heads and screeched E-O-K-A; and we in our armoured car turrets were pelted with stones and bottles.

In the spring we acquired from Peter Purves, the Chief of Kyrenia Special Branch, a pet spy called Phannis, a native of Trypimeni, a hamlet lying in the foothills to the north-west of Lefconico. A disshevelled little Greek Cypriot in his mid-thirties and a former EOKA gangster, Phannis and his brother both defected from the organization after their sister was brutally murdered by EOKA for some disobedience. He agreed to work for the British police provided he was well paid and, more particularly, well protected. His informants were mostly other defectors, Turks and communist party members. Phannis provided the foundation for the vast amount of information that we, as a squadron, built up during 1958, and we had much to thank him for. However, as his English was very poor, we borrowed an interpreter from our brigade headquarters, who unravelled Phannis' some-

1 *The Memoirs of General Grivas*, p.132.
2 ibid., p.132.
3 ibid., p.136.

what erratic, uncoordinated and sometimes contradictory statements. Corporal-of-Horse Godfrey-Cass was the indispensable supervisor of them both.

Our dramatic dialogue with the village of Avgorou began about this time. The men of one of our troops were distributing leaflets explaining the benefits of Macmillan's constitutional proposals when a youth began throwing stones at them. At the troop leader having him arrested a large party of villagers made a rush for him and got him away. The troop was obliged to withdraw with some loss of face. On 3 July, Ailwyn Broughton (now Fairhaven) led his troop through the same village on a routine patrol. On returning to camp Ailwyn insisted to me that he had spotted a wanted man in Avgorou called Karios. (All the officers and NCOs had made careful studies of the photographs and names in the wanted men booklet.) Karios' name had appeared in several police reports after he escaped from a detention camp.

A couple of days later I showed Karios' photograph to each member of the troop under command of David Blake, the most experienced of my troop leaders, and dispatched them to the village to look out for this terrorist. Everything seemed quite peaceful at first, so David parked his vehicles on the village square under guard and gave permission for his men to visit the cafe. A prominent EOKA notice was pinned on the wall opposite the cafe and a youth began pointing at it and leering at the soldiers. Such placards being illegal the troop corporal-of-horse ordered the young man to remove it. He refused and was duly apprehended. As on the previous occasion a large crowd of villagers rushed the soldiers and rescued their young hero and this time escorted him into the cooperative society building on the other side of the road. The crowd, including the bulk of the village women, then closed in on the soldiers with every conceivable hand weapon. The hostile mass had grown to over 150.

David Blake, determined that the first offender should not go free, ordered his car commanders to form a close cordon around the cooperative building, then called up the squadron for reinforcements. Forty minutes later Ian Pilkington's troop, who were on standby, arrived with two sections of assault troopers, armed with riot shields and batons, to join David's cordon on the building. The villagers were now nearer a strength of 200 against the Blues' thirty-three. Corporal-of-Horse Swann attempted to reach the canister containing his tear gas grenades (only the Daimler armoured cars were equipped with these), but was prevented when struck on the shoulder by a rock and on the elbow by a woman with a crowbar, and badly injured. The windscreen of his vehicle was also shattered. The mob – which, according to every soldier's evidence, was intent on murder – was now estimated at 230. David Blake was caught by a brick on his cheek hurled by a youth who had climbed on his Ferret. He decied to fire a warning burst of fire from the vehicle's Browning machine gun. He killed the youth who had been attacking him.

The gun being well elevated, the shots hit a roof. Unfortunately, however, one of them ricocheted and hit and killed a woman in the crowd. The villagers fell back some fifty yards, while David and Ian disengaged and withdrew their troops clear of the village. Meanwhile a company of the Royal Ulster Rifles came up to impose a curfew, while the Blues provided the cordon. (Here are extracts from Grivas's diary on the incident: 'The youth was beaten . . . the armed men began to arrest everyone they could sieze . . . Another boy was mercilessly beaten . . . From the safety of their armoured cars [the soldiers] opened fire on the crowd, killing an old man and a young mother . . . the army then drove out, leaving the bodies of dead and injured lying on the blood-splattered square . . .'[4] All of which was, of course, a travesty since my soldiers could hardly have been more temperate in the circumstances.

In his book *Island in Revolt*, Charles Foley, Editor of the *Times of Cyprus* described the Avgorou fight as 'the fiercest village battle of the emergency'.[5] The incident was widely reported in the British press. On 10 July the Secretary of State for the Colonies read out Foot's report in the House of Commons: '. . . The village of Avgorou has a bad reputation and a long history of EOKA associations. The patrol commander was clearly carrying out his duties, first in ordering the EOKA slogan to be removed and later in endeavouring to arrest the man whom he considered to be the ringleader of the attacks being made against the troops. Throughout the incident he acted with great calmness and restraint, and the moment of opening fire was delayed as long as possible, and was then only done by himself personally, to save the lives of his men and to protect his vehicles.'

The funeral took place on the 6th. Among the wreaths were two bearing the inscription: 'I shall avenge your blood. Dighenis'. 'Three days later,' wrote Foley – an unrepentant sympathizer with the Greek Cypriot cause – 'two National Servicemen were shot, one being the 20-year-old heir of Lord Stavordale . . .' The victims were a most stimulating and witty Blues officer, full of young promise, Stephen Fox-Strangways, and one of our mess waiters, Trooper Proctor. Those two stood at the counter of Pralimnitis' grocery store in Hermes Street, Varosha (the Greek quarter of Famagusta) when the gunmen opened fire in the doorway. Death in both cases was almost instantaneous, though Stephen was quick enough to draw his pistol and face his murderers before dropping.

Naturally this tragedy put the whole squadron in a mood of anger and despondency for a few days. It was a bad time for Blues National Service officers. Just about then Auberon Waugh, who was completing his time as a troop leader with the Nicosia squadrons, suffered a nasty accident during a big cordon-and-search operation. As he stood in front of his Ferret his driver inadvertantly jolted the loaded and cocked turret machine gun, and a burst of fire went into the small of Auberon's back, playing havoc with his innards. Judging by the criss-cross of scars which he displayed for me in hospital a few weeks later, he was very lucky to emerge from that bed alive – and become the celebrated columnist he is.

Later in the week that Stephen and Proctor were killed I had the good

4 *The Memoirs of Colonel Grivas*, p.148.
5 *Island in Revolt*, p.202.

fortune to capture three couriers, a success that led to another Security
Forces triumph. Taking my Land Rover with a corporal and two troopers to
visit a troop position some ten kilometres south of the town and coming to a
rise I caught a glimpse of three men standing over the closed engine cover of
their car on an olive-grove track. I stopped, unseen, but they looked up
nervously at the sound of my vehicle. Leaving a man on the radio I sent the
NCO and the other trooper to outflank the car, first reminding them of the
Greek warning to halt (*Stamata!*) in case the suspects tried to run for it.
Striding forward I signalled the others to close in. We searched the men.
Nothing. Then the car. Under the driver's floor mat were several neatly
sealed EOKA messages. We had the three men in police custody within
twenty minutes.

Under interrogation these couriers gave authentic information concern-
ing a terrorist leader in the village of Liopetri, Christos Samaras, a man with
£5,000 on his head. Accordingly a few days later a snatch party of commandos was dropped by helicopter on Liopetri, supported by an Ulster Rifles
cordon; but Samaras sneaked out while the troops were moving into position. Early in September the village was searched again, and Samaras's
brother, Elias, was arrested. Elias Samaras pointed out a barn where he
thought his brother was hiding. The Ulster Rifles invaded the barn and, after
a tense gun battle, killed Christos Samaras and three members of his gang
(including Andreas Karios, the main influence behind rebellious Avgorou).
The subaltern commanding the storming party was awarded the Military
Cross. Elias Samaras was flown to Britain under protection; but, after several
months, he decided to return to Cyprus to confess his treachery. An EOKA
committee condemned him to death, and he was shot.

Looking back it is rather strange to recall that, amid those violent times in
which we seemed to be ever on the *cave*, there were also happy periods of
play and recreational activity, to remember a journey to Petra, via Jerusalem;
jaunts to Beirut at the invitation of Royal Navy minesweeper captains; Ben
Wilson's wedding in Ankara to Ines, the daughter of the Belgian ambassa-
dor there; cooling August nights in the Troodos mountains; and many,
many colourful weekends in Kyrenia with Thomas and Henrietta Dunne,
Marie Millington-Drake, Julian and Denise Berry and David and Marigold
Wedderburn, among others.

The Foots entertained very generously. Their son, Paul, already a committed left winger and one who regarded the army with the greatest contempt,
was living with them at Government House. I shall never forget Patrick
Beresford and myself and a couple of others being greeted by him for a
party. Looking down on Patrick from the head of the staircase, with all the
disdain he could muster, Paul Foot enquired: 'I suppose you're in the Wilts
[Wiltshire Regiment]?' Patrick looked him up and down with an expression
of even greater scorn. And after a well-timed pause, replied in his slow voice
that seems to come from the chest: 'I'm not ... Are – you?' Collapse of
marxist youth.

The Greeks, who refused to recognize any political rights for the Turkish
minority, were forever accusing the British of contriving to jettison the

concept of Enosis by making too much of the Turkish factor, besides which they rightly smelt in the Macmillan plan a future of partition rather than Greek sovereignty for the island. Meanwhile the Turkish Cypriots who wanted nothing better for Cyprus than the status quo, the existing regime, had given little or no trouble, and Volkan, their militant organization, was nearly all bark and no bite, until the EOKA campaign began to interfere seriously with Turkish village life. In Dr Fazil Kutchuk they possessed a dedicated community leader, while the Turkish Premier, Adnan Menderes, showed from the beginning that he could be counted upon to oppose the union of Cyprus with Greece. And so the cry *Taxim*! Partition! grew into a crescendo. The Greek Cypriots were, on the whole, the cleverer, sharper, more ambitious of the two peoples; they were the business men and artisans, while the Turks were more of an agricultural character. So, fomented by Grivas, the Greeks began a campaign of terror against the Turks.

With the heightening in tension between the communities I had two troops detached every day to escort Turkish workers' buses into Famagusta from halfway up the Karpas Peninsula. This meant a 3.30 am start and we rarely got in from the return journey until after six. All too often we languished on the roadside waiting for spare parts for broken-down buses.

Greeks were now everywhere ejecting Turkish minorities from mixed villages. The homeless Turks had no option but to flee to all-Turkish villages. When, on one such occasion a Turkish shepherd was murdered, his ten-year-old son was also shot at, but escaped to take refuge with his uncle. We then had all the males of the offending village penned behind barbed wire on the adjacent football pitch. The little boy was invited to attend the identification parade from the rear of a police car with a hood over his head. Rejecting that security he asked to face the Greeks openly. It gave us great pleasure to see the boy walk boldly down the ranks, and point a forefinger furiously at his father's assassins.

To record another experience of those days, the Karpas village of Ayios Theodhoras had a population of 782 Greeks and 70 Turks at the start of July By the second week of the month there was not a Turk left and every Turkish house was burned down in the wake of its owners. The refugees evacuated to Galatia four miles away. The last Turk in Ayios Theodhoras was an 80-year-old woman who told the Greeks that, having spent her entire life there, no one was going to evict her now. She was shot in the back at point-blank range by EOKA youths with 12-bores.

Alerted to this infamy we dashed to the scene accompanied by police with tracker alsatians. But the terrorists, anticipating the dogs, covered their tracks with a great deal of pepper and were not brought to justice. We were then bivouacked by the sea, on the golden strand opposite the village of Boghaz, our habitual camping site for operations in the north and north-east of our area. In village raids from that base we arrested between thirty and forty people in EOKA's employment. 'Cassandra' (William Connor) of the *Daily Mirror* spent the morning following the Ayios Theodhoras crime with us. I escorted him to the village for him to see the dismal pool of blood in the old woman's one-roomed shack, the terrorists' pepper grains strewn outside, the black smoke still swirling from the Turkish quarter and the looks of hate on the Greek Cypriot faces. So 'Cassandra' left Cyprus with a somewhat less romantic image of the Enosis ideal than when he arrived in the island.

The monstrous Guenyeli incident also occurred at this time. The security forces drove thirty-five Greek Cypriot suspects to a point close to the Turkish village of Guenyeli. After being debussed, lined up and admonished, these men were told that, as a punishment, they could find their way home from there. Seventy to eighty Guenyeli youths marched out of their village, outflanked the Greek party, set fire to a field of corn between them and the road, surrounded them and literally hacked the whole lot of them to death then and there, which was hardly surprising considering the Turks had seen several of their people tied to stakes and burned alive, having been drenched in petrol.

On 3 October the wives of two sergeants in the 29th Field Regiment, Mrs Sutcliffe and Mrs Robinson, were shot in Hermes Street, close to where Stephen Fox-Strangways and Trooper Proctor were murdered. Mrs Sutcliffe was killed, Mrs Robinson very badly injured. There was no doubt in British minds as to the terrorists' aim in this crime. It was to provoke the Security Forces into violent acts of reprisal which would be represented in the island, in Greece and in the United Nations as a British reign of terror. And EOKA almost succeeded. The three units employed as infantry in the Famagusta area, the 25th and 29th Field Regiments and the Royal Ulster Rifles ran amok with rage.

They sent out their lorries and, meting out very rough treatment, rounded up every young Greek male on whom they could lay their hands, faced them stomachs downwards in their vehicles and drove them to a barbed-wire encircled bunker known as the 'snake pit'. Four Cypriots died in the round-up, one of them a girl of thirteen who had a heart attack, while over 100 ended up in hospital. I was very thankful that the squadron's only part in the operation was to provide road blocks on the routes into the town so we had no contact that night with the citizens of Famagusta. General Kendrew came down a few days later to excoriate all the officers involved. Predictably, EOKA put out a leaflet disclaiming the Cutliffe murder. 'It was a jealous lover, the Turks or some Armenian terrorist organization,' Grivas pretended.

In general the army came out of their four-year Cyprus campaign with an excellent name internationally in regard to their dealings with both communities, particularly considering the often intense provocation. The same could scarcely be said of the police special branch, whose methods were frequently too close to the descriptions used by Grivas in his propaganda leaflets ('medieval torture', etc). In that respect Foot's private secretary, Robert Browning, a personal friend of mine, related an interesting incident to me. The Grenadier Guards were involved with the police that autumn in searching the sprawling village of Kythrea, north of Nicosia. The company under command of Michael Stourton provided the guard on the interrogation centre. A couple of Michael's guardsmen who witnessed the Special

Branch methods of persuasion reported to him that they closely resembled some of those used by the Nazis. Michael took a look for himself and came away appalled.

It so happened he had been invited to dine at Government House that evening and he took the opportunity of relating the circumstances to Rob Browning. Rob had a word with the Governor, who promptly sent for the new Director of Operations, General Darling. Foot ordered his car, and the two men set straight out that night for Kythrea. Fortunately for Special Branch they received radio warning from the outer cordon that the VIPs were heading in their direction, and the interrogated suspects were spirited away just in time. But that was not the end of it for poor Michael Stourton. The army were furious that he had not gone through the 'normal channels' and, accordingly, he was posted home. His commanding officer, James Bowes-Lyon, was, I am told, sympathetic, but was under pressure from the hierarchy; and, besides, feared for the inevitable (Security Forces) obloquy on Stourton, not to mention the battalion.

My squadron became celebrated for new tactics during the autumn of 1958, that was to say the use of donkeys and bicycles in combination with our scout cars. I first hired donkeys from Turkish intelligence contacts for a series of patrols seeking an EOKA gang in the Denarga forest, the central area of which was impassable to vehicles. These animals had the great advantage not only of silence but also in not setting the pye-dogs (the numerous half-starved village mongrels) barking. We carried out a number of most successful cordon-and-search operations using donkey-riders for the inner cordon, and (with those securely in position) scout cars as long stops. We also made much use of bicycles, these being particularly favourite conveyances with two other troop leaders, Mark Birdwood and Tom Harmsworth. Grivas sent word to his followers that the British in their desperation kept changing methods 'such as soldiers on donkey back', but this disdain reflected anxious bravado, and General Darling, who visited Famagusta at the time, cross-questioned me closely on these squadron ploys. 'Softlee Softlee catchee monkey' was a favourite motto of the new Director's. He was a perky little fellow whose eccentric reputation began the moment he stepped out of his aircraft at Nicosia to take up the job. He came down the gangway playfully shadow-boxing at the waiting journalists, jovially asking 'where's Grivas?'

Meanwhile Grivas's guerillas had learned the art of making quite effective mines – pressure or electrically-detonated – which posed a particular threat to my squadron. The explosive was a compound of potassium chlorate (which the Greek chemists bought in large quantities on the pretext of making 'cough drops') and sugar. The police confiscated more than 1,500 kilos of the chemical in Famagusta and some of the larger villages. Those detonating the mines were supported by machine gunners whose job it was to fire on the drivers and crews of the vehicles ambushed. James Wilson, another of our National Service officers and an inveterate terrorist hunter, was the first mine ambush victim. James contacted the police who were quickly on the scene with a tracker dog which led them to a house in an orange grove. There the three responsible saboteurs, too shaken by their deed to post a lookout, were captured.

In the same week two British septuagenarians, Mr and Mrs Brooks, Famagusta residents who owned a house in Kantara, just below the Crusader castle of that name, ran their Jowett Javelin over a thirty pound pressure mine. Their car, completely gutted, was thrown forty feet down the mountainside. Brooks, a retired naval officer, was killed instantly. By whatever miracle his wife recovered in hospital.

During a battalion handover later in October we were given the task of 'keeping the roads open' in that same part of the Kyrenia mountains, and that was when James Wilson came in for his second encounter with a mine, this time a pressure mine buried in a narrow loop of mountain track. While James clung, very dazed, to a precarious ledge on the cliffside, his Ferret scout car went hurtling 400 feet into the valley below carrying his driver, Trooper Birch, a very popular National Serviceman from Birmingham, to his death. Travelling only a mile away I was at the scene in about ten minutes and had a helicopter called up within another twenty to carry the concussed James Wilson to hospital. The Blues commanding officer, the greatly loved Julian Berry, and his adjutant, Nick Nuttall, visited the squadron by chance that day, and, as always, were very painstaking and prompt in the support they gave us, arranging for the unfortunate Birch's body to be evacuated, and replacing the ruined Ferret.

Five nights later I was with Ailwyn Broughton's troop in the vicinity of Lefconico when his vehicle struck an electrically detonated mine. Our reactions not being quick enough on that occasion we devised and practised a new ambush drill which was put into practice on 3 November when a troop was surprised near Prastio. One of the car commanders, instantly opening up with his Browning, shot and badly wounded the gang leader, who was then seized. Our last success was scored by the troop led by Henry Herbert (now Pembroke), who caught a courier and sabotage veteran, Antonis Makellis, who had eluded us for months. Makellis received a nine-month gaol sentence, but, along with all the others, was let out soon after the London–Zurich Agreement was signed on 19 February, 1959. Early that month wily Grivas moved from his Limassol hideout to a new secret lair in Nicosia and from there gave EOKA a general cease-fire order. He then came out of hiding to be received by a tumultuous Greek-Cypriot welcome before returning to Athens. On 1 March, Makarios flew in from the Greek capital to start the job of fashioning the new Cyprus. Two months later the Blues handed over to the 12th Lancers before sailing home and entraining for Windsor.

What did the Greek Cypriots gain from all their hatred and bloodshed? In August 1960 the island became an independent republic (and, subsequently, one within the Commonwealth) but by no means in the image intended by EOKA. Fighting soon broke out between the two communities, and Grivas (promoted to general by the Greek government) returned to restore ginger to the cause of Enosis. While he assumed command of the Greek Cypriot army and bullied the Turkish minority, Makarios accused

Britain of favouring it. Finally, the government on mainland Turkey, ex-asperated by the harrassment of its Cyprus people, invaded the island. Now the Turks have secured a state of partition greatly in excess of their modest claims of the 1950s. As for the morally diminished Greeks the majority of them know in their heart that they were far better off in the days before the mid-50s, when Britain ruled them and Enosis was simply a dream that 'must come true one day, no matter how long it takes'.

Whereas, morally, the islanders gained little or nothing from those years of strife, by and large the British soldier benefitted immeasurably. Cyprus was a more enchanting place in its territorially unspoiled 1950s than it is now, harshly divided into national sectors and hideously punctuated by hotels and holiday homes and geared to tourism. It was not only a lovely place in which to serve but the soldier always felt he was doing 'a real job', relatively free of spit-and-polish parades and routine programmes. National Servicemen arriving in my squadron as pink, callow, ingenuous boys, preoccupied with the comforts of home, left eighteen months or so later brown, hardened men, much more self-confident and worldly wise, with vividly exciting memories and many new friends.

Those of us who had never returned home during those three years were not only dazzled by England's vivid green landscape, but could not fail to be impressed by the new Britain of the later 1950s, a fresh nation of super-markets and bright clothes, of a broadening middle class with second cars, washing machines and television sets. London had changed almost out of recognition. Chelsea and Kensington were no longer the quiet grey villages of my boyhood, but, a-glitter with boutiques, Continental restaurants, launderettes, espresso coffee bars and smart stores, were absorbed much more closely into 'the great wen'. And that was when permissiveness began.

Staying a night or two with my mother in Cadogan Gardens and crossing Sloane Square to buy a paper at W. H. Smith's I was accosted by a flower-seller: "'Ere Guvnor, that weren't a very nice thing you did to Clancy last night!' I looked him up and down for a second, then the penny dropped. 'Are you confusing me with my brother?' I asked. 'I believe he's in something on television at the moment.' That must have sounded rather pompous. The flower-seller regarded me with even greater disdain. 'It's no use you tryin' to get off the 'ook, you *jilted* 'er!' I telephoned Moray that evening; he was playing a leading part in *Compact*. Yes, he confessed, he had been obliged to 'jilt Clancy'.

I flew to Spain to stay for a month with various friends. If there was one hour of that visit more magical than any other it was that of listening to Segovia playing his guitar in the Alhambra's Court of Lions. As I sat there enraptured by the music with Eudo and Rosemary Tonson-Rye and their daughter Rohaise (he was the agent to the Duke of Wellington's Granada property) another wonderful thing happened. The bats suddenly flooded out of the walls' Moorish crenellations to go on their nightly hunt, and, within seconds, swallows flew in by the score to roost in the places which had been occupied by the bats. Nature and art combined in those moments to create a strange and rare beauty.

My month, however, was curtailed by a telegram from Valerian Douro (Wellington's son who had introduced me to the Tonson-Ryes) then commanding the Household Cavalry. 'You have been selected to command the Guards Parachute Company. Please say if you accept and, if you do, return immediately.'

Cyprus 1958: anti-terrorist strategem –
donkey patrol for cooperation with
armoured cars.

(*right*) The officers of the Guards
Independent Parachute Company
assembled to mark my relinquishing
command in the summer of 1961. Back
row: Michael Bowater, Malcolm
Havergal, Philip Fazil. Front row: Fitz
Abel-Smith, Myles Lambert, myself,
Michael Nason.

The Guards Parachute Company dressed for 'keeping the ground' at the Queen's
Birthday Parade, 1960. I am seated in the centre (wearing a helmet) next to the
Major-General commanding the Household Brigade (General George Burns).

Gibraltar, 1962: British and Spanish staffs during a visit to the Governor by the Governor of Algeciras province. I am third from the left; the Mayor of Gibraltar, The Rt Hon Joshua Hassan, is third from the right. Extreme left is Richard Dangar, 16th/5th Lancers, ADC.

Rabat, 1962: changing ponies during a polo match against the Royal Moroccan Army.

Herford, Westphalia, 1964: as regimental second-in-command, greeting NCOs of Denmark's Jutland Dragoons during their visit to the Blues. The figure in the left foreground is that of Regimental Corporal-Major Bill Stringer (afterwards Major and Quartermaster and founder of the Weser Vale Bloodhounds in BAOR and, later, of the Windsor Forest Bloodhounds).

# 6

## *Soldiering in the Sixties*

It was good to be back wearing the red beret at Pirbright Camp again. The Guards Independent Parachute Company was still faced with the same eager numbers of volunteers from the seven regiments of the Household Brigade; and we continued to score the highest rate of passes of any unit in 16 Parachute Brigade through those rigorous tests at the Airborne Forces Depot and the parachute course at RAF Abingdon; but still only thirty-five per cent of our volunteers found a place with us. Those who did were well rewarded, for around that time they were on manoeuvres as far afield as Denmark and Northumberland, Cyprus and the Scottish Highlands, Singapore and Norfolk, Germany and Salisbury Plain, Tripoli and Snowdonia. It was my job to see that we were the fittest and most battleworthy unit in the Parachute Brigade, and so (we liked to think) it proved, whether the tests were of tactical initiative and discipline, aircraft drills, parade precision and smartness or physical endurance. In all this we were most ably supported by our company sergeant major, a Coldstreamer by the name of Channon who came to us after instructing at Sandhurst. He was the most intelligent and capable warrant officer I ever encountered. Extremely ambitious – and seeing comparatively little opportunity of advancement in the Foot Guards – he eventually applied to me for a recommendation for transfer to the Parachute Regiment, in which he was to rise to the rank of lieutenant-colonel.

Taking into account how seldom the Paras had been employed in an airborne role since the Second World War; and seeing that the prospect of them air jumping into battle grew increasingly less likely – owing to a modern enemy's greater capability of acquiring early warning of the approach of low-flying air convoys, coupled with the new surface-to-air missile factor – I was of the opinion that the Company would be of greater use to its brigade with a more positive ground role. I envisaged it as the formation's hard-nosed medium reconnaissance and surveillance force. I therefore applied for Ferret Scout cars. The brigadier, Napier Crookenden, agreed to this idea, provided the vehicles could be parachuted into action. We carried out a number of tests, the Ferrets being successfully dropped by parachute from Beverley aircraft on heavy-stressed platforms. So the guardsmen, to their delight, became armoured cavalrymen as well as pathfinders, each of our three sticks being mounted in three Ferrets and a Land Rover. For the first time guardsmen were trained as radio operators, scout car drivers and machine gunners by the Royal Armoured Corps at Bovington. We also had

trained a team of free-fall paratroopers, and were given a clandestine role to
go with it.

We were always on three or four days standby notice as a contingency
against the sudden eruption of a 'trouble spot' – except for the last couple of
weeks of May and the first one of June when the Household Brigade secured
the services of our Foot Guards element to 'keep the ground' for Trooping
the Colour. (Judging by the prominence given to the Company's name in the
official programme the pundits at Household Brigade headquarters considered our presence to be a great bonus; but most of the company guardsmen found those three weeks of drill and spit and polish rather tiresome.
They would get their fill of that, they reckoned, when they returned to their
respective battalions.)

In 1960 I proposed that the Company, by then twelve years of age, should
have its own Colour, or flag, a wish that the Queen soon granted. On 21 June
1961, General Sir Charles Loyd, the Colonel of the Coldstream Guards,
handed the colour over to me at a parade watched by numerous former
members of the Company. He prefaced the ceremony with these words:
'Without doubt your Company offers as exciting and varied a life as any
other unit in the army. All members are picked men. After their parachute
course they have to learn the specialized pathfinder techniques and must
now know the skills of the armoured cavalrymen as well as those of the
infantryman . . . the Company combines all that is best in the Household
Brigade and the Airborne Forces . . . From the earliest times all organised
armies have carried emblems in battle as rallying points. The Romans had
their eagles and the armies of the Middle Ages had their banners. You will
see that your Colour embodies the Brigade Star, symbolizing that you are
firstly guardsmen, and Pegasus to mark the special duties undertaken by
parachute troops. The design has been approved by Her Majesty the Queen
in whose name I now present it . . .' (Sadly only fourteen years of life were
left to the Company. In the flush of economies inflicted on the army in 1975,
it was disbanded at another parade at Pirbright Camp on 24 October that
year. But a Company association was formed, and a dinner, always very
strongly attended, is held at Pirbright annually.)

Endeavouring to compensate for that sportless Cyprus phase, and making
use of the Household Brigade Saddle Club horses at Melton Mowbray, I put
in a good many days' hunting with the Belvoir, Cottesmore and Quorn
during my Pirbright years, and in mid-summer regular afternoons on the
polo grounds at Smith's Lawn, Windsor Great Park. Being in the Airborne
Forces way of life I imagined myself to be at the peak of physical fitness, but
soon discovered that being riding fit is a thing apart; and that, while I could
manage fifteen-mile route marches in full equipment, make brisk road runs
two or three mornings a week and double up and down hills, without any
trouble, at the start of the 1960 polo season I was puffing and blowing by the
end of chukkas. And so it was for the first week or two of the summer of
1961. For the·next fifteen months after that, however, it was easy; in June I
handed over the Company on being posted to Gibraltar as Military Secretary

to the Governor and Commander-in-Chief. From Gibraltar a dozen of us in the garrison played polo two or three afternoons a week across the Spanish frontier, near La Linea, almost all the year round. I went with the Gibraltar team to Tangier and Rabat – once in rather strange circumstances.

In 1962 a very pushy acquaintance of mine had just married and was proceeding on his honeymoon to Morocco, via Gibraltar. A couple of days before the Gibraltar team was due to sail across the straits to play the Royal Moroccan Army at Rabat, he went to call on me at my office in the Convent (Government House), which I shared with the ADC, Richard Dangar, a 16th/5th Lancer who was, among many other 'extra-mural' things, in charge of the polo programme. I being out, he said to Richard, though quite unannounced: 'I'd like to play some chukkas this afternoon; you can take it from me that Johnnie Watson wouldn't mind if I borrowed his ponies.' Not being notified of this presumptuousness and not being able to play until the evening, I arrived at the ground, booted and spurred, only to witness the said acquaintance galloping furiously up and down on my second pony, having already exhausted the first. 'I must keep it up,' was his only explanation grabbing my towel and rubbing himself down, 'otherwise I'll be totally unfit by the time I get home!'

Completing our journey to Rabat, we looked in on the British Military attaché, who was liaising with the Moroccans to finalize the schedule of matches and social programme. We told him that, as there were five of us, one would always be available to umpire. 'Oh, you needn't worry about that,' said the attaché, 'your friend from England arrived yesterday telling me you'd agreed for him to represent you as umpire.' We looked at one another incredulously and exchanged similar double takes when we met our friend, not only dressed as an umpire on the polo ground and blowing his whistle at us to line up, but again, with his wife, at all the various and sumptuous entertainment laid on by our Moroccan hosts.

Nor was that the end of Moroccan adventures for the pushy acquaintance and his wife. He had been informed that the romantic thing to do on a north African honeymoon was to watch the sun set over the Rif mountains. Well, he had a fetish for vintage cars, and, alas, his 1930s Bentley (I think that's what it was) sank, in its climbing endeavour, up to its axles in the sand. The couple flew home to Britain, but were soon back in Gibraltar awaiting the car's recovery. We all kept a close eye on our ponies.

'I hope you're going to like Gibraltar,' Charles Keightley (His Excellency the Governor and Commander-in-Chief) wrote to me just before I left Pirbright. 'I'm afraid it's not really cavalry country.' That life in the lower regions, the all too thickly inhabited parts, of that bold black headland promontory was constricting and rather claustrophobic was true enough; but service on the Rock had its compensations, not the least being the study it offered of a colourful and tumultuous history, a history that seemed to be placed at a new turning-point in 1989 when the Foreign Secretary announced that the garrison infantry battalion was to leave. I then thought back to the early 1960s when I was Military Secretary and the 700 men of the 1st battalion of the Somerset and Cornwall Light Infantry, the first line of

Gibraltar's land strength, were installed there. Their guard-mounting ceremony, a flurry of white drill tunics, gleaming rifles, drums and brass music, usually witnessed by the Governor, his ADC and myself from the Convent balcony, took place in Convent Square immediately below. Those men seemed like a *sine qua non* of eternal British colonial entrenchment. Had the Gibraltarians been told then, when Franco ruled in Madrid, that their beloved battalion was to go in the 1990s – whether or not that they could have known, too, that Spain would eventually join NATO – they would surely, with utter despair in their hearts, have forecast total British abandonment followed by Spanish sovereignty over the Rock at least by the year 2000. For they were aware that the Spanish government, incorporating Gibraltar nationally, would exploit it, morally and economically, to the dire disadvantage of all its inhabitants.

Little Spanish blood flowed in the veins of those people. After the Carthaginians, the Romans, the Goths and the Visigoths, came the Moors. The Moorish general Tarik took Mons Calpe, as the ancients called it, from its Gothic rulers on the last day of April 711, hence the name Gibraltar, from Gebel Tarik, the Mountain of Tarik. The Spaniards captured it in 1462, holding it until 1704 when Admiral Rooke's squadron of the Royal Navy, in conjunction with an Anglo-Dutch army stormed and grabbed it during the War of the Spanish Succession. As the population was severely depleted owing to the conflict, the new British regime, wanting a prosperous colony, encouraged traders from Italy, Malta and Morocco to go and settle there. Hence the present racial hotch-potch. Spain attempted to re-take the place many times, the nearest they ever got to it being at the great siege of 1779–81, of which the first of many heroes was the commander-in-chief, General Elliott, and the second, a Sapper, Sergeant Ince, under whose expertise the Galleries – that were to hold the guns that inflicted most punishment on the besiegers – were tunneled from the face of the limestone. During the next century and a half Gibraltar became riddled with tunnels which, by the middle of the Second World War, contained a hospital, a barracks and numerous gigantic storage spaces.

The real strategic importance of the Rock was reflected in the Royal Naval dockyard and the comings and goings of our warships. The British army looks up to no one great hero in the way that the Navy reveres Nelson. The Naval officers of Gibraltar sit down to dinner every year on 21 October, Trafalgar Day, to do honour to their hero (whose body was brought ashore on the Atlantic coast not far away). When I attended in 1961 a drunk waiter dropped a tray of glasses immediately behind the Flag Officer just at the climax of that admiral's blandeloquently commemorative after-dinner speech, a moment when some of the officers seemed to be on the verge of reaching for sentimental handkerchiefs. There was then a terrible silence during which every watery eye was fixed on the erring able seaman – a hush broken by the Flag Officer's sonorous admonition: 'And, young man, my Lord Nelson would not have approved of *that*!' I felt that H. M. Bateman might have found good copy there.

Lying more or less at sea level, directly adjacent to the town, the Convent is perhaps the most unusual of all British colonial government houses. It was built (soon after Spain took Gibraltar from the Moors) by a community of Franciscan friars, and has been the Governor's official residence since 1728. A new wing containing the banqueting room was put on in the 1860s. The ballroom was built from the nave of the lovely old chapel, in which the Anglican establishment – the men well polished, the women painstakingly behatted – were always careful to be seen by the Governor on parade for Sunday Matins.

The Governor's military number two, the Deputy Fortress Commander, was a brigadier, the Flag Officer a rear-admiral and the officer commanding the RAF contingent – an understrength squadron of Shackleton aircraft – an air commodore. I used to organize, and take the minutes of, the heads of services committee meetings, the committee being presided over by the Governor and otherwise composed of the three aforementioned men, the Colonial Secretary and Joshua Hassan, the Chief Minister and Mayor (who was to hold that post for almost another thirty years). I was responsible for co-ordinating the activities of the armed services and for checking on the smooth running of their many functions, also involving the civilian organis-ations. And there were many mundane tasks such as, at investitures, reading out names and citations and handing medals and other awards for the Governor to pin on breasts, or pass into proud perspiring fingers.

Gibraltar was, I think, rather too small fry for Charles Keightley, who had been commander-in-chief of the Rhine Army, the Far East Land Forces and the Middle East Land Forces, his sojourn in the latter post also just about finishing with his command of the Suez operation of 1956. The colony was a place in which he could not sufficiently spread his wings. He possessed a stimulating and extremely forceful personality, but gave himself unduly grand airs on social occasions, invariably and loudly hogged the conver-sation and, being also somewhat bombastic, more devious than was good for him, obsessively intolerent and given to frequent dispensing of leaden jokes, he was by no means universally popular on the Rock. Moreover, he had a highly suspicious nature, which I might exemplify by mentioning that he requested me on several occasions to investigate certain windows – outside, and high above, the Convent walls – from which he imagined (I am sure quite erroneously) he was being spied upon. His mistrust became positively phobic. His artlessly charming and very handsome wife, Joan, however, was just the right partner for, and foil to, him.

With the ADC, Richard Dangar, I drew up programmes for the many visitors to the Convent. The late Princess Royal stayed twice during my time there. We were responsible for putting a typed summary of our careers, together with notes on the various dinner guests, in her room in order to help her in dialogue; so when I sat next to her I expected a stereotype of questions. Not at all: she gave me a monologue on her two sons, in particular how, when they were in their twenties, Harewood House was a hideous babel of music, classical from one door, jazz from another. Her second visit, six months later, was from *Britannia*. Entertaining on board she gave me that account of her sons a second time. After dinner at the Convent, when the guests were ranged around the drawing-room with coffee, she and her lady-in-waiting, Lady Margaret Hawkins, both got out their knitting and were much more preoccupied with that important pursuit than talking to their neighbours.

Mountbatten came in his capacity as Chief of the Defence Staff. I escorted him up the hill to the Flag Officer's house, the Mount, where he had stayed briefly as a boy when his father was Admiral of the Fleet Prince Louis of Battenberg. At Mountbatten's behest I told the driver to stop the car at a certain loop in the road. The great man got out and surveyed the bay. 'When my father was commanding a squadron of armoured cruisers,' he said, 'he stood me just here on the occasion that the whole of the Mediterranean Fleet came in for review. I think it was the most impressive sight I ever witnessed. Of course everything is larger than life at that age,' he added, shaking his head as he stepped back into the car. The Windsors came over to lunch from the Golf Club at Marbella. The Duke, talking to me and pointing to a portrait of the Queen at the head of the Convent dining-room, commented with heavy-lidded disdain: 'Very poor likeness of my niece'. As for the Duchess, having been told on good authority that she'd had no fewer than five face lifts, I found myself searching for the scars, which I might just as well have done considering she didn't listen to a word I had to say, except at the end of her prattle when she asked whether anything had been laid on for the afternoon. 'A Rock tour, starting with the apes . . .' I ventured. She leaned across to her husband. 'I guess we've seen the apes, haven't we, honey?'

One seemed to be forever conducting VIPs around the Rock features. Apart from the Barbary apes (which Churchill – half believing in the superstition that if they became extinct, Gibraltar would fall into enemy hands – had replenished during the war) there are three other main attractions on the Rock: the eighteenth-century gun emplacement galleries; the floodlit St Michael's Cave, where the remains of Neanderthal man were found, and which, with its vast stalactite columns, resembled nothing so much as a Gothic cathedral; and the remarkably well preserved Moorish Castle, then over 1,200 years old. In spring the upper rock is ablaze with flowers, and a great many species of wild birds, including hoopoes, golden orioles and bee-eaters may be counted there. Gibraltar was at its climatic worst during the Levanter, the wind of that name driving against the east face to produce the black cloud which, when sultry weather followed, hung like a cap over the Rock for days, rendering the town humid and its people ill-tempered.

That was a time to be in Andalusia, picnicking in the cork woods, shooting on the snipe marshes, visiting Seville, Granada, Cordoba or Jerez, going to the *ferias*, or, for some the bullfights, though the *corridas de toros* held no delight for me. I went once or twice, but, while appreciating the ceremony and the colourful ambience, I felt nothing but compassion for the bulls. It is interesting to note that during the Peninsular War when British cavalry officers were invited to attend bullfights they walked out with displays of disgust at the treatment of the *picadors'* poor mounts.

I had a similar experience when Colonel Henry Birch Renyardson, a widower and the father of an old school friend of mine visiting the Rock, asked to be escorted to the *corrida* 'for a little local colour'. This foxhunter, game-shot and stalker was so appalled he started railing against the participants in a loud voice – 'damn bad show, totally unsporting, ought to be ashamed of themselves' and so on. All eyes for thirty yards around on the stands were upon him, and I must say he looked the very acme of the explosive retired British officer with his red face, white moustache and an Eton Ramblers ribbon around his panama. He asked to leave, and I offered to take him to the local hotel where the *toreros* strode in to recline after their performances and to be showered with carnations by admiring girls. Yes, he said, he'd prefer to wait there. And he gave each one of them a good piece of his mind, too.

I had a great love for Andalusia, especially the places left behind by the Moors, their gardens and tinkling waterways, their castles and other monuments; the horses of the *rejoneadors* and *caballeros* at the fairs and the carriage horses; *flamenco* performed on the sawdust floors of remote *posadas* and *hospederías*; the musical festival held annually in Granada's Alhambra; and the colour throughout the province, its landscape, its *pueblos* and its people. The most beautiful drive I have ever experienced was in heading for the *feria* in Jerez in late March, through cork woods punctuated by flitting orioles, hoopoes and bee-eaters, then debouching onto a moorland that was a blaze of pink, yellow and purple.

There were little more than 25,000 inhabitants in Gibraltar in those days (now, I am told, there are over 34,000, with the high-rise accommodation climbing every year). The leading families were called Russo, Capurro, Gaggero, Norton and Imossi. Such bigwigs sent their sons and daughters to the top English catholic boarding schools; all strove to create a smart British image (like the Latin-looking policemen on Main Street, dressed exactly in the guise of London Bobbies); all wanted to be 'in' with the Governor; all had done well for themselves in what was euphemistically known as 'the import-export trade', but which Franco would probably have summed up as *contrabando*. The Spanish government were perpetually furious at the contrast between the prosperous shoppers on Main Street and the peasantry in adjacent Andalusia; just as they had been momentarily livid with rage at the visit to Gibraltar, in 1954, of the Queen and Prince Philip when Franco whipped up anti-British feeling throughout Spain. Franco revived the Spanish claim to Gibraltar, based on the assertion that Britain, in granting the Gibraltarians autonomy, was in breach of the Treaty of Utrecht; he endeavoured very hard to back this claim in the United Nations; and he could never contain his anger that the Rock was not his.

The Spanophile, colourful and eccentric Rowland St Oswald (of celebrated Nostell Priory, Yorkshire), who often waxed eloquent in the House of Lords about Gibraltar, spent a lot of time with his beautiful Polish wife at their home above Algeciras. Being an ardently political man, a determined and thrusting one and a friend of the Spanish Foreign Minister, he thought he had all the answers to the international controversy, and was forever telephoning me asking to see Charles Keightley, offering to act as intermediary with Madrid and to pour oil on the waters. He was a most benevolent and hospitable man but rather an embarrassment. It was at this Gibraltar junction that I started an enduring friendship with Paul and Maisie Makins, a most distinguished and entertaining couple who lived first in Gibraltar and then on the Spanish coast. Maisie's first husband, Major Bowen, of the Irish Guards, was killed at Narvik, one of her sons being Micky Bowen (now Archbishop of Southwark). After Maisie died Paul lived, as he still does, at Sotogrande, but pays frequent visits to London when I generally dine with him.

The local Spanish military governor of the region next to the Rock, which is known as the Campo de Gibraltar, would not have welcomed anything but the *status quo*, not the least reason for that being the Royal Naval dockyard found employment for 10,000 Andalusian workers who journeyed across the bay from Algeciras every day. (Whenever I was asked how many Gibraltarians, given a plebiscite, would opt for union with Spain, I always replied 'one hundred and ten per cent against' the added ten being the Spanish workers.) It was my job to write to the Spanish chief of staff inviting the military governor and his entourage (including the local admiral and air chief) for their annual visit to the Convent, and those officers revelled in the pomp and ceremony of it. Lavishly bemedalled, swords a-glitter, they sailed over in patrol boats, with scarlet-and-yellow pennants fluttering and a large crate, a gift for His Excellency in one of the sterns, while a gun salute boomed from the Rock and a guard of honour awaited inspection on the quayside. When the drawn-out luncheon was over, we all assembled for a group photograph, one which doubtless takes pride of place on the walls of many retired Spanish officers to this day.

Notwithstanding all that local traditional conviviality the Spanish government made things difficult at the frontier throughout my time at Gibraltar. Their consulate was closed; their nationals were not allowed in without a permit, which was almost impossible to obtain; and, while Franco attempted to squeeze the Colony's economy by every means he could think of, the frontier control people made long and quite unnecessary delays. (But with a Convent pass I was fortunate to be ushered straight through). Anyhow I left the colony at the same time as the Governor, which was just as well since Franco imposed his blockade within weeks of our departure.

I had made quite a determined, though not very successful, effort to learn Spanish, my tutor in Gib being a cheerful little Andalusian called Luis Morales (known, inevitably, on the Rock as 'Loose Morals'). After handing over as Military Secretary I followed this endeavour up with a spell of tuition from another reputed teacher, one of the inmates of the monastery at Chipiona on the Atlantic coast, then with a fortnight at the language school run by Alastair and Diana Boyd at their home, the Casa de Mondragón, a beautiful old Moorish house in Ronda. (More about the Boyds in due course). Meanwhile I had been posted to Windsor where the Blues were posed to fly out to Germany to take over the Life Guards' armoured cars.

Leaving Windsor for the Army of the Rhine in the autumn of 1962 my squadron, the Blues advance squadron, immediately met with the international crisis of the moment. Following the discovery that Castro's Cuba was bristling with Soviet missiles the United States navy blockaded the island, and the world was wondering if and when the dogs of nuclear war would be unleashed. Facing the East German frontier we were starkly aware that we would be taking it on the nose. I addressed my squadron, briefly explaining the political situation and ending with the injunction that, if the buttons were pressed, everyone was to act on their orders quicker than they had moved for anything in their lives. Who would be the first to open Pandora's box, the Russians or the Americans? Either way, in retrospect what that implied for us scarcely bears thinking about.

The Soviets then deployed 175 divisions against NATO's twenty-three (though if NATO had reorganized along Russian lines the divergence would have been a good deal less wide). National Service, which had begun in 1947, had just ended and the Rhine Army had been cut to an all-time low of about 50,000 men. In the previous year the Russians had set off a 50-megaton hydrogen device to make the biggest explosion ever recorded, and the greatest volume of radioactive fallout, too. Both sides possessed great arsenals of intercontinental ballistic missiles. The Russians being overwhelmingly superior in conventional forces, the NATO Allies had adopted a policy of massive retaliation, that is to say dependence upon the nuclear deterrent.

It was fairly certain that, if our enemy was looking for a conclusive and immediate settlement to the cold war at the time of the Cuba crisis he would have ordered his superior forces forward with relentless speed and on a wide front, through Western Germany, the Netherlands and northern France, to seize the Channel ports. He would then have hoped to present his principal antagonist, the United States, with a *fait accompli*. Anticipating such aggression the NATO forces facing the East German frontier would have carried out a brief delaying, or 'trip-wire' role, giving time for the Allied nuclear weapons – including the V Bomber force and Polaris – to be moved into a state of readiness for the promised massive retaliation to be launched. It would then have been hoped that the Supreme Soviet, seeing the Western powers were not bluffing, would have called a halt and offered negotiations.

Had war seemed imminent during that tense last week of October we would have gone through the procedure (not a particularly quick one) of unlocking our live ammunition compound (some distance from the barracks), getting our Saladin armoured cars 'bombed up' and proceeding in co-ordination with Rhine Army's other two armoured car regiments, to surveillance positions beyond the river Weser, which was a few kilometres east of our base at Herford. As the Russians advanced I suppose we would have attempted to withdraw to fresh positions, first overlooking the Ems and then the Rhine, but doubtless we would have been surrounded and cut off before that. (This concept was soon to change. With the innovation of tactical nuclear weapons NATO adopted a policy of 'flexible response' in which the enemy was to be engaged and destroyed as he invaded, not on a front line but in fighting of a fluid character between battle groups and combat teams here there and everywhere.)

I wonder how many of us serving in Germany then and later on were sometimes plagued by nightmares in which bright crimson skies were filled with nuclear missiles hurtling east and west, while all around, on devastated battlefields foetid with radioactive fallout, soldiers lay ghoulishly scorched or blasted to death; in which nuclear-blasted roads were cluttered with shattered fighting vehicles and phantom columns of tortured refugees; and in which legions of tanks and gas-masked Russian soldiers flooded over us, ineluctable as ocean breakers – nightmares culminating in the fragmentation and blowing apart of the whole world. I know I had such dreams. Anyhow, by the end of October Khrushchev withdrew his missiles from Cuba; Kennedy smiled; and, while the dreaded holocaust was averted we breathed contentedly again – and got on with the business of peacetime soldiering.

I toured the Berlin Wall in 1964, when it had been up three years. It seemed the most terrible symbol of tyranny in Europe – worse even than the high wire dividing East and West Germany, because the Wall kept such tight concentrations of thousands of compatriots, including a host of blood relations, apart. It throbbed with cruelty, giving vent to the West Berliners' indignation daubed all over it. *Die Trañen Mauer* (The Wall of Tears) and *Schand-Mauer* (Wall of Shame), they called it, and inscribed the words on the concrete. Later that year Blackwood's published my story *Across the Wall of Tears*. In writing it I sensed that the events of 1989 would come sooner rather than later. And so did those West Berliners who, contemplating the dismal grey barricade with me, repeated their faith: 'That which is unnatural cannot endure!'

Life Guards officers warned us of a lesser and more domestic – if, in its way, equally bizarre – hazard. 'Do be careful,' they advised, 'If you happen to be invited to a Scots Greys guest night. There is a wild subaltern there by the name of Ranulph Fiennes, who always keeps a .38 revolver handy. If you are shut in a loo he wants to use he threatens to shoot out the lock; while his brother-officers play 'Are you there, Moriarty?' with rolled-up newspapers, Fiennes prefers his .38; and he has a habit of hoisting himself onto the ante-room chandeliers and shooting through the flex until he crashes to the floor.' When I dined with the Greys the future ace explorer though large as life was not so entertaining – the poor fellow had been forbidden to keep a weapon in the mess. ❧

Our barracks at Herford, which had quartered *Panzergrenadiers* in the 1930s, though as bleak and uninviting looking as any barracks can be on the outside, had been rendered comfortable enough indoors and were centrally heated (overheated most of the winter). In the officers' mess we had our pictures and silver from Windsor and took the leading sporting and social magazines and all the British newspapers; so we made the place quite like home. But we spent a good deal of time dressing up in tank suits and climbing in and out of our armoured vehicles and Land Rovers. For the generals, imagining the soldiers would be reduced to a state of *ennui* and low morale unless kept in continuous activity, had us out on manoeuvres for most of the time between May and October, the winter and spring being devoted to individual, troop and squadron training. Inter-regimental rivalry reached its zenith each year with the tank and armoured car shooting competitions at Hohne ranges. As an armoured car regiment we were employed, too, as we had been in the late 1940s, in patrolling the gruesome East German border, with its crow's-nest look out posts, each with a heavily armed sentry; its guard dogs and its electric 'iron curtain', the scene of many ingenious, daring and bloody escapes.

So we got to know the topography of North Rhine Westphalia and Upper Saxony – and the villages with their pervasive odour, a blend of *Sauerkraut*, lager, *Bockwurst* and home-grown cigar – quite well, if not the inhabitants. Fraternization was certainly not discouraged, but nor was there much provision to promote it. Very little attempt was made, either by officers or other ranks, to learn the language. Few soldiers found German girl-friends; the men were granted leave only on dates that suited the regiment. For those with steady girl-friends at home the most popular place in Rhine Army was Gutersloh airport. By and large the British army mixed almost exclusively with the British army.

The German image had changed from one of deprivation and destitution when the regiment last knew them at the turn of the 1940s to one of high prosperity. Yet the people of the Federal Republic must have sensed, quite rightly, that the men of the Rhine Army still looked down on them as the defeated race, and so found them aloof and arrogant. They were well aware of being disdainfully referred to as 'huns' or 'krauts' – even 'jerries' was not intoned with an affectionate ring. Senior NCOs, who had fought in north-west Europe or with the occupying forces, thought it rather tiresome – or, indeed, quite wrong – that they must seek permission of a *förstmeister* before bivouacking in a wood, or of a landowner before occupying his farm buildings, or cluttering up private drives with their troop vehicles; or that they had to refrain from being noisy in the *Biergartens*; and were required to be deferential to the *Kreis-polizei* if they committed traffic offences. On the other hand the young officers, with no previous experience of Germany, mostly showed the same expedient diplomacy as they would have done in Britain. We were on particularly good terms with Herford's *Oberbürgermeister* and his officials and with the *Bundesgrenzschutz*, the West German border police.

Taking a broad look at the army in Germany it was very noticeable that, conscription having been eclipsed, professionalism had taken a big jump upwards. Naturally we saw more of the Royal Armoured Corps (the old cavalry of the line) regiments than other arms of the Service. In those early 1960s the time-honoured feudal concept of a landowning class claiming first place in the cavalry's officer cadre, had faded out only relatively recently. The massive growth in the power of the middle class, coupled with the replacement of the horse by the fighting machine, had produced a distinct change in the overall character of the cavalry officer. Whereas (until quite recently) having private means, they perhaps only stayed with their regiments for a few rather amateurish years before retiring to run family properties or businesses, now, despite the still abysmally low pay, most looked ahead to a full professional career. The great thing about the regimental system was (and is), that each – by recruiting officers of much the same background and outlook – achieved a happy harmony. There was, too, the factor that, in the post-war years the standard of education among the rank-and-file had risen appreciably, and officers who were not fully qualified for the posts they held, were less readily tolerated by their subordinates.

While the Rhine Army Corps commander and his relevant subordinate formation commanders were ever eager to have us out on repetitive exercises in all weathers – and hardly a month went by without one of them, or some top brass from Britain, coming to inspect us – we were at pains to keep the soldiers amused. Besides the inevitable inter-squadron sports consisting of football, cricket, basket ball, boxing, athletics, go-karting and swimming, equitation featured large. We stabled a useful quota of regimental horses, ostensibly to give preliminary training to those selected for a tour of duty with the mounted squadron in London, but less prosaically employed for cross-country competitions and gymkhanas, staged by ourselves and other cavalry regiments. Some of the officers, myself included, frequently rode with the Munsterland and the Hubertus hounds, drag hunts with forty or fifty obstacles to jump and carried out in phases, each phase ending in interludes in which girls in bright traditional aprons carried round trays of *Schnapps* and bunches of oak-leaf sprays for our buttonholes. The final phase usually finished with everyone galloping round a field to be the first to 'catch the quarry' which meant grabbing the fox's brush hooked to the 'quarry rider's' collar. Showing the British flag we wore our scarlet coats and top hats and were thought very eccentric by the German sportsmen.

There was, too, an activity known as adventure training which could take the form of anything from canoeing on the Weser to inter-squadron trekking in the Italian Alps. I revived the Pentathlon in the Blues and we won the Rhine Army event in 1963. I flew the team to England to compete in the British Championships at Aldershot, and while there booked myself into King Edward VII's Hospital (Sister Agnes' in Beaumont Street) for the first of many nose operations. I shared a ward with Nick Paravicini, of the Life Guards. It was the time of the aftermath of the Profumo affair and, from our windows we had a good view of the flat occupied by Christine Keeler and Mandy Rice-Davies, and diverted ourselves by watching their comings and goings to court, accompanied by police escorts and by much bustling of reporters and photographers. Nick's mother, Elizabeth, the daughter of Somerset Maugham and her husband John Hope (afterwards Glendevon), amused by this pantomime brought along two pairs of outsize binoculars for us on their second visit to the ward.

I was one of those in Germany who managed to put in some polo, and some flighting on the north coast, while others skied in the Hartz mountains and Austria or spent weekends in Berlin. Prompted by a tour of the notorious concrete wall, which the East German government had erected three years previously, I wrote, as I have already mentioned, a story with an east-west Berlin background, for *Blackwood's Magazine*. Over the next four years Blackwood's published upwards of a dozen long stories of mine, the first of which, with a Middle East setting, won me – remarkable beginner's luck – one of their two 1964 literary prizes.

At the top of each squadron barrack block was a recreation room where weekly so-called 'smokers', squadron socials, concerts and whist drives, took place, much beer being drunk and many ditties sung. My squadron's signature tune was 'The Wild West Show'. A Trooper Clark, a cockney, was the leader of the solos: *In the next case, ladies and gentlemen, we 'ave the oomergoolies bird. The oomergoolies bird is a bird what 'as very short legs and big you-know-what. It flies at supersonic 'eight an' lands at very great speed. An' when it lands its famous cry can be 'eard all through the jungle, oomergoolies, oomergoolies, oomergoolies!* . . . Gales of laughter from his mates, who give a chorus of *sing us another one, do!* followed by:

> *Oh, we're off to see the Wild West Show,*
> *The Elephant and the kangaroo-oo-oo,*
> *Never mind the weather, as long as we're together,*
> *We're off to see the Wild West Show!*

And so Trooper Clark introduced the 'Show's' next weird and wonderful creature, and much fun was had by all. There were all ranks dances, too (heaven knows where the girls came from) and all sorts of troop outings. When I instructed my troop leaders to think up ways of finding extra recreational amusement for their soldiers, one of them, a very generous millionaire twice over (quite a thing for a young man to be in the 1960s) simply bought a minibus and made a present of it to them. The same subaltern set his sights on winning Sandown's Grand Military Gold Cup. And I well remember his voice on the mess telephone instructing his trainer to buy a horse that would do just that, money no object. He flew home, rode the horse and won the cup.

There were over a hundred Blues families occupying houses in Herford's residential areas. The officers' wives gave precise replicas of the little dinner and drinks parties they might have given in London, only buying their provisions at the NAAFI shop instead of at Harrods or Fortnum's, and they forged friendships to last a lifetime. But perhaps the NCOs and their families made more of their time with the Rhine Army because, on the whole, they absorbed themselves totally in the domestic life of the regiment, not hankering to return to England. Most of the wives took an active part in the regimental wives' club thereby offsetting boredom and ensuring that they enjoyed a warm social existence. There was a wonderful community spirit, a happy cohesion, from the top to the bottom of the regiment. After two-and-a-half years I transferred from what was then the army's most technical and potentially most explosive sphere to an equestrian-ceremonial role which had continued in London in much the same style for some three hundred years. I went home to command the Blues Mounted Squadron.

The old Victorian Hyde Park Barracks, cobwebby, draughty and unhygienic, with their tall-ceilinged echoing stables we loved so well, were to be razed to the ground. In their place would be the concrete hideosity, badly

constructed to Sir Basil Spence's design, with which Londoners are familiar
today (many taking the view that they have ruined the Hyde Park landscape). Early one autumn morning in 1965 the mounted squadrons rode out
of the old buildings in Knightsbridge for the last time, to occupy Wellington
barracks, which, being a stone's throw from Buckingham Palace is one of the
Foot Guards' two traditional London homes. Apart from the flimsiness of
the prefabricated stables and riding school which had been put up for us
there, the main impact felt in the change of scenario was a sense of nakedness; for, at Knightsbridge, all our barrack activity was concealed from
public view, while pedestrians now gazed through the railings on the
Birdcage Walk side of Wellington barracks to witness almost our every move
as though we were zoo animals; and, indeed, I imagine we provided a
similar sort of entertainment.

The routine within those railings was much as I have described it at Hyde
Park Barracks fifteen years before. The Queen's Life Guard, alternating daily
between the Life Guards and the Blues, travelled to Whitehall every morning, going under Horse Guards arch on the stroke of eleven o'clock, save
that the journey was, of course, very much shorter now. And the barrack
routine was much the same, too. Stoney Castle Camp, in Surrey, the
traditional autumn camping-place of the mounted squadrons was under-
going a number of improvements at that time. So, at the invitation of John
Egremont (Harold Macmillan's private secretary) I took the Blues squadron
for their annual fortnight under canvas, in 1965 and 1966, to Petworth Park,
in Sussex. And we had a most enjoyable time organizing exercises in the
countryside I had known so well as a boy, including treks south over the
Downs to swim the men and the horses in the Channel. On one occasion
when Bing Crosby, an old friend of the Egremonts, was staying at the
house, he came across to sing to the soldiers, several of whom got out their
mouth organs to accompany him. The landlord of the pub in the adjacent
village of Tillington did us the honour of changing its name to *The Horse
Guard*.

Reflecting a general relaxation in protocol and formality in British society
by the mid 1960s there was distinctly less rigidity regarding the off-duty way
of life and appearance of officers of the Household Division than when I was
a subaltern at Hyde Park Barracks around 1950. Officers were then more
appraisingly or critically aware of whether their brother officers were doing
'the proper thing', the conventional diversions, hunting, racing, sailing,
skiing, shooting, fishing, stalking, playing polo and attending the right
parties. Now their off-duty lives were more private and independent. Fifteen years previously you were committing a social offence if you were seen
walking out of barracks without a dark suit, stiff white collar, bowler hat and
furled umbrella. Since then there had been a semi-liberation from the old
off-duty uniform. Most officers were now only wearing hats with civilian
clothes for equestrian activity, or to attend race meetings. (Perhaps Prince
Philip, essentially a non-hat man, did something to set the fashion of the
naked head?) Along with these signs, I believe, and not entirely by coincidence, went a certain new brusqueness, a diminution of thoughtful

good manners and other social punctiliousness, throughout Britain. We had entered the age of hi-tech, combined with Harold Wilson socialism.

With the army showing greater indulgence, the troopers had a less rigorous life. The barrack rooms at Wellington were lighter, airier, more spacious and at some distance from the stench of the stables. The men, being a bit better paid, not many (in debt) had recourse to gratifying homosexuals as had been the case a decade and more before. The taking of drugs by a very small minority was a new pitfall. Junkies were dealt with severely and the persistent ones removed from the service.

As regards ceremonial performances the first intimation I had of the new self-glorification of the media was when Richard Baker interviewed me the day before a Royal escort occasion. He surprised me by giving the impression that his coverage of the event was to be much more important than the smooth running of the day itself. He was far less concerned with the conventions of the ceremonial, or the lives of the troopers than with the possibility of disasters occurring, such as men falling off their horses or assassins appearing in the crowds. In other words he wanted sensation. But that is something we have come to live with.

My counterpart as squadron leader of the Life Guards was Ronald Ferguson (later to be celebrated as the Duchess of York's father), and the two of us took turns commanding the Sovereign's escorts, including those for Trooping the Colour, the State Opening of Parliament and the various State Visits. On the occasions when there were two Royal coaches, and both regimental standards were carried, one of us would be alongside the Queen's coach and the other by Prince Philip's. There was a comic incident on one such occasion when we waited together on our horses opposite Victoria station for the arrival of King Hussein of Jordan and his (then) English Queen Muna. The escort wore cloaks against a hard-driving rain. Ferguson, noticing that the bottom button of his cloak had come undone and having no hand free to do it up (one holding his reins, the other his sword), he signalled with his sword to a staff officer (also in his relevant full dress and standing under shelter) to come over to him. That officer, thinking Ferguson was the harbinger of some emergency message, duly made the thirty yards walk through the deluge and the puddles. His nose was rather put out of joint, to say the least, to find his mission to be that of a valet.

Ferguson's name had been closely associated with polo from his subaltern days onwards, and, in the barracks, in uniform or out, to keep his hitting wrist strong he was forever swinging a sawn-off polo stick with a lead weight on the end of it. He was a very good regimental officer, well liked by his soldiers (with whom he was never arrogant), his career being only cut short by his inability to pass his promotion exam. He never rose higher than temporary major, despite the intervention on his behalf of the then honorary Colonel of the Life Guards, Lord Mountbatten.

My own military life was drawing to a close, too, partly as a result of my severe hearing loss, caused by gunfire. This started as far back as my activity with the Eton Shooting Eight and progressed through much more competition shooting at Bisley and elsewhere and, of course, with armoured vehicle guns. I was medically downgraded for that. And on another score too – sinusitis and kindred afflictions, stemming, I think, from breathing in too much dust in the Middle East. For these I underwent a total of seven operations between 1964 and 1968. My last eighteen months in the army were spent at Bovington Camp, in Dorset, training Junior Leaders, potential NCO volunteers, for the armoured regiments – at the end of which I was invalided out. I must confess, looking back, one great weakness of mine as a soldier. I always became very frustrated after a time with routine. And routine – as it is with cuckoo clocks – is very much the way of the army.

The army has changed enormously since my day, yet *plus ça change, plus que c'est la même chose*. Nowhere does that dictum ring more truly, I notice, than in the Household Cavalry and Brigade of Guards, which, along with every other corps, have become more hard-working, more professional, more technically minded. And because the Household Division is the most conservative institution in the armed services (probably, too, in Great Britain as a whole) the lead it has given in modernizing is all the more remarkable. Far fewer of its officers are coming from 'traditional Brigade' families, far fewer from the leading public schools, and yet the image is essentially the same, with all the familiar discipline, panache, pride and style. The fact that the rank and file display the habitual smart front, quick response, punctiliousness, buoyancy and personal enterprise indicates that officer recruiting (so widely broadened) and officer training must be at least as well conceived and well conducted as it was in 'the old days'. And the regimental system is as strong as ever.

On the other hand, through regimental associations and other military contacts since the early 1970s I have seen that the profession's sharper edge has produced one rather unattractive feature, and that is the jealously watchful eyes that are manifest in the race for promotion. In our time we were more inclined to enjoy the regiment for its own sake than for any advancement it might bring. Jockeying for career positions between officers was relatively rare. But, for three reasons that scenario was bound to change: officer's private incomes, where they apply at all, are smaller; the promotion pyramid has narrowed; and the chances of finding amenable and profitable employment in civilian life have been greatly reduced.

Ancient institutions that are a part of Britain's heritage of pageantry, like the Household Cavalry, being vulgarised by advertising and media people, become easily taken for granted. If familiarity does not, in the case of that corps, quite breed contempt, at least it breeds some loss of mystique and magic. It may take a terrible tragedy to concentrate the nation's attention again, perhaps to re-evaluate that particular institution. Such a tragedy struck the Household Cavalry on 20 July 1982. That morning the IRA detonated a gelignite bomb, full of nails, opposite the Queen's Life Guard when its members had reached a certain point on Hyde Park's south carriageway, killing the officer, the corporal-major, a lance corporal, a trooper and seven horses. Three horses, Eclipse, Copenhagen and Sefton were close to death, only being saved by quick and careful veterinary attention.

Outraged animal-loving Britons who had witnessed on their TV sets the

Ronda, Spain, 1965: with (*left*) Alastair Boyd at the start of one of our Andalusian rides.

1967: A Sovereign's Escort commander. HM The Queen is accompanied by King Faisal of Saudi Arabia. As for the mare, she was always a bit camera shy.

The four joint-Masters posing on my Sinnington day in 1971. (*left to right*) John Shaw, Anne Feversham, David Westbury and Roddy Heathcoat Amory.

1974: with Lavinia at Pannett's Shipley.

1971: Lavinia with the Radnor and West.

reat black bleeding bodies of the horses straddling the road – some dead, some kneeling, some prostrate, attempting to raise their heads, with eyes of terrible bewilderment – wanted to focus their attention on one of those horses, an animal hero who might symbolically transcend the act of terrorism, inflict a moral victory over the Irish fanatics. And Sefton, who had lost over a gallon of blood, undoubtedly the greatest character of all the victims, was the horse they chose. Among the get-well cards pinned on his loose-box door was one epitomising the national feeling. 'Cheat the bastards!' it read. 'Live!' Similar spirit was displayed when the Task Force had sailed for the Falklands a few weeks before. 'Cheat the bastards!' – people felt, even if they did not express – 'drive them off those islands!' In fact both those events, the bombing of the Queen's Life Guard and the South Atlantic War, were Blues and Royals' dramas for 1982. For the IRA victims were from a Blues and Royals Guard while the Falklands' Blues and Royals detachment, the Task Force's only cavalry (under command of my wife's godson, Mark Coreth), covered themselves in glory. ○

The following spring I had the honour to be invited to write Sefton's biography; and if ever I was faced with a labour of love this was it. It was not difficult to discover when, where, and who by, the horse was bought in Ireland; the very fields in which he grew up; the day of his purchase by the army; the week he crossed the Irish sea; the months and the circumstances in which he lived at the Remount Depot at Melton Mowbray; his chequered career as a trainee horse under his particular 'rough rider' in London; his mischievous behaviour on his first Trooping the Colour; his impish antics as a riding-school horse; his posting to the Army of the Rhine; his supremacy there in competition and in the hunting-field; his being overworked and thus broken down in Germany; and his return to ceremonial duty (including a part in the wedding of the Prince and Princess of Wales) at the new Hyde Park Barracks. Fortunately there was as much of colourful interest to say about Sefton as there was about any other horse in Knightsbridge stables; and, for anyone who had loved those big black troop horses as I had, it gave no trouble to do him justice. Some extracts from my book *Sefton: The Story of a Cavalry Horse* – with a foreword by the Master of the Horse, David Westmorland, who had been equitation officer during my early Knightsbridge days – published by Souvenir Press in June 1983, may explain why people were at once very shocked and angry, very compassionate and sentimental, following the outrage:

'I was dazed, I did not know what the hell had happened' relates Trooper Pedersen [his rider]. 'Sefton just stood there, head hanging, feet splayed, gushing blood. I heard voices through the smoke telling me "get off your horse".' Nails had penetrated Sefton all over his off side, the most serious going deep into a point above his stifle. A six-inch nail was driven through his bridle into his head. Fireballs had scorched his eyeball, there were chips of car metal across his neck. Worst of all, a razor-sharp chunk of car metal had severed his jugular vein. Those four white socks that were chalk-powdered to snowy perfection a minute ago, were now bloodstained almost beyond recognition. The old gelding was losing blood fast ... Sefton, weak and shattered, one eye closed up so that he could hardly see on his offside, was led slowly back towards the barracks. Halfway down the road a regimental horsebox arrived for him. He ambled up the ramp, was held steady in the vehicle and was soon in the sanctuary of veterinary care ...

If ever Sefton received strong mental images of his past would they not have been particularly vivid after the horror of July the 20th. Possibly his whole life, from colthood in County Waterford to glory on Royal Wedding day, streamed across his consciousness, as a motion picture flickers on a screen. He stood in the shadow of the valley of death. Most horses as badly injured as he was would have succumbed. Not resilient Sefton; he was eating a bran mash by the evening. Did he know that an act of man, not of God, had mutilated him. Whether or not he knew, in his fine heart there was no trace of hatred for man ... Soon police notices appeared all over London ... MURDER announced the placard, depicting a bearded man ... Apart from relations and friends of the men who were killed and wounded, animal lovers in particular would not forgive – not in a thousand years ...

By September [Sefton's] success was such that, when the director of the Horse of the Year Show ... applied to the Household Cavalry for Sefton to star as 'the Horse of the Year', sanction was granted ... At the end [of the Musical Ride] the cavalrymen charged up the arena to halt dramatically in front of the Royal Box. The lights were then turned off, and the Ride divided and single filed down the long sides of the great arena, and so out of the doors at the opposite end. Next, a spotlight was beamed on the entrance, and in came Sefton, led by Pedersen. When the applause began, the old hero responded with a buck and a whinny of joy – beautifully timed! – and the cheering eddied out to a prolonged and colossal roar.

Nothing like it had ever before been heard at Wembley. Notwithstanding the dim lights you could see pocket handkerchiefs spreading through the stands like the start of snow on hillsides. The sobbing was contagious and quite unashamed. The scene was witnessed by millions of others on television sets. Sefton was England's darling and England was not too coy to show it. Never had Ronald Duncan's panegyric, written a decade before, in honour of the Horse of the Year Show, seemed more appropriate:

'This Cavalcade of Grace now stands, it speaks in silence. Its story is the story of this land.

Where, in this wide world, can man find nobility without pride, friendship without envy or beauty without vanity? Here where grace is laced with muscle, and strength by gentleness confined.

He serves without servility; he has fought without enmity. There is nothing so powerful, nothing less violent; there is nothing so quick, nothing so patient.

England's past has been borne on his back. All our history is his industry: we are his heirs, he our inheritance. Ladies and Gentlemen: THE HORSE!'

Spectators searched through watered eyes for Sefton's scars. The powerful spotlights could not pick out a single sign of them on that glossy, ebony body. He was as impeccable, as smart, as glowing in health as he had been when he left the barrack gate, destined for a Whitehall box, at 10.35 am on July the 20th, 1982. It seemed like a miracle ...

At the time of writing (1990) Sefton, aged twenty-seven, is still in retirement at the Home of Rest for Horses at Speen, Buckinghamshire, and, I suppose, largely forgotten.

Returning to my days as the Blues squadron leader, straight after the State Opening of Parliament, for which I commanded the Sovereign's escort, in 1965 I flew to Andalusia at the invitation of Alastair Boyd (now Kilmarnock) whom I mentioned earlier in this chapter. He had proposed a fortnight's ride for us from his home in Ronda to Arcos de la Frontera, Jerez, Algericas and the Mediterranean coast, then home across the *sierras*. It was very pleasant after the fast jolting sit-down trot of the ceremonial seat in crowded noisy London to meander through the silent corkwoods and olive groves at the *paso castellano*, the smooth Spanish equine amble. The horse is easily the best vehicle by which to tour any rural district. There is less hazard of disturbing the wildlife, while the slowness of the conveyance allows you time to contemplate everything of beauty and interest that passes. In Andalusia you have the added advantage of knowing that every village you approach when you are tired and aching after fifteen or twenty miles' ride will have stabling for your horses as well as rooms for yourselves.

It was during that enjoyable journey that I first heard of the murder, in 1941, of Alastair's uncle, Joss Erroll, in Kenya, interest in which was revived in the 1980s with *White Mischief*. I learned then, for the first time, too, of the close involvement with Erroll and Diana and Jock Delves-Broughton of my cousin – a first cousin of my father's – Dickie Pembroke. A regular in the Coldstream, stationed in London in the late 1930s he had been having an affair with a brother-officer's wife. His regiment being offered a vacancy on the army staff in Nairobi, promptly dispatched Dickie. From boyhood I remember a man of great charm, good looks and dry wit, and however closely associated he may have become with the 'Happy Valley' set, I think he had a very raw deal at the hands of *White Mischief*'s author.

But that is enough digression. Ali Boyd suggested he and I might combine to write a book on travelling by horse throughout Spain. We discussed the project at Collins with Mark Bonham-Carter, who undertook to commission such a work. But, as I then decided to delay my departure from the army it came to nothing; except that Ali made a number of limited rides with his wife, which resulted in his *The Road from Ronda* (Collins, 1969). Anyhow, following our excursion of 1965, we wrote a substantial article for *Country Life*. Having that entrée I wrote to the editor when I left the army, three years later, enquiring whether by any chance he had a vacancy on his editorial staff. He suggested I should join straight away. I asked if he would allow me a year's grace for something I had long wanted: to attend an art course. And for nearly a year I was at the City and Guilds of London Art School studying figure drawing, sculpture, painting and history of art, before starting a new career as a journalist.

Most tragically, in the very week I started work at *Country Life*, my mother was killed in a motor accident at the early age of sixty-four.

# 7

# *Country Life*, Club Life and Wild Life

Looking back over the eighteen years I spent as a full-time magazine journalist I feel that the moral effect of certain buildings upon the people who work in them may be much underestimated. From the time I first entered Edwin Lutyens's ornate and handsome doorway in Tavistock Street, Covent Garden – the door to the building which he designed for the *Country Life* editorial offices – I sensed a great veneration for the heritage of the magazine (notwithstanding the fact that it had already lost its independence, having become absorbed into the IPC empire, which is itself a part of Reed International). In those far-off Covent Garden days all of us, from the Editor, John Adams (essentially 'Mr Adams' then) downwards, were ever conscious of *Country Life*'s enlightened creation, in 1897 by Edward Hudson; and of its original emergence from *Racing Illustrated* (for that era a very lavish journal), which Hudson put out from his presses at Hudson and Kearns in Southwark Street. We were always at pains to continue the same bright thread that he and his immediate successors weaved. Consequently, the greatly enlarged sepia photograph of the founder in John Adam's office, was an inspiration, while the volumes room in which every issue since the first (8 January, 1897) was kept, was treated like some holy tabernacle and regularly referred to so that the traditional style and spirit of the paper was faithfully maintained. I believe the moral and spiritual endowment of Lutyens's walls in Tavistock Street had something to do, too, with the extraordinary care and respect with which the work of the regular contributors to *Country Life* was treated. Writers such as Mark Girouard (architecture), Eiluned Lewis ('Countrywoman's Notes'), Frank Davis (showrooms), Pat Cotter (bridge), Ian Niall ('Countryman's Notes') all declared that they were never looked after so well by other publishers and journals.

The change of temperament occurred eight years after I joined the editorial staff. In 1976 IPC lifted us from our Covent Garden roots, pitchforking us into the open-plan twenty-second floor of the newly erected King's Reach Tower, a forbiddingly stark, grey cubic beacon standing south of the Thames, close to Blackfriars bridge. From that day forward attitudes began (almost imperceptibly at the time) to change. Although the *Country Life* ideals were neither forgotten nor entirely forsaken, the staff – as perceptive outside contributors gently remarked – paid less attention to those ideals, were rather less faithful to them; for, while the magazine remained the central and most prestigious jewel in the IPC crown, it was caught up in the hasty Philistinism of that soulless building into which all the corporation's twenty and more magazines were then locked.

Sport and country matters were the *Country Life* themes at the end of the last century and the beginning of this one, with racing in the lead. It was not until well into the Edwardian era that architecture came out in front (which it did with such great distinction that a certain Cabinet Minister dubbed the magazine 'the keeper of the architectural conscience of the nation'). Once learned discussions on, and beautiful photographs of, the great houses became the principal feature, the estate agents regarded *Country Life* as the number one platform for the sale of properties, and that subject remains its chief strength today. Although it is now a somewhat less talented magazine than it was in the Covent Garden days and has lost a portion of its old diversity (at the expense of long, colour-laden articles) its circulation, under the inspiring editorship of Jenny Greene, is at an all-time high; and if a referendum were to be taken as to which is the most rewarding of all the weeklies in the world I wager *Country Life* would still win the vote.

John Adams (to whom I probably owe a larger debt of gratitude than to any other man in my middle years) gave me the responsibility of editing all the material on natural history, field sports, equestrian activities and animal and sporting art, and of writing reviews for military books as well as all those other subjects. Also of editing Ian Niall's (real name John McNeillie) 'Countryman's Notes', (which made way twenty years later for 'A Week in the Country' to which I myself now contribute). I regard Ian Niall's effort in turning out 'A Countryman's Notes' week after week, without fail for nearly forty years, as one of the great feats of twentieth-century journalism. Goodness knows why he has received no national honour. When Lavinia and I visited him in North Wales we had expected a sprawling farmstead with a jumble of outhouses, sheep on a lonely hillside and a trout stream in the dingle below; instead of which we traced him to a suburban house on the edge of Llandudno (albeit with a wilderness just beyond) with his fishing tackle and animal skins in a tiny hut and his hawks and beehives all standing on little more than half an acre. But once he moved into a much more spacious property in Buckinghamshire he found rather less to write about, and hence was reduced to contributing for only one week a month.

I relished those early days as a journalist, spent proofreading; telephoning contributors; choosing photographs; composing captions and article titles; rushing (a weekly is always in a hurry) downstairs to the art room and upstairs to the photographic library and the volumes room; visiting the Fleetway printers; catching the milk train on Monday mornings to cope with 'late pages'; staying up till seven or eight of an evening waiting for 'finals'; and, in the lunch hour, trying out different restaurants and pubs or visiting exhibitions with my editorial colleagues.

Magazine journalism is a great apprenticeship to one who aspires to authorship. The work is rarely monotonous (as so many of my army parade hours were); and it provides the opportunity to criticize, to appraise and to learn from, the writings of others. You pounce like a hawk on unacceptable clichés; and you take a delight in clipping the work of contributors who cannot economize with their phrases and sentences. You have plenty of spare time in which to practise your own craft; and, all through your working life, you are in the company of agreeable and intelligent men and women whose business, like yours, is words and pictures.

Sometimes, when I had an hour and a half or so to spare in the middle of the day I crossed the rubicon of Charing Cross road to lunch at the Guards Club, in Charles Street, or Buck's in Clifford Street. (Household Cavalry officers were eligible for either the Guards or the Cavalry. I chose the Guards in my Parachute Company days but resigned a little while after the two clubs amalgamated in 1976.) I had joined Buck's in 1950 when I was twenty-three, when the annual subscription for members under the age of twenty-six was – a now almost unbelievable – £6. Herbert Buckmaster, the founder, served in the Blues during the First World War; his old commanding officer, 'Beef' Tweedmouth, had been the club's first president and chairman; and for many years it was a great stronghold of the Household Cavalry. Buck's first claim to fame, before establishing his club on the Clifford Street corner, was that of being married to the celebrated actress and beauty, Gladys Cooper. (On his first morning in the trenches, in 1914, he overheard one trooper inform another: 'Mr Buckmaster's come out.' To which the reply was the bright question: 'And 'as 'e brought that Gladys Cooper with 'im?')

He was also a considerable horseman, athlete and backer of sports; and, through those interests, formed friendships with many American sportsmen, beginning with the members of the United States polo team who were in England contesting the Westchester Cup in 1921. He started an American membership of his club, which still stands at about 150 out of the 750 members today; and their number contains some of the nicest citizens of that nation you could hope to meet. Up to the early 1960s, when a high proportion of Blues officers, serving or retired, belonged, he entertained them to champagne before the annual regimental dinner. Now their number has dwindled to a tiny proportion, and like so many of the London clubs, Buck's is represented more nowadays by city types than sportsmen and soldiers. The ladies' annexe (it was the first club, I think, to have such a thing) is a charming little place with all the tables against the walls and each with glass side-screens giving an added feeling at once of intimacy and sociability. But it is spoilt by two liberties, one (a relatively recent one) being that members' wives may have hen parties there and the other that smoking is allowed at all times. Up to the mid-1970s, when the club closed for its late summer recess we could use the St James's, in Piccadilly, a most delightful club, the elegant premises of which, alas, were then bought up, and members obliged to find sanctuary elsewhere. Most went to Brooks's. Now when Buck's closes we use one which opens its doors to several other clubs during that interim – the Cavalry, which thus becomes subject to a cacophonic babel, the sort of noise you might expect in some august hotel in a beleagured city.

Pratt's, in Park Place, whose doors only open for dinner, has been a favourite haunt of mine for many years. It has two small basement rooms and a single dining-room table, and unless you have brought a guest along, you never know next to whom you will be sitting. When Harold Macmillan dined there he used to wait until he had the whole table's attention, then hold forth at length. The steward has always been known (whatever his real name) as George, and his female successor answers only to Georgina or Georgie.

A decade or so ago when our grounds in Sussex were invaded by a plague of feral cats we were supplied with cage traps by the RSPCA who would send an inspector out in the morning to dispose of them. On one occasion when I went to dine at Pratt's, Lavinia, at home, was having great trouble with a particular cat in a particular cage. She telephoned the situation to George and got him to ask me to call her. When I arrived at Pratt's, George, a sentimental animal lover, expressed great horror at the cat's predicament. It was early for dinner and the only other member present was Lord Hailsham, apparently deep in the Parliamentary pages of *The Times*. I had some difficulty with the public telephone, which is upstairs. Every time I passed the Lord Chancellor he looked up from *The Times* with an anxious face to ask: 'Has your wife got rid of that bloody cat yet?' As I left the room for the third time he enquired of George: 'Do you happen to know what that member's wife is doing with her cat?' And during dinner he cut off a conversation he was having with his neighbour (about the Reverend Ian Paisley) to put the question to me again: 'Hope your wife's keeping that cat quiet? They can be such a bloody menace, can't they?'

Later on I joined White's. Clubs are inclined to become renowned for the scurrilous stories surrounding them. Osbert Lancaster's cartoon immortalized the occasion, in 1950, in which John Fox-Strangways (the uncle of Stephen in chapter 5) kicked Aneurin Bevan down the front steps of that club. The highly eccentric and volatile Fox-Strangways, who had suffered badly in the Second World War, was sitting in Brooks's when another man, who was a member of both clubs, informed him that – horror of all horrors – the socialist who had described Tories as being 'lower than vermin' was standing at that moment at the bar of White's. Furiously, Fox-Strangways flung his paper to one side, sprang to his feet, strode across St James's Street and helped Mr Bevan down the steps with a kick in the pants. I believe Labourites condemned their Minister of Health for being seen in the chief stronghold of the Conservative Establishment a good deal more than they blamed Fox-Strangways.

When I reminded an old barrister friend of mine, Alexander (Alister) Wedderburn, about that fracas, he countered with another club story about Fox-Strangways. Calling in at Brooks's one day Wedderburn enquired of Newman, the much loved hall porter, 'How is Mr John? [the appellation reserved by all the Brooks's servants for Fox-Strangways].' 'It's quite a coincidence you should ask that, sir,' replied Newman, 'me and Mr John had words only last night.' Wedderburn broke the pause. 'Well – and how was he?' Newman looked nervously right and left, then, *sotto voce*: 'Excuse me, sir, but . . . Mr John asked me: 'Newman do you know where I can get a f. . .?' Wedderburn looked duly shocked: 'Oh, how awful, Newman, how awful for *you!*' Newman put on a pained expression: 'Well, I wouldn't have minded at all – not at all, sir – *had I not been helping my Lord Halifax on with his overcoat at the time.'*

Whenever John Adams lunched with me at Buck's it was rarely long before he reciprocated with the honour of an invitation to the hallowed Athenaeum, (a place at which I hope the hall porter is never thus shocked by members' behaviour?).

One autumn day in 1969 John suggested I might try my hand at some hunting articles. Up to then he had been paying an outside contributor, whereas he wouldn't be obliged to pay me; it would be part of my editorial job. By tradition, *Country Life* hunting articles concern particular packs, and although they deal comprehensively with the personalities, the kennels, the hound breeding, the country and the author's day out, the history had always had the main thrust. My first visit that winter was to Shropshire, to Sir Watkin Williams Wynn's, for which I stayed with the hon. secretary, Philip Warburton Lee and his wife, Hetty (now Fetherstonhaugh), whom I had known since childhood. Then, by way of moving into the role by easy degrees I applied to Masters who were old friends, or army acquaintances, such as Max Gordon (Badsworth), Rupert Buchanan-Jardine (Dumfriesshire), David Black (Garth and South Berks), John Williams (Four Burrow), Tony Murray-Smith (Fernie), John Shaw (Sinnington) and Tony Younghusband (Bicester and Warden Hill); and I travelled to Germany where the Blues and Royals had put together their bloodhound pack hunting the 'clean boot'.

Up to the end of the 1969–70 season, hunting had only featured in the magazine once a month. By chance, at about that time, John Adams chose a spring issue into which to insert pre-paid postcards inside subscribers' copies enquiring which were their favourite subjects. Frank Davis, Ian Niall and the correspondence pages competed for first place, but, less predictably, hunting was close on their heels. So I was invited to step up the quota to two a month. From 1970 I added to the articles' visual assets by including historical pictures – vintage photographs, or portraits – to support that part of the text, and by inserting a map of each country under discussion along with the adjacent hunts surrounding it. Up to 1969, too, the magazine's coverage had only been for foxhunting. I extended that to deer and hare hunting. By 1985 the editor of *The Guiness Book of Records* was writing to me to say 'We understand that so far you have hunted with 212 different packs of hounds in Britain, Ireland, America and Europe. May we include this record in our annual publication?' Or words to that effect. At the time of writing (1990) the score has risen to 270, a figure not including my regular discussions on hound shows and hunting in general. John Adams asked me, as a shooting man, too, to report the Country Landowners' Association's Game Fair which I have continued to do annually since 1970. Until that year *Country Life* carried only one polo article a season, an account of the premier British tournament, the Cowdray Park Gold Cup. With the increasing popularity of the game I was encouraged, when appointed polo correspondent, to step up the number and there have since been eight to ten articles a season. Then came a steady flow of my articles on wildlife conservation, nature reserves, animal welfare and animal and sporting art. My appointment as sub-editor was therefore very soon altered to that of Senior Feature Writer.

Among the scores of places I toured throughout the British Isles, and described for the magazine during the 1970s and 80s, were Brownsea Island, the Norfolk Broads, the Cairngorms, Loch Leven, the New Forest, Upper Teesdale, Burnham Beeches, the Ribble Estuary, Grizedale, Windermere Forest, Lundy island, Wicken Fen, Thetford Forest, Lyme Regis Undercliffs, Wyre Forest, the Wexford Slobs and the Solent shores.

Instinctively, and from the beginning, I have always felt a much deeper concern for the conservation of the natural environment, and also for the wellbeing and kind treatment of animals, whether domestic or wild, than with country sports, although those have taken up rather more of my journalistic time. I am often asked how I reconcile the apparent contradiction of these interests. The conservation part of the equation is easily answered, the animal welfare sphere of it less so. I have my own philosophical conviction with regard to God's motive for life on earth in general. It is this. I do not believe – whatever the Bible says on the subject – that it is His intention that mankind should, by any means, own and govern the biosphere entirely for his own benefit; or that he should transform the largest, and easily the best, part of the planet's surface for his own race, or species; nor that ecosystems that He has created should be destroyed, to the detriment of billions of creatures, from insects up to mammals; nor that people should claim privileged 'souls' denied to other creatures. All life possesses 'soul', mankind's portion of it being only proportionately important in relation to his size and biological development. It infuriates me to hear environmentalists complain about oil spillages entirely in terms of the fishing industry – what about the ocean life in its own right? Or to see greedy landowners creating treeless, hedgeless corn prairies for food that is probably not wanted anyway. Or to hear of dollars going to clear the Brazilian rain forests, with all the destruction of wildlife, not to mention the impairment of the world's climate which that implies, to raise meat for American mouths. Or to hear a priest tell me (as happened at home recently) that God – in comparing the same degree of pain or emotional stress in a human with that of an animal – regards the human suffering as infinitely more serious. What ridiculous conceit! My opinion is that all the world's religions, in their attitudes to other forms of life, reflect the gross arrogance, vanity and avarice of mankind, defects which never fail to amaze me whenever I contemplate how much more attractive the animal world is, generally speaking – in terms both of candour, innocence and sincerity, as well as beauty – than the human race.

Much of my time as a feature writer has been devoted, as I say, to the promotion of animal welfare. I have championed those societies committed to the causes of creating better conditions for farm and zoo animals, and of the banning of animals in circuses; I have, time and again, urged the case for a national dog licence and registration scheme; and I have written against fur farming, seal culling and whaling, all of which I find abhorrent.

How can those sentiments coexist with approval of field sports? I believe that, collectively, the properly and moderately conducted diversions of the fisherman, the game-shot and the hunting man have done more (in Britain anyhow) to promote 'green' interests, more to preserve the quality of the lakes and rivers, to guard the remaining wild corners of the land, and to further the coexistence of farming and wildlife than all the nature protectionists *per se* put together. And that, if those pursuits were to be prohibited, the countryside and all those forms of life that help to make it aesthetically pleasing – from butterflies and songbirds, from wild flowers to deer – would be appreciably diminished. A generation and more ago this was a widely accepted fact. Since then, however, Britain has become an urban dominated society in which, increasingly, townspeople, having more leisure time, money and mobility, have been attempting to impose their attitudes on the rural areas; in which people with urban or suburban backgrounds have gone – along with their city prejudices and habits – to weekend in the country, or to commute from it. Some or their sons and daughters are going to our universities, in many of which youthful heads are filled with false concepts of 'liberty' and 'anti-Establishment' distastes, liberty being stretched, anthropomorphically, to animals, and the word Establishment being made to embrace so-called 'privileged' country folk who can afford to indulge in 'blood sports'.

Admittedly, at first sight to deliberately kill wild mammals and birds, to chase them with packs of hounds, to hook beautiful fish out of beautiful rivers, seems dreadful, but that is only to look at one side of the coin. The great majority of those who set their hearts against the country sports have failed to think the issues through. Anthropomorphically and subjectively blinkered, they see men with guns on grouse moors as callous Philistines, not appreciating that the grouse has a life expectancy of about three years, if that, and then it probably dies of disease and starvation; whereas the men who promote grouse shooting and care for the heather quadruple the numbers of those birds (and much reduce the incidence of disease) along with all the other moorland life. Similarly the more enlightened keepers of game coverts are far more effective guardians of the habitats than nature wardens, whose work is more of a passive kind.

Those who oppose foxhunting rarely stop to wonder why landowners and farmers permit the trampling hooves across their valuable territories. They do so because they want the numbers of the marauding predator reduced. If the chase were to be prohibited that decorative mammal would be persecuted far more ardently than he is at present by domestic fowl- and sheep-farmers – with the shot gun which as often wounds a large mammal than kills it, sending it away maimed, or to die slowly of gangrene; or with the snare or trap, which catches by the leg and tortures more often than it extinguishes; or with gas which leaves its survivors in torment for the rest of their lives; or by poison, probably the cruellest instrument of them all. But hounds kill instantly, or not at all.

It is now largely forgotten that, in 1951, a board set up by the then Labour Government and known as the Scott Henderson Committee, enquired into 'practices or activities which may involve cruelty to British wild mammals'. This committee, composed of vets, naturalists, zoologists and ethnologists, judged that 'the control of foxes by shooting, gassing, trapping and poisoning entails greater suffering than hunting with hounds, which is at once the most effective and the most natural method of control so far devised.' The people involved were well aware that, in non-hunting countries fox populations had not only been decimated, often almost to the point of extinction, but that there the species suffer lingering deaths much more frequently from poisons, snares and gunshot wounds. It is also interesting to note that, until relatively recently – and until swayed by its ill-informed council – the RSPCA concurred with these views.

Most countrymen agree that, both ecologically and aesthetically, it is a desirable thing to have foxes, evenly distributed, at reasonable population levels. During the past decade or so the fox population has risen dramatically. The hunts account for quite large numbers of cubs during the autumn. By paradox they also preserve foxes, sometimes constructing artificial earths for them. From the conservation point of view, that is no contradiction. I do not pretend that the foxhunter is foremost a conservationist, but by coincidence his work as protector of the fox coverts renders him a very good one.

I have always disliked the digging and bolting of foxes. Ideally, for me, the sport should be concluded when the fox, eluding the pack, finds a refuge. During the late 1970s and early 1980s, witnessing an excessive amount of digging, I attributed this partly to the growth in membership of hunt supporters' clubs. It seemed to me that foot followers, raising large amounts of money through a variety of fund-raising events, were demanding their little bit of extra sport in terms of terrier work. I sensed that this was getting out of hand and a letter of mine expressing these sentiments, though couched in very moderate terms, was published in *The Field* in October 1982. The vehemence of the response was quite extraordinary. The chairman of the British Field Sports Society wrote me the most vitriolic letter I have ever received in my life, while the chairman of the Masters of Foxhounds Association demanded to see me immediately. If I had any complaints to make, he said, I was to make them through him. Let those who follow me be warned: the fact that you are set up as a spokesman for hunting does not mean you have the liberty of free speech!

But to return to the 'antis'. The townsman, who thinks the rat an ugly beast, does not mind how many of those are killed by poison, or shot, or even caught by terriers. Would he mind a little more if he knew that rats are relatively intelligent mammals and no less subject to pain than foxes? Probably not – rats, being in his eyes, so much less endearing than other creatures in his estimation – do not really matter. Unconsciously, he is guilty of double standards.

Another very significant factor on the 'antis' side is their objection to the enjoyment of those quarter of a million or so folk in Great Britain who hunt.

Is this, as they claim, because it's a crime for people to take pleasure in the stress of a hunted animal? Or is it really because 'privileged' countrymen and women are finding stimulating diversion in something which they, the antis, do not really understand? If there are hunting men or women who are gratified by the kill, I have, in a lifetime of hunting, only met a handful of such people. They are certainly the exceptions that prove the rule. Hunting enthusiasts indulge in the sport for the thrill of watching hounds work and for the exciting uncertainty of the day (factors not applicable to the drag hunt); also, of course, for the stimulating fresh air and exercise and the comradeship; and, for those with horses, the wonderful gift of being able to ride over someone else's land!

The hare's defence is camouflaged stillness and, secondly, flight. Unfortunately neither of those gifts are sufficient to save it and its leverets from the hectic and relentless pace of modern agriculture. The hare thrives on mixed farmland. After the monoculturist farmer, its principal enemy is the fox, which accounts for a great many of its young, these being born above ground. Its third most dangerous antagonist is the man with lurchers. It has been amply demonstrated, too, that hares survive better on land where they are hunted, simply because the hunting fraternity, followers of harriers and beagles, are, so to speak, the watchdogs of its survival. But the hunts account for only a tiny fraction of the hares killed in Britain.

Perhaps the simplest of all branches of venery to defend is deerhunting. The three Somerset and Devon staghunting counties are mostly divided among a great many small owner-occupiers, hill farmers who make a living under the duress of considerable economic pressures, at the same time suffering seriously from deer damage, especially in the winter. Almost without exception the farming community supports the hunts and nearly all of them follow with car and field glasses if not by horse. Were it not for the compensation of the sport the chances are the farmers would shoot the marauding deer to the point of extinction, a point which, in the past, has been dangerously close whenever hunting has stopped for long, or declined. Owing to the high price of venison, poaching is rife and, although the farmers co-operate as best they can to protect the deer, the three hunts frequently dispose of beasts that have suffered from poachers' gunshot wounds. The hunted stag or hind, on the other hand, suffers very little and is never touched by the hounds. Its end, with a humane killer, is always swift. Hunting the fallow buck in the New Forest is a part of the culling programme. While the Forestry Commission, which is the official monitor of the deer, takes its toll where necessary there with the rifle, its keepers act as harbourers to the New Forest Buckhounds. Despite all this evidence I suppose the day will come when the vote-thirsty politicians, responding to armchair-critic constituents, will endeavour to see Acts through Parliament to prohibit the hunting of live quarries. If that ever happens successfully it will certainly be to the dire disadvantage of the animals.

Having said this, I would add that it is my belief that – unwittingly and most unfortunately – legal hunting's darkest side is that it gives encouragement to the men who indulge in such evil practices as badger-baiting, cock fighting, the digging out of fox cubs, dog fighting, indiscriminate shooting and all sorts of harrassment of animals in the name of sport.

I am also convinced that public opinion and British society at large, unimpressed by the arguments I have deployed, is against the hunting of wild animals with hounds; views it, indeed, as a barbaric anachronism, however well the restrictive rules are enforced; and that it will only be a matter of time before these sports are prohibited by law. Although many of the hunts vow that, in such circumstances, they would never go 'drag', I believe they would in fact opt for the drag-line if the choice was left between that and going into suspended animation. Rather than see them fighting a losing battle against the politicians I would prefer them to go drag before. There need be no loss of face. (Otter hunting was not stopped by law, but by the otter hunters themselves who thus scored a conservationist moral victory.) The foxhunters and harehunters could very plausibly present their reasons for converting to drag-lines as the ever-increasing danger of the roads, the sensitivity of farmland and the potential hazard of rabies. Although, following drag-lines, the old quality of the sport would be missing, the tradition, the pageantry and the fraternity would remain. Whether the quarry is live or false Britain's precious venatic thread would survive.

In 1977 Jomo Kenyatta made a significant decision for the protection of Kenya's wildlife. He declared that, by 12 March 1978, curio shops throughout his country were to be cleared of all wild-animal articles, and that they were not to be stocked with them again. That month, to mark the occasion, I flew, with Lavinia, to Nairobi to make an in-depth study of the state of Kenya's fauna for *Country Life*, my findings being published in three long and liberally illustrated articles over May and June that year.

Guided by a white hunter we began with several days and nights in the Aberdare mountains. ('The trees close by our tent rang every morning like a school for wind instruments,' I wrote, 'with the piping chorus of shrikes, and the incessant call of hornbills and the parrot-like turacos ... Camping can bring you very near to the wild. At night we were sometimes aware that buffalo were sniffing and shuffling against our guy-ropes, and when abruptly woken, we found ourselves wondering whether that close, blood-curdling scream was only a hyrax or really a baboon with a leopard tearing its back ...')

Having hired a Datsun we toured Nairobi National Park; took a cabin in the Meru reserve; drove down to the Tana river; spent a night in Mount Kenya's Mountain Lodge; breakfasted next morning with that colourful old white hunter, Colonel Hilary Hook; and journeyed on to visit Lake Nakuru, Thompson's Falls, Lake Baringo and Naivasha. ('Fringed with gently swaying papyrus and shallows filled with blue water-lilies, Naivasha is the most beautiful of the Rift Valley lakes and to see the best of its impressive variety of 340 birds you cannot do better' – was my opinion – 'than hire a motorboat, as we did, to Crescent Island.')

Having been informed that there was a good deal of migratory movement in the Masai Mara, whose southern boundary is contiguous with Serengeti, we now pointed in that direction. Travelling over the Mara desert we narrowly avoided disaster with a party of heavily armed Masai tribesmen who, thanks to Lavinia's quick action at the controls of the car, lost the fight to snatch my camera after I had given them some biscuits and then (most unwisely) attempted to photograph them. The rains came early that year and our Datsun had to be towed over the Mara river's several swollen torrential fords before we reached Keekerok camp. Our sojourn there – less successful than the other reserves because the lions were hidden from view by the unexpectedly tall lush vegetation – ended with the news that the fords on the Narok road were now quite impassable. So we were obliged to abandon the Datsun and fly back to Nairobi and the sanctuary of our base, the Muthaiga Club. Then we took seats in another aircraft for Lamu, the old Arab island two hundred miles north of Mombasa, the last leg of that Kenyan interlude.

Meanwhile I had interviewed many representatives in the country from such organizations as the World Wildlife Fund, the East African Wildlife Society, the Association of Wildlife Clubs and the Professional Hunters' Association, not to mention half-a-dozen game wardens. The pessimism of my conclusions and prophecies regarding the conservation of Kenya's wildlife in general has by no means proved false. As a start the land is covered with only a very thin layer of nutrient-filled topsoil. The main adverse factor has been the rise of population, owing largely to the white man having shown the African how to resist disease. The second relates to his showing him how to immunize his cattle.

By virtue of modern medicine, Kenya's population rose from nine million in the year of her independence (1963) to eighteen million at the time of our study. Now the townships have grown out of all proportion to their state in the colonial days; and, increasingly, places where wild beasts could once roam free have been taken for cattle or, worse still, for goats which, reaching high up into the foliage of the trees and shrubs, often succeed in killing them and leaving deserts in their wake. And the Africans are continuously cutting back those vital watersheds, the forests, and then wondering why their droughts are so much worse than they used to be.

Kenya's elephant population had been reduced from 160,000 at the end of the 1960s to some 50,000 when we were there, upwards of 10,000 a year being slaughtered by poachers for their ivory. The black rhino, the leopard and Grevy's zebra were at the top of the list of other animals under severe exploitation. Kenyetta's closing of the curio shops was a useful move, and a more effective one than his ban on hunting in 1977 (which had some use as a public relations exercise, little more.) By paradox carefully limited and controlled hunting helped the wildlife. It bolstered the anti-poaching campaign in that those landowners leasing shooting blocks took great trouble to see they were not trespassed, while the hunters acted unwittingly as anti-poaching patrols.

In the decade and more since we were there, of course, we have been reading how the Somali poachers have made such inroads on the elephant and black rhino populations of Kenya that both those species are almost in danger of extinction. But I believe the public outcry would be much louder and fiercer, and the funds raised from charity for protection measures much larger, if less emphasis was laid on the actual conservation factor and more on the appalling agonies suffered every day by wounded beasts, often leading to excruciating lingering deaths. It is, I believe, compassion for the animals that touches most people's hearts rather more than whether or not there will be the same variety of beautiful creatures for the eyes and cameras of the next generation of tourists.

Within a week of returning from that trip Lavinia experienced a comical dialogue with the Prince of Wales at a London cocktail party. He was chatting with me about the 1978 polo prospects when Lavinia chipped in with this comment: 'I believe you camped on the same site that we've just left in the Aberdare Mountains?'

'Oh, really?' said the Prince.

'Our white hunter told us you were unlucky enough not to see bongo,' Lavinia went on. [She referred to the handsome white-striped red antelope that secretes itself in the bamboo cover of the high ground there.]

'He's wrong,' replied Prince Charles. 'My binoculars showed me fifteen of them.'

'Well, we saw twenty-two,' she countered. [At this point the conversation promised to develop into a fierce challenge which the heir to the throne took up.]

'I bet you weren't chased by buffalo?' he ventured.

'No.'

'Well, I'm one up on you there. Just made the Range Rover in time. Another two seconds and he'd have had the seat of my pants off.'

'Did you see leopard?' asked my wife. [Leopards generally put in appearances only at dawn and dusk.]

The Prince's face now wore an expression of suspected defeat. 'No, I didn't. That was the one great disappointment of my East Africa safari. No leopards.'

'Neither did we,' answered Lavinia, in a somewhat anti-climax tone.

Seeing the game was up in Prince Charles's favour, an equerry then moved in and steered him elsewhere.

Attitudes to 'hunters' – the label given in the United States and Canada to sportsmen with rifle and shotgun, as well as those who ride to hounds – are rather different as I discovered when I journeyed through North America, on the Travelling Fellowship with which I was honoured in 1982, by the Council of the Winston Churchill Memorial Trust, in recognition of my writings on animal welfare and wildlife conservation. In America the State Fish and Wildlife Services openly applaud and encourage the field sportsmen as being in the vanguard of the conservationist movement. And the class jealousy factor, which is such a strong one in Britain, hardly appertains at all. Field sports, having always transcended class, colour and income brackets, enjoy a deep-rooted respect in Canada and the States. Teddy Roosevelt and Ernest Hemingway, both ardent (and indiscriminate) big-game shots, are upheld by all stratas of society as being in the best hunter-conservationist tradition. In Tennessee, where about 400,000 hunting licences are (or were then) issued annually, I was told that at least half the rural population indulge in some form of field sports. In Missouri I recorded a dialogue I had with an official of the Department of Conservation, in which he told me: 'Only the superficial condemn hunting outright, the wiser heads know better. The hunter has an odd love for his prey species that most of mankind doesn't understand. This respect for and love of a wild creature has made conservationists of hunters. It was hunters' money which created the agencies to manage wildlife and see to it that creatures were protected. We would be poorer today in wildlife if there were no hunters . . .'

All the same I'd hate to see the *ad lib* transatlantic approach to field sports introduced into Britain. My tours were co-ordinated and arranged through the generosity of the World Society for the Protection of Animals, the International Fund for Animal Welfare, the United States Humane Association, the Canadian Federation of Humane Societies, the United States Fund for Animals, the Toronto Humane Society and several State societies for the prevention of cruelty to animals. I visited a large number of zoos, aquariums and wildlife parks; birds of prey rehabilitation centres; animal hospitals; a hearing dog centre; laboratories whose work included animal experimentation (far too much of it carried out by students); farms where veal calves were in crates, hens in battery rows, pigs in strawless metal sties and turkeys crowded into tiny compounds; and – perhaps saddest of all experiences – abattoirs. I also spent hours with a great many very colourful conservationists and welfarists, such as Professor Bernard Rollin (Colorado State University); John Walsh (who headed the Western Hemisphere office of the WSPA); in New York, Cleveland Amory, author of 'Man *Kind?*' and owner of the militant conservationist ship, *Sea Shepherd*; in Toronto, Madeleine Burns, who runs a private wildlife film unit, and Stephen Best of the IFAW; and, in Washington, John Hoyt, President of the United States Humane Society, and Christine Stevens, who is known as 'the Godmother of American Animal Welfare'.

Accompanied by Neal Jotham, head of the Canadian Federation of Humane Societies, I spent a rather harrowing day with a Canadian trapper. Jotham's organization had come to terms with this practice through the Humane Trapping Association, but the younger, more militant humane societies said 'there's no such thing as humane trapping,' with which I agreed. While trapping is largely abhorrent to the European mind, in up-country Canada and the United States it is all part of the Frontier Romance. From the weekending policeman – whose quarry was mostly muskrats and who I watched setting traps – to the Hudson Bay Company, the scale of commercial trapping is immense: seventeen million skins a year in the United States, five million a year in Canada. The volume of the so-called Romance may be judged visually at the Hudson Bay's headquarters outside Toronto where many thousands of pelts of a large variety of wild animals hang in tight rows in buildings resembling aircraft hangars. Those great halls are a truly dreadful indictment.

I was not quite so appalled, though nearly so, at the Newfoundland seal cull; and after my return to Britain was incensed to read a letter in *The Times* from the Minister for Cultural and Public Affairs at the Canadian High Commission in London saying that 'the actual killing methods [used on the seal pups] are more humane than those used in commercial abattoirs every day.' *The Times* published my reply as follows: 'Having spent some time earlier this year on a Winston Churchill Travelling Fellowship, in the context of animal wefare, I can assure your readers that this is simply not so. In most Christian countries meat animals are slaughtered by the captive bolt, implying instant oblivion, in which the animal does not see its killer; whereas the young seal sees, all too clearly, the man with the club, who often takes two or three blows to kill it. What is more the act is nearly always carried out in the presence of the dam, whose wailing as she follows here clubbed pup and the man who drags it across the ice is probably the most tragic aspect of the cull. Another point is that, while it may be argued that mankind needs the meat of farm animals, at no stretch of the imagination are seal fur goods "necessary" to anyone. My impression – after talking to numerous Canadians, both interested and impartial – was that, while their people as a whole deplore the cull, the Government regard the livelihood and goodwill of the Newfoundland fishermen as being of far greater importance than humane considerations.'

The British animal-loving visitor to the United States is rightly disgusted by the commercial roadside zoos in which, as I all too often saw for myself, the animals mostly live in cramped and filthy cages, alongside hamburger and candy floss stalls, and are never free from the noise and dust of traffic. The rodeo is still very popular in the USA and parts of Canada. It has a tough 'John Wayne, mighty-high-in-the-saddle', heroic symbolism, but it is a cruel sport mostly owing to the cinch which is strapped tight around the horse's loins to make it buck. I also hated to see calves chased around the arenas, thrown by lasso and branded. Dog fighting and cock fighting were then, and still are, widespread in the USA, though illegal. There are several magazines devoted to both. Good fighting dogs were fetching $600–$700 when I was there; they are worth a good deal more now. My impression was that both Americans and Canadians have a far lower sense of responsibility regarding dogs and cats than we, in Britain, do. Far more people there buy them 'to match the curtains', as a status symbol, or so that their 'kids can witness the miracle of birth', and for many other vain reasons. The police have a terrible stray dog and cat problem, and, in particular, with packs of feral dogs. Pathetically, most of the American stray dog shelters are filled to capacity. Americans buy (and often abandon) parrots, monkeys and all sorts of other exotic pets, mainly to show off to their neighbours; and, because they rarely know individual requirements of the birds and beasts, the collective suffering is lamentable.

Just before leaving Britain I read a book giving a rather vague reference to a resolution by the Pilgrim Fathers undertaking to be kind to all animals. Determined to trace the source of this, when I reached Boston I put the question to David Claflin of the Massachusetts Society for the Prevention of

Cruelty to Animals (afterwards President of the WSPA). 'Why don't you attend the Quaker meeting here in Boston, Sunday,' he suggested, 'someone there's sure to know.' So I sat through the Quaker service, with its long silences and some of its members standing to quietly hold forth on disarmament (there had been a CND march through the town the previous day). Over the coffee and biscuits that followed I asked the organizer about the Pilgrim Fathers. 'Reckon you'll have to contact our headquarters in Philadelphia,' he advised; 'but . . . that lady over there' – he pointed to a corner of the hall – 'left the Episcopalians for the Quakers on account of animals. Try asking her.' I duly introduced myself. 'Oh yes, sure I resigned the Episcopalians,' she admitted. 'They say you can't be a true member of their Church unless you worship that *man*. And I can't worship that *man* on account of his attitude to animals . . .' 'Who do you mean by "that man?"' I asked. 'Why Jesus Christ, of course,' she replied. 'First there were the Gadarene swine. He made those poor pigs mad and sent them to their death over a cliff just to help out a crazy fellow human. Then there was the feedin' of the five thousand. Just think of those fish gaspin' on the shoreline for breath. And there was the Passover, the lamb. I guess He didn't mind kosher killin . . .'

I never did discover about the Pilgrim Fathers incorporating kindness to animals in their character!

Towards the end of my Fellowship travels when I was staying in a Washington hotel our Task Force sailed to the Falklands, and it seemed to me that Americans had not demonstrated stronger pro-British feelings since the Second World War than they showed that morning. I opened my curtains to see the walls beside the streets below emblazoned in several places in enormous white letters with the words 'Cry for yourself Argentina!' The three or four people sharing the lift when I went down to breakfast beamed at hearing my accent, and one of them, a woman said: 'You a limey? Well, you just kick those goddammed Argies off those islands and hold their heads under the sea till they drown! The big machoes, we just hate 'em. We're with your Task Force body and soul.' I felt that, at any moment, they might vent their feelings by carrying me, wrapped in a Union Jack, through the city shoulder high!

It was not long after my return that the IRA bombed the Queen's Life Guard and Souvenir Press commissioned me to write the Sefton biography. That autumn Batsford (who had already brought out my *Book of Foxhunting* and my photographic collection *Victorian and Edwardian Field Sports*) republished the first 115 of my *Country Life* accounts of hunting visits, in two volumes, under the title *British and Irish Hunts and Huntsmen*. The third volume was to follow in 1986. It is to behind the scenes of those hunting accounts that I shall now turn.

# 8

# From the Hunting Field

Talking to Major Eric Comerford, Master of the Woodland Pytchley, at their opening meet a few seasons ago and glancing across a field of some eighty followers I enquired how many of those were the sons and daughters of former subscribers to the hunt. Searching the tight equestrian throng for a few seconds Comerford pointed towards a young woman (she was called Patience Wallis): 'Her parents hunted with us . . . That's all', he added.

The fact that he could, in such an illustrious hunt – the Woodland Pytchley is judged by many pundits to be a 'Shire' pack – only identify one second-generation follower is not difficult to explain; for foxhunting has suffered many drawbacks since the Second World War. For one thing, in most of lowland Britain, there is twice the acreage of plough; there is a great deal more barbed wire, so that the joy of taking one's own line is almost a thing of the past; restrictions on riding over farmland are, in general, tighter; a great deal of Britain has become unhuntable since the 1960s, owing to motorways and conurbations (hence the many hunt mergers that have been effected); and, last but not least, the groundswell of public opinion against the sport has put its devotees on the defensive. They are less inclined to nail their colours to the mast.

Owing to the economic revolution of the past half-century many of those families who followed in the 1930s, found by the 1950s or '60s that they could no longer afford to keep horses and pay increasingly heavy subscriptions, while a host of new faces with little or no hunting background appeared at the meets. Many of the *ancien régime* who might have indulged in the pursuit, finding a high proportion of their friends had deserted the hunting field – and that there were thus fewer kindred spirits with whom to socialise at covertside – switched their allegiance to pheasant shooting or other diversions. Among the new-rich taking up the chase were much larger elements from the farming community who were by then blessed with more time as well as more money to spare. Many farmers have found places in joint-Masterships, which has proved an excellent trend from the public relations viewpoint.

To my eye those eighty Woodland Pytchleyites were of a rather different stamp from the Midlands foxhunters of half a century ago, not only in turnout (they were to a lesser or greater degree mostly careless of the old dress conventions) but also in their approach to hunting, which was seen more in terms of having a good gallop (where they would not normally have been permitted to ride) rather than in the fascination of watching the huntsman's skill and hounds working; whereas their predecessors – given the more cohesive stability of rural communities half a century ago – would probably have been brought up with a love of venery for its own sake, which would have been inculcated in the Pony Club branches as well as in the family. But now, alas, the Pony Club has sacrificed itself, to a much greater extent, to competitive sport, with all the unfortunate spirit of 'the-devil-take-the hindmost' which that engenders. Anyhow, it seems that as many riding-club as Pony Club children take up the sport nowadays.

'Everbody can see that the people who hunt are the right people', says Lady Utterwold in Shaw's *Heartbreak House*; 'and the people who don't are the wrong ones.' And Evelyn Waugh, looking back on his hunting days, is on record as saying, 'I didn't enjoy it, I only did it for social reasons.' Lady Utterwold would receive little support for her comment from a social point of view in our day, while Waugh, had he lived a generation later, would certainly not have bothered to risk his neck. For, however glamorous the sport may look, there is not much social prestige to be gained from it nowadays.

Venery, whether in ancient Rome, Continental Europe or medieval times or twentieth-century Britain, has always been a highly ritualistic occupation. Ritual, ceremony and strict conformity go hand-in-hand. As in other rituals the conventions are diverse and complex, the regulations rigid. But the less the participants involve themselves in the actual purpose of the chase, the movements of the quarry, the actions of the huntsman and the hounds, in the different climatic and enviromental conditions of each day, the less they will feel a part of that procedure. And this will be reflected in the way they look. For example Frenchmen and women do not ride with their staghounds for the equestrian joy of it as such, but to relish the venery and the colourful ritual that goes with the sport. The details of their elaborate dress, worn according to their place in the hierarchy, is intensely important to them. By contrast American foxhunters being little interested in Reynard or the antics of their hounds, are there for the gallop. Consequently, in the United States there is relatively little ritual, nor is there much attention paid to the sartorial niceties. (Let me here pose and analogy. In Britain dinner parties are inclined by tradition to be more formal then they are in other countries. For such occasions we sometimes change into 'black tie'. This is now very rarely done elsewhere in the world, where dinner is more of a casual, less of a ritualistic affair. In Britain the old rituals die hard.)

In Britain, a generation or more ago, the different orders of dress in the hunting-field – women in bowlers or sidesaddle habit, farmers in butcher boots and velvet caps, male subscribers in black or red coats, squared or cutaway, and top hats – each carried its own convention with a set pattern from head to toe. And the same went for the pride taken in the turnout of the horses (plaited manes, oiled feet, careful grooming, smart tack). It is not only because we live, in universal sartorial terms, in a most inelegant age that those standards are seen to be relaxed or ignored. It is my theory that carelessness, shoddiness and disinterest in hunting dress has also been brought about partly by the lowering of interest in the venatic purpose at the expense of the preoccupation with cross-country riding. In this context a remark made to me by a woman with a renowned venatic lore, Pearl Lawson-Johnston, a pre-war Master of the Oakley, when I rode with that hunt in 1981, was significant. 'The knowledge of foxhunting here,' she said 'has passed to the foot followers. The riders don't care.' It would be a gross generalisation to say that she might have been speaking for the whole of the Midlands and the south of England, but there would be a lot of truth in it all the same.

Yet, as regards the professional sphere, as I have witnessed closely since the 1960s, the Master of Foxhounds Association has seen to it with a style of authority not unlike that of the Jockey Club – that standards have been rigorously maintained. For the most part professional huntsmen who have not kept their kennels immaculately or cared attentively to their hounds, or who have failed too often to be punctilious and efficient in either the field or the kennels; or kennelmen who have not carried out their tasks to the letter, have lost their posts or been warned that this could be their fate. They are still expected, too, to turn out like the proverbial new pins at every meet and to show an old-fashioned deference to subscribers as well as Masters; which is scarcely surprising, even in this egalitarian age, when one considers the hosts of applicants and the relatively short supply of appointments.

That situation is partly owing to the fact that in the past three decades or so the number of sportsmen combining the roles of Master and huntsman has increased. In former times most Masters (who wanted to hunt hounds, too) had not only to mount themselves, but also to continue to pay heavily for the privilege of being an MFH. Now many hunts not only waive the Master-huntsman's subscription, but mount him, too. In cases where hunt incomes are very low, however, they prefer to have a man who does not require a salary, a situation leaving only the kennelman/whipper-in to be paid. On the other hand there are quite a large number of affluent organisations who prefer an amateur huntsman, if one is available, who can combine very superior talent with really enthusiastic organising ability as a Master or joint-Master. All of which has pointed to fewer places for the professionals.

For a number of social and economic reasons the character of Masterships in general has changed considerably during the past few decades. In the old days a typical Mastership was composed of a man who was at once a hunting devotee and highly respected in his own right in the local county or district hierarchy, one with plenty of money to contribute annually to the hunt and preferably one who was likely to remain in office for a decade or more. The typical modern Mastership, on the other hand, may be made up of three, or perhaps even four, men and women, whose names are relatively unknown outside the hunting (or farming) world, who are probably 'acting for the committee' and who only undertake the appointment for four or five seasons. So the prestige of 'MFH' has declined to a great degree since the Second World War.

Owing to intensive farming and other influences the face of lowland Britain has become much less diverse since the War. A great deal of moorland, scrubland, woodland, marshland and other wild corners have been reclaimed for agriculture, and that factor, coupled with the spread of barbed wire, more extensive use of fertilisers and pesticides and more traffic (and thus more fumes) on the country lanes, has rendered it a good deal more difficult for hounds to stay with their foxes. This in turn has led to the development of a more stereotyped hound, one at once athletically built for speed, perseverance and the capacity to wriggle through difficult obstacles, and possessing a good nose; that is to say a hound whose low scenting and quick intelligence can keep level with its fast pace: in other words a 'hard-driving' hound. Pioneers such as the American Ikey Bell, Sir Peter Farquhar and Major Bill Scott began to breed such a hound between the wars, and since then Captain Wallace, Chairman of the Masters of Foxhounds Association, the late Duke of Beaufort and others have improved on it. Since the Duke's death, in 1984, Captain Wallace has stood supreme as the arbiter of the successful breeding of foxhounds, with such figures as Captain Charles Barclay of the Puckeridge, Captain Ian Farquhar (the new Master of the Duke's) and Mr Timothy Unwin, of the Cotswold, all doing as well by emulating his example. (I have often been asked by outsiders why so many Masters call themselves 'Captain'. A retired brigadier sitting next to me in Buck's Club who posed this question recently, added 'It isn't done you know, except for Majors and above – and then only regulars.' I replied that the hunting world was a law unto itself. He had no answer to that!)

Competition at the regional hound shows – Ardingly, Builth Wells, Honiton and Harrogate – is never less than very keen, while at the top challenge, the Royal Foxhound Show at Peterborough, the air is electric. The Duke of Beaufort and Captain Wallace who used to alternate, almost without exception, in winning the championships right up to the time of the Duke's last entry, were to be seen glancing jealously and surreptitiously at one another during the judging (doghounds in the morning, bitches in the afternoon) and make the sort of nervous gestures you'd expect of schoolboys awaiting exam results. During the mid-1970s I wrote enthusiastically in my Peterborough report for *Country Life* about the West Kent Payment, which surprised all present by snatching the doghound championship from under the noses of Captain Wallace (Heythrop) and the Duke. Soon after publication I heard from the latter as follows. 'Dear Watson, Having read your article on last week's Royal Foxhound Show, in which you rightly extoll the qualities of the West Kent's winning entry, I thought you might be interested to know that Payment, and indeed all the recent principal rosette winners at Peterborough, are descended from my Palmer '59 . . .' He wanted the last word on the subject and he got it!

## Dashing Midlands

Up to the 1950s the five Shire hunts – the Belvoir, Cottesmore, Fernie, Quorn and Pytchley (and questionably, as I said, a sixth, the Woodland Pytchley) – then occupying wonderful grass countries, helped set the tone for foxhunting Britain as a whole. 'Nimrod', writing in the 1820s, said that 'both nature and art have contributed to render Leicestershire *the* county for foxhunting.'

But since the last war all of them have lost country, all have lost grass. The three converging on Melton Mowbray, the Belvoir, Cottesmore and Quorn, present a somewhat different face from other hunts, because their old 'country' character has faded (a great many of their adherents are visitors belonging to the Melton Hunt Club), and partly because hunting there is even more of a race over fences than in other Midland counties. The respective huntsmen, being required to show sport at all costs, must lift their hounds and press on – on moderate scenting days – more regularly and sharply than those outside the Shires would do. So the Belvoir, Cottesmore and Quorn in particular have become increasingly untypical, unrepresentative of foxhunting Britain. That is not to assert that the Meltonians do not derive enormous enjoyment from their sport. It is only to say – loosely speaking – that they enjoy it in a different way from those in the provinces who are nearly all native to their counties.

For our visit to the four-day-a-week Quorn Lavinia and I drove in a peasoup fog up a long gated mudtrack to stay with the hunt secretary, Charles Humfrey, and his wife. No 'hon.' secretary he. Returning at midnight with us from dinner with the senior joint-Master, Ulrica Murray-Smith ('I'm the longest serving Master of this hunt since Hugo Meynell'), Humfrey was met with a series of ansaphone messages, mostly instructing as to what arrangements to make for certain American, and other foreign visitors planning days with the Quorn. He seemed like an overworked business manager receiving orders from the chairman.

The committee certainly have some bizarre problems to cope with. I never heard the end of that recent case of a Quorn man, the owner of a large estate in their Friday country, who, being refused the place he coveted in their Mastership, shut his gates to the hunt. One day, when a fox, found elsewhere, ran over that land, a whipper-in received a number of shotgun pellets on his leg. The Prince of Wales was riding nearby. Michael Farrin, the huntsman, will have a few tales to tell by the time he hangs up his boots. Some of his predecessors would turn in their graves if they knew how old he was at the time he was put on as huntsman of the Quorn in 1968. He was, so I am told, in his early twenties.

'Hounds found two outliers on Mr Herrick's land' I recorded of my day with Farrin from Kinoulton, in the Monday country; 'and hunted one of them over the Standard and across Muxlow Hill, pointing towards Nether Broughton, over Mr Eggleston's farm – again with plenty of jumping, not queuing up but spreading to find our own place, with the smell of grass all the way, we eventually followed them to a drain by the Smite – a quick thing of thirty minutes . . . then back towards Hickling where second horses were waiting.'

What sparkling tittle-tattle one hears as a hunting correspondent and how much one would have liked to include some of it in the contributions. Sir Henry Tate, who had been a joint-Master of the Cottesmore from 1946 to 1958, and his wife, Lillian, entertained us and fed us some good gossip from the 1930s when they were at the centre of that hunt's social life and there were rather more high jinks in the Shires than nowadays. Lady Tate, a most

amusing raconteur, gave us a splendid account of the Cottesmore phase of
the Hilton-Green saga. 'Chetty' or 'Chatty' (the diminutive of Chetwode)
Hilton-Green crops up all over the place in hunt history (starting with the
Eton Beagles in 1913). Having been Master and huntsman of the Meynell
and wanting a position in the Shires he applied, in 1930, for the Cottesmore
when James Baird announced his intention to resign. The Cottesmore refused to take him until he made an honest woman of his paramour, (a twice
divorced grand daughter of the 1st Duke of Westminster, twelve years older
than himself). Having satisfied the hunt committee on that one and having
then shown the Cottesmore six years' scintillating sport, in 1938 Hilton-
Green dispensed with his wife in order to marry Lady Helena (popularly
known as 'Boodley'), daughter of the 7th Earl Fitzwilliam and one of the
most daring horsewomen of the Shires.

Hilton-Green's love life was clearly as colourful as his style as an amateur
huntsman. Lady Tate's graphic account was faithfully recorded for Lavinia's
diary: 'All the Cottesmore girls loved Chetty and fought to be seen riding in
the lead with him . . . Boodley kept the hunt going when he was away with
the Army during the war. When he returned he took up residence with
another woman in the country. The committee told him that 'owing to your
immorality you must resign.' But he refused to answer the telephone and
locked himself in his house. Two committee members who paid him a visit
to take him to task, were greeted only by his current mistress in a nightdress
waving her arms at them from an upstairs window and telling them to go
away . . . Anyhow,' concluded Lady Tate, 'we thus lost a combination of best
huntsman and most entertaining personality we'd ever had.' In 1946 Hilton-
Green entered a joint-Mastership with Captain Berkeley of the hunt of that
name and, divorcing Lady Helena in 1948, ran off with Mrs Berkeley, a
daughter of Lord Dormer, and married her. He and Mrs Berkeley were
joint-Masters of the Old Berkshire (whose kennels are near Faringdon)
between 1948 and 1954; and, when I had a day with those hounds, in 1976,
their veterans told me that he had by no means lost his touch as a huntsman,
although he was sixty by the time he left them. In 1966 Boodley married Lord
Daresbury of Belvoir and Limerick fame.

The Cottesmore Masters at the time of our visit were Mrs Hellyer, David
Samworth and Mrs George Gibson, a sterling character, a great equestrian
show judge and wife of the celebrated stud vet and horse diagnostician. She
recounted for us a recent and wry example of hunting spite. One day when
the Cottesmore hounds met on the then boundary with the Quorn a certain
Quorn woman, who for some reason had it in for the Cottesmore, hid in a
nearby Quorn covert hoping the Cottesmore would draw it, simply so that
she could report the matter to the Quorn Masters and bring their wrath
down on the Cottesmore Masters. But the woman, who was well known for
this stratagem, was discovered in her hiding-place by a Quorn foot follower
and – concluded Mrs Gibson – 'she was exposed for her deviousness all over
the Shires . . . what made her reputation worse was that she cubhunted with
our hounds because we charge no cap in that season.'

The Pytchley claim Frank Freeman, who carried their horn from 1906 to

1931, to have been the greatest huntsman of all time, greater even than the Quorn's Tom Firr. But who can really compare them? Freeman's last day's hunting is commemorated in a Lionel Edwards portrait of the Queen, then the five-year-old Princess Elizabeth, watching him from her pony with hounds in full cry. The duo Freeman formed with Lord Annaly as field Master was said to be one of the most effective teams ever produced in the hunting world.

The Reynoldses who were then joint-Masters, put us up for our 1979 Pytchley day, and took us to tea at a house that is steeped in Pytchley history – Althorp. Lord Spencer gave us a great welcome, his wife, Raine, less so, since she found hunting talk very dull. So much so that, wanting to be rid of us, she gave Johnny Spencer a reproachful look when, at the end of tea, he offered to escort us over the house, and a fiercer one when he stood up to do so. We had a grand tour, during which he regaled us with stories of the time the pretty ex-circus act foxhunting Empress of Austria came to dinner at Althorp in his great-grandparents' time and, among other eccentricities, shocked them by smoking large cigars. (Among the host of pictures I admired was a portrait of Eleanor Needham, mistress of Charles II's eldest son, James, Duke of Monmouth, my biography of whom, *Captain General and Rebel Chief*, had been published by Allen and Unwin in the same month. It was one of those maddening things that can happen to an author. Had I known of that picture six months earlier it could have been in the book.) We thought we had seen the last of Lady Spencer but she rejoined us at the end of the tour just as her husband turned to me with 'I expect you'd like to see the Stubbses? They're all in my study, which is not open to the public'. Admiring them, I commented that Stubbs must have been much influenced by the French animal artist, Jean-Baptiste Oudry. Raine Spencer's face became quite suddenly radiant: 'Oh *Oudry*! Johnny and I met under an Oudry!' On which note she turned abruptly on her heel and left the room. Recounting the Althorp visit to my brother, Michael, a week later he recalled how more than thirty years previously he received an invitation from Raine's mother, Mrs McCorquodale (Barbara Cartland) to escort her daughter to a London dance, with a dinner party first. Officers were still wearing uniform off-duty at that time, a hangover from the war. Michael went dressed in the green patrols of his regiment, the 60th Rifles, to find a party composed of mother, daughter and three officers of the Foot Guards, who were also to squire the dizzy debutante that was Raine. Safety in numbers. . .

Nerina and Patrick Bowlby kindly put us up for the Belvoir during which sojourn we spent an hour or two at Belvoir Castle, and the Duke of Rutland was most assiduous in helping Fiona Anderson – my photographer that season (1977–78) – with her ladder and lamps and tripod when she took pictures of the family hunting portraits. The Rutlands' parting shot was to stick a printed injunction on our car: 'Save it – the Vale of Belvoir!'

As for the day's hunting, these extracts from my report give an idea of its flavour: 'Waiting by the lane as Jim Webster cheered his bitches into Melton spinney, and looking east over the valley through which the Melton brook winds, we were enjoying what many foxhunters describe as the best view in the Shires. And the outlook was enhanced the moment a fox ran out of the covert's south-east corner, when reins were quickly shortened for the pipe-opener which followed, with thrusters taking their own line right across the landscape (and proving that good advice in *Baily's*: "a blood horse with bone is required, a flyer for the Leicestershire side... There is wire, but the wire Committee have no trouble about procuring its removal in the season")... Jim's fast and beautiful Belvoir-tan bitches drew on between Waltham and Chadwell, where at about one-thirty they found an outlier on the old ironstone railway track. This fox was headed at Chadwell, but, with a fine crash of music, they quickly recovered the line, racing on through Goadsby Gorse, across the Eastwell road and the old railtrack beyond it; and giving us another marvellous fifteen minute gallop...'

That enchanting Leicestershire courtesan, 'Skittles' (Catherine Walters) played a prominent part in the early history of Fernie's hunt. She began following the Quorn hounds in the 1850s when Lord Stamford was Master. Lady Stamford, another belle but one with less charm than Skittles (but also, incidentally, like her and the Empress of Austria, a former circus eques-trienne) was furious when the eyes of the Quorn men turned away from her and on to this newcomer. She persuaded her husband to have Skittles banned. 'I don't know what right Lady Stamford has to object to me,' retorted Skittles, 'She's not even the head of our profession, Lady Cardigan is!' Anyhow she crossed the border to hunt with the Billesdon, the southern, neglected part of the Quorn country, which was on loan to Mr Tailby. A brilliant Master, Tailby made Billesdon meets very popular, but from the time Skittles arrived on the scene the fields swelled out of recognition. In 1888 the Billesdon country became, under Mr Fernie, totally independent of the Quorn, and has ever since been known as Fernie's.

Tony Murray Smith having retired from the Blues just before I joined I did not meet him until I stayed at Gumley for my Fernie day, but he was one of the Olympian figures of the Quorn when I rode regularly with their hounds in the late 1940s and early '50s. He was later their Master, in tandem with his first wife, Ulrica, until they parted. She then stayed on in that regime, while he went into a Fernie triumvirate and hunted their hounds for a time, Gumley being one of that establishment's best centres. The blonde and exquisitely pretty Sally, who had been married to James Hanbury of the Belvoir, smashed her head in a point-to-point just before marrying Tony and was never quite the same again after that. She died in her forties leaving him, for a long time, a sad and lonely man. An experienced huntsman and houndsman, war hero, yeomanry colonel, magistrate and deputy lieutenant for Leicestershire, Tony was the epitome of the *ancien regime* Master, and was upheld as the model in the post-war years, for field-Masters. A joint-Master of his at the time of my Fernie visit was Archie Clowes, whose place was to be taken the following season by Brian Bell from the Cotswold. In my article I wrote that Clowes was 'to be replaced by Mr Bell'. On publication Clowes telephoned me with apoplectic rage saying 'My friends will think I've been sacked... I shall have no more to do with you again, in any hunting context, you can be sure of that!' The draft had already been approved by Tony and the hunt secretary. Some Masters are more touchy than others.

The Atherstone, a hunt lying adjacent to the Shires – and owning at least as good a country as most of them, and almost as illustrious a history – is celebrated for Siegfried Sassoon's comments when he went there just before the First World War as the guest of his Master-and-huntsman friend Norman Loder (Denis Milden in *Memoirs of a Foxhunting Man*, in which the Atherstone was the 'Packlestone'): 'The Packlestone . . . appeared to be a paradise of jumpable fences, and compared with the well-wooded Ringwell [Southdown] it was a tip-top country. For the first time in my life I was able to sit down and jump a dozen clear fences without pulling up . . .'

The Masters of the Atherstone in the mid-1970s when I rode with them were cast in a rather different mould from Loder. They were called Travers ('Buzz') Lisney and Graham Arm. Lisney and his girl-friend 'Frosty' visited me in my *Country Life* office to size me up, and got married just before Lavinia and I stayed with them. Lisney and Arm thought they'd have a bit of fun with me. They mounted me on the most terrifying horse of my career. It bucked and pranced as I attempted to talk to the photographer, Jim Meads, at the meet and started away in a thick lather of sweat. Then, at the first obstacle, a fly fence, it galloped straight into it as though blind, turned upside down in the nearside ditch, but, madly and immediately, got to its feet, charged the brush and careered on – with me puffing along on foot behind. The animal being caught, a kind woman rode up to me with the words 'what a horse to give a visitor! Here take mine, I'll have a go with that one.' But the man who caught it said 'No you won't Mary, this is a well-known *killer*!' I kept, like a coward, very strictly to the gates for the rest of the day.

Bob Hoare, of the South Notts, another hunt on the fringe of the Shires, was coming to the end of his long venatic career (West Norfolk, 1937–58, Cottesmore, 1958–69, then South Notts), and it was a great joy to listen to his lilting voice on our scentless day, but sad to see him dismount in arthritic agony at the end of it. He had recently engaged a huntsman, through a *Horse and Hound* advertisement without knowing that the individual in question had left his previous job under something of a cloud – having, in threatening earnest, pointed a loaded humane killer at the Master's head. Anyhow, Bob being a man with a flow of witty stories to tell, and his wife, Betty, a delightful hostess, we had a most enjoyable couple of nights at their home, the Hall, near Oakham. He was particularly amusing about his stay with his cousin, Uvedale Lambert, to hunt with the Old Surrey and Burstow ('First we were on his land there was a special tantivy for Uvy, then we were on Diana Barnato Walker's land, and there was a tantivy for her. . .' and so on). He died five years after our South Notts visit, having just triumphed by raising – as the organiser of the British Field Sports Society Fighting Fund – an astronomical sum of money.

Adjacent to the South Notts on its north side the Barlow country stands studded with Chesterfield, Sheffield and Derbyshire's High Peak. Old Elsie Wilson, Master since the death of her father, Major William Wilson, and a granddaughter of the hunt's founder was still in command when I hunted there in 1986. She owned and kenneled the hounds at Horsley Gate, a few miles south of Sheffield (and her farmhouse smelt overwhelmingly of cats!); but the power behind the throne was her joint-Master, a young woman of the most striking beauty, Mrs Gilbert Hinckley, who kindly had me to stay. She kept the hunt horses in the unique castellated stables below her home, Amber House, Kelstedge. Mrs Hinckley not only organised the hunting (with the exception of the hounds), supervised the stables with the hand of a perfectionist, and rode like an angel, but also holds a high national reputation as a breeder of Irish draught horses.

The Fitzwilliam country lies on the east side of the Cottesmore and Woodland Pytchley. It is centred on one of England's very great houses, Milton, which was our billet to watch the Fitzwilliam hounds in action when, in the spring of 1976, Tony Warre, the late Tom Fitzwilliam's joint-Master, mounted me on his good little ex-polo pony. If there is any house in the world with more spacious rooms than Milton I have yet to see it. (Castle Howard I know is a larger house, but its rooms cannot, I believe, have more expanse than Milton's). This palace's principal drawing room contained, among many other priceless paintings, eight huge Canalettos, and there were six Stubbses in the dining room. For each room there was a leather folder with a list of the pictures, giving descriptions and dates, and often also original bills or notes from the artists concerned. Our fabulous bedroom suite coupled with the valeting service, certainly outdid that of the comfort of any other hunting house we have ever stayed in. Joyce Fitzwilliam who referred to her husband as 'Tom cat' was first married to Lord FitzAlan of Derwent. Their younger daughter's husband was Vivian Naylor-Leyland whose son, Philip, became a Fitzwilliam joint-Master in 1987, and inherits Milton. 'I wonder for how much longer I shall afford to sink £30,000 a year into the hunt?' Tom Fitzwilliam mused to me. It was extraordinary to think that, only sixty years before, when the family also owned the palatial Wentworth Woodhouse in Yorkshire, his cousin the 7th Earl had been Master of the Fitzwilliam (Wentworth), the Grove and the Coollattin, in Co Wicklow, an imperial foxhunting record not easy to outrival.

Before leaving the Shires and their environs I would mention the Meynell and South Staffordshire whose country lies adjacent, on the east side of the Quorn and the Atherstone. That was where the founder of modern foxhunting, the great Hugo Meynell came from, the man who, in the mid-eighteenth century, made Quorndon in the Quorn country his headquarters, from which he was the first to hunt, not the gorged dawn fox that retreated straight to its lair, but the fast mid-morning quarry that fled like an arrow. And, breeding hounds with sufficient speed and stamina to catch it, he increased the equestrian tempo of the sport to make it popular and fashionable diversion it soon became. But what would Meynell think of the Quorn country now? I believe he would prefer his native Derbyshire, which, by comparison with most of lowland Britain, remains a paradise of grass. The Meynell joined forces with the South Staffordshire in 1970 and thereby the

Meynell 'old-and-bold' had a tale to tell me. Soon after the amalgamation some rich Birmingham men, formerly of the South Staffs, were cursed by a Meynell farmer for riding over his crops. The farmer could hardly believe his ears when he heard their explanation. 'But we've always thought of that as the best fun in hunting – taking the micky out of bolshy farmers,' they told him.

There are at least two exclusive Midlands hunts that have been inclined to look down on the Melton organisations during the post-war years. The first is the Duke of Beaufort's, which has been in the hands of the successive Dukes since the eighteenth century. And the second is one which broke away from that hunt in 1835, namely the Heythrop, whose hunt staff have ever since worn the Beaufort green. The 'blue-and-buff', which is awarded to the Duke's select subscribers, is arguably the most distinguished sartorial accolade of British hunting. The Beaufort hounds were widely regarded as being among the two or three most superior packs in the world under 'Master', as the 10th Duke was known to his friends, and so it continues under his heir and his heir's joint-Master, Ian Farquhar, the houndsman son of the hound-breeding genius, Sir Peter Farquhar.

*Country Life* having allotted me two pages of coloured pictures, besides two pages of black-and-white, for my Beaufort article I stayed at Badminton for a couple of nights prior to my hunting visit, the mission being to select some of the famous family pictures for the camera. To partner me for dinner on my first evening the Duke and Duchess invited Daphne Moore, who stands unrivalled as the greatest living authority on hound pedigrees, and who, for most of her life, has been the guardian of Badminton's prolific and immaculately kept kennel lists. The Duchess, sitting on my left, was very quiet until she whispered loudly to me 'We haven't really had a chance to chat, have we, Daphne does bang on so?' When the cheese was brought on, an elegant silver holder, its compartments filled with a variety of biscuits was placed at my elbow, at which signal half-a-dozen dogs, ranging in size from border terrier to mastiff, scampered up to the Duchess, putting their paws on her shoulders, on her arm, on her knees, on her lap. And slavering. 'Please pass me some of those biscuits!' she said. And more and more and more, until the elegant silver container was empty (but the dogs, of course, were by no means satisfied). The photographer arriving next morning, the Duchess escorted us first to 'Master's' bedroom, where, behind the bed-head, hung Lionel Edwards's famous 1923 study of the Duke leading hounds through a gateway, watched by his father from a car. 'I haven't been in here this year,' the Duchess told us, 'I wonder what we'll find?' Almost every square foot was covered in dog. The photgrapher looked terrified. 'Wait down the passage,' advised my hostess, 'while I drive them out.' Ten minutes elapsed before the last one, with a deep growl and a most indignant look in its eye, was extracted from the room. Apparently the Duke, who was president of the Battersea Dogs Home, could not visit that sad institution without taking particular pity on some mongrel or other and bringing it back to Badminton.

My day with the Duke's finished breathtakingly close to the M4. Between the bitch pack and the danger of its destruction, however, stood the stout wire fence, seven feet tall (with an overhang), twenty miles worth of which the Duke had erected along the motorway embankment against such hazard.

I could quote many instances showing the anti-hunting lobby to be largely composed of lunatics with a universal hatred in their hearts for anyone they deem to be 'privileged'. One of the most odious of such examples was the action, in 1985, by a party from an organisation calling itself the Hunt Retribution Squad, who attempted to dig up the Duke's coffin, and who succeeded in badly desecrating his grave.

Returning to Daphne Moore, one of the most formidable figures at Peterborough, and, as I said, a woman with a greater knowledge of breeding hounds than anyone around the ringsides, her name cropped up when I asked Prince Charles whether he had ridden with more packs of hounds than his great-great-great grandfather, Edward VII, when he was Prince of Wales. To which he replied: 'Well, I believe I've just overtaken him [this was in the early '80s]; but, if you want to be sure, check with Daphne Moore, she's keeping the record. . .' The Prince paused with a grin, then added: 'And she can probably tell you a good deal more about my pedigree than I can, too!'

As with the Beaufort followers so the Heythrop see themselves as belonging to Britain's premier hunt. This is not only owing to their very rich heritage and splendid country in Oxfordshire and Gloucestershire, but also to the shining reputation which R. E. Wallace helped bestow on them during the quarter century (1952–77) when he was their joint-Master and huntsman. Enjoying the soubriquet, among his faithfuls, of 'God', Wallace has also gained a high reputation as chairman of the Masters of Foxhounds Association. He surveys foxhunting Britian as a spider surveys its web, and plays a close and influential part in the appointment of hunt servants, the solving of hunt disputes, issues arising on the political front and many other problems. No one could manage the job better, nor could anyone hope to improve upon his success at the Heythrop, with which his name became so synonymous. Stephen Lambert went there in 1981, with a fine reputation from the Warwickshire, and was at the helm at the time of my 1982 visit (he had also hunted the Marlborough College Beagles, then the Trinity Foot, followed by the Taunton Vale Foxhounds and the Warwickshire); and inevitably I heard him compared, poor fellow with Wallace.

Lambert and his hounds, however, gave me a stimulating day. 'With his bitches drawing over Upper Slaughter Farm on December 4,' I wrote, 'Mr Lambert had his first fox afoot at eleven-thirty. It circled, via Redesdale covert, parallel with the Fosseway, in the Bourton-in-the-Water direction, the followers spreading across the farmland, thrusting at the walls and timber. Headed by car followers he turned via Lower Slaughter to Kirkham and Copsehill, and was caught in the open just short of Upper Slaughter, the time being thirty-five minutes from find to finish. . . The next find was at Gashouse at 12.20. On no more than a serving scent, hounds stayed close up to this one until two-fifteen when he was lost in Swellwold. The last was alerted in Swellwold Quarry when twilight was upon us and this one was given best in the pitch-dark, deep into the North Cotswold country, thus concluding a very busy and enjoyable day. . .' But there was a small drama awaiting me.

Mrs Willes, a former wife of Wallace's, became joint-Master in 1977. At the end of my day's hunting I was holding my (second) horse beside its box, which it shared with Mrs Willes's, waiting to load up when, startled by the lights of the traffic, it reared vertically and with such violence that the halter rope was snatched from my hand (as it would have been from anyone else's, too), and it careered full tilt down the road. Mercifully, being a grey, it was soon retrieved, unhurt, and brought back. As I led it towards the box Mrs Willes, not recognising me, said scathingly 'did you see what that bloody idiot from the *The Field* did? He let his horse go.' I replied *'Country Life* actually.' Obliged to have me squeezed in next to her in the horse box cab and looking intensely embarrassed, she uttered not another word as we drove to the stables.

Two very famous establishments in the south Midlands were fused in 1986, the Whaddon Chase with the Bicester and Warden Hill, which was started by John Warde ('the Father of Foxhunting') in the 1770s. An amateur, Tony Younghusband, an old friend of mine and rather a wild one, was hunting the Bicester and Warden Hill when I rode with them in 1970. The committee, finding it difficult to keep Tony in horses, which he rode rather too hard, he moved on to the Mendip in 1975.

The Whaddon was founded by Bill Selby-Lowndes during the middle of the last century, and came to be known as 'the Londoner's Leicestershire'. Captain Pennell-Elmhirst ('Brooksby'), probably the most entertaining of all hunting correspondents, wrote, in the 1880s, that 'Londoners can run down from town on the morning of hunting, leaving Euston Square at the comfortable hour of nine; a slip carriage drops them at Leighton, or a train sets them down at Bletchley in time for all meets; while the up express stops especially for them in the evening, and brings them back in time for dinner. . .' But, within a century of that, the growth of Milton Keynes and other bugbears were beginning to spoil the fun. The grandson of the founder, another Bill Selby-Lowndes, an irascible man, took control in 1908, and was successful in every respect except in his relationships with his subscribers to whom he was often very rude. But he was not as unpopular as Lord Dalmeny (afterwards 6th Earl of Rosebery) who, having a great deal of money behind him bought more and more of the Whaddon country for his father's Mentmore estate and for his own hounds' sport. Eventually, in 1923, he became Master of the Whaddon, renting Selby-Lowndes's pack to begin with. One day several members of that pack were destroyed in a railway accident, at which the subscribers composed a little rhyme:

> *A train ran over some hounds*
> *That belonged to Bill Selby-Lowndes.*
> *If the train had gone faster*

*It would've run down the Master*
*Then we'd have given the driver ten pounds!*

Then there is that charming vignette of one exotic subscriber, Nubar Gulbenkian (son of the omnipotent Calouste) as recorded – when Dalmeny had gained considerably more respect – in his autobiography, *Pantaraxia*. 'Lord Rosebery [the Lord Dalmeny referred to] was a terrifying person, but a very good Master of hounds and a great nobleman. He was no respecter of persons and could afford to blast not only his field, but all farmers, tenants and policemen... On my first day out with the Whaddon Chase I was subjected, as were all new members of the hunt, to a searching scrutiny. "What is that flower you're wearing in your buttonhole?" I was asked. "An orchid," I replied, "I have always been very fond of them." "Oh, an orchid! Well, I've never before seen anyone out hunting with an orchid" my questioner persisted. "Ah," I said, "but have you ever seen an *Armenian* out hunting before?" This reply . . . was enough to establish my reputation with the Whaddon Chase. . .' That gifted man, Dorian Williams (Master 1954–80, the same tenure as his staunch huntsman, Albert Buckle) came to dinner with our Whaddon host, Peter Stoddart, looking, I fear, very ill. He died soon afterwards, a great loss to the equestrian world.

Our friends, Dick and Anne Hawkins, had us to stay for my day with the Grafton (the hunt from which the Whaddon country was originally taken). Colonel Neil Foster, a fine horseman (I believe he passed out top of his Weedon course in the late 1930s) was field Master, and a very disciplinarian one. When we crowded on the edge of a ploughed field at one particular check, some of our horses' hooves had strayed onto the young corn. Neil Foster rode back to flip the thong of his whip, with remarkable precision an inch or so short of our horses' legs, shouting with cold fury, 'I told you to keep to the headlands!' We reined onto the grass very sharply. I wrote my article next morning in Dick Hawkins's study and might have composed a better one had I not succumbed to his offer of port, which arrived in an enormous glass, topped up several times – soon after breakfast.

John Berkeley was Master of his ancestral hunt of that name whose country lies against the Severn estuary and whose livery is the Berkeley yellow. John has two houses, Berkeley Castle, on the Severn banks (scene of the murder of Edward II in 1327) and Spetchley Park, in Worcestershire, where we stayed. We were wonderfully looked after by him and his wife, Georgina; and also by my brother-in-law, Arthur French, who for many years, kept a horse in the Berkeley country. In those days Prince Charles's hunting tours were organised with great skill and confidentiality by the Crown Equerry, Sir John Miller. John Berkeley entertained us with an account of the Prince's visits to the Berkeley. On more than one occasion Miller telephoned to say '*you-know-who* would love a day tomorrow if it could be arranged,' and Berkeley would proceed to persuade a number of his faithfuls to turn out (probably tired) horses at short notice for the impromptu meet. Word soon got round the countryside, and publicans, wanting the honour of the Prince as their guest, would appear at the

December 1977: over a Galway Blazers' Wall.

November 1978: with the Cottesmore.

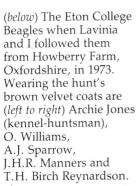

(*below*) The Eton College Beagles when Lavinia and I followed them from Howberry Farm, Oxfordshire, in 1973. Wearing the hunt's brown velvet coats are (*left to right*) Archie Jones (kennel-huntsman), O. Williams, A.J. Sparrow, J.H.R. Manners and T.H. Birch Reynardson.

(*above*) Tyrone and Caroline Waterford with (middle) their son, James, on my day with the Waterford foxhounds in 1983.

February 1981: Anthony and Fiona Martyn of the Glamorgan, leaving the meet at which he was presented with a portrait of himself. I am in the top hat just behind them.

doorways at lunchtime with 'Would you care for a drink, Sir?' And Berkeley's 'No thank you very much' would be capped by HRH's 'Well, how about a very quick one?' And in they went.

There is one rather uncanny object at Berkeley Castle and that is the stuffed head of the hound Cromwell (entered 1855) in a glass case. When Lord Fitzhardinge (Master 1805–57) lay dying he asked his huntsman, Harry Ayris, to bring some of his favourite hounds to his bedside, and in they came, led by Cromwell. 'There are no better ones, Harry!' are said to be the old Earl's last words. It was his successor, Admiral Berkeley who had Cromwell's head mounted like that. I have never seen such a thing before or since.

The Vale of Aylesbury wear the yellow coat, too, because one of the three hunts which amalgamated in 1970 to form it, the Old Berkeley (the other two were the South Oxfordshire and the Hertfordshire) was formerly in the domain of the Earls of Berkeley, who once hunted the fox, in nomadic fashion, all the way from Berkeley Castle to their London property, Berkeley Square. The senior Master of the VAH, Alistair Mann, one of three renowned hunting brothers (the others were Jock, of the VWH and Douglas, of the South and West Wilts) asked us to stay at his home, Wheatsfield House, near Oxford. And there I discovered what a foxhunting empire of that size and complexity – taking in places as far afield as Dunstable, Hemel Hempstead, High Wycombe, Aylesbury and Oxford – involves, with three different hunt clubs, and two point-to-point courses in a country measuring some forty miles by forty. Jim Bennett, the huntsman, a tower of strength in every way, started in that role with the Old Berkeley in 1952 and did not retire from the VAH until 1987 – which meant thirty-five years in charge of the same kennels; not a bad record.

The three hunts that went to make the VAH were fortunate to retain their identities in separate clubs. One with a golden heritage (to the west of the Pytchley), namely the North Warwickshire which I visited three months before its disbandment, in 1985 – and hunted with on foot from their frostbound last meet – was unable to find such a marriage partner. The extension of the M40 was to go slap through its country to link up with the M42, while its conurbations, around Leamington Spa, Solihull, Rugby, Warwick and Redditch, were growing at an alarming rate. Fusion with either the Warwickshire, Worcestershire or Atherstone was mooted, but ruled out as any such amalgamation would have rendered the resulting country too unwieldy. In the event the North Warwickshire country was split two ways, the western portion going to the Worcestershire and the eastern to the Warwickshire, which is one of the proudest of the Midland hunts and which we had visited five years before when Stephen Lambert was joint-Master and huntsman. The Warwickshire people were then in the middle of one of the milder of their hunt rows, of which they have a long and bitter record. The issue that split the committee in this case was as to whether Lambert should be invited to hand over the horn to his kennel-huntsman, Clarence Webster, who until then had been perfectly happy with looking after the kennels and turning hounds to the Master. Or whether he should stay as amateur huntsman. 'For many years now, at the Warwick-shire, there's been a hornets' nest waiting to erupt and go on the attack,' as Stephen Lambert put it to us. He left for the Heythrop the following year, which, in the ordinary circumstances he would not have chosen to do, not least because the offices of his real estate business were then in Kineton village (a few miles south of Stratford-upon-Avon) where the Warwickshire kennels are situated.

The kennels were built in 1839 to house eighty couple, and, in the words of the contemporary 'Cecil' (*Records of the Chase*), 'the materials were drawn to the spot by the united efforts of 180 farmers, who collectively had at work 553 wagons . . . What can be more conclusive of the good feeling which the Warwickshire farmers entertain for foxhunting than that they should come forward as they did, at a time when they were busy with their corn harvest?' The Warwickshire's rich history is particularly distinguished by the in-clusion in its roll of Masters of four towering foxhunting names, from the same family, between 1839 and 1935, the 17th, 18th, 19th and 20th Barons Willoughby de Broke, all of them highly influential hound breeders. Towards the end of the nineteenth century, during the reign of the 18th Baron, the hunt regularly swept the board at Peterborough:

> 'Warwickshire first'. See the Secretary gives it
> Out to the crowd at the Peterborough Show
> Warwickshire first, see the gallant pack lives; it
> Shows they are bred both to gallop and go.
>
> Come with me further, and watch them careering
> Over the heart of the Warwickshire Vale
> Mark how his lordship is riding and cheering
> Mark the bold riders, that keep within hail!

That hound-quality tradition has endured without a break. but 'the War-wickshire Vale' is not quite the same, as we learned when our hosts, Martin and Mish Dunne – he was joint-Master, 1976-79, and had been in the Blues with me in Cyprus ) took us to tea with gallant old George Gillson at his cottage 'Tally ho!'. Gillson, whose hunt service began in 1919 and continued as whipper-in to the great Frank Freeman, was huntsman to the Warwick-shire (except for his war service) from 1935 to 1956. A mist comes into a hunt servants' eyes when he speaks of lost favourite hounds or lost treasured coverts, a mist such as a parent shows in memory of a child. Gillson's mist welled into pools when he told us that 'There was no wire when I started here; then it was 98 per cent grass, now it's 70 per cent plough; mechanical hedge-cutters have ruined the fences; nearly 4,000 acres of that lovely old Red Horse Vale have been taken up; and just look what they've done to Shuckburgh hill . . . it's a disaster!' But that is the story since the Second World War of much of the English countryside.

Lincolnshire's reputation for flat, heavy land has not much detracted from it's name as a hunting county, and it boasts the oldest heritage. The Brock-lesby hound lists, kept by Charles Pelham, go back to 1746 and the most famous hound portraits of all by Stubbs (including that of Ringwood, in

1788) are of Brocklesby hounds. We stayed with the Yarboroughs in a bedroom overlooking the kennels and enjoyed the accompaniment of hound song at dawn. At breakfast John Yarborough recalled an occasion sitting on the terrace with his father and an American visitor, and his father saying: 'Just listen to that lovely music!' And the guest replying, 'Gee, I can't hear no music, just them old dawgs!.' With their strong old-fashioned tricolour, silky quality and level conformity those hounds were a lovely sight as they trotted off to the meet in the sunshine under their huntsman, Cooper Atkinson.

While I was hunting Lavinia helped to organise the photography in the house. 'Portraits of late earls and countesses and late hounds had to be photgraphed, and this took all afternoon,' she wrote in her diary. 'Lord Y helped occasionally by pretending he was Aladdin and holding up flash lamp equipment. Then Hughes [the photgrapher] announced the film had broken and we had to go through the whole performance again. I thought Lord Y would explode, but he simply retreated quietly to his enormous study where he continued perusing the racing form. . .' Having around 30,000 acres and one of the best shoots in the county John Yarborough put down a huge quantity of young pheasants every season. Regarding predators, however, he refused to have any fox killed except by his beloved pack, and was obliged to dismiss a keeper who shot one. His head keeper, he told us, rode regularly to hounds, and indeed was out on my day.

South of that lies the Burton which lists such impressive venatic names as Monson, Osbaldeston, Chaplin and Bentinck in its roll of Masters. They staged their hunt club dinner on the eve of my day with their hounds and invited me to speak for ten minutes, which I did in hot rivalry with four other orators. Arthur Lockwood – who took over the Mastership from his father, William and who was to hand over, in 1981, to his son, John – provided my bed. I was fortunate next day to ride Justice, an ace gelding which had carried Peter Wright, the Cottesmore huntsman, for three seasons. South of the Burton comes the Blankney, where pretty Mrs Richard Parker and her shooting husband were the soul of hospitality at their fine home, the Manor, Metheringham, close to Blankney village. Ruth Parker, a truly dedicated foxhunter – she put in a day a week with the Quorn, as well as two at the head of Blankney field – has been in the Mastership since 1983. She lent me her favourite gelding, Nicky, for the last meet of the 1984–85 season, and a spirited woodland Saturday followed, which prompts me to quote a caution from Brooksby during the 1880s: 'Saturday is *par excellence* the day of the Blankney. Keep your best horse for it and smoke one cigar less overnight than is your rule!'

The South Wold occupy Lincolnshire's coastal country between Grimsby and Skegness, and, happily for them the best part of the Lincolnshire wolds. Martin Trollope-Bellew, a West Countryman had just taken over as Master and huntsman when – mounted on Mr Bob McGowan's splendid grey, Santa Claus – I went out with them in February, 1989. Martin was also celebrating his engagement to Penny Littleworth, a grand daughter of Charlie Littleworth of York and Ainsty (South) fame. I renewed two old acquaintanceships there, the first with the kennel-huntsman, David Anker (who was whipping-in to the Sinnington when I rode with them in 1971 and carrying the horn at the time of another Yorkshire venue of mine, to the Cleveland); and the second with Carol King who turned hounds to her husband with the Tickham, in Kent, when I went there. Looking very dapper in scarlet she played the same role with aplomb for Martin Trollope-Bellew. We were on James Heneage's 5,500 acres at Hainton. 'There seems to be a plague of foxes round here' he told me over coffee at Hainton Hall. And foxes were indeed all over the place, but all too wily that day to be caught by the South Wold.

'The further, in the Midlands, you travel from London the more enjoyable your sport is likely to be,' is a maxim I have heard on the lips of many foxhunters. And, in that respect, the west Midlands hunts, which are inclined to be more parochially exclusive than their neighbours in the east, less inclined to attract Saturday visitors, are more congenial socially to their natives than those closer to the Great Wen. I have greatly enjoyed my days with the Gloucestershire hunts, with the Berkeley when Chris Maiden was standing in as huntsman for their injured Tim Langley; with the Duke's when Brian Gupwell carried the horn; with the VWH when Jock Mann was in command; with the Croome and West Warwickshire where I was looked after beautifully by Maria Coventry; and with the Cotswold, first under the Mastership of Brian Bell in 1970, and again with Tim Unwin during the 1980–81 season. But what most impressed me in that vicinity was a little three-day-a-week country running from Gloucestershire into Worcestershire and embraced entirely within a twelve-mile radius of the market town of Broadway. I refer to the North Cotswold, which dates from 1868, when the 9th Earl of Coventry began hunting there following the break-up of the old Berkeley country. When I rode with the North Cotswold, in 1989, they had just come under the inspired Mastership of Mr and Mrs Nigel Peel. Nigel Peel went there from the Chiddingfold, Leconfield and Cowdray and hunts hounds in the exquisitely unspoilt Broadway country – a tract nicely divided between vale and wold – with the same buoyant and determined style that he showed in west Sussex. His wife, who, as Sophia Lambert, was Master of the Old Surrey and Burstow (as her father had been before her) is a fearless, hard riding field Master with much charm and a fine manner of command. I hope this popular couple will go from strength to strength.

Old friends from Cyprus days Thomas and Henrietta Dunne (he is the brother of Warwickshire Martin) had us to stay in their glorious Elizabethan home, Gatley, embosomed in Herefordshire's back-of-beyond, for a Radnorshire and West Herefordshire visit when he was joint-Master; and he was numbered among the field when I was out with the Ledbury six years later. I wrote in my Ledbury report as follows: '... At the very moment I was wondering how my mount's legs would stand the [slippery] going a voice beside me said, "Ah, I see they've put you on the Wild One. I hope you're used to broncos? No one's ever stayed on that tornado's back for more than twenty consecutive minutes." It was Captain Thomas Dunne, Lord Lieutenant of Hereford and Worcester, once Master of the Radnor and West and a celebrated wag, who eyed my grey with a mischievous grin. As he well knew the subject was Thistle, a horse on permanent loan to the Ledbury from Major Robin Bucknall. And (albeit he is no flyer) a quieter, better mannered or more willing mount – or one who makes so little of the Ledbury's thorn fences – you would not hope to meet. He was the perfect visitor's hunter . . .'

My Ludlow visit, in 1976, was abortive. We met at Downton Hall, which is the spiritual home of the hunt as well as being the home of the then senior joint-Master, Miss Mary Rouse-Boughton (whose father, Sir Edward, had founded the North Ludlow in 1932). We waited, mounted, on the terrace below Downton for a dense fog to lift. The joint-Master and huntsman, Brigadier John Stephenson (who, alas, was killed in a motor accident the following year), kept driving down to the valley below to see if it was clearing. But in vain. Next day he drove Lavinia and me over to see the nearby Titterstone, the steep slope in the Clee hills, all the way down which William Childe of Kinlet galloped, to the marvel of his friends, on a loose rein one day in the 1770s. Childe, the man who first introduced foxhounds to the Ludlow country, then went to join Hugo Meynell, in Leicestershire where – owing to his penchant for jumping the Quorn enclosures – became known as 'the Flying Childe'.

I have always found the summer hound shows auspicious occasions on which to make overtures to prospective Masters for visits the following season. One of the countless invitations I have received following such encounters came from David Parker, Master and huntsman of the Clifton-on-Teme, which, pivoted on Bromyard, lies sandwiched between the Ludlow, Worcestershire, Croome and North Herefordshire. Swelled with pride after securing a couple of very creditable rosettes at the 1987 Peterborough, he suggested I follow his hounds the following season, and I duly stayed with him and his wife, Linda, at the end of February 1988 in their kennels bungalow at Tedstone Delamere. It was not so much the unusual hunt breakfast at the Lion inn – in the village from which the hunt takes its name - that made the visit so special, as the experience of listening to Mr Parker's hounds vocalising to him. I will explain. For ten years he held a place in the Welsh Opera Chorus, singing principal tenor roles in many productions. And there can be no question about it – his hounds know that he appreciates their kennel yodel, because without fail at around midnight they set up a joyful melody. When he is ready to sleep he flicks a bedside switch to throw a beam on the kennels, and they stop abruptly, until first light when they greet him with a dawn chorus. And in the hunting-field he reciprocates with his dulcet voice and rhythmic horn-notes which send them delirious. Hunting devotees cannot ask for better sound empathy than that!

The Cheshire, I think, ranks with Sir Watkin Williams Wynn's as the grandest set-up in the West Midlands. Its traditions are traced to a son of the 4th Earl of Barrymore, John Smith-Barry, who bred hounds of such exceptional speed that he aroused the envy of Hugo Meynell, who challenged him to a race 'on a hot drag-line over the Beacon course at Newmarket, each Master to run two couples'. The young Cheshire bloods who went to back Smith-Barry had a song to accompany their support:

> They talk of Hugo Meynell and what he can do;
> But we'll ride 'em or fight 'em this Leicestershire crew,
> And we'll teach 'em eh ho!
> How the Cheshire will go!

The first single hound to pass the winning-post first was to decide the issue. During six weeks' training the Cheshire put their entry on a diet of sheep's feet, oatmeal and milk. The race was run on 30 September 1763. 'The pace was so terrible' said an eye-witness, 'that, in three miles half the horses were beaten... At the finish Cheshire's Blue Cap came away from the Leicester-shire entry and won by 100 yards...' Poor Blue Cap – he was so fleet of foot that on hunting days, he had a weight tied around his neck to prevent him outstripping the rest of the pack! Every student of hunt history should visit the Cheshire kennels at Sandiway and read the inscription on the obelisk erected to him:

> This obelisk, reader, is a monument rais'd
> To a shade, tho' a hound, who deserves to be prais'd;
> But if Life's but a stage whereon each acts a part,
> And true greatness a term that's derived from the heart;
> If fame, honour and glory depend on the deed
> Then O! Blue Cap, rare Blue Cap, will we boast of thy deed!

Those interested in the English hunting heritage ought also to take a look, too, at the Cheshire's Tarporley Hunt Club room, whose walls are adorned with portraits of names famous in the the hunt annals, such as Cholmonde-ley, Grosvenor, Delamere, Bromley-Davenport, Trafford, Warburton Eger-ton, Tomkinson, Combemere, Greenall and, of course, Smith-Barry.

'Never overstay your welcome!', is an essential commandment in the hunting correspondent's list of dos and don'ts. At the start of my career in the late 1960s I did just that at Broad Oak, Redbrook, Shropshire, the home of Philip Warburton Lee and his wife Hetty (née Armytage, now Fetherston-haugh) for a Boxing Day meet with Sir Watkin Williams Wynn's. At the end of that wet day I slid from my horse with a shuddering fever, then collapsed into bed with a temperature of 103 degrees, and the most virulent attack of flu I have ever suffered. A tight programme of parties ensued until the New Year, and my hostess and her daughters did not thank me for having to carry trays to my room for the next four days. The Warburton Lees had their doctor in to inject me with antibiotics and got me away on the fifth day, free of infection but feeling weak as water. On the credit side they had a splendid library of hunting books, half-a-dozen of which I absorbed from end to end.

*Proud South*

'Never hunt south of the Thames!' a nineteenth-century father advised. And indeed the establishments close on the south side of the City have been regarded in more remotely rural parts – from Victorian times onwards – as somewhat inferior. They owe that notoriety partly to their proximity to the metropolis, which attracts business commuters to their fraternities; partly to their overdeveloped countryside and close network of roads; and partly to that 'South of the Thames' stigma. But it applies to all the Home Counties hunts. Surtees made his comic hero, the Cockney grocer, John Jorrocks, Master of such a pack; and the Old Surrey and Burstow proudly claim to have been in the mind's eye of the author when he devised a country for Jorrocks's motley pack. The OSBH call their supporters' club the Jorrocks Hunt Club. (The green collar that adorns their subscribers' scarlet is said to originate from the anxiety of City men to arrive on 'Change by four o'clock, and appearing to wear their business green under their overcoats, attempting to give the impression they had been at work all day).

Diana Barnato Walker – celebrated as a wartime air ferry pilot and breaker of the women's air speed record before she became an MFH – was the one who looked after me during my 1978 visit, while Tony Wilson mounted me with his good Jubilee, and the great Jack Champion, then approaching the end of his 30-year tenure as huntsman, gave us a very spirited day from Marsh Green, Edenbridge. Before leaving the OSBH I would comment on the comedian, Jimmy Edwards, another joint-Master. I cannot remember ever meeting a more vain man. Whenever an opportunity occurred on my day he would trot onto the road, hold up motorists and peer, grinning, into their windows. And he was not happy unless he was greeted by them with the ecstatic looks of adoring fans. Had he lived a century and a half earlier I am sure he would have provided useful copy for Surtees's pen.

The patronising and somewhat incredulous smiles with which Lavinia and I have invariably been met by hunting folk in more remote parts of the British Isles whenever we have confessed to living in the Crawley and Horsham country have served as a perpetual reminder of the sporting reputation (or rather the lack of it) of the Home Counties hunts. And yet as we witness, whenever we are at home on hunting days, the Sussex sportsmen and women usually have at least as much activity, and just as much fun with their venery as any Leicestershire thrusters.

The Grand Old Lady of the Crawley and Horsham was Mollie Gregson with whom I had a close dialogue until her death in the mid-1980s. Riddled with arthritis she was always bed- or chair-ridden during the years I knew her, though she was habitually converted to her Range Rover; and, ensconced in that, was a familiar figure, behind very dark glasses at the Ardingly Show where she was determined to see 'm-y h-o-u-n-d-s' – she spoke with a rich drawl – carry off the lion's share of the rosettes. Following a youth mainly devoted to hunting she took over the acting Mastership of the C and H from Guy Cubitt, when he went off to fight in 1939, and remained in control up to 1961, after which she continued to breed the hounds (keeping a close liaison with the Duke of Beaufort and Ronnie Wallace) until a few years before she died.

Rupert Buchanan-Jardine, of the Dumfriesshire, had put in a few Crawley and Horsham days during Mollie's Mastership in the 1940s. Mollie, hearing a few years ago that he was to stay with us for Ardingly, invited us to bring him over to dinner. 'Will you be sure to see that he takes a look at Benton's before he comes here,' she said, (Benton's being one of her favourite fox-holding coverts). Rupert duly made a walk to that copse at the crack of dawn, and was able to greet Mollie in the evening with 'I made a tour of Benton's this morning – it still looks a marvellous covert!'

When she was relieved of the hound-breeding role she invited me over to her home at Warnham on the pretext of showing me some Lionel Edwards paintings (in connection with my biography of the artist), but really so that I could share a grudge ('between you, me and the gatepost' her confidences always began), and she went on to complain of 'the rude and undiplomatic way in which I had m-y h-o-u-n-d-s taken from me after all my years of dedication.' She won nearly everyone's sympathy on that score. A cruel and mysterious incident occurred at the C and H kennels which also upset her terribly. It was in 1984 just at the time of the departure of the then huntsman, Dick Chapman, to the Meynell. Two of the best hounds were poisoned, one of which was Brandon, who had won the doghound championship at Peterborough.

'. . . When Jack Clarke cheered hounds into Wickwood,' I reported for the magazine about a C and H day, 'one of a brace led hounds away with as forceful a drive as you could hope to see foxhounds go, through Tory Copse, over the sound pasture which Mr Phil Edwards rents from Sir Walter Burrell – with its hunt tiger-traps always apparently in the right place to let you over – past New Barn, Woodman's and Perrylands until, after fifteen minutes race, they were seconds behind his brush at an earth on Hooklands. . . The third was signalled by a *holloa*, and away they sped with a really lovely chorus over the road above Blonks, across a sea of plough to Faulkner's bushes and onto Ingram's Firs, where the pack divided, two and a half couple of veterans pointing for Major Martin-Bird's well-reputed Coolham Gorse. . .'

University and polytechnic students play a larger part than any other section of the community in anti-hunt demonstrations and disruption (mainly from a left-wing stance against so-called 'privileged capitalists', though of course they pretend it is from an altruistic animal welfare motive). The best revenge I ever heard of was the occasion when such students spent an afternoon in acts of violence against the Eton beaglers and their hounds during the 1978–79 season. The Master and huntsman was a son of Edmund Vestey, the chairman of one of the largest commercial corporations in the world. That corporation had reserved places on its staff for graduates of the university concerned. Those reservations were immediately withdrawn. Talking of that I witnessed a comic scene during an afternoon with the Christ Church and Farley Hill beagles, when Alexander Fitzalan-Howard was carrying the horn. The saboteurs were out in force with their tin whistles and horns. Lavinia had our terriers on a lead, and when the 'antis' came close the terriers went growling towards them. 'Don't go near them!' was my wife's caution; 'they do nasty things to dogs like you!' At which one of the demonstrators turned away on mincing steps repeating Lavinia's words with a sarcastically la-di-dah lilt. . . Thus followers and 'antis' were brought together for one moment by a mutual laugh! The two hunts suffering worst of all from the antics of hunt saboteurs have probably been the New Forest foxhounds and the Surrey Union. After riding with the New Forest in 1982, I was given a fascinating discourse on how the fox fits into the Forest's ecology by Newton Rycroft, the Master, a man with a considerable affection for all animals and an extremely knowledgable naturalist. It seemed the greatest irony that his, of all hunts, should be singled out for so many vicious assaults.

Days with the Eridge and the Southdown prompted me to return to the autobiographical pages of Siegfried Sassoon, for the great author's initial hunting experiences were with the Eridge (the 'Dumborough' of *Memoirs of a Foxhunting Man*). He took the character of Lord Dumborough, from Lord Henry Nevill (afterwards 3rd Marquess of Abergavenny), Master from 1893 to 1929, and 'the most terrifying man I ever encountered'. As a young man Sassoon left the Eridge in favour of the Southdown (the 'Ringwell') where his friend Norman Loder (Denis Milden in the book) held sway, and knowing that part of the Downs as well as I do it is not difficult to imagine and share his exuberance: 'The mornings I remember most zestfully were those which took us up to the chalk downs. To watch the day breaking from purple to dazzling gold while we trotted up a deep-rutted lane, to inhale the early freshness when we were on the sheep-cropped uplands; to stare back at the low country with its cock-crowing farms and mist-coiled waterways; thus to be riding out with a sense of spacious discovery – was it not something stolen from a lie-a-bed world. . . I would be dragged out of my daydream by Denis when he shouted to me to wake up and get round to the far side of the covert; for on such hill days he often went straight to one of the big gorses without any formality of a meet. . .' Recalling the Sassoon connection with both hunts it was fitting that the Southdown and Eridge joined forces in 1978. As I mentioned in the last chapter he followed Loder up to the Atherstone ('Packlestone') in the 1913–14 season.

The Southdown was Arthur Dalgety's longest tenure. Endowed by a family that had made millions in the wool trade and ranking on a level with Bay de Courcy Parry and Chetty Hilton-Green among the nomadic amateur huntsmen in the pre-war and post-war days, Dalgety began with the Dunston harriers in Norfolk, in 1923, and went on to join the roles of Master and huntsman with the Vine, then the Southdown (which he combined with the New Forest foxhounds for a season or two with Jock Buchanan-Jardine), the Hursley (with his brother, John), the Isle of Wight, and finally to Tipperary and the Ormond, which he had from 1965 to 1973. His son, Hugh, shares that passion for foxhunting. He, too, hunted the Hursley from the family home, Lockerley, where he and his wife, Ann, had us to stay during the season prior to the hunt's fusion with the Hambledon in 1978.

Mounted by General Barry on his nice mare, Arabella, I went out with the Hampshire Hunt (HH) for their 1977 traditional Boxing Day meet at the Butts, Alton, and there witnessed the Masters and hunt servants parading the hounds, as they always do on that occasion, through the wards of the

Lord Mayor Treloar hospital. The HH button carries the three feathers insignia of the Prince of Wales (deriving from the days when the Prince Regent kenneled hounds in that region). And I wrote in my subsequent article that 'the HH hope it will not be long before His Royal Highness honours them by spending a day in their company.' Meeting the Prince at a cocktail party the summer after he had been given his HH day I asked him how he got on. With a wry smile he showed me the thumbs-down sign. Recounting this to Bill Montgomery when staying with him at Grey Abbey on Ulster's Ards peninsular for a North Irish tour, Bill added a sequel to the cameo. The Prince told him that, to compensate for his boredom at covertside on his blank HH day, he began doing exercises, leaning back on his horse's quarters, swivelling from the hips, arms outstretched, touching his toes, and so on. And, to his embarrassment, looking round he saw three middle-aged men imitating his every movement, as though obliged by protocol to follow the Royal example! I felt how well a comic draughtsman, such as Snaffles or Cecil Aldin, might have captured that moment.

One of the most enterprising and successful post-war ventures has been the foundation by the late Ken Goschen (a former HH Master farming 600 acres near Alton) and his wife of a new pack in 1965. 'This popular hunt' said Ken's *Times* obituarist (31 May 1989), 'has introduced many people to the beauties and pleasures of the English countryside, which Goschen considered incomparable anywhere in the world. He had a shrewd knowledge of foxhounds and judged at shows in this country as well as in Canada and the USA. In 1983 he was made President of the Peterborough Royal Foxhound Show and received the Queen Mother as guest of honour. He also gave valuable service to the Hunt Servants' Benefit Society . . .'

Having borrowed country from the Chiddingfold, Leconfield and Cowdray and the Garth and South Berks, the Goschens secured the Bisley and Sandhurst domain from Major Fulton when he disbanded in 1975. In that year, too, Michael Porter, another ex-Master of the HH, joined them at the helm. My day with 'Mr Goschen's', in the old Cowdray country, was just after the great storm of 1987, and the beautiful hounds which they bred had to contend with the awful challenge of a confusion of fallen trees and branches. If the Goschen hounds – which are all, without fail, of superb quality – possessed a little more bone and substance they could be taking the top prizes at the shows. On the other hand, as their owner pointed out to me, if they carried such extra bulk they would not be able to negotiate the trappy woodlands and other wild corners of that country nearly so well. 'A hound for the country' is the Goschens' motto.

Mention of that leads me to wonder whether bloodhounds hunting the clean boot (ie the scent of a man) are not the best answer to the problems of venatic sport in some of Britain's most highly developed regions. My old friend Bill Stringer, who had been a corporal-of-horse (equivalent of sergeant) in my squadron in Cyprus, and who rose to the rank of major and quartermaster, was a co-founder, in 1969, of the Household Cavalry's Rhine Army bloodhound pack, the Weser Vale, which hunted the clean boot from their barracks at Detmold, and with whom I had the honour of a day in 1971.

Posted home that year Bill went on to establish the Windsor Forest blood-hounds. He and his joint-Master, Willie Loyd (another Household Caval-ryman, who had been adjutant of the Mounted Regiment when I commanded the Blues squadron and who kenneled the bloodhounds at his home Cowarth Park Farm, at Ascot) invited me to follow the Windsor Forest in 1979. Their most celebrated hound, by name Sanguine Sarjent 73, was the one with which Clement Freud helped to advertise on television the dog food Mince Morsels for Quaker Oats. That proved a good saving on kennel cost because as a result, Quaker Oats supplied the Windsor Forest with this product (which was the hunt's staple diet) free of charge. Poor Sarjent, however, died just after my visit.

Bloodhounds' noses – carried below those substantial folds of pelt on their foreheads and jowls that are said to accentuate their keen-scentedness – are probably as sharp as any in the canine world. But the breed is also compara-tively delicate. In particular it is prone to atrophia, the ingrowing eyelash, from which blindness can come quickly. The other chief physical liability is bloating, the blowing up of the stomach, a malaise that all to often brings death in bloodhound kennels. Also the breed moves rather awkwardly and is inclined to be aggressive in kennels. For those reasons, combined with that of a desire for greater pace, and greater beauty, too, Neil Wates – of the Coakham, whose meets are in Surrey, Sussex and Kent – went for a blood-hound-foxhound cross. In 1976 he secured one-and-a-half couple of dog-hounds and a couple of bitches, all bloodhound-Dumfriesshire foxhound crosses, from Reginald Wright, who was then disbanding his North War-wickshire clean boot hunt. (It is not surprising the Dumfriesshire cross proved such a successful nick, considering there is a strong element of bloodhound in their breeding.) And from those beginnings Wates built up a healthy and fast pack.

The Coakham is the only example of that cross I have witnessed in action, and, with their low scenting and extra speed, they seemed to offer the ideal sport for equestrians who only have a few hours of a Saturday afternoon to spare. As Andrew Drysdale, the Coakham's chairman (since Master) put it to me: 'They have none of the waiting at covertside, often cold, wet and bored, that is so often endured by foxhunters. Instead they gain all the galloping and jumping for which foxhunters yearn – compressed into the convient space of two or three hours. They do not share the foxhunters' concern for the abundance, or lack as may be, of quarry-holding coverts. Nor, since they operate on carefully defined lines, agreed with the farmers concerned, do they have to worry about the proximity of railways, motor-ways or built-up areas. On the other hand there is none of the artificiality of a drag hunt, in which failed, discarded foxhounds get excited about a bag of aniseed. Our sport is natural hunting . . .' In built-up, intensely farmed, and excessively motorised southern Britain I envisage the foundation of more packs like the Coakham and more and more horsemen and women wishing to risk their necks at the sport.

East Anglia, taken as a whole, being very open, is more a hare hunting than a foxhunting part of the world (the foxhunting becoming more scant the further north you travel in those regions). Essentially and traditionally, too – and very generally speaking – it is more celebrated for its game shooting than its hunting. Yet, as I have seen from riding with every pack in that part of Britain, their followers are as proud of their sport as anywhere else. Norfolk and Suffolk have between them the highest concentration of harrier packs in mainland Britain and I have stayed with several delightful Masters to hunt with them, including Anthony Harvey (Easton), Bill Somerleyton (Waveney) and Mrs Anthony Gurney (North Norfolk). Not far to the west of the Easton Harriers are the most famous of all, the Cambridgeshire, under the Mastership of the woman who is widely known as 'the Queen of the Harriers', the greatly loved Mrs Gingell (née Betty Marriage). She had completed over thirty years in that role when I had a day with her hounds in 1973; and 1992 will mark her half century. For nearly fifty years she has been a consistent winner of championships and other awards at the shows; her sires are easily the most widely used in harrier Britain and countless hounds bred by her have been exported to Canada, the United States, New Zealand and elsewhere. (A note from Lavinia's diary: 'Mr Gingell is very much the Master's husband. We noted that he greeted his wife at breakfast – without a trace of mockery – with "good morning, Master"!')

The northernmost of the East Anglian foxhunts is the West Norfolk for which we stayed with Mrs Francis Don at Elmham House, Dereham, for a meet at the hunt's time-honoured rendezvous, the Litcham Bull inn. Sandringham lies in the country and Mrs Don told us how, in the 1920s and '30s, the Princess Royal and Edward VIII, who were regular followers, would drop in for hunt teas at the end of their days, and 'were welcomed with no more formality than anyone else'.

There is a warm 'county' feeling in the Essex hunts. Two charming hosts were Mr and Mrs Guy Lyster, joint-secretaries of the East Essex (she is the daughter of the late Mike Gosling who was Master for twenty-three years). Hounds put a fox to ground at three-thirty from a meet at the Gosling home, Dynes Hall, for which I rode a marvellous 16.2 hh chestnut called Dick. My report continues: '. . . this was a quick thing with some hard galloping, during which Mr Gerald Ruggles, the secretary of the Hunt Supporters' Club, fell onto his face near Little Lodge, ending the afternoon with ten stitches in his nose. But for the rest of us that hunt was not the conclusion. At four o'clock they found just below Byham Hall, in Mr Christopher Gosling's kale. This one pointed for Links Hill, and it was Mr Gosling, Mrs Lyster's brother, who *holloaed* him away. Given the improved scent which accompanied the evening's drop in temperature, hounds ran with an unbroken chorus and close as termites as they steered past Great Maplestead churchyard and Barratt's Hall Grove, and it was good to watch these Essex sportsmen taking thorn fences in as free a manner as you would expect in the Shires. Hounds lost their fox over foil on Purl Hill, but not before they had run four twisty miles and given us twenty-five minutes of the best . . .'

After following the Essex, whose coverts lie south-west of that, I reported as follows: 'The mugginess of mid-week had been blown away by a sharp north-east wind and replaced by twenty degrees of frost; but the drought had been so longstanding that when our impressive column of ninety mounted followers – as well turned out a field as I have seen for some time – left Roxwell Green at eleven o'clock and struck out behind Tom [Watchorn, the huntsman] on the ploughed field edges for Boynton Cross and Newland Brook, despite the frigid surface they created as much dust as cavalry in August. Whereas what the Essex need for scent is rain, rain, and more rain . . . And it was not until about one o'clock when we were standing along the lane leading south to Bushy Hayes that a fox lying snugly in a drain near Torrell's felt hounds too inquisitively close for comfort, and bolted across the cold and dusty arable, setting his mask towards Rowes Wood, to give us the run of the day. And as those Essex foxhunters shortened their reins and glanced for likely routes round the restricted farmland, one sensed the special animation which especially comes, I find, from a sporting fraternity which takes pride in its old traditions and whose own spirit is essentially right . . . That drainpipe fox described a forthright circle by Rowes Farm. And as hounds checked on the plough just south of it, a *view holloa* rang out from Mr James Radbourne, the hunt chairman, who spotted him leaving Rowes Wood. Hounds were soon gaining on him when we heard a number of *holloas* from the road, and saw car followers pointing excitedly towards Skreens. Piloting them round Skreens Park he headed north by Tye Hall and found his favourite form of bolt hole, a drain at the back of the Old Skreens drive where he was given best . . . and we hacked back to the boxes in a blinding snowstorm.'

So there is often more activity in a day's hunting in East Anglia than most people would imagine. But I would not recommend the southernmost establishment, the built-up Essex Union. At the end of my article on them I forecast that they could not survive except by joining forces with the Essex Farmers' Hunt. And they did so for the following season. One is filled with admiration for the way such other hunts close to London's north side as the Enfield Chace and the Aldenham harriers, keep going.

We have moved to Devon. It is the year 1831, and Henry Philpotts, Bishop of Exeter is travelling along the Torridge Valley on a tour of the parishes, soon after his appointment to the diocese. Suddenly a pack of hounds careers across the road in front of his carriage, followed by a number of sportsmen all in black coats. The highly principled, deeply compassionate prelate leans to his chaplain with a solemn whisper: 'Dear me, this neighbourhood must have been visited by some fearful epidemic. I never saw so many men in mourning before.' The chaplain, identifying the mourners as bretheren of his cloth and personal friends, shook his head: 'My lord, the only bereavement these gentlemen suffer is not being able to wear pink.' Flabbergasted, the bishop watched them pass, one after the other: the Rev John Froude (of whom his biographer wrote 'he was well known for his utter disregard of Episcopal, and indeed all human, authority . . .'); the Rev W. H. Karslake, a fanatically keen Master of harriers; the Rev Harry Farr Yeatman; the Rev Peter Glubb (who 'kenneled a very killing pack near Little Torrington'); most celebrated of them all, the Rev Jack Russell, of terrier fame; and more. Not present that day, though just as keen among West Country hunting vicars were the Rev William Clack (in mid-Devon), Parson Hole (North Devon) and the Rev E. C. Forward (East Devon). When the Bishop took Russell to task, the riposte was 'There are many other clergymen in your diocese who keep hounds, my lord; why am I singled out among so many?' Upon which, his lordship's chaplain tells us, 'the bishop groaned in despair'.

After the Rev Peter Glubb became Vicar of Little Torrington, in the 1820s, he wrote to Russell: 'Here the sport of legitimate foxhunting, being utterly ignored by the majority of the natives, it is their practice to kill a fox whenever and however they can catch him. Foxes are tracked to ground, the church bells ring and the village turns out with picks and shovels . . .' Russell, who succeeded Glubb in that village, gave admonitory sermons on the subject and even threatened to horsewhip a party of fox diggers, after-wards claiming that 'from that day forward I secured for myself and my successors not only the goodwill and cooperation, but the friendship, too, of some of the best fox preservers that the county of Devon, or any other county, has ever seen . . .' Russell continued to draw coverts in what are now the Stevenstone, Tetcott, Torrington Farmers and Eggesford countries until 1853. I believe the eccentric George Templer, of Stover (in south Devon), Russell's chief venatic mentor, may be the real pioneer (between 1815-25) of foxhunting in the county, but there is no doubt it was that great association of churchmen who converted Devonians as a whole to a love of venery. And it is with this knowledge that the student of foxhunting in Devon must start.

A combination of black coat, velvet cap and brown breeches – usually a well weathered combination at that – is the regular order of dress in the county (I don't remember seeing a top hat west of Somerset in twenty seasons' worth of visits), and it is mostly the farmers who now hold sway. Exmoor is better known for its staghounds than its foxhounds, though its reputation for the latter has blossomed since the advent of Ronnie Wallace. Dartmoor, however, is essentially a foxhunting place. In 1979 I wrote in *Country Life*: 'For the foxhunter whose idea of heaven is *not* interminable flights of fences laid over endless grass, it would be difficult to imagine a more desirable place to live than on the fringe of Dartmoor. For it is the only land area in the British Isles - the Lake District, the Yorkshire Moors, the Scottish Lowlands and Exmoor included – where there is practically no wire, nor for that matter any other man-made obstacle, and where you can ride in perfect liberty from end to end. It must be one of the very few tracts in all Europe where the horseman feels a true sense of illimitable space, coupled with that air of primal beauty which wild moorland gives . . .' Away from the moors Devon was once a good horseman's bank country, but the banks – being now mostly topped with thick shrub or tree growth (often kept in check by automatic hedge-cutters) – are generally impossible to negotiate. Here is part of my description of a day with Spooner's and West Dartmoor, when a fox led us off the moor towards the Lamerton country in 1982.

'Trotting over the River Lyd we rode in bright sunlight onto Doctor Common, where hounds picked up the drag of a fox, and traced it to a big badger sett on Brat Tor. While Mr Bellamy then drew over the majestic height of Widgery (or Jubilee) Cross we were given a lovely perspective across the heather and the granite rocks, the white grasses, mossy bogs and gorse whins of wild Dartmoor, and north-westwards towards the Quiltwork farmland of the country hunted by the Lamerton ... The fog was coming down now and nearly everyone hacked back to the Inn. But, drawing the whins towards home, Mr Bellamy and his hounds were soon onto their fourth fox. Only the Master, Alan Lewis, Mrs Beverley Murphy and I stayed on to savour this last run of the day. What a dramatic three miles it was! West over the A30, down a tortuous course of farmland paths, across a dozen water splashes, under the canopy of Leawood, and, with a clatter, up the narrow tarmac of Buddlebrook until scent ran raw out in the woods of Bearcott. As Mr Bellamy blew 'home', we heard the Lamerton hounds hunting their last fox just over the hill ...

'I enjoyed the privilege of riding the same 15 hh dun, Haven Dale, which Mr Bellamy – a Duchy of Cornwall tenant – lent the Prince of Wales when he rode with Spooner's and West Dartmoor two seasons ago. When the agent informed the Master that HRH wanted to pay him a visit, Mr Bellamy muttered to himself "Oh hell, I suppose the rents are going up!" It was more than a relief, it was a golden surprise, to know that all Prince Charles wanted was a day with Spooner's. Doubtless his impression – like that of most visitors – was that this hunt seems to belong to the moor as closely as the sheep and the wild ponies that scatter, as that wonderful pack with their music echoing down the deserted combes, careers past them on winter and spring Tuesdays and Saturdays ...' Before leaving Spooner's and West Dartmoor I cannot resist this memoir provided by the Morleys (he had just been appointed Lord Lieutenant of Devon), with whom we were staying. The country concerned was hunted with harriers, between the 1770s and 1823, by a Colonel Arthur Kelly. He departed this life concurrently with the favourite cat of a local versifying carpenter. Hence this little ditty:

> *Here lies my old tom cat I tell 'ee*
> *He died same day as Squire Kelly.*
> *One hunted hares, t'other rats,*
> *Squires must die as well as cats ...*

Harehunting was the West Country Squires' sport until the nineteenth century, the wiry, rangy, hard-driving West Country harrier being the hound they kenneled. But during the Victorian era – at the same time that more intensified bank enclosure rendered the quarry more difficult to keep up with – hares became scarcer, foxes more prolific. Gradually harehunting (anyhow its mounted form) became the exception rather than the rule, and the squires converted to foxhounds. But Russell and his associates had all pursued the fox with the old West Country harrier, and many have done so since their day, most notably, perhaps, the Masters of the Cotley, a hunt whose little country is positioned where Devon, Dorset and Somerset meet, a hunt that has been in the hands of the Eames family, of Cotley House, since the eighteenth century. Colonel Dick Eames, who was at the head of affairs at the time of our visit in 1973, began (in 1949) crossing his white harriers with College Valley (a Northumberland blend of Border, Fell and Foxhound Kennel Stud Book blood) and the result proved just right for foxcatching in the tightly bank-enclosed Cotley country. '. . . From the other side of the combe,' I wrote (from the 1973 opening meet), 'we saw their twisty fox make four or five great circles; we saw three roe deer cross their line and two fresh foxes roused in thick-bottomed Whitehouse, but no hound rioted, none was distracted. We saw each member of the pack momentarily checked as it struggled with the banks; and yet the white hounds of Cotley followed the line in single file, giving the semblance of a string of white beads, or drops of milk flying from a tap, until at last they overhauled him at Brockfield . . .'

Turning to Somerset, even that proudest of hunts, the Taunton Vale harriers (for which, in 1984 I had the loan of Mrs Tim Mostyn's fine horse, Prince) was prompted, by lack of hares, to convert – in 1955, at the start of Mr Michael Roffe-Sylvester's Mastership - to foxhounds. While retaining, like the Cotley, their strong West Country harrier quality, they are liberally crossed with College Valley blood. The Minehead harriers, however, though now a foxhunt, are still pure West Country.

If Melton Mowbray is the birthplace and heart of foxhunting in the Shires, Steepleton, between Blandford and Shaftesbury, deserves the same accolade for the sport in Dorset and Somerset. Steepleton House was the home of Thomas Fownes, who, according to the *Old Sporting Magazine*, kenneled 'the first real steady pack of foxhounds in the Western part of England.' This was between 1730 and 1745, the year in which Fownes sold Steepleton to Julines Beckford, whose highly academic son, Peter, was to set the tone for hunting in those parts, and to pen the most important British treatise on the sport, *Thoughts upon Hunting* (published 1781). Peter Beckford died, aged seventy, in 1811. Perhaps the most important single copy of his classic was the one inscribed to his young protégé, James John Farquharson, who established kennels at his home Eastbury, in 1806 (when he was twenty-three), and at Cattistock. Farquharson went on to forge a foxhunting empire that embraced the whole of Dorset, besides substantial corners of Wiltshire and Somerset. Why his claim to have the hunting rights in so many vast neighbouring estates went virtually unchallenged for half a century is something of a mystery; but the fact remains that it was not until 1856 that neighbouring grandees turned their impatience with his presumptuousness into action. That was the *annus mirabilis* in which several of them decided that enough was enough. Lord Portman then started up a private pack, with country centred on Steepleton; Lord Pottimore founded the Cattistock; G. D. Wingfield Digby, the Blackmore Vale; and J. S. W. Erle Drax, the Charborough country. Farquharson withdrew to what he called the East Dorset (later South Dorset), which, when the old man sold his hounds the same year, was taken over by Charles Radclyffe. These hunts stemming from the wealthy squirarchy – in contrast to most of those of Devon and Cornwall – therefore possess a smarter (what might be called a 'top hat') tradition.

The West Country has perhaps the strongest record of successful amateur

(*above*) Mrs Mollie Gregson, the Grand Old Lady of the Crawley and Horsham presenting a cup to the Eridge huntsman, John Cook, at a South of England hound show.

Derek Gardiner, huntsman to the Goathland (mounted), pointing out some of his hounds to me at a meet in the 1986–7 season.

Mrs John Hannum, Master of Mr Stewart's Cheshire, over a typical American stake-and-rail at the time of my Pennsylvanian tour in 1974. Her neck support is from a broken collar-bone.

Ben Hardaway, Master and huntsman of the Midland since 1950. I rode with the Midland from both his Alabama and Georgia Kennels in 1974.

huntsmen and the name Alastair Jackson springs particularly to mind. In his student days he hunted both the Radley and the Royal Agricultural College Beagles. Ronnie Wallace, talent spotting, suggested a full venatic career for him. Jackson (then briefly with the West Percy) said he couldn't afford it. Nonsense, replied Wallace, amateurs, if they're really good, will be paid like company directors in the future. And I believe that Jackson, of all the post-war amateurs, has most satisfactorily followed such a vocation. Certainly when we visited him and his wife, during his South Dorset Mastership, he was very much in that bracket; and but for a stint as an Exmoor hotelier he followed until quite recently the same life's work with other packs. He showed me a wonderful day: '... through the kale at Kingscombe and, with thirty of us still behind them, over the Ansty road at Cheselbourne. Riding a fast galloper and bold jumper belonging to Miss Sarah Hayward, I was fortunate enough to see these wonderful bitches hold the line with great tongue round the rim of Henning Hill, until in the gathering dusk their pilot was given best above Melcombe House. That was eight miles as hounds ran and a point of four ...'

I had a red-letter day with the Taunton Vale foxhounds (not to be confused with the Harriers which, as I say, also now hunt fox) at the end of 1988 during Robin Cursham's last season as joint-Master there. He is one of those dedicated and gifted amateur huntsmen with very little money behind him who has given of his best to one hunt after another. Starting with the Taunton Vale Harriers in 1966 he went on to the Radnor and West where I first met him and his wife, Sarah (cleaning out the kennels – I believe they had no help). He was later with the North Herefordshire, the Blackmore and Sparkford Vale (where in 1981 I again enjoyed a taste of the wonderful sport he showed) and, for one season, a pack in Canada. He began with the Taunton Vale foxhounds in 1987, but was always aware that the committee were looking for someone who did not require so heavy a guarantee. Such a man offered his services just after my visit and, although the committee turned that one down there remained a lobby against the poor Curshams, so they were obliged to seek pastures new. They had a couple of mares at stud and decided, instead, to expand on that business. My Taunton Vale day was from the John Cely Trevilians' lovely Elizabethan house, Midelney Manor: '... Hounds found at three o'clock in Mrs Maude-Roxby's Ash Wood. From there they careered via White Cross over Andrew Dixon's Stream Farm, turning left-handed for Redlands, a thick-bottomed wood, where they checked for twenty minutes, with the field – who had ridden hard to be with them and jumped many formidable lengths of timber – pausing in a pall of steam on the opposite hillside. Hitting off the line again, in the direction of Midelney they perservered with great tongue through Shutters, until at last at four-thirty they marked in Lower Burrows, deep into the Seavington Country, making a total run of seven miles. My most sincere thanks are due' – my report concluded – 'to Mr Peter Hartnell for providing me with his five-year-old chestnut, Cheval, a wonderful performer from which to witness the Taunton Vale at their best.'

Although, among huntsmen, a sharp line divides the amateurs from the professionals there is one man who has shown how it can be crossed. That is George Hyatt who when I first followed him, was carrying the South Devon horn as a joint-Master (and doing practically all the work in those kennels). When I next met him he was touching his cap and calling everyone 'Sir' and 'Madam' (and being paid as handsomely as a huntsman can be paid) in his first season as professional to the Avon Vale (a hunt with a large revenue) and he seemed very much happier in his new circumstances. One wonders whether men like Robin Cursham would not, by paradox, enjoy a freer existence as hunt servants?

In bank-enclosed Cornwall, which as a hunting county is something of a law unto itself, the most prominent establishment is the Four Burrow. That is synonymous with the Williams family, the county's leading tin miners since the eighteenth century and men who bred hounds – such as Whipcord '05, Pleader '38, Filbert '39 and Life Guard '39 – whose names resounded through foxhunting Britain. John Williams, representing the fourth generation to breed the hounds and carry the horn, was our host in 1972. During another Cornish tour in 1984 I took in the Western and the North Cornwall. The Western country occupies the tip of the Cornish peninsular (from the Four Burrow boundary to Land's End). I stayed a couple of nights in the farmhouse bungalow of John Thomas, who combined his Mastership with business as an agricultural contractor and the horse trade. He made bi-annual visits to the southern counties of Ireland where he bought (perhaps he still does?) some twenty animals a year, brought them on in the hunting-field, then sold them throughout Cornwall. He lent me a fine one, chestnut Porky. It was a filthy stormy day, I remember, one that prompted three professional long-line fishermen, who could not get their boats out, to saddle their hunters and attend the meet. But by four o'clock the tempest had abated and 'by that time,' I wrote, 'the sky was clear, and looking across Mount's Bay as we rode towards Sheffield, we saw St Michael's Mount thrown into dazzling relief. It is a lovely part of the world in which to be astride a horse.'

Cross from Land's End to the westermost tip of Wales and you're in South Pembrokeshire, which was my destination early in 1987 when I was the guest for a day's hunting with Mrs Brian Evans (née Auriole Allen) of Cresselly, a woman – like Molly Gregson, of the Crawley and Horsham – with an intense devotion to her hounds and pride in her hunt, but one with a strong family background in it, and a more worldly woman than Molly, too. The Allens of Cresselly have lived on that site since medieval times, though the present house was not built until the 1770s – by Mrs Evans's great-great-great grandfather, John Bartlett Allen, who founded 'the Cresselly Hunt' in 1789. Captain Seymour Allen changed the name to 'South Pembrokeshire' in 1844. 'I'll really have to give up the hunt next year,' Mrs Evans told me, 'I can no longer afford to sink £25,000 into it year in, year out.' And true to her word she resigned in 1988, after forty-five years in the Mastership.

Mrs Evans was a woman who refused to be responsible, she told me, for a hunt that could not 'do everything in the right style'. By contrast there was a veteran further up the coast – in Cardiganshire, a few miles north-east of Aberystwyth – who was determined not to let lack of funds deter her. Marjorie, Lady Pryse became joint-Master with her husband, in 1930, of the Gogerddan, a hunt which could be traced back through the Pryse family to Norman times. She was sixty-nine when we followed her and her hounds in January 1976. She gave up riding in 1973 when her old mare retired, but continued to carry the horn on foot. So she dismounted the hunt completely. To accompany her scarlet coat and velvet cap she donned voluminous white cotton breeches and what looked to me like racing boots.

Lavinia's diary describes our arrival at the kennels: 'Eventually we found a rotten iron gate fastened with a cracked-leather dog collar. In the pouring rain we worked our way along the potholed drive to a ramshackle farm cottage on the edge of a steep hill. The back door was a broken gate. The reek of hounds' urine in the dim dank passage was revolting. We were escorted into a tiny room with two high-backed seats, scant lighting, and piles of old photographs and books. Weatherbeaten Lady Pryse, who welcomed us, had, at the age of thirty-two, married the then 74-year-old third baronet. . . On our way out (we were to stay, thank goodness, in an Aberystwyth hotel) we caught a glimpse around the kitchen door – unbelievable filth everywhere, remains of hound food, calves' feet, sheeps' legs and cows' heads, mingled with rusty tins and garden tools . . . The meet next morning was at Nant Eos (Brook of the Nightingale). We followed Lady P through dense pine plantations, thorn thickets and barbed wire entanglements, but she didn't turn a hair. One very fat old black bitch from Dumfriesshire kept close at her heels all the way. She explained that it had got locked in the flesh hovel all night and, having gorged itself, didn't feel like hunting. . . .' Age was not the explicit factor that prompted the Master to disband her hunt in 1987 (though by then she was over eighty). *Baily's Directory* explains: 'The Gogerddan hunt has been disbanded on the retirement of Marjorie, Lady Pryse . . . who cites fox destruction societies, wire, forestry plantations, the registration fee, local private packs and rheumatism as reasons for her decision . . .'

Fox destruction societies? The mammal being as great a threat to livestock as it is anywhere else in Britain – owing to the Welsh forest and mountain fastnesses, in which it can usually hide, forage and breed with impunity – it is regarded among many farming communities as a menace of great proportions. Some of the old farmers' conventional hunts, besides several new ones, kennel a few hounds which they follow up on foot with guns (and spades). Foxes, not being easy to destroy with shot guns, except at close range, there must be many that escape severely wounded. It is this (coupled with the facts that it is against old Welsh country tradition, and often interferes with the activities of the mounted hunts) which renders the gun clubs so unpopular with the men and women who ride to hounds.

But there are many in Wales who take every bit as much pride in the smart presence of their hounds, horses and followers as any in the English Midlands. The Pembrokeshire, Curre, Llangibby, Tanatside, Flint and Denbigh, Brecon and David Davies are half a dozen I recall in that category. And, best of all, I think, the Glamorgan, which were, and still are at the time of writing, under the Mastership of a former High Sheriff of the county, Mr Anthony Martyn (formerly of the Downside Beagles and the Wheatland foxhounds) and his wife, the splendid Fiona (a pillar of the local branches of the Pony Club and Riding for the Disabled). The day I rode with the Glamorgan, in 1981, coincided with a presentation to Tony Martyn of a portrait of himself to mark his first twenty seasons. When told he could choose anything he liked he expressed a wish for a picture depicting himself riding his favourite hunter and accompanied by a few of his favourite hounds – by Peter Biegel. Unfortunately, however, Biegel – being then a sick man and having just turned down a similar request to paint the Duke of Beaufort – said no. Someone in the Glamorgan then happened to see a good likeness of the Prince of Wales (dressed as Colonel of one of his Welsh regiments) and recommended the same artist, who was duly commissioned. The picture was ceremoniously handed over by Glamorganshire's Lord-Lieutenant, Sir Cennydd Traherne at the lawn meet at his home, Penllyn Castle, which I attended, with a large throng of the hunt faithful forming a half-circle, astride their horses, to hear the speech. The gift was a waist-low portrait of Tony (no hounds, no horse), a rotten likeness and hands like bunches of bananas. A low groan arose form most of those who had subscribed to it. And, as we rode away to the first draw the recipient asked me: 'What would you do with it if it was yours.' I replied that I would consign it either to a dark passage or the loo. 'Good idea,' Tony agreed.

Nose, cry and perseverance: those are the three great qualitites of the Welsh hound. His shortcomings are lack of stamina, and a tendency to independence and babbling, to compensate for which several nineteenth-century Welsh Masters brought infusions of the best English blood to their kennels. But none with such resounding and immortal success as Edward Curre of Itton. In 1896 he went to the head of a heritage that was born in the eighteenth century, for he took over the Chepstow Hunt, which began as harriers under his great-great-grandfather, John Curre. In 1869 the Chepstow, having a very small country, amalgamated with the Llangibby but separated again a decade before Edward Curre took over from Squire Lewis of St Pierre. He re-named the hunt 'Mr Curre's', and was Master for thirty-four seasons.

'I wanted a hound' he explained at the end of his career, 'that had drive and voice and speed. I wanted them all of a type, without the woolly Welsh coat – which to me was unsightly – and I wanted them *white*, so that I could see them in the distance; for, even in my country, hounds often ran in places where a horse could not follow, and it would have been difficult to see the darker-coloured ones. But I did not want to lose "the hound of the country" ... By using stallions from the long-established Welsh packs that possessed the most drive and speed, and crossing the produce with English stud book hounds, which possessed low-scenting qualities, and had plenty of tongue – and, wherever possible, the light colour which I wanted to get, I gradually acquired a type of my own; a type which, as you can see, reproduces itself generation after generation ...'

Establishing his kennels during the last years of the century with the best Welsh strains – some of John Lawrence's 'killing Llangibby', the Glog and the Neuad Fawr, during the pre-First World War era, Curre crossed these with such influential sires as the Milton Potent '01, Belvoir Weaver, '06 and Watchman '07, the Duke of Beaufort's Leveller '10, and, most extensively of all, with his favourite, the redoubtable 'hard-as-steel' Four Burrow Whipcord '05. Up to the war, it was Belvoir, Belvoir, Belvoir. Practically every prize-winner at Peterborough was bred from the sacred 'Belvoir Tan'. But owing to over-breeding and over-emphasis of certain points, the Belvoir had not only become lumbering caricatures of their antecedents, but had lost much of their working qualities: their nose and cry had deteriorated. Hound breeders began to search for a lighter, more active hound.

At this time the Curre blood was becoming famous, and year by year an increasing number of English bitches arrived at the kennels that Sir Edward had built along the road from Itton Court in 1906. The die-hards were horrified: 'The Welsh cross is a blot on the escutcheon, a mésalliance' complained Lord Bathurst, 'a marriage without quarterings'. But the progressives held sway. 'Always on the look-out to improve my hounds,' wrote Ikey Bell, 'I soon paid Sir Edward Curre and his hounds a visit. I was astounded by their cry and their work in the field . . .' The Curre Fiddler '09 is said to be responsible for Bell's conversion to the Welsh cross, a conversion which marked a salient turning-point in the evolution of the modern hound.

Then that great Anglo-American sportsman, A. H. Higginson, tells how, when he was out with a pack hunted by a 'brilliant amateur', he saw a hound make a hit across some plough when nothing else in the pack would own the line, and was informed that 'it went back to some of Teddy Curre's blood'. He goes on to relate how he owed the succes of his own pack in America – the Middlesex – 'to the infusion of Sir Edward Curre's blood . . . It *made* my pack, I know that. And when I came back to England . . . I found that many of the best working packs in the land used some of the Itton Court stallions . . .' He could have added that it was originally Curre outcrosses, more than any other, that were responsible for the swing from heavy Belvoir to the foxhound we know today. Curre blood permeated nearly all forward-looking kennels in Britain. And still does.

I had a wonderful day with the Curre hounds from an Itton Court meet in 1973 during George Headdon's illustrious time as huntsman (Charlie White took over in 1976). My report concluded as follows: '. . . It had been fascinating to watch these rather short-legged, close-coupled and unusually agile hounds wriggle and persevere through the thorn and bramble brakes of the conifer plantations in which this part of Wales abounds. And considering it is such a tiny county, it was heartening to find so much widespread determination that the hunt shall remain independent – and shall never cease to breed the stamp of hound Sir Edward bred, hounds whose blood has suffused every corner of the world of foxhunting for the past half century.'

When the Banwen Miners hunt – whose country in west Glamorganshire, lies around Swansea and Port Talbot – was started up in the early 1960s it was welcomed by the hunting world at large as a force to help improve the image of the sport – which still presented itself to most outside eyes as a diversion for the rich and privileged – and foster too, good relationships between town and country. The embryo of the Banwen was a small and motley pack belonging to George Crisp, secretary of the local branch of the National Coal Board. This was taken over in 1962 by the Banwen founders, Tom Hopkins and Tom Jones, both mine owners at those collieries. The Duke of Beaufort gave them twelve couple of hounds together with exclusive sporting rights on all his extensive estates in west Glamorgan. The Duchess, also proving her enthusiastic support, boxed a horse from Badminton for a day with them, and the occasion is commemorated in a cartoon in the Pantyddraeren Arms at Banwen. It depicts a miner's wife holding hunting clothes in one hand and miner's overalls in the other and shouting out: 'Dai! Are you working today or tally-ho-ing with the Duchess?' Alas by the time I rode with them in 1988, only one miner could be counted in the mounted field, while the hierarchy was mostly composed of businessmen and solicitors.

I have many rather bizarre memories from Wales: such as losing my way with the Pembrokeshire and being faced by an apoplectic farmer with a pitchfork; getting lost again in a conifer forest when Lord Davies had the David Davies hounds still running under the moon; spilling my early morning cup of coffee on a precious bedroom carpet when the guest of the Bonner-Maurices for a Tanatside day; putting the son of a famous Master of the Carmarthenshire to great trouble having a Lionel Edwards portrait of his father photographed and then seeing it reproduced in *Country Life* the size of a postage stamp; taking to the magazine a photograph of Sir Edward Curre, inscribed, signed and given by the great man to one of the Curre joint-Masters, Mrs Meade, when she was a child, and it being torn up by an 'anti-bloodsports' enthusiast at the printers; and of standing on a station platform near the west coast for some forty minutes (when a train I was due to catch was cancelled), and listening to a certain Master's daughter-in-law, who was seeing me off, enquire whether I advised her to leave her husband ('You saw quite plainly throughout the weekend how things were between us'! she said). Fortunately the next train arrived before I committed myself to any rash suggestions.

But what stands out most happily from my Welsh memories is the beauty of the landscape, as evinced by these notes made after some of my visits: 'The country hunted by the David Davies, which lies astride the river Severn in south Montgomeryshire, is a most charming one to ride over. The springy sheep pasture and the bracken moorland heights are divided into expansive hedged enclosures with plenty of gaps and gates and hunt jumps, and so are the vivid cattle fields surrounding the isolated farmsteads in the valleys below ... The Flint and Denbigh country is one of small enclosures in steeply undulating farmland and big dingles that lead on in the climbing south to a wild expanse of moorland ... I was struck by the clean and vivid beauty of the Llangibby farmland, composed almost entirely of neat grass enclosures, more for sheep than cattle ... The visitor to the Pembrokeshire soon sees what a lovely tract it is, all gorse and bracken brakes, wild,

high-banked lanes and old pastures undulating into deep, woody dingles
... We were riding over the lovely hilly pastures (hardly a yard of arable
to be seen in Carmarthenshire) in the Towy Valley, just east of the county
town...'

And the same with the Brecon, even on a filthy day in 1986, such as this:
'Anyone who recalls the conditions of western Britain on December 21 will
have images of a remorselessly wet and windswept day, preceded by a night
that should have kept all but the most urgently hungry foxes underground.
"It's too bad to go out on the Beacons," so Mr Williams, my kind host
informed me at breakfast; and there was no intention of drawing on those
delectable heights. But John Davies had scarcely cheered his hounds into the
dingle of Lower Cantref when they spoke to a line, and, in a moment were
pursuing their fox over the hill towards Cwm Oergwm. By stony paths and
across many ditches, along woodland tracks and over bracken slopes we
cantered above them onto the Brecon Beacons. Through the curtain of the
heavy drizzle, blown by a north-wester into a drifting white haze we
watched them in the valley below, still latched to the scent, threading their
tan-and-white column through the thickets bordering the swollen stream.
Back down the hillside we rode and another thirty minutes went by before
their fox was given best in the dingle by Tregaer. The climate was so rough
by one-thirty that most of the field then pointed their horses heads for
home.' The beauty of the wet and cloud-dark panorama was in its uninhab-
ited wildness.

### Golden North

A ubiquitous hunting correspondent is sure to be asked, time and again,
where he would hunt if his sport was to be confined to a single county. And
my answer to that has always been Northumberland (though I must admit
that parts of Yorkshire and the Scottish Lowlands would come close
behind). It is not only that Northumberland hunt provinces are largely
comprised of unspoiled, and easily negotiable, grass terrains over which the
sport enjoys long and rich traditions. It is also because in the north of Britain
– and most convincingly, I think, in Northumberland – hunting is part of the
way of life to all manner of countrymen, landowners and cottagers, tenants
and tradesmen, children and retired folk, its interest bringing all these
strands together in close fraternity, transcending class, professional and age
differences – the poet laureate John Masefield had something to say on this
in the introduction to his narrative verse, 'Reynard the Fox' – 'Hunting
makes more people happy than anything else I know. When people are
happy together, I am quite certain that they build up something eternal,
something both beautiful and divine which weakens the power of all evil
things upon this life of men and women.'

If I were to cite an example from my experiences of the impact of this spirit
it would be from my visit to the Percy in 1982, when those hounds were the
property of the 10th Duke of Northumberland. They were out four days a
week, the meets invariably being at one or other of the Duke's tenants'

houses, and the days finishing at the home of a different tenant. I enjoyed
the privileges of both the Friday, when the Duke carried the horn to the
dog-hounds, and the Monday when his huntsman, Don Claxton, hunted
the bitches. I have never met such a diverse and yet intimate assortment of
people as those assembled at Richard Green's Heckley High House. Among
fifty others there was Danny Moralee, the field Master, who, for five successive years in the 1950s had been Britain's amateur champion jockey; the
bold-riding Anne Hale who had then completed thirty-seven years as hunt
secretary; Ralph Tulip, whose mare had recently given birth to a splendid
foal the night after a long day's hunting; septuagenarian Harry Sordy,
whose first Percy day was before the Great War; Judy Kinghorn, the dedicated Pony Club district Commissioner; Robert Matterson, the Duke's
agent; Colonel Peter Bridgeman the hunt chairman; and, of course, the
Duchess, the enchanting Elizabeth, who, as one of the farmers put it to me,
'is a fine horsewoman and a rare one to go'. (She confided to me that, during
her early married life – her husband being very much 'a man's man' –
hunting proved to be the best social outlet from the claustrophobia of the
castle.) Every tenant farmer knew how to mix a Percy Special (a desperate
concoction, not unlike the True Blue with which NCOs in my regiment
attempted to put officers under the table) and none better, so I was told, than
our host, Mr Green. Anyhow, Percy Specials or not, the atmosphere of high
morale was terrific.

A month prior to that meet, after a snowy (foot) day with the Morpeth I
visited Alnwick Castle to take a look at the family hunting pictures with a
view to selecting a few for publication. Hughie Northumberland was not
well; he was suffering from a hernia. After showing me the Alnwick painting he said 'There's another you really ought to see, it belongs to Simon
Browne at Callaly Castle. The Percy stems from the Browne family hunt. I'll
drive you over there . . .' I then met the Duke in the hall, doubled up with
pain. 'I'll be all right' he assured me (his face contorted), 'it's only a hernia.'
Although the county was deep in snow he drove his Range Rover to Callaly
at breakneck speed. Ushering us in, Major Simon Browne (who was then in
his late eighties) offered refreshments. 'Have you got any of that good old
brandy, Simon?' enquired the Duke. Browne fetched a bottle of the golden
stuff and invited the Duke to say 'when'. Half a tumblerful was splashed
out. The Duke downed it in two and left the room. Browne said to me, 'Do
you know how old that brandy is? It's 1821 . . . Poor Hughie with that hernia,
I must get Elizabeth to book him in for an operation.' With that he proceeded
to give me a taste of the Napoleon – enough to wet the bottom of my glass.
To see the picture, which was a life-size one, of Simon Browne's grandfather
with hounds crossing the River Coquet, made the expedition thoroughly
worthwhile. The Duke got us back over the icy roads to Alnwick in a time
that was ten minutes shorter than the journey out.

When I stayed at the Castle in the following month he lent me, for bedtime
reading, a copy of the ghost story, *The Shadow on the Moor*, written by his
father for *Blackwood's Magazine*. It concerns a sinister, if brilliant huntsman,
'Black Tom', who believes he has got away with the murder of his whip-

per-in until the younger man's widow puts a curse on him. Then, at the end of a long and nightmarish hunt, Black Tom is lured to his death over a precipice by the whip's ghostly *holloas*, coupled with, behind him, the shadow of the story's title and, in front, the wiles of the fox, the dead man's reincarnation, which keeps running back to entice Black Tom in the fatal direction. Hughie Northumberland told me that it was the lyrical voice of the 8th Duke's first whipper-in, Sidney Pilmore, that inspired the character of the *Shadow on the Moor's* phantom whip. The following season, when I was out with the West Percy, hounds ran into their fox at Reavely Glitters which is just opposite Ingram Glitters, the precipice down which the 8th Duke had Black Tom career to his death.

Before I left, Hughie asked: 'Any chance of you're giving the Border hunt a spot of publicity next season?' When I enquired why he replied: 'Oh, the Master's a tenant of mine, I think he likes to be taken notice of.' Considering the kennels in question were some forty miles north of Alnwick I would have thought this request rather showing off had it not come from the self-effacing 10th Duke of Northumberland.

The Border is a real hill farmers' pack with which the names Jacob Robson (Master 1879–1933) and his son ('young Jake') and Hedley (Ian, father – Michael, son) are most closely associated. 'The meet was at Buchtrig where Roxburghshire adjoins Northumberland,' I wrote, 'where the farm road peters out in the high Cheviots, where human habitation is a rarity, and the only sounds on the naked hillside are curlew cries and babbling burns, the occasional bleat of sheep and the whisper of the wind in the heather. Lady Goodson was there (on her feet) and Bobby Bruce and Colin Campbell (both mounted), old acquaintances from my days with the College Valley, Buccleuch and Fife, respectively . . .'

The College Valley (now united with the North Northumberland) lies just to the north of the Border hunt country. Lavinia and I rode with them during the 1972–73 season, staying for our visit with the late Sir Alfred (Bill) Goodson, and his wife, Enid, at their home Corbet Tower. Both suffered acutely from hearing losses and there was much shouting and non-comprehension. Goodson was – like his friend and fellow Border baronet, Jock Buchanan-Jardine – fascinated by experiment in the breeding of domestic animals in general. His family were from the West Country, but when, in his early youth, his father asked him where he would like to settle, he replied 'where your ewes come from', and he duly began to farm on the borders of Northumberland and Roxburghshire, breeding Aberdeen Angus cattle and Cheviot sheep. This happened to be a corner where the Border, North Northumberland and Duke of Buccleuch's hunt countries met and which were all neglected. The upshot was that Goodson and his friend and neighbour, Claud Lambton, put together the College Valley hunt, the hounds being, in the first instance, mainly crosses of Jacob Robson's Border breed (which was virually fell) and Buccleuch. The best results of these crosses were put to a couple of Goathland bitches (whose country is the North York Moors). Their progeny formed the foundation of the College Valley. A few years later, when the great Ikey Bell watched these hounds in action he confided to Goodson that he wished he had used fell blood, instead of Welsh, when he bred the South and West Wilts (the strains of which, more than any other, were to mark the turning-point in the character of the modern foxhound).

From the age of six Bill Goodson had also bred bantams, and he possessed a beautiful collection of them at Corbet Tower. Showing them off to Lavinia and me he suddenly turned his back and thrust the current exhibit back in its cage on the unexpected arrival of his wife. 'She hates me spending so much money on them,' he whispered. At dinner the old man asked Lavinia, 'Do you wear your nightdress under your evening dress? Mary Beaufort always does, she told me at Badminton the other day where they had Ronnie and Rosie Heythrop (or whatever their name is) staying . . . We don't often go away now. Find these new motorways a bit tricky. Tried the M6 and saw a sign to Preston. The old lady said "we always went through Preston". So we did. Added a bit to our journey, I'm told.'

At our departure Goodson's butler inadvertantly packed his dinner jacket shoes, together with my own, in my luggage, so we had to post them back. When we stayed with the Goodsons for my visit to the Duke of Buccleuch's later that season there was another dinner party and, as the butler - who enjoyed an ongoing banter with his master - appeared behind my place Goodson pointed derisively at him, shouting 'That's the bloody fool who sent you home with my evening slippers!' Nor did he mince his words when the Master of the Buccleuch, Hugh Arbuthnot, arrived for dinner looking very scruffy: 'Really, Hugh, when I said "don't change" I didn't mean you were to come in your kennel clothes!' He then regaled us with his account of Arbuthnot's reaction when, soon after the latter took over the Buccleuch Mastership, he attended a dinner party at which the Lothians were fellow guests. Arbuthnot was not aware of their Christian names and when someone talking to him from the opposite side of the table referred to 'Peter and Toni' he asked 'Oh, are they the local queers?' This became quite a *cause célèbre* throughout the Borders.

Moving south I had good fun on a very windy day with the Tynedale when Ian Williams (son of the legendary Tipperary Evan, who rode the winner of the 1937 Grand National) was carrying the horn; but, in 1984, a meet planned for the Braes of Derwent (whose country lies in Co Durham as well as Northumberland), when we stayed with that engaging couple, Emma and Charles Stirling, was cancelled owing to a heavy snowfall; and the same thing happened to our visit to the Zetland, with whose hounds I had so much excitement in the early 1950s when the dashing Colin McAndrew was hunting them. But for the South Durham, in the middle of the 1988–89 season, owing to the generosity of the amateur whipper-in, Alan Mason, who mounted me, I had a most enjoyable ride: 'The meet was at Mr Wade's home, Howe Hills Farm. Fred who carried me, is accustomed to travelling up with the pack, which is where his owner advised me to stay all day. I am glad I did so because the best way across the country is over the hunt's liberally distributed post-and-rail fences, and Fred combines a facility for timber jumping with as steady a temperament as I have ever encountered – the perfect visitor's horse'.

If I was obliged to name Yorkshire's most distinguished hunt I would reply the Sinnington. (Its old-and-bold also claim it to be Britain's oldest, though the case is tenuous, to say the least). It is still run by the squirarchy, there are large funds supporting it, the hounds are bred to a high quality, things are generally done in style and it has a wonderful country, grassy hills and moorland north of the A170, vale to the south. (This is not to say that many of the other Yorkshire hunts do not have such attributes, but the Sinnington stands out). I savoured several days there in the early 1950s and first rode with them for *Country Life* in 1971 when an amateur, the moustachioed, swashbuckling and entertaining David Westbury carried the horn. I followed again, from a moorland meet when a new joint-Master, Major Alastair Stewart, a most upright personality and true sportsman, was hunting hounds. His appointment, however, caused such controversy that a small, but influential, faction would have nothing more to do with the hunt. Among other bitternesses the row set up a barrier between Lady Feversham, a former joint-Master, and her daughter, Clarissa Collin (my hostess for my second visit, who had then just resigned from the committee after twenty-four years); while Major John Shaw who had then also been in the joint-Mastership for a long time, refused to allow the Sinnington over his land and, for a period would not speak to his erstwhile best friend, Colonel Max Gordon, the honorary secretary. Having discussed the issue with many Sinnington foxhunters I came away amazed that so many middle-aged people were capable of such pettiness. But there can be no greater rancour than that generated by hunt disputes in general! (Alastair Stewart resigned from the Mastership in 1989 his place being filled by Adrian Dangar, the son of my old Gilbraltar friend, Richard.) 🐾

In terms of high style the Middleton is on a level with the Sinnington. Nick Crossley, one of the four joint Masters, hunted their hounds on the occasion I watched them in action on a splendid point just short of four miles, seven as hounds ran. The late Lord Halifax, who bred them, told me that every bitch of his went back on tail-female to Warwickshire Comfort 1822, and I believe the present regime continues to adhere strictly to her lines. The fine kennels at Birdsall, built in 1858, are among the oldest in Britain. The house is the ancestral home of the Willoughby family, from whose title the hunt took its name. The circumstances are romantic. One night, early in the eighteenth century, Thomas Willoughby, second son of the 1st Lord Middleton whose estates were in the Midlands, was caught in a fierce snowstorm as he rode through the night from Hull to Malton. Coming to Birdsall Brow he spotted a light in the valley below. By painful degrees he led his horse against the tempest towards this ray of hope. There a groom relieved him of it, and a footman answered his hammering, heaving the door against the driving snow. To greet him in the glow of the hall – and to change his life – was the beautiful Birdsall heiress, Elizabeth Sotheby. Through the marriage following this happy encounter Thomas Willoughby brought into his family her estates on the Yorkshire wolds, which their son, Henry, who became 5th Baron Middleton (on the failure of his elder brother's line) united with the other Middleton lands. It was the 6th Baron who, in

1832, gave the hunt the name 'Lord Middleton's'. The 12th Lord Middleton, who was out hunting on my day, was then vice-chairman of the committee.

Max Gordon, whom I mentioned in a Sinnington connection, and who was my first squadron leader in the Blues, was joint-Master and huntsman of the Badsworth when I rode with them early in 1970. He gave up hunting hounds the following year, the main reason being that, owing to a war wound, he was obliged, when riding, to wear a surgical collar; and, because he couldn't twist his neck independently of his shoulders, he couldn't always 'lend a direct ear to his hounds', as he put it. Another old Blue, George Lane-Fox, had us to stay at Bramham Park for the 1971 opening meet of the Bramham Moor, of which he was field Master. The kennels at Hope Hill, then in the care of old Tom Cody, are large and very impressive. Lord Halifax was their hound-breeding mentor.

Simon Roberts, formerly huntsman to the Ampleforth College beagles, had just taken over the Derwent (east of the Sinnington, north of the Middleton), at the age of twenty-six, when we stayed for a lawn meet at Roxby Manor, Thornton-le-Dale, the home of the Ashley Burgesses, whose daughter he was about to marry. Our hosts related for us this weird tale. As one of the Derwent's most famous characters, old Robin Hill, lay dying, in 1956, he vowed to have just one more day's hunting and, if he was denied that, he promised to return and give it as a fox. He died the night before the 1956–57 opening meet, at which the then Master, Charles Chafer, requested two minutes silence in his memory. A week later, when Lord Feversham was hunting the Sinnington hounds, their fox (as Feversham's widow records in her *Strange Stories of the Chase*) ran into the Derwent country. That evening a tired fox was seen retreating into Brompton cemetery where Robin Hill was buried. It is widely believed, or conjectured, among the Derwent faithful that this was the reincarnation of the old sportsman, a man who, 'through his whole life', said Ashley Burgess, 'showed the most uncanny knowledge of the run of a fox.'

Lord Mountgarret who gave the meet for my York and Ainsty, North, day (in January 1983) had just been convicted of loosing off his 12-bore at some people suspended in the basket of a hot-air balloon and deliberately disturbing his grouse moor. But he looked very happy all the same, and described how his father, the hunt's founder, who hated jumping, had easily-latched gates inserted in every enclosure. His son recalled that 'There was only one occasion on which my father left the ground. That was when his mare was threatened with assault by a passionate stallion, to escape which he jumped her over a thick blackthorn hedge with perfect safety.' Major Roderic Bailey, the Master at the time of my visit, was a regular soldier who combined his sport with the role of army recruiting officer for Yorkshire (a mainly summer occupation).

Although there is a North and a South York and Ainsty they were never formally divided and there is still a central committee, though the respective Masters carry on as though they are independent. The man at the South's helm when I rode with them was James Bloor, a very experienced amateur huntsman who showed me some good sport with his pure-bred English hounds – Brocklesby and some Belvoir (via Limerick). This was the hunt that suffered the terrible drowning accident in February 1869 when the grossly overcrowded Newby ferry capsized and among others, the Master, Sir Charles Slingsby was swept away in the current and drowned with his horse, Saltfish.

The least blessed of the Yorkshire hunts, in territorial terms, has to be the Cleveland, which lies in the county's far north, adjacent to Middlesborough. Its Masters, Messrs Fletcher, Muir and Munro spelt out the problems with passionate pessimism on my day there in 1985. Not only had they to contend with ever increasing conurbation and the blight of the Whitby-Middlesborough railway, but also with a good deal of selfishness. ICI for example, owning 2,000 acres of their best country preserved it all as a shoot for its executives and kept the Cleveland out until the end of January. Another of the best tracts belonged to a keen shooting man who says to his keeper, 'If I see a fox on this land, you're fired!' Yet the said landowner had the temerity to box his horse for a day's hunting in Co Durham every week. 'Why don't you complain?' I asked the Masters. 'Well, he might then put his land out of bounds to us altogether,' they replied. On returning south I mentioned this to the Director of the British Field Sports Society, who was equally appalled. He promised to suggest to the Masters of the Co Durham hunt (the Zetland) that they ban the Yorkshire landowner concerned.

By contrast, just along the coast from the Cleveland there are several excellent hill countries hunted by farmers' packs, the Bilsdale, Farndale, Goathland and Staintondale. The most celebrated of these, I think, is the Goathland, which has had several names well known in the hunting world in its Masterships, such as Gerald Gundry, Maria Coventry, David Westbury, Nigel Peel and Jamie Cameron. I had a spirited gallop with the Goathland in 1986, but the venture was a little marred by the fact that a Mr Toulson Clarke, who had been briefly in the Mastership wrote me a vitriolic letter demanding to know why his name had been omitted from my article. I replied that, regretfully, not everyone can be included in such a short space (in fact my hosts had explicitly requested me not to mention him). Refusing my explanation Mr Toulson Clarke wrote furiously to the editor, and he received no change from her either.

In the whole history of the British climate there cannot have been such curious weather conditions as those prevailing during my two decades and more as a hunting correspondent: open winters mainly, all too often too warm for scent, or too windy. A Bedale day in 1974 was not untypical: 'A howling gale the previous night kept most foxes tight underground' says my journal, 'and there they remained. So strong was the blast that hounds were hunting the scent fifty yards off course of the one that was *holloaed* away from Bedale wood. But working on it tight as leeches, they hunted him for forty minutes and over two miles, as far as Holtby Hall, we following, with heads into the north wind . . .' And sometimes, on warm days with not much doing, there would suddenly be a drop in the temperature and improved scent to end the day, such as this one recorded from my Hurworth visit: 'We knew from the start that scent would be poor from Appleton Wiske; the muggy atmosphere and the deep blue on the Cleveland hills told us as much. But . . . Foster blew for home at three-thirty and was heading for the kennels when hounds found in a pile of straw bales. The temperature had plummetted, scent was strong and there was no stopping them. Following a hard-galloping evening burst they won their reward on a railway embankment . . .'

I started hunting with the fell packs in 1970, concluding my last report in 1974; and since all are on foot, over some of the most rugged terrains in the British Isles, I am glad this was when I was a bit younger! These extracts from my journals sum up my research and impressions. First from the Melbreak: 'We do not know when the tradition began, for the early records are thin. But when Hutchinson wrote this note on the inhabitants of Loweswater in his *History of Cumberland*, published in 1794, one assumes the roots were already deep. "The people live in harmony and they express contentment. The peasantry have one enjoyment here, which is prohibited to most men of their class. Through the liberality of their lords a hound is kept in nearly every house. Two or three qualified inhabitants take licence to kill game and command the pack. As soon as harvest is in, an honest cobbler shifts his garb and becomes huntsman, and every second or third morning collects the dogs and calls the sportsmen to the field; the cottagers climb the mountain-side where they can view the chase, and without much exertion enjoy the pleasure of the hunt; after which they retire with cheerful minds and invigorated constitutions to their peaceful homes."'

From the Coniston: '. . . A fell huntsman that can kill foxes is indeed a hero to the farmers. Nor would any disagree with J. W. Allen, the large-scale sheep farmer, who is chairman of the Westmorland Agricultural Executive Committee. "Hunting is literally the only effective form of fox control we have in the fells." he says. "that is why these packs hunt well on through lambing, into May. . . Good fell hounds show certain distinct qualities: an extreme lightness to compete with slopes and walls, a long pastern to minimize concussion, a sound hare foot to grip the rocks, a big well-placed shoulder for mountain strength and a very well let-down hock for speed, combined with a superlative nose and a loud cry."'

From the Ullswater: '. . . Then there are the ever-changing contrasts of colour and scene, only known to the genuine foot follower: here bracken (which slows hounds up so badly) bronzed from the frost, and jumbles of boulders (where the cavernous borrans that serve as fox refuges are concealed); here Herdwick and Swaledale sheep, grazing on dew-drenched grass, with buzzards and crows circling above them, hoping they will die; and there, round the shoulder of the fell, past an outcrop of that thickly lichened volcanic stone, which makes Cumbria what it is, to an expanse of heather from which, with their tuneful scream, grouse intermittently explode and quickly vanish. Here perhaps, the heather and bracken give way to bog, to sphagnum moss, a rosy-verdant squelch, with cotton-grass and bent-grass flying against the wind; and then, around another bend, into a steep-sided ghyll, with lone and stunted hawthorn and ash trees contriving a life from the stone, and tinkling waterfalls to mark the ascent. Car followers have none of this, nor the self-satisfaction of physical exertion, nor the melody of hounds and huntsman.'

From the Lunesdale: 'If you can imagine a steep and barren bleached-grass moorland, without a sign of human habitation or activity, except for an occasional flock of sheep and, once in a while, a stone wall – which these hounds jump like gazelles – you begin with a basic idea of typical Lunesdale country. In the weather of 20 March it took on a tundra quality: the gale doubled flat the bent-grass and cotton-grass; the tiny waterfalls marking the becks were a stalactite pattern of icicles; your feet crunched into the soft ice covering the yellow-green sphagnun moss, the bogs were frozen over, and the high tops were silvered with snow. "What way?" The familiar fell-hunter's request rang out from the direction of a rocky outcrop 400 yards away. But you need not reply, for, suddenly, round the shoulder of the silent hill, come a piebald and skewbald vortex of hounds, flashing in circles, telling you they had lost that drag from Taythes Ghyll.'

From the Eskdale and Ennerdale: 'In the whole world of sport, from tiddly-winks to ocean racing, probably no greater pride, in either their old heroes or their contemporary gladiators, is expressed than that felt by the fell hunters of Lakeland. And the hunt hero of each is, without question, second to none. "Could anyone seriously suggest," ask the Blencathra, "that a finer man ever drew breath than John Peel, who hunted our country for fifty-six seasons, still following his hounds on 40-mile chases till the age of seventy-eight? And, if you want a runner-up, take John Crozier, our founder, and Master for sixty-four seasons."'

'"For real good men," claim the Melbreak, "there's none to beat our Benson or our Iredale." But Melbreak sportsmen would scarcely say that above a whisper in an Ullswater pub, when the 'tatie' goes round and the ballads begin; for there Joe Bowman was the champion of *all* Cumbria for *all* time . . . "Bowman?" enquire the Coniston, with a headshake. "Peel? Oh yes, we've heard of them, but they were not a patch on our Tom Chapman, who has always been labelled 'greatest of them all' . . ."'

From the horseman's viewpoint Cumbria is a foxhunting province, Lancashire a harehunting one. John Peel's hounds pursued their foxes over much of what is now the Cumberland hunt country; and Sir Wilfred Lawson (3rd baronet), whose Masterships of the Cumberland Hunt spanned the period 1886–1937 inherited descendants of hounds which his father acquired on Peel's death. In 1923 the eastern end of the Cumberland country was designated a separate entity as the 'Cumberland Farmers', a hunt with which I and a couple of horses from the Household Cavalry got to know very well when I was stationed near Carlisle in the early 1950s and David Brock and George Fairbairn were Masters.

John Brockbank – breeder, maker, trainer and owner of many successful steeplechasers – and his wife kindly had me to stay at their home Westward Park to hunt with the Cumberland in 1985, when Bobby Hudson was carrying the horn, and his daughter, Heather, turning hounds to him. I wrote afterwards: 'This is not a country for people whose concept of hunting is jumping fences, but rather for those who love to cross wild and lovely places, and who regard their horses as vehicles from which to observe hounds working. In contrast to followers of nearly all other packs the majority of the Cumberland field can name most of their hounds. As I experienced, they are trusted to ride up quite close to the huntsman; nor did they fail to express a muted excitement every time hounds hit off a line. All that, surely, is what hunting ought to be about?'

This, I believe, is in contrast to the Lancashire harrier people who hunt for the gallops and the jumps. And what fun they have! Newton Bacon, the man with his hand on the Holcombe tiller when I rode with them in 1974, told me something of the history. The Holcombe claim descent from the pack put together by one of James I's young courtiers, Sir Gilbert Hoghton, after the king stayed at Hoghton Tower, Blackburn, in 1617, and issued a warrant giving his knight extensive hunting rights. He also permitted Hoghton and his hunt staff to wear the royal scarlet, which is why the Holcombe have that colour and not harrier green. The hunt staff, incidentally, were on foot until the 1920s. Though a large country, the Holcombe has the worst of industrial Lancashire, besides the M6 and the M61, to contend with, and the conurbation is spreading badly.

Compare this with the country (half in Lancashire, half west Yorkshire) occupied by the next-door Pendle Forest and Craven Harriers, for which we stayed early in 1987 with Mr and Mrs Simon Towneley, whose daughter, Charlotte, had recently married Lavinia's brother, Arthur. 'Earlier this season,' I wrote, 'someone commented in my presence that England can no longer boast a hunt country with an exclusively grass terrain. And I believed him until last month when Lady Horsfall, the senior joint-Master of the Pendle Forest and Craven, invited me for a day with her harriers, and proved that those hounds and their followers enjoy just such an elysium . . . It really was an education to watch hounds hunting almost continuously across that entirely open hilly grassland.' The PF & C, who are of course, registered with the Association of Masters of Harriers and Beagles, also joined the MFHA in the early 1980s with the express purpose of keeping out a foxhunt foot pack that threatened to share their country.

The Scottish Lowlands are blessed with such lovely hunt countries that comparisons are inclined to be invidious. As I mentioned in Chapter Four I had the privilege of two seasons (1951–53) with the Dumfriesshire, and I described there how Jock Buchanan-Jardine bred, at Castle Milk, his unique black-and-tans for that great hill country which has since echoed to the cry of the same breed under the Mastership of his son, my friend, Rupert. The oldest of the Scottish hunts, the Linlithgow and Stirlingshire, lying adjacent to Edinburgh, is probably the least favoured in terms of country, but I believe they have opened up new tracts for themselves in different parts of the Lothians since my visit in 1977. I have enjoyed some marvellous days with the Fife, Lanark and Renfrewshire, Jedforest and Duke of Buccleuch's, though, in terms of journalism the latter was afterwards somewhat marred by the fact that the *Country Life* printers got the pictures and captions the wrong way round (a photograph of Hugh Arbuthnot fording a river, followed by a posse of female subscribers, for example read 'The Master and huntsman with some of his bitches . . .'). I believe the Buccleuch have been plagued for many years by over-conscientious keepers and thus a great dearth of foxes and that the feeling between the Masters and shooting landowners in some cases remains rather strained.

Best of all were my rides with the Lauderdale – when I stayed at Thirlstane Castle with the enchanting Bunny and Rossie Maitland-Carew – and the Eglinton whose hounds have a magnificent part of Ayrshire in which to show their skills. The late Lord Glenarthur laid the foundations of the present Eglinton pack. With its big woodlands and many river banks presenting earthstopping problems, and its poor scenting conditions, this part of the Lowlands, 'is not a country for a very long hunt', wrote Glenarthur. These facts seemed to me to dictate the necessity for a pack which could really gallop and burst their fox in the early part of a hunt if they were to have the opportunity of catching him later. When I took over we had big hounds with a lot of bone . . . What we have tried to provide is something smaller, lighter, more active. We decided the Crafty '44 line ought to be kept as the mainstay; so it seemed reasonable to base our breeding on hammering back to Middleton Stalwart '07 . . .'

That lithe Eglinton hound elegance which so impresses one at the shows speaks of a really swift one. 'So fast indeed did the Eglinton travel on the scent of their morning foxes on my day' – I said in my report – 'that most of the field were far behind when hounds marked the first to ground . . . and the second was given best after a terrific race from Craigbyre Wood. Their stride, I thought, must be as strong as that of any foxhounds.'

*Merry Beaglers*

In the houses of some two out of three of every Master of beagles I have visited there hangs the print of a famous painting by Harry Hall. His *Merry Beaglers* of 1847 shows three top-hatted men in white trousers, the one in the middle being the Rev Philip Honywood, the man who set the modern beagle on course. The word derives from the Celtic *beag*, meaning small; and the little English dog in those ancient times which had something of a terrier look about it, was commonly known as a 'rabbit beagle'. Honywood crossed his 'rabbit beagles' with harriers. In due course old English harriers were crossed with conventional foxhounds, and what eventually emerged was the minature harrier type of beagle with which we are now familiar. Honywood's home was at Coggeshall, near Colchester; and the Colchester Garrison Beagles (with whom Lavinia and I spent an afternoon whilst the weekend guests of Gerald Charrington and his wife at Layer Marney Tower, where the meet was in 1978) claim a tenuous decent with Honywood's hunt. In 1861 an officer at the infantry barracks at Colchester, an Essex man called Margesson, founded a pack, based on Honywood's breeding, and this has been handed down to fresh generations of soldiers ever since.

Not Essex, however, but the Wirral peninsular of Cheshire owns the best claim to the birthplace of the sport in organised terms. For while Honywood's was very much a private pack, the Royal Rock which was established with 'rabbit beagles' by a young Wirral farmer, by the name of Tinley Barton, became a hunt club in 1845. And since most of its members lived in the vicinity of Rock Ferry – a 'Royal ferry' ever since William IV had used it when he was Duke of Clarence – and because the sportsmen's principal meeting place was called the Royal Rock, that was the name for which Barton and his friends opted. We had a splendid afternoon with the Royal Rock in March 1974, when Terence Harvey, a solicitor and distinguished athlete, was at the helm (he was Master from 1958 to 1983). Up to the time of our visit Mr Harvey had run no fewer than twenty times in the 6¾-mile Cheshire Beagles foot point-to-point and secured the best time more often than any other runner. The Royal Rock also have a Leverets section, their answer to the Pony Club, for 7-to-17-years-olds. '. . . These hounds were so close when their last hare clapped just short of a rhododendron thicket', ran my report, 'that I thought they must have her. But when she jumped into the bushes just ahead of their noses and the one they followed away from there was obviously fresh, Mr Harvey blew "home". And after three hours on the trot we were glad enough to return to Thornton Hough and Mrs Wetherell's sumptuous tea . . .' (Beagling teas are indeed what make the days for many followers of foot packs!)

Beagling was not nationally popular until the present century, and the little hounds that men like Honywood and Barton bred were rather looked down on. ('Beagles! Quite little things' – Surtees put into the mouth of John Jorrocks – 'In fact I doesn't know what to say about beagles. Be rather *infra dig*, wouldn't it?') It was from the southern outskirts of London (from what are now the City suburbs or Greater London, southside) that the sport really spread. Of the ten packs in England in the 1860s, five were between and above Guildford in west Surrey and Bromley in north-west Kent. 'Were there not photographs to support the fact' – I wrote in my report on the Surrey and North Sussex Beagles, in 1972 – 'it would be rather difficult to imagine the pony traps and hacks converging for meets at Croydon and Kingston, alongside the walkers who had come by train from Redhill and Sutton, Victoria and Charing Cross, the men in their tight Norfolk jackets and leggings, the women in nicely tailored tweed coats, voluminous hats, multi-buttoned boots and layers of ankle-length skirts, tripping across the deep plough by Surbiton.'

A certain smart foxhunter – rather agreeing with Surtees and his rumbustious Jorrocks – said to me recently that he was always given the impression that 'the beagling crowd seems to be mostly composed of retired people, middle-aged professionals, doctors, lawyers, etc, and jolly-hockey-sticks women, townsfolk more than countrymen.' I replied that this is a popular misconception, that they come in all sorts and sizes and age groups, and that most of them are at least as genuine countrymen and women – probably more so – than the equestrian hunting tribe. Not being preoccupied with horses they show a closer interest, on the whole, in the venery. They are largely there with the express purpose of watching the houndwork, which cannot be said of most people who ride to hounds.

There is probably no better harehunting corner of the world than the Anglo-Scottish Border country where I hunted a pack of beagles forty years ago. Northumberland is the home of the Beagling Festival, at which, in the autumn, packs from all over Britain are taken by rotation, to be tried for a week or so over those lovely moorlands. The Trinity Foot, the pioneers of these visits, have been making the pilgrimage since 1888, when two North-umberland undergraduates, called Carr-Ellison (uncle of Sir Ralph, Master of the West Percy) and Allgood, first transported the university hounds to kennels at Carr-Ellison's home, Hedgeley Hall, Powburn. 'To beagle in Northumberland is to be transported into another world', wrote the Trinity Foot historian, James Knox, 'where the hares are bigger and stronger, where hounds seem to fly, not just to run, and where the inhabitants welcome the TFB as if it were a homecoming, in short where hunting is life and the country seems to be designed for his very purpose.'

The Festival has been under the aegis of the Newcastle and District beagles since 1946, when Colonel Leonard Gibson became Master of that pack. He first carried a whip to them in 1929, and did not give up until the end of the season of my visit in 1982 – a long innings by most standards. But not so by the measure of John Seymour-Williams, who took on the Master-ship of the Wick and District (on the south side of Bristol) in 1931 and was still hunting when I stayed with him and his wife for a meet in 1983. And even less so by that of old Betty McKeever, who became a Master in Kent aged eight, in 1909, when her father, William Dawes – an Anglo-New Zealand shipping magnate and Master of the Tickham foxhounds – pre-sented her with her first pack. By the age of twelve Betty Dawes was not only quite an experienced huntsman, but clever with a trout rod and shotgun, too. She was still Master and celebrating her eighty-sixth birthday (though travelling in a Land Rover) when we ran with her hounds (the Blean) from a meet near Throwley in 1987. The Daweses were one of Kent's most remark-able hunting families. Mrs McKeever's brother, Sandy Dawes, was also addicted to the chase from early childhood, and became, in his time, Master of the Mid-Kent Staghounds, deputy Master and huntsman of the Ashford Valley Foxhounds and Master of the Romney Marsh Harriers.

As I learned when staying the weekend with the chairman (and former Master) of the Ashford Valley foxhounds, Philip Buckland (to ride Mrs Hibbert-Foy's lovely chestnut mare, Amber, on the Saturday), his family set quite a Kentish record, too. Philip Buckland's grandfather, John, was the first Master of the Ashford Valley (when they were harriers). Then came Philip's astonishing father Harry, who began whipping in to John at the age of eleven. 'Harry's wonderful natural seat on his pony,' wrote his biog-rapher, 'his shrill holloaing, and the pretty figure he cut in his little hunts-man's coat and cap made a picture which old-time harriermen speak of with a sparkle in their eyes.' (Only pale shades there, however, of that infant prodigy, Robert Buckley Podmore, who was Master and huntsman of his own pack of harriers from the age of eight; who whipped in to the Barnstaple staghounds and the Vine foxhounds before he was twelve; and who died, aged fourteen, in 1907.)

Harry Buckland went on to be a champion point-to-point rider and winner of the Belgian international cross-country marathon at Spa. As 'chief honorary trainer and rider' to the Jewish-American magnate, Walter Winans, he broke the world equestrian high-jumping record, and kept it for thirty years, the pinnacle being 7 ft 2 in. (But that career was not achieved without a fractured skull, cerebral and spinal concussion, and his pelvis broken in four places, not to mention his heart knocked out of position. No wonder the doctors declined to pass him for active service in 1914.) He was Master, too, of the mid-Kent staghounds, in which guise we see him, through Sassoon's eyes as 'Buckman of the Coshford Vale'. ('I gazed at Harry Buckman with interest when he tit-tupped stylishly past me at the meet with his velvet cap cocked slightly over one ear'.) In 1913 Harry resigned as amateur huntsman of the mid-Kent to take the East Galway for a season; and he returned to the mid-Kent on the resurrection of that hunt in 1919. He was joint-Master of the Ashford Valley with the American Alfred Chester Beatty in the late 1920s; and his son, my host, was a Master of that hunt from 1961 to 1974. A good measure of the Bucklands' venatic heredity came, I think, from Philip's great-great-uncle, Charles Witherden, whose pride and joy was his private pack of harriers in the same district. If Witherden's hounds were still running when the light failed he would ram a stake into the ground at that point and turn to his followers, saying 'We'll come here at dawn gentlemen, and we'll start again!'

Returning to Kentish beagle packs, another Grand Old Person of the post Second World War period is Phil Burrows, of the Bolebroke. When we ran with those hounds in 1984 he was over eighty and confined to a car – but from which, cleverly positioned, he probably witnessed as much sport as anyone. He began whipping in to them when they were first established, in 1925, by Percy Mann. Burrows bought the pack in 1934, carried the horn and went on to win numerous prizes at the shows – until 1974 (when Tim Lyle and Moreen Hale took over). There are two main object-lessons for youth at the Bolebroke: firstly that of Phil Burrows, whose enthusiasm for the sport was inculcated in boyhood with the Eton Beagles; and, secondly, by the fact that Percy Mann's four dedicated hunting sons – Douglas, of the South and West Wilts, Alastair of the Vale of Aylesbury, Jock of the VWH and Thomas, who died in the war (but had been whipping in to the Trinity Foot in 1939) – were first attracted to hounds through the Bolebroke. On returning from my Bolebroke afternoon I telephoned Alastair Mann, who replied: 'Oh well, you see, our parents were regular mounted followers of both the Old Surrey and the Eridge and very interested in houndwork . . . They thought a pack of beagles would keep us boys out of mischief. We whipped in . . . and their enthusiasm rubbed off on all of us.'

The five school packs have made an enormous contribution to hunting. The senior of them, the Eton, with which I ran during the 1940s, were not recognised by the College authorities until 1860, though various boys kept hounds secretly there throughout the 1850s. The Eton College Hunt must receive the accolade for sending more distinguished names into the adult hunting world than any of the others. The 10th Duke of Beaufort, 'Master', whipped in there during the 1917–18 season; then wearing the famous brown velvet coat, between the early '30s and the late '60s, were the Earl of

Halifax (joint-Master and huntsman 1930–31); Major Gerald Gundry (joint-Master 1930–31); Lord Hugh Percy, afterwards Duke of Northumberland (joint-Master and huntsman 1931–32); Captain R. E. Wallace (joint-Master and huntsman 1936–38); Captain Charles Barclay (joint-Master and huntsman 1937–38); Sir Hugh Arbuthnot (joint-Master and huntsman 1939–40); Michael Holland-Hibbert, afterwards Viscount Knutsford (field-Master 1943–45); Captain Simon Clarke (joint-Master and huntsman 1953–54); Willie Poole (whipper-in 1957–58); Oliver Langdale (whipper-in 1961–62); Charles Stirling (joint-Master and huntsman 1964–65); and Richard Milburn (whipper-in 1965–67).

Ronnie Wallace's tally was probably the alltime record: sixty brace of hares and a fox in his first season and seventy-five brace of hares and three foxes in his second. I suppose it is not surprising that, as chairman of the MFHA, he came to be known as 'God'. I have been regaled with many a good story in regard to that. 'Have you heard the one about the Duke of Beaufort reaching the Pearly Gates?' a Taunton Vale farmer asked me at covertside. 'No? . . . Well, when St Peter welcomed him in, Master said "I don't think I like this place – there's no foxhunting". To which St Peter replied: "Oh don't worry about that, we'll lay one on tomorrow." At the heavenly meet Master, spotting a familiar figure in a green coat on the far side of the throng, accosted St Peter with: "That's looks like Ronnie Wallace, but surely he hasn't died so soon?" St Peter smiled indulgently at the Duke. "Oh no, that one is God, but he *thinks* he's Ronnie Wallace!"' At the end of a 1989 hound show at which Charlie Barclay and Wallace were judging together, Barclay made a speech, which included the following quip. 'When Ronnie climbed into bed with his wife, Rosie, one cold winter's night after hunting, Rosie exclaimed "God, your feet are cold!" To which his riposte is said to have been "you may address me as Ronnie in bed!" . . .' And so the jokes continue.

Dickie Milburn (later co-founder with Roger Palmer, of the Palmer Milburn Beagles) took the Eton pack home to Northumberland in 1967, catching 21½ brace of hares and six foxes in twenty-five days. His colleague, Roger Palmer, was too preoccupied at Eton with other animals – hamsters, ornamental pheasants, domestic rats, budgerigars and monkeys – to have time for the beagles; but, at Cambridge, he became hon secretary and 1st whipper-in to the Trinity Foot. He couples the Palmer-Milburn with Mastership, on Sundays, of the Berks and Buck Draghounds, to which he also carries the horn. And he leads a 6 am – 6 pm City life in between – a life, in other words, that would surely exhaust most men in a matter of weeks.

The second oldest public school pack, started in 1917, is the Ampleforth, with which my wife and I ran when her nephew, Patrick French, who kindly looked after us, was a boy there. I relish the picture of the first Master, 17-year-old Paddy Dunne-Cullinan, going home for the holidays to Co Meath when the First World War was raging, and complaining to his mother that – although the College was set in a potentially wonderful hunt country (the frontiers of the Middleton and Sinnington Foxhounds meet in the valley below the playing fields) – it sported no pack of hounds of its own. And Mrs

Dunne-Cullinan duly sending her son back on the ferry for the following term in the company of four couple of beagles. Thady Ryan, of the Scarteen, Robert Campbell, of the Garth and South Berks, Paddy Hartigan, of the Oakley, and Simon Roberts, of the Derwent, all benefitted by the apprenticeship of the Ampleforth Beagles. And what a wonderful country they had in which to enjoy it.

The Radley pack, another born in wartime, comes next. Towards the end of 1940, when the Battle of Britain was in full swing, three Radley College friends – all followers during the holidays of the East Essex foxhounds, and on school Saturday afternoons of the Christ Church Beagles (then under the inspiring Mastership of R. E. Wallace) – appealed to the school's sporting bursar, Charles Jenner, to support the motion for a school pack. Those boys were Rob Motion, Anthony Round and Nat Sherwood. It was, of course, a time when most packs were disbanding, but Jenner and the Warden (headmaster) were persuaded by the facts that a school enjoyed the advantage of a great deal of 'waste food'. Jenner, who became chairman, opened the minutes book with a quotation from Pope:

> To plains with well-bred beagles we repair
> And trace the mazez of the circling hare...

The boys constructed the kennels, did all the work and took the hounds home in the holidays. There was no kennel-huntsman until after the war. It was all very good practice. Rob Motion became a joint-Master of the Warwickshire hounds and Nat Sherwood, of the East Essex. Two more distinguished old Radleians, who once hunted the school pack are Anthony Hart (Cotswold Vale Farmers, Albrighton and South and West Wilts), the hon secretary of the MFHA; and James Crosbie Dawson (Vine and Craven). Owing to extensive urbanisation around Oxford the Radley have been obliged, like the Eton, to meet further and further away from their kennels. I joined them at Black Bourton, on their westernmost border, between Burford and Faringdon in October, 1986, where I had the great pleasure of meeting, among forty others, their stalwart *sine qua non* kennel-huntsman, Peter Coombes, and his wife.

Next on the school beagles scene, in 1952, came the Marlborough, who (alas) keep going without any kennelmen. The Marlborough beaglers not only feed and exercise the hounds and look after their kennels, they also see to their elementary veterinary needs, breed them, care for them in whelp, send their puppies out to walk, lay on the puppy show, escort them (to the Master's) home in the holidays, and hunt them in north Wales and elsewhere. I say 'alas' advisedly, because I was given the impression, from my 1982 visit (for their thirtieth anniversary opening meet) that all this was a bit too much for them, and rather hard on the hounds!

It was a trio of boys – James Bouskell, Martin Letts and Nicholas Wykes, regular followers of the Tedworth foxhounds on Saturday afternoons, who, in the winter of 1951–52 conceived the idea of a pack of beagles for Marlborough College. Wykes left after the Easter term; but with the advent, in the summer, of a new headmaster, Mr Garnett, who had expressed a wish to see more extra-mural activities, Bouskell and Letts proposed the hounds. The opening meet was in October, 1952. James Bouskell became Master of the Wilton foxhounds in 1983; Martin Letts was consecutively Master of the Northern and Eastern Counties Otterhounds, the Bolebroke Beagles and, since 1964, of the College Valley foxhounds. The principal names to emerge from Marlborough, apart from those mentioned, have been Alastair Jackson (Master, 1961–62), Stephen Lambert, (1965–67), Max Southwell (1959–60) and Jeremy Walters (1964–65).

The last public school to form a pack was Palladian Stowe – in 1962. The initial moving spirit there was Miss Rosemary Hill, a dyed-in-the-wool 'Diana', who was secretary to three successive headmasters, beginning with that visionary academic J. F. Roxburgh. Stowe's third headmaster was Donald Crichton-Miller, who arrived from Fettes in 1958 and who became a regular follower of the Grafton foxhounds. In 1961, Crichton-Miller, when interviewing Colonel Edward Walsh, a retired cavalry officer and a candidate for the post of bursar, asked 'You're keen on hunting, I believe?' Walsh, replying that he was 'very keen indeed' was promptly appointed. John Atkinson from Yorkshire's Colne Valley beagles was put on as huntsman; and while he acquired drafts of hounds from the Bolebroke and the Newcastle and District, Rosemary Hill made friends with the local landowners and Masters of Foxhounds, including Dick and Anne Hawkins who had me to stay for my Stowe Beagles day at the end of 1987. That school pack has been another resounding success story. Among the many familiar hunting names that have featured in their history are those of Charles Bartholemew, of the Avon Vale; the Bell Irving boys, from Dumfriesshire; Roderic Ando, of the Derwent; Tom Bannister, of the Pendle Forest and Craven; Adrian Dangar, of Spooner's and West Dartmoor; Frank Houghton Brown, of the South and West Wilts; and James Fanshawe of the North Cotswold.

Marlborough's Max Southwell and Alastair Jackson each went on to hunt the Royal Agricultural College beagles at Cirencester, a hunt whose history stems from the year 1893. Anthony Fillingham (who later had the Per Ardua beagles), Alan Fletcher (Taunton Vale foxhounds) and John Howard-Jones (South Oxfordshire) are among others who have carried the RAC horn. Luke White (whose great-grandfather, Lord Annaly, formed a famous partnership with Frank Freeman when the former was Master of the Pytchley) was hunting hounds when we had an afternoon at Cirencester in 1982. He went into his Bicester and Warden Mastership at the start of the 1985–86 season.

In 1987 I attended the fortieth anniversary meet of another college hunt for 'mud students', this time in East Kent – the Wye, which was established in 1947 by John Stevens who, later in life became a joint-Master of the Meynell and South Staffs. He had a great ally in Newton Rycroft, founder of the Dummer, to which Stevens had once proved a faithful whipper-in. Rycroft, who in 1947 happened to be busy moving from Dummer House, in Hampshire, to Gloucestershire, found it convenient to lend his hounds temporarily to Stevens, and the hunt was initially known as the 'Wye College and Dummer'.

Oxford and Cambridge, too, have given many future Masters of hounds and amateur huntsmen valuable experience in handling a pack. The Cambridge establishment, the Trinity Foot, stems, rather like the Eton College, from a number of very small student packs in the 1850s. In 1867, a Trinity don, an Irishman called Pat Currey brought some hounds over from Lismore and founded what he called 'the Foot Beagles'. Two seasons later the title 'Trinity Foot' was given. But this pack attracted relatively little attention in the University until the advent, in 1879, of a remarkable young man Rowland Hunt ('Mother' to his friends). Undergraduates who had been acquainted with the brilliant sport shown by Hunt as Master of the Eton Beagles flocked to his meets and the reputation soon spread. (A friend commented that the new Master must have had a compact with the dons, as he was rarely seen at lectures, hall or chapel). Anyhow he issued meet cards, engaged a professional kennel-huntsman, dressed himself and his whips in green velvet coats and generally put the TFB on the map.

From then onwards a bright galaxy of hunting names have carried the Trinity horn – Pease, Fitzwilliam, Carr-Ellison, Paget, Barclay, Holland-Hibbert, Straker, Whitbread, Hoare, Stirling, Cadbury, Kirkpatrick and Lambert, to mention a few. Edward Foster – whose father has been Master of the Wheatland foxhounds (the pack with which, incidentally, Rowland Hunt went on to make another name for himself) since 1961 – carried the TFB horn when we ran with them in 1977. There were still plenty of young field sportsmen at Cambridge in those days; but, sad to say, the following had much diminished when I enjoyed another afternoon with them in 1989 (from Longstowe Hall, the home of Michael Bevan, who was captain of M'Tutor's when I was a Lower Boy). The Masters told me then that they were pushed to find suitable candidates to carry whips. Advised by them, I attributed this in my *Country Life* article to the much greater preponderance of undergraduates selected entirely for their academic grades and the ever higher proportion accepted from the State schools. This received an immediate rebuke (published in the correspondence columns) from the University, in the person of Michael Tilby, the admissions Tutor of Selwyn College. Nevertheless the point I made was, I re-affirmed, irrefutable.

There were also hounds at Oxford, kenneled by undergraduates of Christ Church, from the middle of the last century, beagles, then harriers, then beagles again. In 1896 a second pack was formed by New College men. In 1903 New College teamed up with Magdalen and, in 1912, Trinity was brought in. In 1950 they united with the Christ Church to make a single university pack. Twenty years later the Christ Church and New College, as it was called, amalgamated with the Farley Hill – then under the Mastership of that distinguished breeder, the Hon Mrs Hermon-Worsley – both hunts having become seriously short of country. The combined hare hunting empire then extended into four foxhunting countries, the Bicester, Heythrop, Old Berks and Vale of Aylesbury.

Four Masters of the Eton Beagles followed one another in the Mastership of the Christ Church in the 1930 and early '40s – Charles Wood (afterwards Lord Halifax) and his brother Peter; Lord Hugh Percy (afterwards Duke of Northumberland) and R. E. Wallace. Alexander Fitzalan-Howard – one of three brothers who had carried the horn at Ampleforth and continued in the same capacity at Oxford – was Master and huntsman at the time of my visit, with the stalwart, Raglan Snell, as kennel-huntsman. Snell - whose career began with the VWH (Cricklade), where he was groom to Captain Maurice Kingscote in 1930 – took over the Christ Church kennels from Walter Clinkard at the time of the hunt's fusion with the Farley Hill.

Mention of the name Clinkard reminds me that Roy Clinkard, after working under his father, Walter, at the Christ Church kennels was put on as kennel-huntsman to the Aldershot by Brigadier Francis Gibson in 1958, and became a joint-Master of that hunt in 1971. With over a thousand rosettes to their name during the period 1960–85 the Aldershot must be easily the most successful beagle pack in the showring. They are pretty good in the field, too. 'To follow beagles in a tempest that takes the form of heavy rain, driven by a forty mph gale' – I wrote after following them in 1983 – 'must seem like insanity to those who prefer to put their feet up at the weekend, but . . . if, notwithstanding such conditions, there is a serving scent, good hounds will keep working as happy as sand boys and that rule prevailed on October 15 . . . I am sure I have never before witnessed a pack of hare-hounds hold a line in similar conditions with quite such tenacity for two hours, hunting very close without a lagger, a skirter or a babbler to be seen or heard . . .'

The Aldershot formed in 1970 (and now amalgamated with the Sandhurst) is not the oldest of the army packs; that distinction goes to the Colchester Garrison. The pack at Catterick Camp was 'got together in 1930 for the benefit of the officers of the garrison,' in the words of *Baily's Directory*; 'today the pack is supported by all ranks stationed in the garrison and district, as well as civilians, representation on the committee being approximately equal'. The commandant of the Royal Military Academy gave his blessing to the foundation of the Sandhurst Beagles in 1935 'to give the cadets the opportunity of learning about hunting and hound management'. Owing to urbanisation their country is now an appreciable distance west of Camberley. (The meet was at Stratfield Saye, Berkshire when I followed their hounds in 1985). The infantry, in particular, have a strong beagling background, the Durham Light Infantry, the Highland Light Infantry and the King's Shropshire Light Infantry being three of several regiments that have sported packs. In 1948 the School of Infantry establised their kennels at Warminster, and in 1960 (as I recorded in my 1986 report on that pack) '. . . the Army Beagling Association was formed. Beagling secured recognition as an official army sport, which meant that army packs were not required to pay rent for their kennels, soldiers could follow with as much justification as they could to play football, while Army hunts were entitled to grants from such sources as the Nuffield Trust . . .' Owing to an increasing civilian representation the School of Infantry hunt was re-constituted as the Wiltshire and Infantry in 1985.

The RAF formed their Beagling Association as early as 1951 when the Per Ardua hunt was started by Air Commodore Levis at Cranwell; but owing to lack of support in the Service, the pack was 'civilianised' in 1977. The Royal Navy's beagle hunt, the Britannia, is nearly a century older. When Lavinia and I stayed with the Master and huntsman, Admiral Sir James Eberle, and his wife, he led us to a little eminence a few paces from the kennels, at Dartmouth, and pointing down towards the lower reaches of the River Dart, indicated the point where two wooden-hulled ships-of-the-line, *Britannia* and *Hindostan* were moored from 1862. On board those two ships, he said, every one of the young officers of the Royal Navy, which then deployed the largest and most powerful fleet the world had ever known, lived and received their training (virtually as children). It was on board the *Britannia* that the Dartmouth pack began – at the instigation, during the 1870s, of one of the school's training staff, Lieutenant Guy Mainwaring. He began with a collection of mongrels of terrier strain, the leader of which was named Jim. (Jim Eberle called his history of the hunt *Jim, First of the Pack*, thus at once putting both himself and that mongrel in front). Although the Britannia remains a naval pack in name, Dartmouth has been heavily dependant upon civilian support ever since the cadet entry age was advanced from thirteen to eighteen, and particularly since cadets have been spending less than a year at the college.

Jim Eberle, who was Commander-in-Chief Home Fleet (an appointment also embracing a substantial NATO command) at the time of our visit in December, 1979, was obliged to react in a supportive tactical way to the Russian invasion of Afghanistan at the end of our day's hunting. After following his hounds for three hours of a very sporting afternoon he arrived with the rest of us, tired and mud-bespattered at the remote, pre-ordained farmhouse where the tea was given. Jim, on alert for the political crisis, had left the farmer's telephone number with his Flag Lieutenant. And a call came. 'Yes, no problem', we heard the Admiral reply (followed by an injunction to the following effect): 'send *Hood* and *Ajax*, and if they want a third make it *Achilles*.' That evening the admiral deployed his salt and pepper pots and wine glasses over his dining-room table, explaining to me how ships of the American fleet in the Mediterranean had been sent in a posturing mission to the coast near Afghanistan. Consequently NATO had requested ships from the Royal Navy to fill the vacuum in the Mediterranean. It was gratifying for the sportsmen to know that top international strategy could be conducted by a figure in a muddy beagling coat from a quiet farmhouse on a Devon hillside.

Then there is dear old Bertie Basset! What a gift he has been to cartoonists from the moment he reached our shores and became popular a little over a century ago – particularly the original *basset à jambes torses* with his crooked forelegs, long back and ground-dusting chest, his dismally puckered brow and pendulous ears and flews. The *jambes torses*, however, was never widely popular. Although the French treasured him as a truffle-hunter, they found him too ponderous for their *petite vénérie* (which usually consisted of following up game by scent, driving it from the rough and dispatching it with a gun). And since they found the *jambes droites* too fast for that pursuit they evolved a compromise, *le Griffon-Vendéen basset a jambes demi-torses*.

The first *demi-torses* to arrive in England (in the 1860s) were gifts from the Marquis de Tournon to Lord Galway. Between then and the turn of the century several small packs were bred, one of them belonging to the then Prince and Princess of Wales. Some more dedicated and enterprising hare-hunters were soon finding that the hypersensitive nose, stentorian music and tenacity of the *demi-torses* did much to compensate for his slow pace. The first basset hunt to be registered in *Baily's Directory* was founded in 1889 by Tom and Mornington Cannon, of racing fame. Then in 1891 two other brothers, Christopher and Godfrey Heseltine, established the Walhampton with drafts from the Cannon kennels. At the turn of the century Christopher Heseltine took another pack, but Godfrey continued, on and off, with the Walhampton. During one of his absences (in the 1920s) the artist Cecil Aldin hunted them and wrote this note in his autobiographical *Time I was Dead*: 'It was fun playing hide-and-seek with the timorous hare with those slow little hounds; the pace was never much more than an energetic man could walk, which is, in my opinion, the best pace to hunt the hare.' Put up for auction in 1933 the pack was bought by that distinguished venerer, Colonel Eric Morrison, who changed the name from Walhampton to Westerby, the village closest to their new kennels. Morrison was the man who first speeded up the English basset – by means, first of a harrier cross (the Dunston Gangway '48), and later by using Welsh, fell and other harrier blood. When we ran with the Westerby in 1979 Charlie Bevin was in his twenty-third season as Master and huntsman. 'Everywhere a thick mist lay over the snow,' I wrote. 'But, whenever they ran out of sight, they told you their direction with that song, which is distinctly louder, deeper and more musical than that of foxhounds or beagles. After their cry and low-scenting facility, the qualities which most impress you are their independent deter-mination and lack of flashiness. Far from simply joining the chorus, no hound gives tongue unless it owns the line; so, as they ran over the plough, they were nearly on top of one another, like a trail of termites. "For good honest hound-work give me bassets every time," one follower said to me. He meant, of course, "give me the Westerby".'

In 1988 I carried this story one chapter further on in the pages of *Country Life* through a sixtieth anniversary meet to the West Lodge harehounds held at the home of their Master, Neil Curtis, who lives in the country hunted by the De Burgh and North Essex hounds. (The compromising label 'hare-hounds' is explained by the fact that both hunts have a stronger element of harrier blood in their kennels than most basset packs). The West Lodge were originally beagles, established in 1928 by Sir Douglas Ritchie and disbanded in 1941. They were resurrected, in 1950, by Lionel Woolner, who, in the previous year had acquired a pure Griffon Vendée broken-coated basset bitch from Sir John Buchanan-Jardine's Castle Milk pack and put her to a prize-winning beagle. In 1950 Woolner received a couple of drafts from the Westerby, and later in the 1950s got most of the remainder of the Castle Milk pack, which were by then largely Griffon Vendée-harrier crosses, and were about to be disbanded. The West Lodge still contains a high proportion of hounds carrying the Griffon-Vendée broken coat. At the time of my visit they were going principally to the Westerby for their outcrosses, while the De Burgh and North Essex favoured Britain's premier harrier pack, the Cambridgeshire.

The climate on our 1988 afternoon was boisterous, but at about 3 30 pm the wind dropped and there was a sharp snap in the air. Just then about 100 yards ahead of the questing West Lodge a hare got up and as I recorded 'those long-backed, short-legged, long-eared hounds gave tongue – their deep, bell-like tongue – with real fervour for the first time ... The hare piloted them parallel with the River Stour until they checked for a minute or two. They hit off the line again on freshly drilled ground, bringing her round right-handed over the Cowlinge-Great Bradley road. On they ran uphill, in deep song, leaving Doley Wood on their right as they continued over the valley towards Little Bradley. There was a second brief check when another hare crossed the line, but with tenacious concentration hounds were rapidly closing the gap, and at 4.40 pm they had their reward, making it just on four miles as they ran. And so home to another glorious foot pack tea.'

### Buoyant Ireland

Foxhunting is still as synonymous with Ireland as skiing is with Switzerland or grouse shooting with Scotland. The sport is an integral part of Irish country life. Horses grow nowhere better in the world than on the Emerald Isle's rich pasture or the soft water of its streams, while horse trading plays an important part in the national economy. A love of horses – and hounds, too – runs deep in the veins of the country folk, whose passion for the chase is a byword. And there is little, if any, of the 'blood-sports' controversy – which so embitters the pursuit in mainland Britain – to restrain them from shouting their relish of hunting, so to speak, from the rooftops.

Yet riding to hounds in Ireland is not the unbridled joy it was, say, four decades ago. Stock farming being the principal form of husbandry it remains a land of grass, and, as every visitor remarks, very vivid grass it is. But, as that grass happens to be crucial to the national trade of cattle raising (as well as to foxhunting) the farmers, in their desperation to make ends meet, have discovered ways of increasing the ratio of stock to acres to an extent that would have been unthinkable half a century ago. Stud farms as well as dairy and beef farms have proliferated, and that has meant a massive increase in the laying of barbed wire. Almost every obstacle – whether bank, ditch, wall or thorn hedge – is threaded with that ugly commodity. So riding to hounds in Ireland is often a matter of follow-my-leader over the only accessible places. Electric wire, too, is much more prevalent than in England. And all too frequently it is left on at the main on hunting days.

Hounds that run into electric wire are unlikely to hunt again that day, nor perhaps, for a week or two afterwards. Attributing every sensation, whether of pleasure or of pain, to the men and women who rule their destiny, they look back, on being electrocuted, sterns between their legs, at their huntsman, a question-mark on their brows as though to say 'And what have we done wrong this time?' When I was riding, in 1985, with the Island hounds in Co Wexford, Mrs Charley Skrine, the hunt secretary, decribed to me how, when she had recently released a hound from an entanglement of electric wire, it had staggered on a few paces, obviously in a state of great shock. Then, seeing her, and believing she had inflicted the pain, it attacked her savagely, biting her deeply in both hands. The unfortunate creature was put down, while Rosemary Skrine was taken to hospital to have her hands stitched up.

Huge tracts of conifer plantation have sprung up in many parts since the war. But, although there is very little natural woodland, there are plenty of foxholding places, such as gorse whins, scrubland, thorn thickets and overgrown marshes. The fringes of the Irish farmland are still a joy to ride over. Although one should not generalise, it is about true to say that the Blazers country – Galway being on a limestone base – is more or less all walls; the Kilkenny is more ditches than walls; the Louth nearly all ditches and banks; the Meath predominantly ditches; the Kildare ditches and fences; and the Cork countries are mostly banks; while the Tipperary, Limerick, Wexford and Waterford countries hold a good measure of all four obstacles.

In my opinion the greatest pleasure to be had from Irish hunting is to be astride a good banker, one who knows just how to jump up onto that high bank or broad wall, and how to step nimbly over the ditch beyond. Feel as one with a horse like that and you are at one with the Irish countryside. The best, in my experience, was a grey cob called Paddy, lent me by Mrs Roch-Perks for my United day, and again the following season with the West Waterfords. 'He never hestitated once before those daunting banks,' I wrote, 'and never put a foot wrong in crossing them. I have rarely ridden a hunter that crossed Ireland with such aplomb.' Paddy was on a par with Freddie, the paragon George Chapman lent me for my Island day: 'I was allotted a gallant gelding from the hunt stables, Freddie Heineken, so called on account of his reputation – like that of the beer – "to reach the parts other horses cannot reach" – which was just as well considering there must have been well over forty doubles to be negotiated.'

But there has been quite a lot of rough to take with the smooth, and I have often been in some trepidation as to what sort of mount will be provided. 'We had such a beauty lined up for you,' said a certain Master in Co Cork, 'but, unfortunately it was lamed yesterday. So we've arranged a hireling.' I was greeted next morning by a wild-eyed unshaven coper holding a shaggy dull-coated little beast whose vertical shoulder, narrow front and rusty bit told me the worst. 'Sure, it'll jump over the moon for ye, it's a rare little wonder . . .' But just as I was mounting came this confidential afterthought: 'He does take a little bit of a h-o-u-ld, sorr.' And of course there was no stopping the brute except at the obstacles, at all of which he resolutely jibbed. It was pouring with rain when I found this hireling's box at the end of the day. The coper was in the pub, so I asked a girl who was about to go in there to inform him that I'd returned. A few seconds later she poked her head round the door: 'He says he'll be with you in about twenty minutes. He's finishing his drink.' To which I, by now soaking wet, replied: 'Well, would you be kind enough to inform him that he'll find his horse tied tight by the reins to the box and that I've gone home and the sooner he gets some rugs over the poor thing the better.' He charged £50 all the same.

Most of the harrier packs are now entered principally to fox, the hare – owing to intensive farming and the reprehensible practice of park coursing and other persecutions – having become a relatively rare mammal in most parts of Ireland, north and south. (Park coursing comprises catching up leverets, rearing them to adulthood, then setting them off in a long wire enclosure for the purpose of racing greyhounds at them. The hare, of course, has little or no chance of escape.)

In the mid-1970s the business of fox-pelt trapping began in some earnest throughout the British Isles. When the price offered by Continental furriers was relatively high, snaring was rife in England, particularly, I believe in the West Midlands and East Anglia. By the early 1980s, however, the trade was considerably reduced, except in Ireland, where the boom continued, furriers offering up to £25 a pelt. In many parts, gin traps as well as snares are liberally set, to the extent that dogs, cats – and hounds, too, are caught, along with other mammals besides foxes; and, because the trappers mostly fail to visit their iniquitous contraptions regularly, the victims frequently suffer great agonies before dying, or if they are 'lucky', wrench a foot off, to go three-legged for the rest of their days. The foxhunters bemoan this state of affairs, scarcely on account of the suffering caused, but because their quarry has been decimated.

As I say, there are a great deal more yobbos having a go at the wildlife of Ireland than there are in Britain. Hunting folk there complained to me, in the 1980s, that owing to the high prices paid for fox pelts the Irish countryside at night has been teeming with youths carrying .22 rifles, high-powered torches and vixen whistles, and that these criminals are accounting for far greater numbers of foxes than the traps. When I commented that, potentially, there's far less pain involved with the bullet than the snare they looked at me incredulously as though to say 'and what relevance can that have?'

The most outrageous incident I saw was with the East Down in Ulster, when a fox was put to ground in a bank and the Masters decided to dig. I saw two youths holding lurchers standing among the onlookers. When the fox was bolted these young men surreptitiously slipped the dogs, which, of course, set off with their tremendous stride, leaving the baying pack trailing behind them. The fox twisted this way and that, his brush weaving circles, but the lurchers caught him within seven or eight seconds' race from his earth. 'Why,' I asked the Master afterwards, 'did you not dismiss those two men? Surely they had no business to be at the dig with their dogs?' He gave me a pitiful headshake: 'Sure you can't do that in Northern Ireland. You start ordering fellers like that around and you'll get home to find your house burned down!' Thus, anarchy reaches the hunting-field. On several occasions in the south, when foxes went to ground, I witnessed the huntsman being instructed to lift his hounds straight on to the next draw without a pause in case men with terriers and spades who dug out foxes for their pelts were hovering nearby to spot the point where hounds marked. Unfortunately the pelt men share a fairly sound knowledge of where the used earths are, and I have, on more than one occasion, heard exchanges of intelligence in the pubs. (I am happy to add, however, that by 1989 fox pelts were fetching such small sums that these unpleasant practices were much reduced.)

Whenever possible not only are Irish meets staged at pubs, but everyone finishes the day at the same haven. The hot toddy is the favourite tipple, the sort of potion you might take for 'flu (only with twice the whisky, of course, and no Lemsip!) At the meet the 'Irish', the 'Paddy', is probably taken cold. At the end of the day, while horses are languishing for hours in their trailers and boxes, pubs are throbbing with foxhunters, all largesse, their toddies steaming to the ceilings. In the more remote parts sportsmen and women, in their conversation, express mild surprise that a journalist from England should bother with them. 'Are ye anthin' to do with that Foxford feller from the *Horse and Hound*?' a worthy enquired of me through the whisky steam of a bar in Co Antrim. 'I'm not,' I replied. 'Has he been out with you?' The man looked amazed: 'Oh, God no! No writin' feller's ever bin to the'Antr'm hurriers till y'came.'

Parking my car in Drimoleague (towards the southwest corner of Co Cork) for a Sunday with the West Carbery – the hunt of which that great and witty author, Edith Somerville, was once Master – I saw two middle-aged couples, arm-in-arm, dressed for Mass and heading for the church. On the opposite side of the road a publican stood, arms akimbo, in the doorway of his inn which he'd opened especially for the hunt. The two male churchgoers, seeing the pub open, glanced quickly at their watches, detached themselves from the arms of their wives and stepped smartly across the road, only to be stopped firmly by the landlord: 'Honters only!' he told them, while letting me in with my passport of boots and breeches.

Talking of church and hunting, when Lavinia and I stayed at Scarteen with Thady Ryan in 1973, to see his celebrated Black-and-Tans, he escorted us to Mass saying 'I want to show you how the Kerry Beagle trencher-fed hunting lads go about their business.' We arrived to see a dozen men, close by the church, each holding a hound or two on leashes. Their wives, or girlfriends, were already inside waiting for the liturgy to begin. When the priest finished administering the sacrament in the nave, he proceeded outside, where the foxhunters, each holding their precious charges, had formed their queue to take the host. And each, having received it, lost no time in heading for the meet.

Thady emphasised, as I say, that those hounds were, for the most part, Kerry Beagles, a breed with which southern and western parts of the country have been familiar for 400 years and more, a French breed that reached Ireland from Spain in the sixteenth century. (The term 'beagle' in the old days, referred not so much to height as to any light-boned hunting dog.) In his excellent book *The Ryan Family and the Scarteen Hounds* Major

Michael MacEwan states that an eighteenth-century John Ryan was the family member who used a fresh outcross from France to give the Scarteen Kerry beagles their unique pure black-and-tan. Not unnaturally their appearance is a good deal closer to the French staghound than the English foxhound, and they are famous for their deep resonant cry, their speed and hard-driving quality and the fact that they react more adversely than most to insensitive handling. Joseph Pickersgill, the widely experienced amateur, who hunted them for Thady's father in the 1931–32 season, wrote of their unique manner of casting: 'When the leaders are at fault the tail-hounds fan round them to left and right, driving on at the same time. If they are still at fault, they will make a big cast all the way round, as a pack – not as individuals, as fell hounds do – and most of this at the gallop . . . I don't think I have ever seen another pack of foxhounds do a really big all-round-your-hat cast quite on their own . . .' Thady and Anne Ryan retired to New Zealand in 1987, their son, Christopher, having become joint-Master and huntsman in 1986, to continue a three-centuries family tradition.

One of the most interesting Irish foxhunting sagas is that of Tom and Elsie Morgan, with whose West Waterford hounds I rode in 1983. Married in 1946 in their native Gwent, the Morgans' first pack was in Germany where Tom was serving with the Rhine Army and Elsie was on the European show-jumping circuit. When they retired to Ireland in 1949 he became secretary to the West Waterfords, and when the Masters of that hunt, Major and Mrs Anthony Burke, transferred to the Ballymacads, the Morgans took over, with Elsie as huntsman. To their great advantage that towering American houndsman, Ikey Bell – once Master of the Galway Blazers and the Kilkenny, but more famously, perhaps, of the South and West Wilts – was living nearby, and was immediately impressed by Elsie's horsemanship, her remarkable rapport with animals and her style and flair as a huntsman. During my stay the Morgans showed me her signed copy of Bell's classic *A Huntsman's Log Book*. 'To Elsie Morgan,' runs the inscription; 'after watching you handling hounds in the field, I don't know why I ever had the temerity to write a book. Ikey.' With that statement he turned to her and added: 'I'm going to breed you a pack worthy of your talent.' And he did. He asked his friends the Duke of Beaufort, Sir Peter Farquhar, Sir John Buchanan-Jardine, Sir Alfred Goodson and Colonel Peach Borwick for drafts of hounds 'for this genius woman', as he put it, and it was upon those that the Morgans' pack was composed. Bell had for long harboured an affectionately sneaking feeling for the fell hound. After seeing the College Valley in action he told their creator, Bill Goodson, 'I wish I had used fell and not Welsh when I bred the South and West Wilts.' And he urged the Morgans to make College Valley their base blood. The result was to be one of the most effective packs that ever hunted the fox in Ireland. Little Elsie was just seventy when I hunted with her. 'When she jumped the lofty walls ahead of us,' I wrote, 'there is so little height to her that at first it seemed she was vanishing into pits on the far side.'

As to the comparative standards of hunt establishments, no greater con-

1988: receiving a warm French greeting.

At the start of the *curée* which concluded my day with the Rallye Vouzeron.

A moment during the 1988 Pony Club polo championships. 'Over half our players of 4 handicaps and above emerged from the Pony Club'.

England versus USA, Smith's Lawn, 1988. The tough hurly-burly of high-goal polo bears little resemblance to the game I knew as a player.

trasts can be found in the world than in Ireland. There are kennels like the impeccable West Waterfords, Scarteens, or the Kilkennys – situated at the McCalmonts' home, Mount Juliet, which are on a par with Badminton or Belvoir, and whose inmates also rank with the finest in Britain – and those of some of the more motley harrier packs, whose accommodation may be a dilapidated corrugated iron shed and an earthern floor, rendered deep with mud in winter, kennels which in Britain would be quickly and roundly condemned by the RSPCA.

As for Masters, I have ridden on separate occasions in Ireland with a Canadian, two Americans and an Austrian. Gene Kruger, the bearded billionaire Canadian in whose hands lay the fortunes of the Meath when I rode with them in 1977, owned such an immense tract of conifer forest in his homeland that, by the time one end had grown mature for the lumberjacks, the saplings at the other were well on the way, and so *ad infinitum*. Being in his seventies, Kruger liked to amble his horse from draw to draw, and insisted on the field keeping behind him. A joint-Master – coaxed by the subscribers, who were understandably irked by this dawdling, especially on rainy days – offered to arrange a car and chauffeur to convey him to fresh draws. To which Kruger replied that he was damned if he was going to continue sinking £35,000 a year into the hunt 'if I can't do as I darn well please'. As a matter of fact he had two joints, the other being his Austrian wife, a girl nearly forty years his junior (and some ten inches taller, too), who had been his skiing instructor, then his secretary. Kruger was so tickled by his experience of placating a certain farmer one evening when he first took on the Mastership, that he collapsed in giggles at every few words of the story, as related to us, tears rolling into his beard. The gist of it was that he was surprised to be met at the door by a man with a candle. 'Don't you have electricity here yet?' he asked. 'Ah, sure I do, but I only turns it on to find me candle!'

Another millionaire, the American Thomas Fields Long, a former successful Maryland hunt cup rider, had the Kildares when Lavinia and I stayed with Pat and Celia Conolly-Carew (he was field Master) for a day with them in 1972. It was my first experience in Ireland of hostile farmers, in particular of farmer immigrants from western parts, where there is no hunting tradition, who had been allotted smallholdings by the Land Commission, in old established hunt countries. Fields Long, who had been used to buying people off who frustrated his wishes, met his match with some of these farmers. I remember finishing the day in a real 'birdcage' bit of country the only gap out of which was barred by an irate young man (not the first one of the day) with a pitchfork. Fields Long, by nature rather arrogant, was obliged to eat very humble and apologetic pie.

A charming American woman, Jean Cameron, the widow of an Englishman, Colonel Charles Cameron, was at the helm of the Ballymacads at the time of our visit in 1987. She rode sidesaddle, with a green coat and a blue skirt, and, so everyone told us, 'still goes beautifully', though of a ripe age. Unfortunately – although she dressed up for a photograph at the kennels – we did not see her or hounds in action, as Ireland was snowbound that

January, which reminds me that our Ballymacad host, Commander Oliver Stoney, the hunt secretary, also had Lady Cusack Smith, formerly the legendary Mollie O'Rorke, staying with him and his wife. Mollie had been Master of the Galway Blazers during the period 1939–43 and, with her husband, Sir Dermot, founded the Bermingham and North Galway in 1946, but her hunting days were long over by the time we met her. We made note of the fact, however, that she had a very sporting capacity for the consumption of gins-and-tonics. In her youth, so we were told, she was celebrated for her ability to blow a hunting horn from one corner of her mouth while smoking a cigarette from the other.

Next to the Ballymacads lie the Westmeaths of which Lavinia's mother's family, the Deases, were leading lights and with which we had great fun staying with William and Petia Harvey Kelly, in 1972. I very much like the story of the advent of the American, Harry Worcester Smith, who took the Westmeath Mastership for a few seasons before the First World War. His large retinue included a negro hunt servant who whipped in. A cottager seeing, for the first time, a black face, crossed herself in a frenzy, crying 'Oh, God help the poor feller, let's pray he'll recover by tomorrer!'

While Irish hospitality is rightly famous I have always been wary of Irish bedrooms and creature comfort in general. Frequently the electric fires either don't work or they electrocute you at the plug or on their frayed wires: on more than one occasion, in rooms I have been allotted, several window-panes have been missing: and guest room beds are equipped with duvets, which, being anathema to me, I soon got into the habit of travelling with a couple of blankets and sheets. But I have found a considerably greater contrast in Master's houses over there than in mainland Britain. For example the North Down found me in Bill Montgomery's imposing house, Grey-abbey on Ulster's Ards Peninsular; the West Carberys in a coastguard's bungalow; the Waterfords, West Waterfords and Kilmogannys in the mighty and charmingly disshevelled pile that is Curraghmore with its eleph-ant-foot umbrella stand and cobra lampstand (Tyrone Waterford being an old Blues friend); the Longford harriers in a tiny farm cabin; and the Galway blazers in Peter Patrick and Anne Hemphill's elegant old family home, Tulira. But for a really typical Irish hunting home I would name the McClin-tock's Rochestown, near Cahir, where I stayed for a day with the 'Gallant Tipps', the Tipperarys. The strength of the warm welcome and hospitality was matched about equally with that of the feeling that the house might fall down around one's ears at any moment.

Ireland's grandest hunting base was Mount Juliet, the home of Victor and Bunny McCalmont – he was Master and huntsman of the Kilkennys, and for a time of the Wexfords, too – the house he sold after Bunny's death in the hunting-field in 1987. The visitor found everything done in lavish style, from the valeting of his clothes to the delivery of his breakfast, and that of his wife, to their bedroom, the former's brought in by a liveried butler and the latter's by a well starched maid. I recall what must have been the deepest piled carpets, the brightest and largest chandeliers, the longest dining-room table and the most stunning collection of pictures and porcelain in all Ireland. Bunny rarely seated her guests before ten, nor had them out of the room before midnight. A dinner party generally included an amateur entertainer or two, who were expected to lay on some sort of post-prandial cabaret. For one of our visits she invited the notorious Alexander brothers, Johnny and Broosie, both well-known raconteurs, to stay. We shall never forget the volume of merry mirth when, after dinner, Johnny fell asleep in an armchair during one of his brother's stories, to be awoken by much clapping and laughter from our hosts and the dozen or so other guests.

There being hot rivalry between the brothers, Johnny immediately jumped to his feet, and to the audiences's even greater ammusement, unwittingly related the same story that Broosie had just told. (It was the one about the Millionaire Charles Clore enquiring of the Irish doorman of the Dorchester Hotel what he had been doing lately. 'I've just returned from Rome, and do you know what, sorr, I received the blessin' of the Pope.' Clore was enthusiastic: 'Oh, I'd just love to do that, but of course he'd never receive me, not being a Catholic.' But the doorman was encouraging: 'Sure he would, Mr Clore, all you need do is slip him £1,000 in lire for the Vatican funds.' So away flew Clore to Italy and deposited his donation in the right quarter. When, with others, he presented himself for the blessing, however, the Pope entirely ignored him. And to his further consternation he saw the great man make what appeared to be the sign of the cross over a filthy bearded hippie sitting in the corner of the room on a bedroll. 'How did you get the blessing?' – Clore accosted the ragamuffin as the latter was clambering to his feet – 'and I didn't get it, considering I gave a lot of money for it?' The hippie looked up at the millionaire in amused amazement: 'You 'ave to be jokin', that was no blessin! The old man pointed down at my bedroll and then at the door and though I didn't understand 'is lingo I understood him say: "Pick up your 'effin palliasse and b . . . orf!")' The applause of the McCalmonts' guests at hearing the story a second time was, of course, more in the nature of mockery than appreciation of the joke itself, but none the less keen for all that.

As I say Victor kenneled the best bred and what may have been the most effective foxcatching pack in all Ireland. Towards the end of a day I enjoyed with him, the Kilkenny hounds had been hunting their fox for some twenty minutes when he led the lot of them onto a railway line, down which the Dublin-Waterford express was thundering from the opposite direction. Victor went white with horror. 'My God!' – he turned to me as we galloped parallel below the embankment – 'It'll take me ten years to breed up another lot like that!' By amazing fortune, however, the fox piloted them off the line in the nick of time.

Whenever my memory returns to Irish sporting visits I perhaps recall the brave spectacle of that elegant girl, Antonia Cattell, Master and huntsman of the Muskerrys, faced, one green-gold evening, by the loud and seemingly interminable tirade of a farmer's wife in a gateway, which Antonia, dismounting, ignored without a word, and strode across the adjoining field to call up her hounds to go home. Or that rich sensation of history I felt during our Louth visit, seeing the great doorway at Lisrenny, it old wooden portals studded with foxes' brushes, fresh brushes nailed over the rotting ones below, by generations of Filgates since early in the eighteenth century. Or I may remember the impressive sight of Fergie Sutherland, his wooden leg firm in its leather bucket as he took banks six feet high with the Uniteds; or those bright young rustics, ash plants thrust down their boots, out with the West Carbery, calling ecstatically across their shoulders to their friends after jumping some daunting bank or other 'did ye have that one? Did ye *have* it?' or little Elsie Morgan planting a kiss on the cheek of every member of the West Waterfords before mounting her mare to hunt hounds on her seventieth birthday; or that marvellous stay again at Curraghmore, in 1988, when Tyrone mounted me so handsomely for another Kilkenny day, gave me a day's shooting, and escorted me to hunt with the Kilmoganny when Rory Dicker carried the horn. Or Robin and Lavinia Boyd taking their dogs at midnight to hunt the rats in their stables on our return from a dinner party during my Duhallow visit; or getting in at the kill on a borrowed horse after mine was lamed for the Wexford's longest run of the season; or that long day with the Louth when old Billy Filgate caught his thousandth fox; or Toby Daresbury – of Belvoir, as well as Limerick fame – donning a kennel coat and putting on a kennel-huntsman act, dropping 'sirs' and 'madams' and doffing his cap as he handed us kennel lists on the Sunday morning after our Limerick day. But as any regular visitor would concur, you rarely return from the Irish hunting-field without some adventure or colourful little incident to relate.

### Scarlet Coats Abroad

Not only was foxhunting, the Meynellian science, first cultivated in England but the English foxhound, the English approach to hunting, the English hunting horn and English dress – even down to the mahogany-topped boot, the cut of the scarlet coat and the construction and knotting of the hunting tie or stock – were adopted almost wherever the tentacles of our old Empire reached.

In colonial America the seed was pre-Meynellian. When, in the 1740s, Lord Fairfax, great-grandson of the Parliamentary general, inherited from his maternal grandfather, Lord Culpeper, what was described as 'the most desirable estate in the English Colonies', the north neck of Virginia, he sailed out with a few couple of the old 'Southern-mouthed' hounds. One of his employees was the future founder of the independent nation – the then sixteen-year-old George Washington, a surveyor, who recorded of those days that 'we were much engaged in the hunting of wild foxes'.

When Washington (the father of American foxhunting as well as the founder of the nation) came into his Mount Vernon estate two decades later, he wasted no time in building and filling a foxhound kennels complex. America's native grey fox, decribing a circle like a hare when chased, gave relatively poor sport. Shortly before the Revolution, red foxes from England were therefore imported and released. Soon after the turn of the century they were being pursued by descendants of the 'new English foxhound'. Now, there are many different strains of hounds in the 130 and more American packs, but the British methods of hunting and modes of dress have been followed more or less faithfully since the eighteenth century. The traditional scarlet uniform coat, which had been associated in the American mind only with George III's hated army, was readily adopted for the hunting-field.

English foxhounds first went to Canada with some of the United Empire Loyalist families, who, deserting Washington's regime, travelled north from Virginia to make new homes around Montreal and Toronto. Thirty years later, following the successful conclusion of Wellington's Peninsular campaign, one or two of the regiments drafted to Canada founded garrison packs. The Montreal Hunt, starting 1826, is the oldest of the thirteen surviving Canadian hunts. The hounds and the methods of the chase have remained almost entirely British, and British experts are still frequently invited to judge at the Canadian hound shows.

The same happened in Australia, to which continent English hounds were first shipped in 1810. They were 'entered to' dingo and kangaroo until the 1840s when Thomas ('Gentleman') Pyke, a Wiltshire man, introduced the European fox into the Werribee district of Victoria. A decade later George Watson, a member of the celebrated venatic family of Co Carlow, founded the Melbourne; and, according to the hunt's entry in *Baily's Directory*, 'all our hounds of today can be traced back to the orginal breed'. Australia's other sixteen establishments also kennel English foxhounds and look to the most successful British packs for their outcrosses. Tasmania, like Victoria, is another hunting stronghold. The island had its first convict settlement in 1803. With the convicts came soldiers and with them horses and hounds, although English foxhounds were not imported until 1848, when they came from the Duke of Beaufort's kennels.

The Australian traditions remain British and so do those of New Zealand to which the English settlers introduced the red deer as a quarry species in 1851, and the fallow deer and the hare during the 1860s. Most of New Zealand's twenty-two organisations (while all using English hounds) follow drag-lines, though some still hunt hare.

It seems that wherever the British established themselves, up to thirty years ago, their foxhounds followed. When Iraq became a British mandate in 1919, officers of the Indian Army Service Corps promptly founded the Royal Exodus at Baghdad; and in the early 1930s the British administration in Palestine started up the Ramle Vale; both hunted jackal. The Ramle survived the Second World War, during which it was hunted as 'the Ludd'. The British Army brought foxhounds to Ceylon in 1893, to Hong Kong in 1924 and to Sudan in 1925.

Kenya boasted three packs and Southern Rhodesia another. In South Africa, in the 1880s, the Rand Hunt grew with the advent of British gold prospectors. The Cape Hunt, another essentially English foundation dating from about 1820, still survives in pursuit of jackal and drag.

Of India's eighteen pre-war jackal hunts, sixteen were founded and run

by the British Raj under the auspices of the Masters of Foxhounds Association of India. The only survivor is the Ootacamund, which is supported
and patronised almost entirely by Pakistan's three armed services. They
breed their hounds on traditional lines and occasionally import fresh drafts
from England. As the sun was setting on the old Indian army, the British
Army of the Rhine formed three packs and the British garrisons in Egypt and
Tripolitania two more.

Turning to Europe – first to Russia – the English community at St Peters-
burg introduced hounds to hunt the foxes there during the 1880s and '90s. In
Hungary, the Budapest foxhunt was established under the Austro-Hungar-
ian Imperial regime and run with English hounds and most of the trappings
and style of a British organisation. It was abolished with the revolution of
1918, but revived as the Orkèny in 1927 – until its termination in the Second
World War.

In 1835, George Stanhope, 6th Earl of Chesterfield, who had then just
relinquished his Mastership of the Royal Buckhounds, laid the foundations
of the Rome Hunt (Societa Romana Della Caccia Alla Volpe). He travelled to
Rome early that year on the advice of his doctor, his wife being a victim of
tuberculosis. As he rode along the Appian Way one morning, a fox crossed
his path, and, seeing what magnificent hunt country the Campagna
Romana would make, he wasted no time in sending home for hounds,
hunters, huntsman, whipper-in and kennelman.

That winter, meeting two days a week, Chesterfield was regularly followed by a large group of Italian equestrian friends. When he returned to
England in 1837, Prince Odescalchi took over, and the Rome Hunt has
remained an Italian affair ever since; the professional huntsmen were
always English or Irish (except between 1895 and 1907) until Count Cigala
Fulgosi succeeded to the Mastership in the 1960s and carried the horn
himself. The hounds are still spoken to in English and, says Cigala Fulgosi,
'a sort of pidgin Roman-English is the *lingua franca* in kennels.'

In Andalusia the Calpe hunt originated with the foxhounds shipped to
Gibraltar in 1812 by the Rev Mark Mackereth – chaplain to the Governor, the
Duke of Kent – to deal with a plague of foxes there. The Napoleonic 'army of
observation' having just been withdrawn from the surrounding district, the
Rev Mark's horn was soon to be heard echoing through the Andalusian
corkwoods and olive groves beyond the colony. The hunt assumed the title
'Royal' in 1906 when Edward VII and Alfonso XIII agreed to become its
patrons.

In April 1939, the Royal Calpe hounds met for the last time, but they have
their successors. In 1978 Major and Mrs Peter Hall founded the Guadiaro,
which, from a kennelful of English harriers, hunts the fox in the same
country as the old Calpe, with a strong contingent of Gibraltar officers and
their families in support.

The blood of the several drafts of foxhounds, which were sent to Portugal
in 1810–13 for the diversion of Wellington's Peninsular army, might be
found in many dogs in France, Spain and Portugal today. Their presence

gave rise to two European hunts, one in the French Pyrenees, the Pau, and the other near Lisbon, the Equipagem de Santo Huberto.

The Portuguese were particularly impressed with the *équipage* of the hounds in train of Wellington's headquarters, which were taken to the Peninsula by his two ADCs, Lord Worcester and Lord Tweeddale. The colourful Tom Crane, a private in the Coldstream Guards, and previously huntsman to a Scottish Border pack, exchanged his guardsman's scarlet for foxhunter's scarlet early in 1810. During campaign lulls he soon found himself and his pack at the head of very large equestrian fields, a dazzle of different uniforms.

With the abdication of Napoleon, the accession of Louis XVIII and temporary peace with France, a proportion of Wellington's army settled for the winter of 1814–15 in the French Pyrenees. A regiment stationed at Pau then indulged in some serious foxhunting with the hounds that had followed across Spain with their commissariat. Pau proved such an agreeable resort that several of the officers bought villas there and permanent kennels were built. The town became known as *La Ville Anglaise*, and the hunt as *la chasse Anglaise*, or *le sport Anglais*.

The Pau fell into abeyance during the 1820s, but was revived in 1840 by Sir Henry Oxenden. It then had a succession of English and American Masters, until the Second World War when it was disbanded. In the late 1940s the hunt was restored by the French – with English hounds – but more as a drag than a foxhunt.

The influence of the various packs in train with the Peninsular army was much stronger, if less direct, in Portugal than in France. It is difficult to imagine an instance where the British character has blended better with the exotic than in the case of the Equipagem de Santo Huberto. There was little tradition of venery in Portugal, but one or two of those who witnessed the exhilarating activities of the chase, as displayed by the British army in 1810–11, determined to establish *equipagem de montaría* of their own and to hunt the fox in the *modo de Inglaterra*.

A little later in the nineteenth century three *equipagem* were founded, with English foxhounds and hunt servants faithfully dressed in British scarlet coats and mahogany-topped boots. It was on returning from hunting, in 1908, that Carlos I (the penultimate King of Portugal and an ardent devotee of the chase) and his son were assassinated. Those foundations expired with the Second World War, but the spirits of all three were reincarnated in 1950 in the Equipagem de Santo Huberto.

Drafts of foxhounds were purchased from a variety of British kennels, and a succession of professional British huntsmen were commissioned to carry the horn to them. The founders insisted that everything should be conducted in the English style. Even when, in the 1970s, the Masters were obliged to resort to a Portuguese huntsman, the hunt language has remained in English.

Twice a week, each Portuguese winter, a bright cavalcade of some thirty horsemen and women, following a handsome pack of English foxhounds can be seen winding through the cork and conifer forests, a few miles across the River Tagus from Lisbon. A dozen or so of the cavaliers are dressed in the style of English hunt servants, while others wear black coats with their velvet caps. Their mounts are less stereotyped: some pure Arab, a few Irish, others barb, two or three of the *rejoneador's* sort, and one, unmistakeably of English Thoroughbred strains. This is how Lavinia and I remembered the scene when we sampled a day with the Equipagem in 1974. The Master was an Austrian businessman, a heavyweight of roguish reputation who rejoiced in the name of Baron Frederic de Beck (the title derived, so we were told, from his father, a tailor dubiously granted it by the last – deposed and exiled – Emperor, in default of a very large outstanding bill). De Beck who relished the clamour and guffawing that greeted his outrageous remarks, always sought the largest possible audience to acclaim them. True to form he dropped a good one in our presence. He had provided a horse for John Ure, the newly arrived Councillor at the British Embassy, whose wife, a woman with a cachet for beauty, was to arrive the following week. When Ure duly thanked him in front of the other followers at the meet, de Beck countered in a loud voice with 'not at all, and I very much look forward to mounting your lovely young wife!' And with that amid the appreciative laughter he sought, he ordered his huntsman, José Nogueira, to move off.

The shadows, first of cork, then of eucalyptus, then of pine dappled softly over the equestrian figures, and the forest was so quiet, so little touched by the hand of man that we imagined the scene belonging closer to the eighteenth century than the twentieth. The procession seldom stopped, for the hounds drew on, pausing only momentarily for a fuller investigation of, say a tangle of brambles or bracken, or a broom thicket. Then it was 'Loo in, my bee-ooties!' carefully modulated on José's lips. Riding just behind were the two joint-Masters, de Beck and Senhor Belo de Moraes. A discreet distance behind them came the followers led by the field Master, Senhor Antonio de Brito e Cunha. One young Lisbon blade, impatient with the shuffling trot gave his pretty Arab a zig-zagging pipe-opener between the gorse and mimosa clumps, to be cautioned by Brito e Cunha, when he advanced too far, with 'I say, I say, sta-idy there! H-o-l-d h-a-r-d!' like an imitation of linguaphone Leicestershire.

'Yeet, tray, hay, hay!' urged José as the trotting phalanx threaded through a fresh pattern of cork, whose trunks and lower limbs showed the stark cocoa-coloured underbark, where the cutters had removed the precious commodity. There seemed to be no end to the silence of this unenclosed wilderness. Until gun-shots rang out. Then we knew the forest was shared by other weekend hunters. Baron de Beck leant across from his Irish chestnut to let us know how much he hoped they 'only intend to shoot the birds'. He implied 'and not us'. For these game-shots had a reputation for popping off at anything that flickered; but, when the hunt went by, they called their dogs and gazed up, delighted at the unexpected pageantry. Their display of pleasure was not reciprocated: the sight of the guns reminded the foxhunters that, here, increasing areas of land had been fenced off as shooting reserves, to which horses and hounds were forbidden entry and to which the hunted fox escaped, probably to be shot, to be poisoned or to be trapped by the gamekeepers.

A hound spoke. 'Hake to Playmate, hake!' (None of your Isabel nor Rosario; these are *English* hounds making *English* sport.) The frost that lay in the open during the early hours and the dew in the woody fastnesses had long since dried, and we wondered how the scorching sand could hold any trace of scent; but they were all on now, and the trotting retinue gathered into a canter, permeating through the eucalyptus to the fir. A check. 'Hold hard, I say!' The line was retraced; the hunt proceeded for two miles. Then, 'he has certainly gone to ground', explained the young Count of Monsaraz, Director of Portugal's Turf Club and an amateur whipper-in; but hounds will not mark; they are held back ... 'What measure do you now take in England? ... A terrier? We could not do that; it might catch him. Foxes are too scarce here to allow any killing except in the open.' I rode up to examine the earth. Strange: there were so many foxes' padmarks around the entrances; it looked as though half a dozen chose this retreat.

They hunted two more across three miles with scarcely a serving scent. We were told that conditions were 'quite abnormal'. Never mind, it was a rare privilege to follow hounds through those lovely evergreen woods with their scents of gorse and thyme and eucalyptus in the warm air. At two o'clock Baron de Beck decided it was time for luncheon. He gave José the signal. The cavalcade raced back, without a pause, and it proved advisable to keep well up at this moment, for they cantered nearly all the way, and, without the music of hounds to guide us, it was easy to get lost. In a trice these hounds with the old English look were home in the capacious and beautifully kept kennels at Santo Estavao which were built in 1962 by de Beck, with Senhor Brito e Cunha as architect.

The pre-prandial scene at the adjacent club-house reminded us of the players' section of a polo pavilion; muddy white breeches and sweat-stained boots lay outside the steaming showers, from which poured excited talk of horses and the sport they provide in general. For the equipagem was more than a hunt: it was an equitation club. Next door, below walls hung with foxes' masks and Leech's paintings from Surtees, whisky was ordered and glasses were raised towards the photograph of that august figure, The Countess of Barcelona, co-founder and honorary Master, dressed in side-saddle habit, who if she was never to be the Queen of Spain she should have been, has reigned for four decades or so where St Hubert's spirit moves in Portugal.

The First Troop, Philadelphia City Cavalry, the oldest military unit of the United States, celebrated its 200th anniversary on 15 November 1974, the night Lavinia and I flew into the 'Quaker City'; and, since that band of horse-soldiers was formed from America's first substantial sporting organisation, the Gloucester Foxhunting Club, it seemed an auspicious date on which to touch down for a hunting tour of five of the eastern and southern states, a tour organised by my erstwhile stepfather, Colonel John L. Hornor Jnr, with whom, as I mentioned in an earlier chapter, I first hunted in

Virginia, in 1946–47. We stayed near Philadelphia initially, with Harry Nicholas, their President of the Masters of Foxhounds Association, the walls of whose house were crammed with pictures by Munnings and other British sporting artists. (I was to be astonished, throughout our tour, at the number of good original British sporting pictures hanging in the homes of many of the Master of Foxhounds and others we visited.) On 16 November, we hunted with the Pickering, of which Nicholas had just relinquished the Mastership. It was at the closing stage of the Fall, and how lovely the forests looked, the oaks and chestnuts a myriad of amber and crimson, gold and pink, bright yellow and deep rose.

Although the red fox is indigenous to the north-west and the central plains, he was not known along the eastern seaboard until 1730, when he was introduced from England into Maryland by foxhunters wearying of the little native grey, which invariably describes a circle like a hare. By the time the Gloucester Foxhunting Club came on the scene, the European red was established in Pennsylvania. But now – although the density of foxes is far less in America than in the British Isles – in the northern States there are more reds than greys; and soon after the senior joint-Master, Sylvester L. Quigley, led us away at 9.30 am. from Chester Spring, Phoenixville (a little under thirty miles from Philadelphia), a red fox was afoot in the forest by the Two Churches.

It was astonishing to see hounds hold his scent, for the air was as crisp and dry as you could imagine, the moisture on the ground fractional; but these pure Penn-Marydel hounds never lifted theirs heads nor quietened their tongues until fifteen minutes later, when their quarry found a big drainpipe, and our horses were well lathered from traversing hills of white-green grass and parched earth fields, from which the maize had just been harvested; and (where in England there would have been more gates to open than hedges to cross) jumping panels and 'chicken coops' and post-and-rail fences. They left him in that drain: foxes are so scarce over there that Masters rarely, if ever, use terriers or dig; you never hear of 'vermin control', and American houndsmen set little store by 'Blood'. ('Did you kill?' enquires the British countryman of the homegoing foxhunter, while 'Did you have a good *race*?' is what his American counterpart wants to know).

Penn-Marydel? Founded in 1934, the Penn-Marydel corporation then stated its aim as follows: 'To preserve purity in the bloodline of a species of the American foxhound, which has been found to be the most serviceable, and satisfactory for the club and pack hunting, and which has been bred and hunted for generations through the south-eastern sections of Pennsylvania, Maryland and Delaware . . .' Watching the Pickering pack more closely, with their light frames, long backs, low-set ears on high-domed heads and wide feet on sloping pasterns, as Albert Crosson, their huntsman, lifted them from the drain, I was reminded of those pre-Meynellian paintings of English 'northern beagles' and 'southern' hounds; and, since the Penn-Marydels' ancestors were introduced into colonial America in the seventeenth and eighteenth centuries and the blood kept fairly pure, there is good cause for that resemblance.

They are lower scenting than their modern English cousins; they have to be: the climatic conditions are much less favourable there. While they worked through the next forest, I wondered how they would fare in a tight-brambled English covert; for there is no such challenge in American woodland, where the bottom is never thicker than dogwood and hickory, entangled, perhaps, with wild grape and honeysuckle; the huntsman rarely pauses with his draw. Here they found again, and how their music echoed through the valley, as they swung right round with him to the Two Churches, where the big green fruit of the Osage orange trees littered the avenues like a playground floor, and the still, moistureless air was filled, as it was nearly everywhere, with the faint subtle odour of bittersweet berries; but these Penn-Marydels are ponderous, they dwell on the line, and thus they lost him.

What a stimulating day it was, and what a contrast to my last foxhunting, three days previously, in Sussex with mud up to the hocks, thronging at gates, cars at every junction of the close road network and long waits at covertside. And yet, for us, in America, some essential part of the scene was missing: was it a combination of soaking leaves, greenery and mist, hunting farmers and dedicated local foot followers, who in England help to 'tie the hunt to the land'?

Next day we visited the kennels of the Radnor hunt, whose hounds are Penn-Marydel-English crosses, and from there to the fine 1930s stone-built kennels at Unionville, where Mrs John B. Hannum, Master of Mr Stewart's Cheshire, keeps the largest pack in the United States: 63 couple of pure English hounds, with the blood of the Duke of Beaufort's, Garth and South Berks, Heythrop and South and West Wilts strongest in their veins. From that pack (the ears of every one of which were rounded) John Roche, the young kennel-huntsman (who had been carrying the horn since Mrs Hannum's last crippling fall), drew, for our admiration, Worry '72 – by the Duke of Beaufort's Wafer – the bitch that won the 1984 Virginia championship.

On 19 November we reached Henchman's Lea, Orlean, Virginia, the home of Colonel and Mrs Albert P. Hinckley, who had probably done more for British foxhunters during the previous quarter century, especially for officers serving in Washington, then anyone else in the United States. Colonel Hinckley, by whose house the Old Dominion hounds were kennelled, succeeded to the Mastership of that hunt in 1947 – during the season I first rode with them – and handed over to Mr William W. Brainard, Jnr, twenty-one years later.

There was no love lost between Bill Brainard and debonair, cultivated Al. Al told me how Bill had asked him, Al, to propose him for a certain exclusive New York club. Al put him off ('because he's a parvenoo, I guess . . . and when he wouldn't let me go on that subject, there just wasn't anything for it but for me to tell him he was a parvenoo'!) After dining with the Brainards, Lavinia wrote in her journal of 'the large study crammed with sporting magazines commemorating hound judging, paintings by all the best English sporting artists, foxes dressed like people in Beaufort green or Berkeley yellow, expensive English coffee-table books piled on the bumrack by the fire and an old copy of *Country Life* with Johnnie's report on Sir Alfred Goodson's hounds laid open on the desk . . . In the enormous drawing room a black butler, huge silver-framed photographs and more priceless paintings.'

Al and his wife, Steady, then nearing the end of their days, lived in the *great* Virginian style as we comfortably witnessed, eating off nothing but gold plate, drinking from nothing but sparkling cut glass, and with neatly uniformed black servants (starched caps and aprons) standing behind expectantly at every meal, seeing to their every need. ('My children call me a luxury-lovin' ol' bastard,' Al told us, 'and I guess they know'!) Al and Steady appeared each evening changed into what I can only describe as capacious Chinese dressing-gowns, kimonos, lavishly decorated with a dragon motif, silk on satin. A few years later we found ourselves sitting next to Bill Brainard at the Peterborough hound show. When we asked after Al he muttered only two words as he gazed steadfastly and grimly to his front: 'he's daid!'

The Old Dominion country lies in the Piedmont section of Virginia, what is dubbed 'the Leicestershire of America', in north Rappahannock and west Fauquier counties, at the foot of the Blue Ridge Mountains which – always on the horizon – are sometimes lavender, sometimes indigo but never less than a striking blue. It is a rolling tract of grass, liberally interspersed with forest, the cattle country being enclosed rather less now with stake-and-rail and the traditional and picturesque chestnut-pole zig-zag 'snake fence', than with that woven 'American wire', which is so teacherous to hounds. Although the red-and-white Old Dominion strain, narrow, light and standing only twenty-one inches at the shoulder, could slip through the wire's twelve-inch apertures more safely than most, even he sometimes got himself hung in the mesh by a leg.

It was Ned Chadwell, formerly of the Orange County (a hunt established in Virginia, in 1903), who was put on as huntsman in 1924, when Sterling Larrabee founded the hunt that was to become, in 1931, the Old Dominion (the name given to Colonial Virginia; and it was Orange County hounds, whose blood goes back to the red hounds with white necks ('red ring-necks'), bred by William Early (1849–1934) and Burrell Frank Bywaters (1843–1922) and his son Hugh (1872–1952), that formed the basis of Larrabee's new pack. Early and the Bywaters bred theirs from hounds descended from those imported by settlers two or three centuries ago and sold them, as they sold their cattle, sheep and pigs – mostly to the night runners – the hunters, who still turn their hounds out into the hills after fox by starlight, listening for their cry through the dark and calling them in by horn in the morning.

These Early-Bywaters types were among the most quality-looking hounds I saw in the United States, and the compact and level Old Dominion their best representatives. Brainard, a most successful breeder of animals generally, also kept a pack of English hounds, which he usually hunted himself about once a fortnight.

From the meet, at Mr Joe Hume Gardiner's Cabin Branch Farm, for which I joined them 21 November, the Old Dominion American pack drew through the rambling Bear's Den Forest, and there they remained for much of the day; like most American woodland in the east, it is composed largely of oak, not our oak, but the slim and lofty red oak, white oak, pin oak and chestnut oak, whose long indented leaves, having the texture of maple leaves, form the backcloth of the Virginian fall's dazzling crimson and gold, but which, in that abnormally dry season, lay brown and tinder-dry on the forest floor. Yet, despite the dampless atmosphere, after forty minutes blank, those red-and-white hounds found a fox, which they drove hard through the woods to a creek within half a mile of the Rappahannock River. There they threw up, and Ray Pearson, their huntsman, calling them to him with his 100-year-old cowhorn, lifted them away, because the coverts beyond are well-known deer havens and it was feared one of these might lead them into the swirling currents beyond. (After the Second World War the U S Government restocked several States with the nearly extinct Virginia white-tailed deer, and now, to the discomfiture of foxhunters, the forests are bristling with them.)

Soon they were on to another fox and made a picture of fleeting reddish-tan and white as they spoke to his line; but, although I was riding Colonel Hinckley's sure-footed chestnut, Cracker, I could not watch them for long at a time as the ground was pock-marked with groundhog holes, which are so much more deadly than rabbit warrens, for they are secreted and scattered. The groundhog, or woodchuck, which has been responsible for many a broken cannon-bone or humerus, has one other significance in American hunting: his holes are legion, and the fox invariably improves on them, making them his own, which is one of the reasons why earth stopping is virtually pointless.

Between Independence and the War between the States, the fox was hunted everywhere in charted America, and most of the plantation owners kept packs of hounds. The holocaust and social and economic upheaval of the 1860s reduced the sport to a miserable scale, lasting several decades, but one, at least, of the plantation hunts did survive – that established by the Confederate hero, Colonel Richard H. Dulany, at Welbourne, Virginia, in 1840. The oldest hunt in the United States, this flourishes today as the Piedmont.

At the start of my day with the Piedmont, on 22 November, Mr Erskine Bedford, the Field Master – riding ex-champion steeplechaser, Bon Noval, the property of the Master, Mrs Archibald Randolph – faced us to stress the importance of keeping immediately behind him, in one body, reminding one of the sad fact that there is scarcely a hunt in the United States favouring followers who take their own line; this seems to be more because Americans hunt primarily 'for the gallop' – and are all too prone to overrun the line – than to save the ranches. The Piedmont country is one of big landowners, with what they call 'well-manicured' farms: we rode from Mr Hubert

Phipps' Rockbourn estate to Tan-y-Byrn, belonging to Mr Paul Mellon, the famous collector and a former Master of this hunt, and rarely have I experienced such a sense of open unblemished space; at certain times the plains swaggered, as nature designed them, to every horizon, without so much as a farmstead or a herd of cattle showing but only neat walls and spick stake-and-rail fences as evidence of man's presence.

Yet, alas, that was not typical of north Virginia, for many of the hunts were being pinched by the encroachment of new roads and suburbia; there was little, if any, building restriction or denial in the open countryside; and the Orange County, I was told, would soon be divided down the middle by an inter-state highway. North Virginia, 'the hunt country of America', as they boast it, so reputable, so convenient for Washington and still so beautiful, remained pre-eminent, but how long, I wondered, would it remain so?

Our first run, fifteen minutes circularwise from find to finish, ended by Mr Mellon's celebrated sporting museum at Oak Spring, where hounds marked on a walnut tree. 'There he is!' – Mr Bedford pointed up with his whip – and I trotted forward, curious to see a grey (for only greys scale a tree of that height); but, instead, a wrathful figure, clad in black, white and ginger, gazed down. They had changed in the final dash, from vulpine to feline, and looked, I thought, a little shame-faced as they sidled on towards Goose Creek and Black Forest. But then cats do seem to show an unhappy facility for getting involved in foxhunts in America. Perhaps their movements are a little too like those of the grey fox for their safety?

It was in this country that the famous Anglo-American Foxhound Match of 1905 took place. The challenge – that the American hound could be proved inferior, on its own soil, to the English – came from a name well known in British hunting circles, anglophile A. H. Higginson, Master of a pack coming mostly from Mr Fernie's – the Middlesex, of Massachusetts. The man who accepted the challenge - with 6½ couples from his American Grafton pack, bred in cooperation with B. F. Bywaters (and also from Massachusetts) – was one of the towering figures in the history of American foxhunting, Harry Worcester Smith, who had then been recently elected Master of the Piedmont.

The contest began with a Middlesex meet at old Dulany's house, Welbourne, on 1 November, and, after ten days, with huge fields at every outing, the match was decided in favour of Worcester Smith's lot. National pride reached high fervour and pack breeders soon came to put top faith in the likes of the Bywaters and Early. Nearly every follower at the 'great match' vouched, too, that the country was 'just as fine as Leicestershire'. And that is how, by the time of the First World War, northern Virginia became 'the hunt country'. Not only was it handy for Washingtonians but would soon become the mecca for New Yorkers and Long Islanders who were gradually to be squeezed from their home hunting-grounds.

Founded in 1887, with roots going back to 1807, the Warrenton, whose country lies east of the Old Dominion and south of the Orange County, are next oldest after the Piedmont. Mrs Tyler Wilson generously provided me with as fine a 'coop jumper and flyer as could be desired for my ride with this famous hunt on 23 November, and I was up with Mr Douglas Harcourt Lees, her joint-Master, throughout the day which was mostly spent on forest rides.

Mr Lees, like Brainard, was a strong admirer of the English hound and a close observer of the English and Irish hunting scenes, but his pack were mostly Bywater, a well-matched tricolour lot; and very stylish they looked at 10 am as they moved off from Rappahannock Farm under their huntsman, Fred Duncan.

Virginia was still dry and hot; they could not work out the line of the one that had been in the coverts around Canterbury, they drew blank in Brood Mare Barn Woods, but finding at 1 pm in Charlie Johnson pines, they gave us a good thirty minutes' race before they lost him by the cliffs of the Rappahannock River, and a straight spurt with another red fox which at length found sanctuary in a woodchuck hole in a field at Ashland.

Hacking five miles to the horse-boxes before Mr Harcourt Lees' hunt breakfast, we crossed two roads, passed a dozen modern buildings and dismounted to unchain three gates, which made it the least 'natural' single ride in my American tour. For British foxhunters, that, in five miles, might have seemed nothing, but for Virginia it was bad. With such a precious heritage as theirs, one could only pray that if the country got more 'tied up' and less 'opened up', it would do so by the slowest degrees.

Very early on the Monday morning, we drove 800 miles to southern Tennessee, whose foxhunters were faced by few such threats and who were, indeed, opening up fresh country year by year.

The forests became wilder and steeper as we drove south-west, mounting the high Appalachians, and the open land grew browner, more prairie-like. That russet grass, feathery and waist high, called broomsedge, grows where the earth is sour and uncultivated, where rich grass cannot thrive; *en masse*, it gives the appearance of golden veldtland and looks very lovely as you are hacking home in the sunset. Where the ground rises, the deciduous woodland begins, and this is punctuated with the tall cones of juniper (Virginia red cedar), showing the presence of limestone outcrops, that make for rough riding. Broomsedge and cedar are the hallmarks of wild Tennessee. The red and (more numerous) grey fox live there alongside the opossum, raccoon, coyote, woodchuck, bobcat and white-tailed deer, and the stark and lonely hunting landscape is frequently brightened by flocks of scarlet cardinals and lime-breasted meadow larks or by the dazzle of blue jays and silvery, red-crowned woodpeckers.

In the early 1800s the frontiersmen took this land from the Indians by treaty, and the new settlers cleared the trees from the plains and made them rich. With the War between the States, the agricultural boom ended, but tumbledown log cabins, occasional windowless verandah-fronted villas and long-abandoned churches, with graveyards overgrown with sumac and hickory, tell you that, up to the First World War, quite prosperous communities lived there, farming cattle, maize and cotton. Then the labourers, mostly negroes, went to the towns in search of a living wage, and the countryside at the time of our visit was still relatively deserted. Huge expanses had been bought by men with fortunes, whose limited aim may have been to raise cattle but who, more ambitiously, have developed it for gun, rod and horse. Although some of the remainder of the land carries the soya bean, corn cob, pimento and sweet potato, and much more is wired up by beef and pig farmers, whose stock is their sole livelihood, it still constituted a fine playground for the hunter.

In America, of course, hunting meant duck shooting, coyote chasing or deer stalking, in fact more or less any pursuit with firearm or hound, and the sportsman carries the same licence in his foxhunter's coat as he carries in search of black bear or bobwhite quail.

In Tennessee, the old tradition of foxhunting with packs of hounds expired with the Civil War, and its first new seed was not planted until 1930, when the great Joe Thomas brought his hounds there; then, in 1932, the Hillsboro emerged, under J. Mason Houghland, from the Harpeth Valley Country Club, near Nashville. The only other foxhunting legacy was that of the nightrunners, which, as it involves neither trampling men nor horses, in no way upsets the ranchers; but 'pack foxhunters', with their troop or so of riders in wake, were viewed with suspicion, and Masters opening up new territory had to work very hard to win the farmers' trust.

The first sign of a hunt country was a rash of 'chicken coops', and, under most 'coops in Tennessee, we found barbed wire, for cattle thieving was rife there and no serious rancher regarded an apron of wood, which could be simply pushed aside and put back, as defence against rustlers. To keep the cattle in, the 'coops need not be more than 2 feet 6 inches high, though most were nearer 3 feet 6 inches.

When the red fox invaded the southern states in the 1830s and '40s, he was regarded as a menace by foxhunters. 'Whenever the grey fox was driven out,' wrote the top authority of the last century, Colonel F. G. Skinner, 'foxhunting was a labor instead of a pleasure, for the red devils, with far more speed and bottom than the natives, could easily outfoot the hounds . . . at last all sorts of devices were resorted to to improve the speed of the hounds.' Experiments with English hounds were mostly disappointing: 'Their noses were not cold enough,' complained Skinner, 'and they were too fast and too silent.' Much as Virginian Masters and night-hunters imposed their faith in the Bywaters, the southerners preferred the strains produced by John W. Walker, Colonel G. L. F. Birdsong, Ben Robinson and Colonel Miles Harris. Walkers were then perhaps still the most popular in the South.

It was Thanksgiving weekend when we reached the quiet steep 'hillbillyland' of Tennessee; turkeys were being prepared for full-treatment hunt breakfasts, and, when the Hillsboro met at Cornersville, a sprinkling of children reminded us that the schools had closed until the Monday. The senior Master, Mr Vernon Sharp, who had just taken over from Harry Nicholas as President of the Masters of Foxhounds' Association (founded in 1907) made me a nice speech of welcome at the meet; and it was his joint-Master, Mr George Sloan (twice a Grand National rider), who carried

Competing with the *Country Life* Triathlon team.

Receiving my Churchill Fellowship award from Lord Tonypandy (formerly House of Commons Speaker, George Thomas). In 1982 I travelled extensively in Canada, the USA and Continental Europe in the context of animal welfare.

Talking to the Prince of Wales with Lavinia.

1989: At Home. The terrier is Linnet, one of our Jack Russell bitches.

the horn, because Bob Gray, their English huntsman, was in hospital, having driven a nail through his foot.

Here, with forty years' tradition and the majority of land owned by hunt subscribers, there was scant trouble with access, and, in spite of a scorching day, with the yellow alfalfa butterfly out in force over the golden fields, the combination of a stout red fox and the tenacity of the Hillsboro's Walker-and-Fell-bred hounds provided the straightest run I had in the States – a quickly undulating twenty-five minute gallop.

I also enjoyed a Thanksgiving hunt, with the Mells, which was founded, in 1962, by my stepfather, Jack Hornor. We started up the hill behind the kennels at Waco, and the Mells hounds, which are descended from a litter of Vale of Lune harriers – with Penn-Marydel, Bywaters and Walker outcrosses – soon found a red fox in a piece of woodland that made my memory of Virginian forest seem like ornamental parkland. We crouched low over the withers, screwing and ducking to avoid the three-inch thorns of the honey locust tree and great loops of vine and honeysuckle, then slid down and clambered up near-vertical boulder-strewn gradients, before turning suddenly on to a majestic expanse of pasture, 1,000 yards across the ridge beyond. When I commented on the shortness of American hunting days – most of which amounting to no more than three hours in the saddle – Mr Richard E. Dole Jnr, who was then in his sixth season as Master, as though to modify my verdict, mounted me again, this time for a dripping wet four-hour day in a 'new' woodland area, by no means properly panelled – the Mells country is a multiplicity of small estates – and we were forever dismounting in the rain, looking for passages over or round the barbed wire: no chicken coops, no free way.

My morning with Buck Allison's private Cedar Knob Hunt helped me, more than anything else, to imagine what it was like to follow one of the old plantation packs, for Allison had a charming Southern take-what-you-please philosophy. His friend and neighbour, William Carter and I (the only followers) were in happy conversation as we followed the pack (like the Hillsboro a Walker-and-Fell combination) across that enormous, total wilderness. 'Hey there!' came a shouting whisper from Allason, 'keep yer voices down will yer, you have to be awful quiet if we're goin' to take 'em unawares ...' And then with a voice rather louder than ours: 'Say, Mr Watson, do you hunt the timber wolf in the Old Country?' I explained that there had been no wolves in Britain for over two centuries. 'Do you have a go at coyote then?' 'Certainly not!' 'Waal then, how 'bout bobcat? ... ma hounds had three maybe four mile point after bobcat last week. Only thing was little old bobcat he then stood at bay hollerin' and spittin' and barin' his claws, so I whipped 'em off f'fear they'd have their muzzles ripped. And I just swear I heard the leadin' hound tell his pal 'say, friend, this ain't the guy we oughter be chasin...!'

At that moment the pack showed interest in a stack of logs just ahead, whining and scratching at the timber and giving tongue, at which Allason got extremely excited and broke into a canter. 'Guess ma hounds 're speakin' to bobcat in that little ol' woodpile!' he shouted back. We trotted to catch up;

and, arriving at the timber stack, he said 'Here, take ma horse, will you, Mr Watson, while I get the critter out o' there'. He jumped from the saddle, threw his reins at me and began heaving rocks at the woodpile. But suddenly the pack's attention was attracted elsewhere, and in a trice they were careering in a tight column and in full cry across the wilderness towards the horizon. 'Goddam!' exclaimed Allason, 'Y'know what? They're after whitetail deer. That means we won't see 'em again today, maybe not tomorrow either. Waal . . .' he looked at his watch: 'could do worse I guess 'n head on home for an early lunch.' We'd only left the kennels twenty minutes before. (The Cedar Knob amalgamated with the Hillsboro in 1980, and was then 'recognised' by the MFHA.)

We now motored south, between the red cotton-fields, to Madison, Alabama, where Mr Harry Moore Rhett, Jnr, Master of another private hunt, the Mooreland, kennels a very high-quality pack, established in 1961 and composed of about 65% American and 35% English. Mr Rhett's plantations, which came down to him from an equally sporting great-grandfather of pre-Civil-War days, form the nucleus of a country which is part flat cotton ploughland – admirable for seeing hounds work – and part woodland and pasture, at the tail-end of the Appalachians; and there cannot be many examples of how foxhunting provides a principal winter recreation and initiates local interest in equitation than that shown by the Mooreland: few of the forty followers out on my weekday had ever ridden before discovering the Mooreland, and many took a shrewd interest in the houndwork as two greys and a red were traced to ground.

Lavinia had something to say just afterwards about our Mooreland visit. 'Founded by Harry Rhett, with Jack's help, it is entirely private, no donations, let alone subscriptions accepted. Rhett's guests only. His white Huntsville house is fronted by forty-foot pillars with a wide sweep of steps leading to the front door. A palace-like interior with the walls laden with ancestors – the Rhetts started in America in 1680 – and really beautiful furnishings. The main Rhett fortune was amassed through Harry's great-grandfather banking the proceeds of his cotton plantations in England and thus avoiding the loss of them in the Civil War (the 'War-between-the-States' as they all insisted.) Harry Rhett's wife came from what he described as 'a very good New Jersey family', and, judging by her portrait had been a tremendous beauty. (She shot herself two years ago.) The dining-room wallpaper was hand painted and a floodlit fountain on the terrace outside looked charming. Lunch consisted of mourning doves (quite tasteless) and a dull pudding . . .'

My most spectacular days of all were still further south, with the Midland, which hunt not only Thursdays and Sundays from their Georgian kennels, south-east of Columbus, but also a new tract in Alabama, based on the old Fitzpatrick hunt centre. Their owner, Ben H. Hardaway III, joint-Master and huntsman since 1950, an enormous man both in physical appearance and personality – a great grandson of the founder of 'Hardaway's Rifles', that celebrated unit whose guns first effectively defiladed the Union palisades in the War between the States – had fashioned a pack of 30 couples composed chiefly of American July, and of British Fell blood (coming from the West Waterford and College Valley), with occasional outcrosses of Penn-Mary-del, Bywaters, the Duke of Beaufort's and the Heythrop. The Julys, descended from Irish importations of the 1830s, gain their name from the foundation sire, July 1859, bred in Maryland by Nimrod Gosnell and acquired, as a puppy, by Colonel Miles G. Harris, of Georgia, in 1858. Ben Hardaway was the first to agree with the old hound expert, George Garrett, who advised a would-be breeder, seventy years ago, 'If you want music get Walker hounds; however, if you want action and excution, get July by all means'. Ben was fifteen when he acquired his first Julys from Garrett.

These narrow, long-legged, snipey-faced, and slightly broken-coated hounds are shy and temperamental but, crossed with the intelligent and similarly rangy Fell, produce – as Ikey Bell suggested they would – wonderfully hard-driving fox-catchers; and I never shall forget the way the Midland pushed their grey out of a slash pine and creeper entanglement on 7 December. They say the grey always describes a circle; but not this one; he ran straight as a die into the open, across a great sweep of auburn grass where cotton once grew, and eventually into another conifer copse; here, vainly trying to shake them off, he twisted and turned a dozen times, from corner to corner of the covert, before they ran into him by our feet in a clearing, going forty-five minutes from find to kill.

We then left Alabama for Ben's Georgian home, he and I in front with the hound trailer, Lavinia and Jack Hornor following. We stopped for petrol and, while Ben was paying his bill, the garage attendant, who looked the spitting image of Jimmy Durante, asked me 'What's them dawgs?'. When I said 'foxhounds' he replied 'Foxdawgs? Can foxdawgs do tricks?' He promptly fetched a couple of Dobermanns, which he urged to sit up and beg, while he stood between them imitating their posture, his tongue lolling. That set Ben's hounds howling with such cacophonic alarm that he came running out and starting up the car 'afore we get ourselves arrested for disturbing the peace'. It was dark by the time we reached the town of Columbus. Looking down, after a long silence, on the twinkling lights, he said 'Did you know I own this joint?' I imagined this remark to be some esoteric metaphor – until we proceeded through the streets and I saw that most of the neon advertisement lights bore the inscription HARDAWAY. 'Yes, I see you do own it,' I said. And so across the city limits into the Midland country, onto the Hardaway estate, past Hardaway Hall where Ben's mother lived, between a number of lakes to the mansion which he had built for himself. His pretty wife, a diminutive figure little over five feet tall, but a steely one all the same, and a yoga adherent, greeted us sitting on a table in the hall in the lotus position. She pointed at her watch. 'You're an hour late!' she admonished him. And the huge and formidable man crumpled like a naughty boy.

Straight after church next day he took out twenty-five couples with no whipper-in to turn them to him. Harlot '70 (which Ben later presented to the College Valley) was first to speak to the line they hunted, and when the remainder joined her and raced for half-an-hour on a grey's brush, the Anglo-American chorus was terrific, and the silence as dramatic after they took him in a creek, with thirty of us weaving through the hickory and rattan as we cantered up behind.

How about the hazard of whitetail deer? Ben was in the habit of holstering a pistol on hunting days for the purpose of stinging on the backside any hound that rioted – the ammunition was otherwise innocuous – though he had no recourse to it, I'm thankful to say, on my days with him. Touring his kennels I asked whether there was no more humane, yet as effective deterrent. 'I guess there is another way. Y'see that barrel over there,' he pointed to the corner of the kennels towards a container the size and shape of a churn or large beer barrel – complete with a door and an organ-grinder's handle – cupped on a stand. Waal, I keep an ol' skin of a whitetail there, an' each new young entry to the pack I put in there an' close the door. An' very slowly I turn the handle . . . 'Does that really put them off rioting after the deer?' I asked, duly shocked. 'Waal, I don't know whether it stops 'em chasin' the whitetail' he replied with a rueful headshake. 'But they sure don't want to go in that barrel again!'

At the time of writing Ben Hardaway has just completed forty years as joint-Master and huntsman of the Midland.

'In our journey through the south – during which we were never less than royally entertained and I beautifully mounted – we were told everywhere' (I wrote afterwards) 'that an increasing number of people were taking up the sport, and we gained the impression that there will be a proliferation of hunts in the Southern States during the next decade. The Southerners certainly have magnificently unspoilt arenas for it . . .' And quite a few have sprung up, although by no means all of them are yet entered in *Bailys*.

I wonder in which direction the formal hunting of hounds in north America would have turned if the French had first colonised the eastern seaboard, or even if Lafayette, not Fairfax, had influenced Washington and the other colonial landowners in their mode of sport. Would the deer, now the bane of American foxhunters, have been the primary quarry? Would the forests of Pennsylvania, Virginia, Maryland and Carolina have echoed to the notes of those great circular horns that loop the chests of the French *veneurs*? Would the gold embroidered coat, the winged thigh boot, the tricorne hat and the short sword, all those symbols of *chasse à courre*, have been *de rigeur*?

But such conjecture apart there is no doubt that the hunting of the fox suits the character of the American sportsman in a way that forest deer hunting never could. Americans in general would have had little time for all that ritual, all that trotting back and forth down woodland rides, all that horn-blowing semaphore. Indeed a French hunting visit is something the average British or American foxhunter would not often wish to repeat. For it seems, like most ritual, very repetitive and predictable even for those foreigners who have taken some trouble to unravel the meanings of the music, the niceties of the protocol and the whole nationally esoteric nature of French hunting. Conan Doyle's story about his French hero, Brigadier Gerard, charging and slaying the fox with his sword, during a hunt staged by British officers in the Peninsular War, well sums up the Frenchman's mystification at our national sport. Indeed the contrasts of hunting in France and hunting in Britain, if thoughtfully analysed, go some way to highlighting the differences in the respective national characters. (In that context it is interesting to note from my account of the Equipagem de Santo Huberto how, despite the Portuguese determination that everything shall be done in the English manner, their general unconcern with the hounds, their preoccupation with their horses and their race to return to the hunt club pavilion for the regular gargantuan lunch the moment the Master gives the signal – not to mention their use of showers and changing-rooms there, like so many footballers – shows how removed from the English concept their sport became.)

My first French hunting experience was a day with the Rallye Trois-Forêts – whose woodlands are close to Chantilly – during a British Sporting Art Trust tour in 1979. I did not repeat the experience until 1987. This time it was with the Rallye Villers-Cotterets and the Rallye Nomade, between Paris and Reims. The third occasion was in 1988 when I enjoyed several days much further south (south of Bourges and Nevers) with the Rallye Vouzeron (stag), the Rallye Les Amoges (roe buck) and the Rallye Chapeau (boar). Here are a few excerpts from my records. First the Trois-Forêts: Leaves of beech, oak and birch were falling as light as tissue, while shafts of sunlight beamed so forcefully on the tinder-dry carpet of foliage and pine-needles that few would have been surprised if an unextinguished cigarette had suddenly ignited the forest, when members of the British Sporting Art Trust joined the Rallye Trois-Forêts, some forty kilometres north of Paris, on the first Saturday of last month.

'Il fait trop chaud!' exclaimed the Rallye's President, or Maître de'Equipage, M. Lachaze, with the same pessimistic heel-in-ground and headshaking sniff which British Masters reserve for apologising to visitors for indifferent weather conditions. The animation at the carrefours, the crosspaths rendez-vous in the Forêt d'Ermenonville, swelled around him – not only with cavaliers, unloading their boxes and trailers, and the rather long-legged hounds wearing collars of identification on their thick, rough necks, but also with Peugots and Renaults disgorging bicycles and, by the dozen, hunt supporters, rummaging in knapsacks, ensuring they had not forgotten the indispensable loaf, cheese, garlic and Beaujolais . . .

The privileged members of the Rallye, les Boutons, were dressed in the hunt colours, dark blue breeches and coats, gilets, red waistcoats, adorned with strips of gold braid (galons de vénerie), velvet caps and white hunting ties, fastened by gold pins, mounted with the stag's eyetooth. Some sported the winged thigh-boots which protect knees from branches and from the cold; all, athwart their chests, carried the great circular hunting-horns, the first symbol of la chasse. The women are now very rarely seen in glamorous sidesaddle and tricorne hats, and last month those of the Trois Forêts were more or less indistinguishable from the British and American equestriennes of our party. But the men of the Sporting Art Trust, wearing foxhunting scarlet, produced a incongruous sartorial contrast . . .

This is how I introduced my account of the Villers-Cotterets and Nomade: The method of hunting the red deer stag in the forests of France is not dissimilar to that practised on the open space of Exmoor; yet the character and ambience of the two sports could scarcely be in sharper contrast. In France the *valets des limiers*, accompanied by a 'silent' hound, set out at dawn to discover and select the quarry, *faire le bois*, rather in the manner of the West Country harbourers. The meet is in later morning; and, accordingly, the hounds are cast where the stag was tracked (but 'tufters' – as in Somerset and Devon – are not employed).

If and when the hounds eventually bring their quarry to bay it is dispatched with a humane killer. Until quite recently the stag was finished off with a short sword, and side-arms, though now mostly only ceremonial, are still slung from the gold belts of *les boutons*, the most privileged of the followers, those entitled to wear the hunt coat. Participation, which is strictly by invitation of the *Maître d'Equipage*, is steeped in ritual and traditional ceremony.

Much significance is attached to the sartorial accoutrements: there are those who are entitled to the *bouton*, and those who may wear the *gilet*, the hunt waistcoat, elegantly trimmed with the relevant gold-braid strips (*galons de vénerie*). Any member of the *équipage*, however, may don the winged thigh boot and the gold pin with a stag's eye-tooth that fastens the hunting tie; they may also carry one of those looped, body-encircling horns, *trompes*, with which, perhaps, we in England most closely identify the *chasse à courre*.

They communicate with one another through the day by a musical semaphore that seems to echo back down the ages to the eighteenth century when the Marquis de Dampierre, *maître veneur* to Louis XV, regularised the calls throughout staghunting in France. And, if there is a kill, they sound those instruments – before and after the formalities of dressing the stag and feeding it to the hounds, and the presentation of *les honneurs*, the slots – in a series of distinctive hunt fanfares that record the day's proceedings. Their season is from mid-September to the end of March.

For the Rallye Nomade I was mounted on a very handy chestnut mare, at least as useful and comfortable a ride as my Villers-Cotterets hunter. I was requested by her groom, a bright Scots girl (Christine from the Isle of Lewis) to 'be sure to change to your second horse if they go to the high country; this mare is only fit for half a day in the Gobain.'

And thereby hangs a tale. For the Forêt St-Gobain has a low, flat forest and a high forest, the latter being a much more steeply undulating tract than the Retz, with a going that is deep and miry, a difficult country to hunt and a very tiring one for horses and hounds. Many of us failed to reach our second horses.

Hounds drew through the low woodland first, and drew blank until about 2 pm. A remarkably large host of foot followers stood in groups at the forest cross-paths looking eagerly this way and that for a sight of *le cerf*, no less ardently than the horsemen and women; and, almost whenever we approached a road, great columns of cars were to be seen closed up, bumper to bumper.

The two o'clock find carried hounds on a run that was variously estimated at being between an astonishing fifty and sixty km. Giving that rich and exhilarating music for which they are so renowned, they ran with scarcely a check, winding up and down the clay-soft, often precipitous, wooded hills until, at about 6 pm, their stag reached the swift-flowing river Ailette. He plunged in, was carried 500 yards downstream by the current, scrambled ashore on the same bank and took refuge in a thicket. Hounds – followed now on foot by the *piqueur* and his assistants, for their horses had been led away exhausted – crossed the Ailette by a bridge, and so, I am thankful to record, lost their gallant quarry.

Meanwhile, along with a great many others, I too was hopelessly lost. To be lost in a strange British hunt country as it is getting dark is one thing, to be lost in a vast Continental wilderness at that hour is quite another. And, of course having been nowhere near my second horse, I was riding a mare who was so tired she made it quite plain to me that she did not wish to be taken out of a walk.

It was therefore a monumental relief to meet along a road Vicomtesse de Spoelberch, a celebrated horsewoman and one of the most resplendent figures of the day in the traditional tricorne hat; but now – having been as badly adrift in the hills as me – had transferred from her sidesaddle to her car. She kindly showed me to a farmhouse haven, then drove a great distance to inform M. Maurice Velge's groom where I and my mare were to be found . . .

'There can be no countrymen in the world who show greater reverence for their forests than the French' I wrote after my 1988 visit. 'And none receives stronger affection than that which the *veneurs*, the hunters, bestow upon the Forêt de Tronçais, the mighty tract of oak lying, as the guidebooks say, *au coeur de la patrie* – in the Allier, or Bourbonnais, the province from which the Bourbon kings took their name. The following effusive eulogy by a *veneur* of the 1930s is echoed time and again: *Admirable forêt de Tronçais! Que de beauté, que de richesse, que de charme! Qu'il fait bon vivre dans la Cité des Arbres! Ce Temple splendide de la nature et foyer ancestral de la vénérie!*

'Until the end of the seventeenth century the area had been kept open by herds of ruminant animals, both wild and domestic. Then Louis XIV's all-powerful chief minister, Jean-Baptiste Colbert, having been informed that its soil was the best in the country for trees, gave orders for the cultivation of oaks, to be planted in such a way that they grew straight and immensely tall (for the nation's posterity – they were to serve Napoleon's navy). Tronçais remains the maturest cultivated oak forest in Europe.

'It was not long before this woodland was colonised by the three mammals of *Grande Vénérie*, the red deer (whose stag is *le cerf*), roe deer (*le chevreuil*) and boar (*le sanglier*).

'M. Gérard Vigand, founder of the Rallye l'Aumance, one of the three Bourbonnais *équipages* that I was privileged to follow last month generously invited me to ride from his rendezvous at the Rond du Poteau. By chance, that was the annual joint meet with one of the oldest of France's 260 and more hunts, the Rallye Vouzeron, which is under the Mastership of the

Marquise d'Harcourt. She and her privileged fellow *boutons*, hunt members, wear scarlet coats, which made a bright and happy ensemble with the green of the Rallye l'Aumance.

'M. Vigand started the day by asking Robert, his *valet de limiers*, or harbourer, to proceed with a report on his *quête* (preliminary reconnaissance). *Limiers*, which are 'silent' hounds, play an important part in French hunting. Working on the leash, the harbourer takes them out in search of deer or boar, probably between 8 and 9 am, by which time the quarry beasts will have settled after their night's roaming. The *limier* should be superior in nose and intelligence to the run-of-the-mill *chien courrant*.

'The *boutons* are jealously proud of their place towards the front. The l'Aumance elite rode close behind the hunt's respective *piqueurs* and their hounds, while, initially, we kept a respectful distance behind. The *valets de chiens*, the whippers-in, were on foot. M. Vigand's *piqueur* stopped at the point on the forest path where the *valet de limiers* had left his *brisée*, his broken branch, the sign indicating where hounds should be first cast.

'Everyone knew it was likely to be a difficult day. Not only was the wind in the south and the forest dry, not auguring well for *la voie*, the scent, but there was the added complication of having two *meutes*, two packs, out. However, they were quickly onto the trail, and their first cry had scarcely chimed before the *daguet* and *bitches* were sighted, and shouts of *tayaut!* (from which our *tally ho!* is derived) echoed through the oaks.

'These were quickly followed by a succession of different airs on the body-encircling *trompes*, the horns, which are carried and played, not only by the *maîtres,piqueur* and *boutons*, but also by any other followers, mounted or on foot, who fancy their expertise with these instruments. We heard the *lancer* (the hunt has begun) followed by the *accompagné* (several deer) and the *bien aller* (hounds are running well). As the French metaphor for a hunting forest is a temple, or cathedral, so the *trompes* and the hound music are the organs and the choir.

'The first-time participant in *la chasse à courre à cheval* soon realises that the motives of the sport have little to do with equitation. There is no jumping other than hops over ditches or fallen trees, nor fast galloping in tight throngs over farmland or heathland, to which excitement the English fox-hunter is accustomed. The objects of the exercise are rather the observation of the movements of the quarry and the hounds, the interpretation of the music of the *trompes* and the *meute*, and, of course, the ambience of the forest.

'The hunted stag was on his own now. *La vue* reverberated down the rides, then *l'accompagnè* (he has joined other deer) and *le passage de route* (he has crossed the road). At last, after nearly five hours riding and half a dozen *défauts*, checks, interspersed with much questing through the trees, animated enquiry and cupping of ears as the music unfolded the day's story, the stag entered a lake and we heard the *bat l'eau*.

'No sooner had the *piqueur*, rowed out and very promptly finished it, than every *trompe* present on the shore joined in a great chorus of *hallali*, the kill. (The Marquise d'Harcourt told me afterwards that she and her *piqueur*, one of those *veneurs* who still insist upon the convention of the old death-stroke, recently went to Somerset to witness a British staghunt. When the English huntsman prepared to shoot a beast at bay with a humane killer, the *piqueur* remonstrated that a gun was undignified and cold steel much kinder. So saying, he took out his *couteau*, and killed the stag with one quick stab.)

'Above the shore the climax of the ceremonial, *la curée*, was now re-enacted in precisely the same manner as it has been all over France for centuries. The stag was skinned and the best venison given to *les riverains*, the local foot followers. The head and pelt were then laid across the remainder of the carcass and – while *les maîtres d'equipages* and *les boutons* formed columns in one group and the horn-carrying foot followers in another, to blow the fanfares – a *valet de chiens* took the head by the antlers and shook it at the pack to incite them.

'This was followd by the relating on the *trompes* of the entire day from *le départ* to *l'hallali*. M. Vigand then raised his whip and lowered it – the signal for the *valet de chiens* to whisk off the pelt, and for the *piqueur* to cheer his hounds onto the carcass.

'M. Vigand next invited the guest Master, the Marquise d'Harcourt, to award the premier *pied*, the first slot, which – amid the triumphant blowing of *les honneurs* – she kindly presented to me. At the time of writing it is being cured and mounted for me by Daniel Thominet, *piqueur* of the Rallye l'Aumance.

'*La vénérie* is not only treated like a religion, but is involved with the church. For every hunt in France, the greatest ceremony of the year takes place on the feast of St Hubert, 2 November, or nearest Saturday. At the close of the traditional mass the priest blesses the hounds; those who blow the *trompes* endeavour to put on their very best performance; and the hounds, so I am told, seem to know it is all for them.

'What most impresses me whenever I hunt in France is the warm and happy bond of each fraternity, a bond inspired by a mutual interest in the chase and its national tradition. The firm handshakes, airy kisses, *bonjours* and other salutations, as well as the fond enquiries and the gracious replies, the ribaldry, the playful exchanges and the thoughtful courtesy that always prevails, are so obviously genuine and heartfelt. As I was told last month: *la vénérie est un merveilleux sport, difficile et loyale! C'est une école de modestie, de droiture, de courtesie et de respect: respect envers soi-même, envers les autres boutons, l'environment, les chiens, les chevaux, et bien sur et surtout, l'animal de chasse!*

'Whether attending a meet of hounds, watching the climax of a day's hunting (the *curée*) or visiting kennels,' I wrote, 'the guest of French hunts will doubtless contrast the relationship between the *piqueurs* and *valets de chiens* and their dogs with that of our huntsmen and their hounds. In France, with the *piqueur* always careful to assert total domination, the bond seems to be based entirely on mutual respect. The adoring affection that exists between the English huntsman and his charges is certainly lacking.

'In Britain and Ireland for the most part the hound puppy learns to love humans during its long period 'at walk', when it is sent away to the home of a hunt supporter who feeds, exercises, houses and loves it, and generally introduces it to the outside environment. In France, puppies are nearly always brought up in the stern school of the kennels, while their eyes are more inclined to be kept warily on the whip-hand than on the benign eyes of a loving kennelman. I was strongly reminded of this comparison last month at the Rallye l'Aumance kennels.

'The fundamental blood of the French hound stems from the kennels of the monks at the monastery of St Hubert in the Ardennes. St Hubert himself (AD 656–727) was apparently the first man in the modern world to keep pedigrees. From those derived the three most popular of the later *chiens courrants*, the Gascon-Saintongeois, the Poitou, or Poitevin, and the broken-coated Griffon. All of these were considered too slow, however, and for a long time now they have been crossed with English foxhounds, the Anglo-Français being the strain now found in every French kennels whose pursuit is *La Grande Vénérie*. The original English pack-hunting hounds derived from the *chiens courrants* brought over by the Normans, which became known as Talbots.

'To meet the needs of the speedier, longer-distance mode of foxhunting developed by Hugo Meynell and others in the eighteenth century, the Talbots (Southern-mouthed hounds) were crossed with greyhound types, producing a scent hound of much greater drive, stamina, ferocity and swiftness. It is that blood, added to the superior French nose and cry, that enables the modern *chien courrant* to keep up with and challenge the deer and boar of the great forests. Among the British breeds, the Dumfriesshire black-and-tans – with their bloodhound, Gascon and Anglo-Welsh background combining all the qualities – are most favoured by the Frenchmen.

'M. Vigand's hounds, which are *Anglo-Français* Poitevins, are particularly respected in French breeding circles. With considerable pride, Daniel Thominet, *piqueur* of the Rallye l'Aumance, drew out for me Brigadier, who won first prize at the Vichy show last year. Notwithstanding the strong measure of English blood, the essentially French conformation – long legs, narrow chest and high-domed head, with pendulous, low-set ears, scant stop between the eyes and long, narrow nose – is largely predominant. The French admire a rather larger and taller hound than our foxhunters are looking for.

'I went on to Urcay in the afternoon to visit M. Jacques Gontard's similarly bred Rallye La Folie hounds, which I was due to follow on the Saturday. This *équipage*, which is *créance* (entered) to boar, includes one or two of the highly favoured broken-coated Griffons (originating from Vendée, La Rochelle). Some wolf blood, too, may soon be added to that of the conventional *chien courrant*. The two wolf cubs with which M. Gontard recently returned from Yugoslavia are now well developed, and his *piqueur*, Alan Salle, gave a convincing demonstration of their docility. It will be interesting to learn whether the proposed mating is successful and if so, how the puppies turn out. I then returned to my hotel, the Hotel de Tronçais, which is small, quiet and comfortable and most convenient for anyone hunting in this part of France.

'There was a horse waiting for me the next morning for a meet of M. Pignot's Rallye Les Amognes, founded in 1956, which has hunted *le chevreuil*, the roebuck, in the Forêt de Tronçais since 1972. The hunting rights of Tronçais being primarily for the staghunting Rallye l'Aumance, the Amognes are only permitted to draw in a defined central part of the forest; but once their quarry is started they may follow it to the end, whatever the direction or distance. Unlike *le cerf*, the red deer stag (which tends to keep to its home territory) *la chevreuil* may run straight and far. Shortly before my visit, a buck had taken the Amognes over a course of some forty kilometres.

'The *chevreuil* hounds needs to be one of particular stamina, drive and tenacity. As that great international hound expert, Sir John Buchanan-Jardine, wrote in the late 1930s: "I should say there is no doubt that the best and most carefully bred packs of hounds in France . . . are those hunting roe deer, partly perhaps because the roe is one of the hardest animals to kill with hounds, and partly because no one, unless he is a genuine hound man, takes the trouble to hunt that animal, for it is a type of hunting of which difficult and interesting hound work constitutes the principal charm."

'Mme Pignot, who is at least as ardent a *veneur* as her husband, joined him at the head of the cavalcade when *le départ* was sounded, and, following the faithful guidance of the *valet de limiers*, there was a quick find. This buck gave a run of nearly twenty kilometres – leaving me far to the rear – the end being on the opposite side of the lake to that on which the Rallye l'Aumance *hallali* had been blown two days earlier. Afterwards the *boutons* and other mounted followers were entertained, amid great camaraderie, by *les riverains* in a village hall.

'My third day, which began with a massive midday hunt breakfast, was from a rendezvous near Chateau-Chinon in the neighbouring *département* of the Nièvre, of two boar-hunting *équipages* who always join forces, M. Gontard's Rallye La Folie and the Rallye Chapeau. The latter is under the Mastership of the Comtesse de Monspey, who kennels at her château near Chevagnes. The territory of both hunts extends over two private Bourbonnais forests, the Nièvre and the Saône et Loire. The boars are less numerous and less easy to locate than the deer, so the hunts employ a number of *valets de limiers* to reconnoitre various parts of the country to be hunted. The Masters then settle for the *rapport* appearing to hold the most promise. Apart from this, as I witnessed, the procedure is similar.

'Such opposition as there is to *la chasse à courre* in the Bourbonnais is more to do with manner and method than with principle. Some of the critics, for example, object to the *coup de grace* being administered with the knife rather than with the gun. The *veneurs* counter-claim that while the blade, in the right hands, is quick and clean and certain, the bullet may not always be immediate and may be dangerous for foot followers.

'Paradoxically, the conservationist 'Greens' are often on the side of the *équipages*, for both are against the shooting by foresters and *chasseurs* which is prevalent in many areas. The foresters, regarding the animals as a menace to young conifers, have them shot indiscriminately, and many hunts have to dispose of animals with severe gunshot wounds.

'*Chasse à courre* may seem to some people rather barbaric in its ritual, but there is no doubt that is saves a great many worse cruelties. The pleasure it gives is deep-rooted among the country people, and it does much to promote the conservation of the French forests.'

Owing to the lasting occupation by the French of what is now Belgium the first of that nation's three languages is French, her customs and her culture are more French than anything else and the character of her hunting, *chasse à courre*, is French too, with all the French rituals, horn music and modes of dress. Through the generous *entrée* of our friends Roland and Anne van der Werve de Schilde, I was given a couple of days hunting there in 1984, the first with the Rallye Vielsalm in the Ardennes, near the Luxembourg border; and the second with the Rallye Campine whose northern country lies close to both Holland and West Germany. In our haste to reach the van der Werves in time for the dinner party they were organising for us we started our Belgian sojourn rather shamefully by filling our tank with diesel (it was one of those dimly-lit Continental garages in which the different brands of petrol are not – to British eyes – clearly signed), the result being that we asked poor Roland to arrange our recovery from the motorway. We were not, however, too late for his and Anne's reception and, as the butler handed round a tray of champagne, one wit, a Master of hounds, shook his forefinger at me with 'you be very careful, my friend, not to take ze one with ze diesel in it!' Here are some comments I made after that visit.

'The roebuck is an awkward animal to trace, not only beause its scent recedes as it is hunted, but also because a tired buck too often succeeds in diverting the pack to a fresh one. 'There is no doubt that the best and most carefully bred hounds in France are those hunting roe deer,' wrote Sir John Buchanan-Jardine in his definitive *Hounds of the World*. Sir John himself influenced the Vielsalm kennel in 1946 by giving the present Master, Baron Janssen, one of his black-and-tan Dumfriesshire sires, which contain bloodhound and Gascon strains. But, fundamentally, the pack remains Gascon-Saintongeois, that mixture which originated with St Hubert in the seventh century, and whose blood has not been much adulterated in those 1,200 years. The strain is characterised by great depth through the heart, a long, sloping shoulder, high dome, pendulous ears and a deep, baying voice. Black and white with very little tan, the hounds stand about 24 in.

'Following the winding valley of the River Salm and climbing high into the conifer-clad Ardennes, at 11.30 am we reached the cross-tracks designated as the meeting-place, where horses had been generously arranged for us by M. Eric Janssen, who acts as Maître d'Equipage on his father's behalf, and who was to hunt hounds. The *piqueur* and the *valet des chiens* had unboxed the hounds, and already the horns were sending the notes of the hunt fanfares, *La Janssen* and *Le Rallye Vielsalm*, echoing through the spruces. We were close to the borders of three nations, Germany, Luxembourg and Belgium. Not only are the sounds of horn and hound music quite often heard in all three countries, but the Rallye Vielsalm have been known, too, to run their quarry over three frontiers in the same day. Not surprisingly, there is a special tune for 'change of nation (*changement de royaume*).

'It was foggy in the high Ardennes on our day, and rendering scent even more elusive, an east wind blew remorselessly. But we saw a great variety of country, and hounds did catch a young buck, which, having been duly skinned and taken back to the meeting-place, was devoured by the hounds to the triumphant music of the *hallali*. But that was not before the distribution of *les honneurs*. I enjoyed the privilege of receiving a slot.

'M. Verhaeghe de Naeyer, the President of the Rallye Vielsalm, and his wife kindly put Philippe Casier, Eric van der Werve and my wife and me up for the night. By coincidence it was the fortieth anniversary of the Germans' counter-offensive in the Ardennes, of which Vielsalm was the salient point. M. Verhaeghe de Naeyer told us that, while he was fighting on that front with the Belgian Armoured Brigade (during which time he received the British Military Cross), his château was occupied (unknown to him) in quick succession by the Americans, the Germans and again by the ultimately victorious Americans. In the early morning, we drove north of Liège for the Sunday meet of the Rallye Campine.

'Every year the feast of St Hubert, 2 November, is celebrated in France and Belgium with a mass at which the hounds, and the forests which they draw, are blessed before that day's hunting. Following the Vielsalm hounds we had been fewer than thirty kilometres from the spot where St Hubert (656–727), the patron saint of hunting and founder of what became the conventional *chien courrant* throughout the world, is said to have experienced, on a Good Friday, his vision of a stag with a crucifix shining between its antlers.

'Accepting that vision as a sign from heaven, Hubert abjured his life of venery, hound-breeding and self-indulgence for one of Christian devotion and monastic chastity. He became bishop, first of Maastricht, then of Liège, both of which cities we passed on our drive north to the meet of the Rallye Campine.

'Baron de Fierlant Dormer was recovering from an operation, and unable to attend. His son Baron Charles, who kindly mounted me from his own stables, was hunting hounds that radiant Sunday, assisted by his brother, Thierry, the hunt secretary. Limburg being a Flemish-speaking province, Baron Charles's speech of welcome was in Flemish, too.

'After two hours or more we were galloping between a maze of vegetable allotments, down a village street, and at last to a little acre of softwood behind the houses, close to which two followers with highly lathered horses and smiles of broad triumph called to me, *Hallali! hallali!* The buck was carried back to Bivak-Pexof. The next phases in the day were the preparation and award of *les honneurs* and the feeding of the hounds.

'Then came an even more important ceremony. It had been the first time in the life of the ten-year-old Comte Raphael d'Ursel, the treasurer's son, that he had ridden with the Rallye Campine. He was to receive the initiatory rite that would make him a fully-fledged *veneur*. He was to be blooded. While he entered the circle of spectators and knelt in the middle of it, the *piqueur* cut the heart from the buck and handed it, steaming, to the *Maître d'Equipage*. Having made, with great deliberation, a cross of blood on the boy's forehead, Baron Charles handed the heart back to the *piqueur*. A small piece of the heart was then cut off and placed in the young count's mouth and the boy beamed with delight as the cries of *Félicitations!* broke the silence all around him. It was a scene that might have been witnessed in any Continental forest a thousand years ago.

'Now the pelt was whisked from the buck, and Baron Charles's son and daughter, who had been holding back the impatiently whining hounds, let them surge forward. The carcass was broken up and devoured in a very short time. Drowning the cracking of the last bones, all who fancied themselves with the horn joined in the chorus – retracing the narrative of the day's chase, without omitting a single tune recalling the story, from the move off from the meet onwards to the kill. At length, on the most stirring note, came the *hallali*, then the fanfares of the *Equipage, la Rallye Campine* and *la Fierlant Dormer* and, last of all, in tribute to my wife and me, a faithful rendering of the British National anthem.

'The post-hunting feast is as habitual in Belgium as in France. The Rallye Campine's was held at a Flemish inn that was once a flower-oil mill dating from the sixteenth century. It was just the place to compound the warm atmosphere that the *veneurs* brought to it. There we sensed that now familiarly mutual fondness and exuberant animation, emanating from what is essentially an intimate, family-like concourse. That being so, we felt highly privileged to be included in such a private event. The *piqueurs* of both the Vielsalm and the Campine are now having my slots cured and mounted. I look forward to receiving them and thus being often reminded of those two happy days' buck-hunting.'

The generosity of both Belgian and French Masters is such that they invariably make a point of presenting a slot, *un honneur*, to any guest rider who may be with them. However, many a visitor – having been on the receiving end of the ceremony and blushed at the applause of the hunt members thronging the *curée* – has been embarrassed on proceeding to his car by a tap on the shoulder. It is the *piqueur* holding out his hand. He requires the equivalent of £35, please, since it will be his business to mount the slot. And I beg those hunting in France for the first time not to tell him they had in mind to take it to their taxidermist at home. They might not be invited again!

What, one wonders, will the years ahead in the European Community bring? The future of hunting live quarries with hounds hangs in the balance, as do all other sporting activities in Europe, involving animals. The environment will feature as a crucial sphere in the programme for the Internal Market and both anti-hunting and pro-field sports organisations will be struggling to secure superior positions on the 'Green' bandwagon. The former will proclaim that venery is cruel *per se*, and should therefore be banned totally, while the latter insist that the sports are in the interests of either a culling programme or of vermin control; and, secondly, that they make an important contribution to wildlife conservation. Early in 1989 the British Field Sports Society appointed a leading political consultancy to support its European operation in Brussels. The Society has been in close cooperation with the Irish Field and Country Sports Society, so I am told, and the European Community's Federation of Field Sports Organisations (FACE) produced, in 1989, a manifesto setting out a field sports policy 'for the conservation of natural habitats and wildlife'.

There will be all sorts of political pitfalls to be overcome. For example, a report by the Community's Environment Committee called for legal action 'against activities involving cruelty to animals', with bullfighting as the primary target. Then, for fear of being seen to be prejudiced against Spain, the morality of sports in other countries was called into question, and the report proceeded to cover hunting and coursing. I predict the making of many controversial movements such as the animal rights lobby attempting to have legalised a ban on all hunting of live quarries with hounds – and some idiot of a committee approving the recommendation to the Parliament. But they will soon realise how easily oversimplified such a resolution can be. Does that include minkhounds? they may be asked. Yes, of course, they will reply, all hunting with hounds is cruel. Yet, as all good countrymen in Britain know, the mink is a pest which has ravaged the wildlife of Britain, small mammals and birds, too, not to mention farm livestock, and there is no more effective way of destroying these voracious exotics than by drawing up the waterways for them with hounds. And who is to say that it is not the best way of culling the fox and West Country deer populations? And rats? Will Europe forbid us to set dogs on the rodents that infest our barns and stables. And how about gundogs used to flush game? The European Commission will find 'blanket' resolutions to be extremely invidious and contentious.

Of one thing I am certain that, in Britain, the welfare of neither the red fox nor the brown hare, the red deer of Exmoor nor the fallow deer of the New Forest, will in any way be enhanced by the banning of venery.

# 9

# *To the Polo Ground*

My polo career goes back to my army days in the 1950s when, in nearly all the garrisons, officers enjoyed a good deal more leisure time than they do now and the game was generously subsidized by the saddle clubs. I began in Cyprus and continued at Smith's Lawn, Windsor Great Park, during the early days of the Guards Club when the small playing membership there was composed mostly of serving officers and the average handicap was extremely modest. The Duke of Edinburgh, through whose influence and initiative the club was largely founded, was a regular player, and I frequently found myself on the same side as him for practice games. He was very patient with tyros – showing none of the brusqueness I witnessed on regimental occasions – and I recall being often taken on one side by him after matches, with other members of the team, when we were gently though firmly shown the error of our actions. Service in Gibraltar, during the early 1960s, found me the whole year round two or three evenings a week with rough little Andalusian ponies on even rougher Spanish pitches, interspersed with visits to the clubs at Tangier and Rabat.

Then I played regimental polo in Germany for a couple of seasons – Rhine Army manoeuvres and other duty permitting – before returning to England and finishing my active polo days with the Blues team, my last two matches being, I think, against Cambridge University, and, in the inter-regimentals, against the Irish Guards. I may add that – largely because I am naturally left-handed (a left-handed tennis and squash player) and polo must be played with the right hand – I made little progress during all those years. Following my discharge from the army, I assumed my involvement in the game must then be over for ever, not imagining for one moment, in 1968, that I was to endure a long career as a polo correspondent. John Adams, the then editor of *Country Life*, sent me to write up the premier British tournament, the Cowdray Park Gold Cup, in 1970; and, from 1971, he extended the magazine's polo coverage to five tournament articles a year. By 1980 that increased to seven or eight.

In 1978 the Home Editor of *The Times*, Charles Douglas-Home, was looking for a correspondent to succeed Colonel Andrew Horsbrugh Porter (a pre-war international player and a good reporter, too) and invited me to take the post. Since the *Country Life* hierarchy was at that time jealous of other publications using the names of their contributors in their by-lines I asked Charles if he would accept my reports under Lavinia's name. After a couple of seasons, however, *The Times* sports editor urged me to drop the pseudonym, which I did and *Country Life* overlooked the matter. *The Times* gave me my first experience of telephone reports on tight deadlines. Since the interest of both publications has been confined to the British high-goal scene, and to a lesser extent medium-goal challenges, my experience of the grass roots of the game, low-goal club polo, has been scant, although I have made a close study of the Pony Club element, of which more anon. Up to a few years ago *The Times* was the only newspaper reporting polo, but in the late 1980s the *Telegraph* began featuring it.

Cowdray Park, Sussex, Smith's Lawn, Windsor, and Cirencester Park, Gloucestershire – those have been my principal stamping-grounds as a polo journalist, and year after year, for more than twenty years, I have been preoccupied in June with the tournaments for the Queen's Cup and the Royal Windsor Cup at Smith's Lawn, and the Royal Warwickshire Cup at Cirencester; in July with the British Open Championships, and the Cowdray Park Challenge Cup at Midhurst, and the Hurlingham Association's International Day at Smith's Lawn; in August with the Pony Club Championships at Midhurst; and, in September, with the Guards Club's medium-goal autumn championships. This work has been regularly relieved, however, by coverage of such other *Country Life* interests as hound shows, animal and sporting art exhibitions, the Game Fair and more recently my 'Week in the Country' contributions.

From the time polo became firmly established in the 1880s and '90s at Hurlingham, Ranelagh and Roehampton it quickly acquired, throughout Britain, a brave and glamorous image, an image that carried a certain social prestige. Ever since then rich men – apart from taking up the game for the sheer love of it – have vied with one another to find places in teams that have been potential winners, or, if unable to participate, at least to patronize and field such teams. Glory has been the name of the game. I do not believe the majority of the general public understand why polo is so closely associated with affluence. The reason, which is the same in the 1990s as it was in the 1890s, may be summed up in the one word 'ponies'. (Strictly speaking – measuring an average of 15.2–15.3 hh – they are horses, but the traditional 'pony' survives the days when there was a height limit). A player pays heavily for his mounts, which, depending upon his handicap and stake in the game may number anything from two well-trained animals (low-goal tyro) to fifty (high-goal player-patron). Nor have the costs of grooms, stabling, fodder, horse boxes and saddlery ever been cheap.

Up to the Second World War, when big money was mostly 'old money' in the hands of a few, polo was almost as exclusive as the smart regiments (which, incidentally, produced a large number of the higher handicap players), the leading public schools and the London clubs. ('A game played by peers on the other side of the ground,' said the cynical.) That general principle more or less applied just after the war when John Cowdray led the game's revival in England, with Prince Philip as the figurehead, while Sunny Blandford, Johnny Macdonald-Buchanan, Charlie Smith Ryland and Billy Wallace (none of them by any stretch of the imagination, yuppies) were typical of the young men starting on the handicap ladder.

When, increasingly, from the 1960s the *nouveaux riches* hankered after the old institutions for their sons and daughters, and it was new money that more often than not talked loudest, a host of parvenu faces appeared in the polo clubs. With the coming of the yuppie age, new-rich men, no longer in need of parental propulsion, wanted polo along with the manor house and the extensive acres, the BMW, the yacht and Bermuda. Thus the clubs became glutted with new aspirants in their thirties and forties a great many of whom bought the game as a status symbol, prompting Colonel Alec Harper (hon secretary of the Hurlingham Association until 1990) to write in the HPA handbook: 'A lot of them are of very low handicap, and one wonders whether the motive is to play polo or to put a pair of boots on and a Lock hat in the back window of the Porsche.'

The other side of the coin, however, shines most brightly and honourably. Quite a large number of British players who are genuine sportsmen have made it, through sheer devotion, to the top echelon, men like the Hipwood brothers, Alan Kent, Paul Withers, John Horswell, Charles Beresford, Oliver Ellis, Martin Brown, Patrick Churchward, Philip Elliott, Martin Glue, Andrew Hine, Robert Graham and the Lucas and Seavill brothers. Most of those owe their livelihood to polo, whether in play or in the pony business. Players such as these, five-goalers and above – and many four-goalers, too – have little time for the glitzy, vain side of the game. They are too preoccupied with maintaining or improving their handicaps, keeping themselves riding fit, planning their travels in autumn, winter and spring around the polo circuit, South America, Mexico, Australasia, Malaysia and the United States. And a great deal of their time is spent supervising the care of their precious ponies, ever sensitive of the animals' welfare, their injuries and ailments or the least loss of condition, always conscious of any deterioration in their performance.

Over half our players of four handicap and above emerged from the Pony Club, whose annual championships have been attracting some sixty-five team entries, 260 young people. Let no one think that participation in Pony Club polo is cheap. For the very young challenges, in which a match consists of a single chukka, only one small pony is required, but as the child grows into a hefty teenager, taking part, say, in the tournament for the highly-prized Rendell Cup, he or she will need to draw upon two, or perhaps three, and as the boy or girl becomes increasingly 'hooked' on the game, parents must delve deeper into their pockets. Be that as it may the Pony Club, with its beautifully organized championships, stretching over more than six weeks of the summer, its well-conducted courses and its HPA scholarships to South America and Australasia, is the best hope for the future of British polo. (A great deal of the credit for the wonderful success of Pony Club polo must go to John ('Buff') and Liza Crisp.) Enduring affection for the game, however, poses a dilemma for most of the young with real talent. The ones attending university will probably have their sights set on a regular career, which means that the game must be more or less abandoned until they are really well established and financially secure. (Although, in the case of those going to Sandhurst, they will doubtless be eagerly recruited into regimental teams.) Others may be torn between the prospects offered by working in the polo yard of some patron, hoping thereby to find a niche in a good team and thereby struggling up the handicap ladder and becoming professionals on the cheap; or taking some other job in the expectation of earning enough money to return to polo at the earliest opportunity.

Switching to the high-goal scene let us take a cursory look at the patrons and their contribution to the game. In 1988, thirteen teams entered for the British Open, in 1989, when the Argentines were allowed back (after seven persona non grata years following the Falklands war) the number rose to twenty-one. The re-entry of the Argentines has proved a great bonus for polo – for the British players have much to learn from them. Their gift for ball control and game-sense rubs off easily on their team-mates, to whom they also show how to extract the maximum speed, tightness of turn and quickness off the mark from their ponies, and several useful tips in horsemastership, too. There is no doubt the standard of polo at the high- and medium-goal standards has risen since the Argentines came back to our shores – and probably at low-goal level as well, because the tyros learn much from watching the high-flyers. As against all that several Latin Americans display a habit that is inimical to British eyes: that of disputing umpires' decisions, raising their sticks to appeal for fouls at every given opportunity and sometimes showing marked signs of being bad losers. They are also, collectively, the main offenders of the 'manufactured foul'.

The return of the men from the Buenos Aires Clubs has not been the only reason for the unprecedented entries for tournaments. There have been more rich patrons entering the game, and the Gold Cup has become a more highly-prized trophy than ever (although, financially, there is everything to be lost and nothing to be gained for them by winning pieces of polo silver – except prowess and glory. And the patron who achieves the Gold Cup for the British Open will probably have spent around a quarter of a million on his way there.) In 1989, the Australian billionaire Kerry Packer purchased seventy and more Argentine ponies; and he signed up the eight-goal New Zealander, Stuart Mackenzie, on a three-year contract to be the pivot of his team, Ellerston. But Ellerston came nowhere, and one can readily understand why. The ponies, being bought late, were not acclimatized until towards the end of the season, and the players never looked like a particularly close-knit unit. (The four members of a successful polo team should be as closely integrated in play as a fisherman's rod, reel, line and hook.)

The most successful team of the late 1980s was Tramontana, who carried off the Gold Cup in four successive years between 1986–89. They deployed what may have been (given the conditions of HPA tournaments) as near a perfect 22–goal combination as one might hope to find. This was composed of its two patrons, Anthony Embiricos and David Jamison, each providing superlative strings of ponies and both playing off respectable three-goal handicaps. They fielded a couple of ace Mexicans in support: Carlos Gracida, a ten-goaler (arguably the best player in the world) and one of two of his six-goal compatriots, Valerian Aguilar or Roberto Gonzalez. Gracida is not only a magician with the ball and the possessor of a brilliant tactical intuition but he also has the gift of endowing every team member with a sense of superiority and of team unity. Moreover Tramontana has been a squad that has practised its strategy and interplay *ad infinitum*.

The patrons who fail to take the glittering prizes are, on the whole, those with moderate handicaps (in high-goal terms) who – more from vanity than any conviction that they are good enough – insists upon including themselves in the line-up. Whatever fun such men may get out of the chukkas themselves, it must be admitted that they not only fail to contribute properly as cogs in the team wheel, they also get in the way and cause fouls; and, because of their ineptitude, they make a mockery of the game. When, in one of my reports, I passed a derogatory comment on the play of such a patron at Cirencester, the club committee was so angry at my having had the effrontery to criticise one of their most useful financial benefactors that they deliberately omitted my name from the sponsors' lunch and went out of their way to say why! But after I had made a general comment to this effect in *Country Life* at the start of the 1989 season several aficionados greeted me warmly in the stands at Cowdray Park to concur with what I had written.

I am writing this at a most auspicious time for British polo, and astonishingly so considering it is little more than two years since the financial crash of October 1987, which many believe sounded the death-knell of Britain as a great International centre of the game. 1989 witnessed record entries for all the senior tournaments sanctioned by the HPA who, in response to patrons and players wanting more chukkas, persuaded the leading clubs to organize their challenges on the basis of leagues rather than knock-outs. And despite a summer almost unbroken by rain, club managers were at their wits end to find grounds to accommodate all the matches involved.

In addition to the tight and exciting programme of play at the top end of the game record numbers of tyros have been entering at the bottom end, and several new clubs have sprung up to cater for the influx. Nor has polo ever attracted such formidable public interest as it does now, and, in that respect, the most vital factor is the Royal involvement.

The Duke of Edinburgh's participation attracted the crowds during the 1950s and '60s as the presence of no other member of the Royal Family has done before or since. The Prince of Wales has proved a colossal draw, too (but, as I say, not so great as his father was). The polo hierarchy, ever conscious of this trump card in attracting sponsorship, etc, are naturally at pains to maintain and succour the Royal patronage, a fact reflected most of all in the trouble taken to gear tournament draws and timetable matches to suit Prince Charles's programme. Unfortunately for the Royal Family they pay as large a moral price for all this as in any other sphere of their lives. I refer to their exposure and the vulgarization of them: witness the gawping at Prince Charles in the pony lines and at other members of his family in the boxes, the sponsors jockeying for favourable positions and the armies of photographers and the (usually facetious and irrelevant) pictures and captions in the tabloids next day.

For many years I have been less than happy about the treatment by a few players of their ponies, which are all too often made to work far beyond their endurance and stamina, too often not properly cared for in the lines or the stables and not regularly inspected by a vet. I have seen animals injected with dope in the lines by people who are clearly unqualified to administer it (if indeed such doses are called for at all); and time and again I have seen ponies in play which are either clearly unfit or which carry signs of some unhealed injury. At the end of each season too many ponies are broken down or at best show signs of utter exhaustion. And again too often I have seen players using their whips and at the same time pulling on their ponies' mouths to 'put them on their toes', and ponies showing on their flanks the bloody traces of having been raked by spurs. But, as I have suggested earlier, the polo world is full of men who are not really horse-lovers and, in their yearning for personal prestige, hardly mind how much their animals suffer on the way. It should go without saying, however, that in principle the more valuable a pony is the better it will be cared for. Money speaks. It is the less high-calibre animals we should worry most about.

Polo has burgeoned and blossomed to the extent that the HPA hierarchy has begun to look rather archaic. It requires a stronger and more decisive authority. A single reason from many I could cite of this is the Association's failure to exert the discipline that is necessary in the matter of umpires, who are all too often late or inadequately mounted or not properly dressed and equipped. And, because umpires lack staunch backing from the ruling body, they are frequently cowed by high-tempered players. The stamp of firm government would help put all that right. The HPA needs, I believe, to be reorganized and streamlined in much the same manner that proved necessary for the Jockey Club. Their administration should be run by a dynamic professional with a sure grasp of polo's fundamental problems. But the fact that this is now urgent simply mirrors the triumphant direction in which the game is heading. For when the tail is wagging the dog clearly a great new exuberance resides in the dog.

My friend Jilly Cooper's host of admirers are now eagerly awaiting her latest novel, which is to have a polo background, and I much look forward to seeing how she applies her unique narrative skill and imagination to the story. What wonderful ingredients are hers to play with! Cosmopolitan millionaires and impoverished girl grooms, glamorous high-goalers and glitzy girls, animal beauty, courage and suffering, the exuberance of Pony Club polo, villainy in the pony lines, gossip in the pavilions, jealous rivalry, high tempers, up-market ribaldry and loud vanity – with, overall, an aura of colourful romance. For a novelist, rich pickings indeed!

# 10

# *Sussex Then and Now*

Now I come full cycle. The first chapter of these memoirs began with my father and so will the last. For – although we were based in Chelsea (and London claimed him for much more time than he would have wished) during his last few years before his death, near the Franco-Belgian border in May, 1940 – he enjoyed regular intervals with his family in his remote little house in West Sussex, a house devoid of electricity and to which the main water supply had only recently been extended. My father fashioned a garden, with terraces and shrubberies, ornamental trees and brilliant borders, from the primeval land, and since we were surrounded by silent pastures and undisturbed woodlands, almost the entire character of the district was still and quiet, except for the sounds of Nature (the dawn chorus was a cacophony in those days). In due season the meadows, woods and waysides were vivid with a profuse variety of wild flowers, a galaxy which was to be severely diminished, in due course, by agricultural sprays. The flight of an aircraft over Wickers, as it was called, was such a rare occurrence that we all looked up following its course, as though mesmerized, until it was out of sight; if two cars passed down the adjoining lane in a day it was one more car than usual. We saw few other people than Margaret, the cook, and Kenward the gardener, or more occasionally, old Brooker the keeper (who taught me many a thing about the fauna and flora. He showed me creatures that I hardly ever see now, otters and yellow-necked field mice, long-eared bats and harvest mice, hobbys and merlins, slowworms and natterjack toads.) Or when the hunt met close by to invade the tranquility. Or in the summer when we joined other children at tennis and tea parties. My best friends, after those I have mentioned, were Judy, our beloved brindled bull terrier, and 'Mr Smith', the old Siamese cat who came down from London to make himself thoroughly at home in Sussex, especially in spring and early summer when this elderly sealpoint moggie (well known in Smith Street, Chelsea) would sit patiently by the mouths of rabbit burrows and take a young one or two as they emerged.

Petworth, our local market town, was a relatively smart place, I suppose, but still little more than a large village. The A272 which now runs so menacingly through its centre, was hardly noticed as a main road in the 1930s, and probably no more than two of the thirty and more antique shops (for which it is now so celebrated) existed. It has since served as a prosperous middle-aged retreat, but in those days it contained a much younger (and much smaller) community, committed mostly in one way or another to the farming and forestry of the Leconfield estate. Everyone knew everyone else, knew their business and their calling, too, and greeted all and sundry with a 'good morning' and a warm smile, while the shop assistants took a close interest in their customers' needs and were always courteous and helpful. Letters were invariably acknowledged by return of post and telephone messages promptly followed up. If shopkeepers or tradesmen were guilty of errors they made duly humble and sincerely contrite apologies, and promised that such negligence would not re-occur. There was much generosity, much neighbourliness and little of the materialism that was to come. There was courtesy on the roads. No-one bothered to lock their front doors or their cars, let alone their bicycles. And, reflecting the community spirit, Sunday mornings always found the church full, everyone happily celebrating matins in their Sunday best.

But Petworth, with its modern impatient bustle and rich man's image, would be alien to my father if he returned to see it now. And, if the Sussex home of which I have written, were to go on the market at the present time anyone intending to 'get away from it all', as my parents did, would do better to seek an equivalent in Scotland or Wales. Because its solitude has been stolen by progress.

I have gone back to boyhood in this way in order to draw comparisons and contrasts; for the house in which Lavinia and I live is little more than twenty minutes drive away from there and it shares the same developing environment. The peace of our sky is all too often broken by the monsters from Gatwick and that of the lanes with the roar of impulsive traffic – the little cottages quaking and shuddering at the approach of the engine-throbbing leviathans – while the farm machines (it is nearly all contract farming here now) race about their business as though their drivers are in a life-or-death contest, and they leave not so much as an inch of the traditional headland, while tossing lumps of clay under our post-and-rail fences onto our lawns with their frenetic blades. The serenity of weekend evenings is too frequently broken from the pub by drunken revelry and screaming motor bikes, Sunday mornings shattered by the commotion of the clay-shooting club drowning the church bells, other days by that most antisocial creature, the chain saw.

The village is filled with retired folk save for its new spick estate which houses flourishing nine-to-fivers. Some of the old labourers' cottages are havens for the elderly, but many more have been bought by whizz kids and other young high-flyers with BMWs and Porsches, who have developed and extended these dwellings almost out of recognition, and who contribute ostentatiously to the social life of the district with sophisticated little dark-suit dinner parties on Friday or Saturday evenings. One of them, living only a few hundred yards away, takes off for work each weekday morning in a helicopter. Everybody seems to want to save time and then wonders why life slips past so quickly. Because these unattractive conditions burgeon only by gradual degrees it is not too difficult to learn to live with them. But, as I say, had it been possible for my father, who died before his fourth decade was quite out, to be resurrected in the Sussex of half a century later he would doubtless wish to be restored to the grave without delay; and who of the older generation would blame him, notwithstanding the fact that, conversely, the quality of life has improved enormously in many other ways? He would probably notice in particular the drastic recession of wildlife in the last half century, the extinction of so many wild flowers, done away with by herbicides and development; the sad abatement of avian music, because more than half the songbirds' nesting-places, hedges and corners of wilderness, have been removed, and the magpie and other corvid populations are such that the small birds are losing more of their eggs and fledgelings than they ever did. Of the mammals I think the one most notable for its absence is the hare, with which the Weald of Sussex once abounded. I have never seen a hare in the area where we live now. Unable to compete with the pace of modern agriculture, they withdrew to the Downs long ago.

I am sure my father would comment, too, on the virtual elimination of the local patois, the slow Sussex burr, with its rich accent and lilt, somewhere between Devon and Norfolk, now, alas, taken over by the universal, much less colourful Home Counties voice with which the media and mass communications in general have endowed the South of England.

The original two-up two-down half-timbered wattle-and-daub part of our house was built, virtually without foundations, in the mid seventeeth century for the parish cordwainer, the supplier of boots and shoes, who, being called Arthur Pannett, lent his name to the place – Pannett's Shipley. Our dining-room, with its inglenook and bakery oven, was the Pannetts' living-room and kitchen; their shop is now the hall dividing that from our drawing-room. Their water came from a well thirty feet deep (its beautifully brick-built sides are still watertight). The extensive additions to the seventeeth-century sugar-loaf dwelling did not come until about the time of the Second World War or after. With the whole site more than trebled in size there is ample room for the two of us and our guests, while the garden boundaries have been pushed out to two acres where once there was only half an acre. (Lavinia is an avid and irrepressible gardener despite her arthritis.) We used to open to the public under the National Gardens charity scheme, but since this meant doing all the work – notices, teas, car parking and entrance money – we have transferred our allegiance to the local Red Cross, who lay on everything and, in addition, set up a profitable shop in a summer house. It amuses us on those days to watch our visitors and observe the things that absorb them most. The main attractions seem to be not so much the many facets and features of the garden itself as the surrounding farmland, the quaint composition of the house, the fantail pigeons, of which our dovecote holds about fifty, the inmates of our ornamental duck enclosure and, above all, the dogs.

Our ornamental ducks suffered an appalling disaster recently when their enclosure was invaded by an entire family of mink. They must have felt like American frontiersmen when the Indians crept over the palisades with their tomahawks. Bodies lay around with heads missing or were stuffed, tight as sardines, up drainpipes serving as mink larders. By the third morning the entire splendour of our collection was gone, with the exception of one brave male mandarin; and the pond, once happy with wild song, was quiet as a morgue.

'How can we improve our defences?' I asked the expert, Fred Hobgen – a man deeply versed in the wiles of all predators – who arrived with his traps the morning after the first blow was struck. He glanced around our foxproof fence. 'Short of constructing an impenetrable enclosure with overhead netting like a fruit cage, you can't,' he replied. 'Little devils, they'll climb trees and drop in from the branches; they'll burrow beneath your underground wire netting, they'll crawl through narrow pipes, they'll even scale your fencing. They'll laugh at Fort Knox,' said Fred. Be that as it may I have now restocked the pond and we are praying no more of these vicious invaders will be trying their luck too soon.

Life at Pannett's Shipley revolves around our springer spaniels and Jack Russell terriers. Grizel, a loner among canines if ever there was one, came of Leicestershire hunt terrier stock. Her daughter, a most engaging bitch, Gannet – so called because she sported dark rings around her eyes like the sea-bird's – gave her name to my novel, *Gannet: The Story of a Terrier*. Tragically, she was drowned having tumbled into a lily pond on a black wet November night in 1984 and left no trace of herself until her cold little body surfaced three weeks later. Now we have her niece, Linnet, Grizel's granddaughter, a red-and-white terrier of exquisite symmetry and good looks, who last autumn won one of the prizes presented at our local 'fun dog show' from a field of nearly forty in the class for 'the dog with the most appealing eyes'. The illustrator of my Gannet story, Helen Backhouse, used Linnet as her model.

How different are our dogs in their personalities, as well as in their appearance, at least as diverse as people! The deeply-wise gaze of the quiet old tricolour spaniel, Boadicea, a great-grandmother – who won the blue rosette in the veteran class at the same show – follows our every move. (Her signature song could appropriately be the American *I've got my eyes on you, I'm checking on all you do from A to Z* . . .) She used to be an absolutely brilliant catcher of rabbits, so it is rather sad to see her in her old age outpaced by all the others and eluded at the turn.

Boad's daughter, Bundles, is an extrovert, full of humour, frequently a buffoon. And she sings for joy, nose pointing to the sky like a wolf, when she is about to be taken for a walk. 'If it smells nice and presents a challenge take it to bed with you!' seems to be one of her mottoes. Hedgehogs must be like nectar to her, because, before retiring to her kennel of a winter's night she frequently visits a corner inhabited by these little mammals, and, with a mouth apparently quite immune to the pricks, carries one to her straw. Fortunately we always know when that happens since a hectic barking ensues. I then go down to her kennel armed with a torch and thick pair of gardening gloves. There, sure enough she is, her straw kicked to one side to expose the poor creature, while she points her nose at it yelping furiously. Then she glances up with a pained expression in her eyes as if to say – like a schoolgirl for whom an apple-pie bed has been made – 'I say, just look at this, some joker's put a hedgehog in my lair!' So I pick up the barbed ball and carry it to the ornamental duck enclosure, the only place entirely inaccessible to the dogs. I have lost count of how many have ended up there. She is very insistent that her back be scratched of an evening. While the others may beg for food Bundles will importune, with much tapping of my elbow with an animated forepaw, and, when patience is running out, guide my hand to her back with a wet nose, then whine in ecstasy when the treatment is given.

Bundles's first mate was another good spaniel, but she was got at the night following her marriage, by a roving farm dog. The result was that rare phenomenon, a dual conception, with a litter of eight mongrels and three spaniels to show for it. We kept Bright, who remains the prettiest of our four black-and-white spaniel generations and the one with the sweetest nature, too. Bright's daughter, Brambling (Bling), is a delightful blend of character, sometimes playing tip-and-run by the hour with little Linnet, sometimes mounting a manure heap or other mound to bark at the others with her version of 'queen of the castle', often simply lying on her back, paws dangling, neck outstretched, tongue lolling. She possesses a 'wall eye', otherwise known, I believe, as a 'fish' or 'pearl' eye; it is the colour of the sky on a summer's day, so that the dark brown of the natural eye contrasts starkly with its cerulean. When she is hunting she outstrips all the others and her nose, ever close to the ground, betrays the carefully bred gundog acuity prevalent on both sides of her proud pedigree. (Her sire came from the famous Bricksclose field trial champion breed.)

While I am all for the Christian ethics the more I get to know animals and the more I observe the ways of the natural world the less I believe that the Creator ever meant man to be the world's supreme being. Or that man was made in the image of God. Or that only man inherits eternal life. I believe that God looks upon man as the vandal element in His creation, in evolution. And, as for life everlasting, if there is such a thing I am convinced that all life is its beneficiary. I believe that no man or woman who sees the essential good in the animals he or she owns or who has a truly close affinity with Nature, can honestly claim that they or their fellow humans are 'better' creatures.

We are indeed privileged to be allowed to exercise six dogs off the lead on the adjacent farmland. They rarely have less than two hours' walk a day; but as the shooting interest has been greatly increased on the estate, we have to be more careful than ever, especially in the spring (for there is nothing that intrigues the dogs more than ground-nesting birds) and in the early autumn (when the young pheasants and partridges leave the release pens and are not too sure of themselves on the wing). And in winter, of course, we must give the shoots a wide berth. The new feverish farming activity is another factor that makes dog-walking a more precarious activity. Where last year there was grass now there is corn; where this morning there was stubble this afternoon there is plough, where twenty minutes ago the field was empty, now it holds a hundred head of cattle; and when there are no vehicles tilling, others will be dredging or hedging and ditching. There are nearly always farm noises (engine – not animal – noises). For the past few years large flocks of sheep have been introduced to shave our surrounding pastures bare, whereas in the past the sheep was not a Wealdon beast. And now the estate, to make ends meet, poses more threats to us local residents.

'Diversify!' cry those who audit the estate accounts. 'Diversify!' repeat the agents (with an eye to a monumental rake-off). 'Diversify!' echo the young men who have inherited the land, (for quite apart from profit, it is the fashion). The one whose property surrounds our plot owns the sites on which a trio of adjacent villages lie; he has substantial housing projects in hand for all three. He plans to convert his ancestral home into a hotel with a golf course in the park, fishing on the lake and a commercial shoot. His mind's eye sees eight sturdy barns developed into weekend cottages or permanent homes; and, (worst of all, from our point of view) he proposes to dam and flood several pretty little valleys for angling and wildfowling, with club houses and car parks for those who would take rods and guns on the beats.

It is heartening (at the time of writing) to hear of the Government planning policy on the protection of the countryside, launched by the new Secretary of State for the Environment, a policy highlighted in the same week by the rejection of his predecessor's approval to build a massive housing estate at Foxley Wood in Hampshire. I very much hope this new national conservation policy will be felt throughout rural Britain.

What is not apparently vogueish in our vicinity is 'set aside'. Our countryside has been ruined by intensive farming, by the heavy hand of agricultural man, producing the vast expensive surpluses of food that nobody wants. I would like to see – as the Nature Conservancy Council and all the wildlife conservation bodies would, too – large tracts of farmland restored to Mother Nature and thus the return of all that fauna and flora of which the farmers have deprived us. If I were influential in the judiciary I would impose the most terrible penalties on farmers who pollute, along with other rural criminals such as badger-baiters, and poachers of the rivers and woodlands. However, I think it is wonderfully encouraging nowadays the way the schools emphasize the importance of the wildlife conservation. Not a single lesson was given at my prep school on natural history or on the wealth of Britain's rural heritage; but at the Horsham primary school, of which I was a governor for twelve years, such subjects are allotted quite a prominent place on the syllabus.

What a confusing lot of conflicts there are in modern Britain's rural areas! In the mid eighteenth century an imaginative ancestor of another landowning neighbour of ours, Harry Goring, planted up Chanctonbury Ring, that great beech clump that breaks the skyline close to the South Downs Way above Worthing. When the hurricane of October 1987, blew half the trees down, leaving that once smart landmark looking like a man who had lost, overnight, all his hair and half his teeth, the distraught Mr Goring announced his intention to replant more or less right away. But bureaucracy stalled him. Bronze Age Britons established a fortified village on that very site, and, smack in the middle of it, the Romans built a temple. 'You mustn't touch it until the archaeologists have had a go!' the Ministry, having consulted English Heritage, told Mr Goring. The dig should have begun in the summer of 1989, but the necessary funds were not to hand. When *will* they be available? At the time of writing no one can give the answer to that. So I suppose we must endure a long wait for the excavation to commence – which few Sussex folk care tuppence about (for all its great academic importance) – and a very long time indeed before the widely known and greatly loved landmark is restored to its pristine effect. For beech grows slowly.

Having been rather too disparaging about our corner of the county I would add that, despite all the pressures, it is also a wonderful corner, and how lucky we are to occupy a house embosomed in two acres of garden with fields and woodland all around. Our village, ten minutes walk across the fields from the house and standing in a loop of the River Adur, may well lay claim to being one of the half-dozen most interesting, historically, in Britain. Having been a Roman settlement the plot was given by William of Normandy to one of his favourite barons, William de Braose, who built the first Knepp Castle, the ruins of which can be seen on their hillock from the Worthing road. In 1208 King John confiscated the castle from the de Broase of the time and made frequent use of it as a hunting lodge. Early in the twelfth century Shipley was the site chosen by the Knights Templar for their most important preceptory in the south-east of England, and they built the church, St Mary the Virgin. Following the destruction of that Order by Edward II, the Knights Hospitallers occupied the Templar buildings.

Shipley's ruling family from the mid sixteenth century were the Carylls, ironmasters and also staunch Catholics, and for that they were persecuted and suffered such fines that they were persuaded to sell up towards the end of the eighteenth, since when the Burrell family – living in the 'new' gothic, Nash-designed Knepp Castle, the house now earmarked to be an hotel – have held sway. The Adur being once a broad tidal stream Shipley was then a little port from which oak was sent for shipbuilding at Shoreham, and supplies came up from the coast, including, in great quantities, those of smugglers. Leading off from Shipley is a long straight old smugglers' lane, depressed between the fields and flanked by trees which has since served well as a public footpath. The Quakers' principal meeting-house was in this part of Sussex and William Penn lived less than a mile from Pannett's Shipley. Alexander Pope spent part of his life in the adjacent West Grinstead Park and Wilfred Scawen Blunt's house, Newbuildings, is also in the parish.

Shipley's focal point is less the Templars' church than the windmill, of which I am a trustee. At a cost of some £150,000 we are having it restored, and, at the moment, it looks rather forlorn with its weatherboarded smock tower bereft of sweeps and fantail. Nevertheless it attracted some 600 visitors on its 1989 open days and we are hoping for many more when it returns to its full glory. It once belonged to Hilaire Belloc who, in 1906, bought it with the adjacent house, King's Land, and where he lived until his death in 1953. By agreement with the miller his children were accustomed to swing on the sweeps to their hearts' delight. Belloc, who was born in 1870, was in infancy when he lost his father, a barrister broken by the Franco-Prussian War. Madame Belloc, an Englishwoman, then left France with her little son for England, and Hilaire had long been in love with the Sussex Weald by the time he first arrived at Shipley in 1906 (riding a bicycle with hs wife, Elodie, in a trailer behind it). His property stretched to 120 acres. He kept some cattle, helped to reap the hay (of which crop he was particularly proud) and grew vegetables that suited his taste for French *cuisine*. With his idealistically pastoral view of the countryside he is another of a past generation who would doubtless turn in his grave if he were to witness the changes that have occurred, and are threatened, in Sussex, and indeed the lifestyle of the villagers, which, considering his philosophy, I am sure he would condemn as 'artificial'. Anyway it is gratifying to think that we tread the paths that Blunt and Pope and Belloc trod, pick blackberries from the brambles that they may have plucked in the September sunshine, listened to the birdsong that they heard.

Belloc must be counted as one of the two or three most prolific writers of the twentieth century. Much of his stuff was repetitive, badly researched and badly composed (most of it, in his old age, dictated at great speed to secretaries) but one cannot help admiring the sheer volume and variety of his good writing, drama and verse, biography and travel, history and fiction. It is more because Belloc lived only ten minutes walk across the meadows from our house and his spirit still somehow pervades the village (and because I have made a particular study of his best work) than for any other reasons that I often compare the lot and condition of authors of his era with those of today.

There are now infinitely more writers, more publishers, more books, more bookshops, the trade in Belloc's day being tiny by comparison. There are also a great many more authors competing for the honours, far more struggling for positive recognition whatever their special fields of endeavour. The literary world of half a century ago was much kinder, much less cut-throat, too. Jealousy has since played a more bitter role in the game. I have dealt with half-a-dozen and more publishers, the first of which, during the 1970s, was Batsford. My editor there warned me that I mustn't be surprised if my 'opening' book failed to receive a review at all in one or two of the relevant specialist magazines, or (if it did gain a notice) if it was condemned out of hand or, at best, damned with faint praise. 'Why is that?' I enquired. 'Petty jealousy,' she replied. 'Either the editor or the reviewer will wish he or she had written the thing himself or herself, or will be annoyed because it has come out before a similar book by one of that publication's own contributors. And (your book perhaps having been allotted a few disdainful lines), the next thing you'll see,' said the Batsford editor, 'is a two-page spread extolling a (probably) inferior book on the same subject by one of the said editor's favourite contributors. And thus that magazine's readership is misled.' I looked at her in astonishment. But in fourteen years of writing books I have found that she did not exaggerate at all.

What a cankerous evil thing jealousy is and how far-reaching its tentacles! But, considering the plethora of books with which editors are faced nowadays I suppose authors are, on the whole, dealt with quite reasonably and fairly. Whatever cavalier treatment our books may receive at the hands of reviewers I, like most authors, are happy in the knowledge that, so far as we are concerned our efforts have been truthfully and imaginatively created; and constructed to the best of our abilities. The satisfaction of that should outweigh the damage done by spiteful reviewers. The only general complaint I have regarding the reception of books is that, in the 'serious' newspapers far too much space is given to novels of doubtful merit, and highly academic works (often painfully indigestible and of interest only to the few) at the expense of too many 'popular' books of intrinsic literary worth, which are nevertheless dismissed by the *literati* for being Philistine. I wonder if it is a matter of undue intellectual snobbery? It is the same in the world of the fine arts.

I have loved good prose for as long as I can remember; and have always been a story addict. My brothers and I were fortunate to have a father who enjoyed reading to us. Jeffrey Farnol, Charles Kingsley, Captain Marryat, G. A. Henty, Walter Scott, Rudyard Kipling and R. D. Blackmore were among the mixture of authors he chose for our delectation. I was spellbound by the stirring tales those men spun and weaved. After my father died (when I was twelve) story-reading became such an obsession with me that, at school, I frequently retreated into a fantasy world of fiction, which was one of the reasons I was such a bad scholar. I spent evenings copying out passages from novels (anything from *David Copperfield* to *Gone With the Wind*) when I should have been studying physics, trigonometry, or whatever. During the 1960s, when I was writing 6,000–9,000-word stories for *Blackwood's Magazine*, old Douglas Blackwood wrote saying he thought his publication was the only one that would accept the old-fashioned style and character of my narratives. I replied that this was probably a case of arrested development, so influenced was I by the author-heroes of my boyhood, rather than those of the fiction I read afterwards. As for the novelists of our generation I must confess an inability to get along with such luminaries as Amis (either of them), Murdoch or Drabble, but I greatly enjoy Brookner, Golding, Greene, Lively and Tremain.

Many of my most fertile ideas surface on dog-walks, for which I always carry a piece of white card and a pencil to record them. I have never veered from my original method of writing. I make three, sometimes four, drafts of everything I write, the final longhand proof being on the right-hand page of an exercise book, the left page being kept clear for additions or conclusive corrections. I have never used a typewriter, let alone a word processor. Lavinia does nearly all my typing, correspondence as well as manuscripts, often making very rude red-ink comments in the margin insisting that I take this out, add that or change this.

A big proportion of my time is still spent contributing to *Country Life*. I told the Editor, Jenny Greene, recently that I wished to reduce my hunting articles by half. The reasons I gave were Lavinia's resentment at my being away too many winter weekends and the inordinate lengths of time spent in driving, for which I have little liking especially at night. Another reason is that, ever since I took on the role in 1969, I have been obliged to turn down numerous shooting invitiations and I now hope to devote a few more days annually to that pursuit. Anyhow Jenny has recruited an assistant to alternate with me through the season. With him visiting the more famous hunts that I concerned myself with long ago, I am now content to go out with those in the backwaters of hunting Britain and Ireland. We have yet to see how that works out.

The diminution of my hunting commitment has by no means reduced the necessity to keep riding fit, for which support, over my twenty seasons, I have exercised a number of neighbours' hunters two or three mornings a week. My nice nineteen-year-old current hack is beautifully mannered in every respect except that he frequently reacts to perfectly harmless objects, such as drain covers, pieces of paper or plastic, or traffic signs as though they are dragons or boaconstrictors. Without any warning he will stop dead in his tracks, and in the same movement rear or shy at right-angles across the road, a habit that might end in a very serious accident for us both. I prided myself in being his only rider who had never been thrown, until November 1988, when I was flung most painfully on the tarmac. He galloped straight back to his stables, crossing a main road en route, and I trembled to think of the result if that moment had coincided with the demon traffic. (My experience has been that the most thoughful road-users, from an equestrian viewpoint, are farmworkers, postmen, haulage drivers and tradesmen. When I mentioned this to Lavinia the other day she asked who were the least considerate. 'Women in private cars' I replied without hesitation and with at least a grain of truth. 'Absolute nonsense!' was her instant retort.)

The vacuum left by the cut-down in my *Country Life* hunting programme has been fruitfully filled. In 1988 I commenced my regular 'Week in the Country' contributions, for which I usually cover four different subjects for the page concerned in the space of some thousand words. And there is no shortage of topics in our neck of the woods. I watch the herons fishing, the martens building, the kestrels hunting and the foxes playing; I attend terrier shows, ploughing matches, agricultural shows, point-to-points, horse shows and meets of the mink hounds; I pass the time of day with the keeper, the pest control man, the forester and the huntsman, duck breeders, cat breeders, pony breeders and goat breeders; and I join boat parties to view the waterfowl at Chichester harbour or see what the county naturalists trust is up to. I watch closely the seasons' changing moods and I always make time to watch a dramatic going down of the sun. Though Lavinia and I have seen a thousand sunsets in the Mediterranean and the Orient that are far more sensational, for us the sunsets of Sussex have never been surpassed as the sweetest and most glorious in the world.

# *Index*

Abel Smith, Col Sir Henry (RHG), 44, 46
Abel Smith, Capt. Richard (RHG), 56
Acton, Major-Gen. Thomas (Rifle Bde), 35
Adams, John, Editor, *Country Life*, 100, 101, 104, 208
Agnew, Sir Geoffrey, Eton master, 26–27
Aguilar, Valerian, polo player, 211
Airborne Forces Depot, 56
Aldenham Harriers, 141
Aldershot Beagles, 169
Alexander brothers (Ireland), 179
Allison, Buck, MFH (USA), 193–94
American hunting, 32–34, 185–196
Ampleforth Beagles, 165–66
Ampleforth College, 28
Amory, Cleveland (animal welfarist), 112
Animal Welfare, 105–109, 111–114
Anker, David (South Wold), 132
Annaly, Lord, MFH, 121, 167
Arbuthnot, Sir Hugh, MFH, 18, 154, 160, 165
Arm, Graham, MFH, 123
Ascot races, 48
Ashford Valley Hunt, 42, 163–64
Association of Wildlife Clubs (Kenya), 110
Atherstone Hunt, 123, 137
Athenaeum Club, 104
Athlone, Major Gen. Earl of, (LG), 62
Atkinson, Cooper (Brocklesby), 131
Avgorou incident, 72–73
Avon Vale Hunt, 146

Bacall, Lauren, actress, 45–46
Backhouse, Helen, artist, 217
Bacon, Newton, MH, 160
Badsworth Hunt, 156
Bailey, Major Roderic, MFH, 156
Baird-Murray, Douglas (Middlesex Yeo), 13
Baker, Richard, commentator, 95
Banwen Miners' Hunt, 149–150
BAOR, 35–44, 88–93
Barbary apes (Gibraltar), 86
Barcelona, Countess of, MFH (Portugal), 185

Barclay, Capt. Charles, MFH, 118, 165, 168
Barker, George (Quorn), 51
Barthorp, Major Michael, 35
Basset hounds, 170–72
Batsford, publisher, 114
Battersea Dogs Home, 125
Beaufort, 10th Duke of, MFH, 118, 125–26, 135, 176, 187
Beaufort, Mary, Duchess of, 125, 154
Beagling Festival, 163
Beaumont, Hon. Richard, 22
Beck, Baron Frederic de, MFH (Portugal), 184–85
Bedale Hunt, 157–58
Bedford, Erskine, MFH (USA), 189–190
Belgian hunting, 204–206
Bell, Brian, MFH, 122, 132
Bell, Ikey, MFH, 118, 176, 195
Bellamy, W. P., MFH, 143
Belloc, Hilaire, 25
Belvoir Hunt, 51, 118
Bennett, Jim (Vale of Aylesbury), 129
Beresford, Lord Charles, polo player, 210
Beresford, Capt. Lord Patrick (RHG), 70, 74
Berkeley, Hon. Mrs, MFH, 120
Berkeley, John, MFH, 128–29
Berks and Bucks Draghounds, 165
Berlin Wall, 90
Berry, Lt-Col Hon. Julian (RHG), 74, 78
Bevan, Rt Hon. Aneurin, MP, 103
Bevan, Michael, 168
Best, Stephen (IFAW), 112
Bicester and Warden Hill Hunt, 127
Biegel, Peter, artist, 148
Birch, Trooper (RHG), EOKA victim, 78
Birch Reynardson, Col Henry, 86–87
Birch Reynardson, William, 18
Birdwood, Field-Marshal Lord, 47
Birdwood, Hon. Mark (RHG), aft. Lord Birdwood, 77
Birley, Sir Robert, Eton headmaster, 29
Black, Sir David, MFH, 104
*Blackwood's Magazine*, 90, 92–93, 152

Blake, H. D. (RHG), 72–73
Blandford, Marquess of (LG), aft. Duke of
    Marlborough, 45, 209
Blankney Hunt, 131
Blean Beagles, 163
Bloor, James, MFH, 156
Blue Ridge Hunt (USA), 33
Blunt, Wilfrid, 27
Boadicea, a spaniel, 217
Bogart, Humphrey, actor, 45–46
Bolebroke Beagles, 164
Bonham-Carter, Hon. Mark, publisher, 99
Bonner-Maurice, Major Edward, MFH, 150
Border Hunt, 153
Borwick, Col 'Peach', MFH, 176
Bouskell, James, MFH, 167
Bowen, Rev. Michael, Archbishop of
    Southwark, 88
Bowes-Lyon, Lt-Col James (Gren. Gds), 77
Boyd, Hon. Alastair, aft. Lord Kilmarnock,
    88, 99
Boyd, Robin and Lavinia, 180
Boyle, Sir Edward, Bt, 23
Brainard, William W., MFH, 187–188
Brambling, a spaniel, 218
Brecon Hunt, 151
Bredin, Col H.E.N. (Para), 64
Bright, a spaniel, 218
Britannia Beagles, 170
British Field Sports Society, 107, 123, 157,
    207
British Sporting Art Trust, 197
Brock, D. W. E., MFH, 54, 159
Brocklesby Hunt, 130–31
Brockbank, John, MFH, 159
Broughton, Hon. Ailwyn (RHG), aft. Lord
    Fairhaven, 72, 78
Brooks's Club, 102, 103–104
Brooks, Mr and Mrs, EOKA victims, 78
Browne, Major Simon, 152
Browning, Robert (Colonial Service), 76, 77
Brownlow, Major William, 18
Buchanan-Jardine, Sir John, MFH, 54–55,
    137, 153, 160, 171, 176
Buchanan-Jardine, Major Sir Rupert, MFH,
    41–42, 54–55, 104, 135–36, 160
Buckhunting, 108
Buckland, Philip, MFH, 163
Buckle, Albert (Whaddon Chase), 128
Buckley, Major Kemmis (WG), 64, 66
Buckmaster, Capt. Herbert, 102
Bucknall, Major Robin, 133
Buck's Club, 102, 104, 118
Bülow, Baronin Hedda von, 37–38
Bundles, a spaniel, 217–218

Burnaby-Atkins, Andrew, 22, 25
Burrows, Philip, MH, 164
Burton Hunt, 131
Butler, Major-Gen. Hew (Rifle Bde), 35
Butler, Brig. Mervyn ('Tubby') (Parachute
    Brigade), 64, 67
Butterwick, Michael (Rifle Brigade), 34
Bywaters hounds (USA), 188, 193, 195

Café de Paris, The, 48
Caldwell, Edmund, artist, 9
Calpe Hunt (Spain), 182
Cameron, James, MFH, 157
Canadian Humane Trapping Society, 112
Cantrell-Hubbersty, Mrs (Quorn), 50
Carey, Capt, Darel (RHG), 65
Carr–Ellison, Sir Ralph, MFH, 163
Cartland, Barbara (Mrs McCorquodale), 121
Casier, Philippe (Belgium), 205
Castro, Fidel, 89
Cattell, Antonia, MFH (Ireland), 179
Cedar Knob Hunt, USA, 193–94
Cely Trevilian, John, 145
Chafer, Charles, MFH,156
Champion, Jack (Old Surrey & Burstow
    Hunt), 135
Chanctonbury Ring, 219–220
Channon, CSM (Coldm Gds), 81
Chapman, George, MFH (Ireland), 173
Chaworth Musters, Robert, MFH, 18
Chelsea, 10, 12
Cheshire Hunt, 133–34
Cheshire, Mr Stewart's, Hunt (USA), 187
Chesterton, G. K., 25
Churchill, Sir Winston, 31, 86
Churchward, Patrick, polo player, 210
Christ Church and Farley Hill Beagles, 136,
    168–69
Chrysler, Walter P., 33–34
Cirencester Park Polo Club, 209, 212
City and Guilds of London Art School, 99
Claflin, David, WSPA, 113–114
Clarke, Jack, Crawley & Horsham hunt, 136
Clarke, Capt. Simon, MFH, 165
Cleveland Hunt, 157
Clifton-on-Teme hunt, 133
Coakham Bloodhounds, 139
Cockfighting, 113
Colchester Garrison Beagles, 161, 169
College Valley hunt, 153–54
Collin, Lady Clarissa, 155
Coniston hunt, 158, 159
Connor, William ('Cassandra'), journalist,
    75–6
Conolly-Carew, Hon. Patrick (RHG), 177

Conolly-Carew, Hon. Mrs Patrick, 177
Constantinou, Alexander, EOKA terrorist, 71
Conybeare, A. E., Eton master, 22
Coombs, Thomas, 42
Cooper, Jilly, author, 213
Cooper, Gladys, actress, 102
Cooper, Maj.-General Simon (LG), 20
Coreth, Capt. Mark (Blues and Royals), 97
Cotley Hunt, 143–44
Cotter, Pat, writer on bridge, 100
Coventry, Lady Maria, MFH, 132, 157
*Country Life*, 9, 22, 29, 99, 100–103, 109, 114, 118, 123, 142, 188, 208–209, 212, 222–23
Coward, Noel, 23, 64
Cowdray, 3rd Viscount, 209
Cowdray Park Polo club, 208, 209, 212
Crawford, Lt-Col J. D. (Carabiniers), 53–54
Crisp, 'Buff' and Liza, Pony Club polo, 210
Crosbie Dawson, James, MFH, 166
Crosby, Bing, 94
Crossley, Major Hon. Nicholas, MFH, 155
Crystal Palace, 10, 11, 24
Cubitt, Col Hon. Guy, MFH, 14, 135
Cumberland Farmers' Hunt, 54
Cumberland Hunt, 159–160
Cursham, Robin, 145, 146
Curtis, Neil, MH, 171
Curre, Sir Edward, MFH, 149
Cusack-Smith, Lady (Mollie O'Rorke), MFH, 180
Cusack-Smith, Sir Dermot, MFH, 178
Cyprus, 59, 60–65, 68–79
Cyril, a squirrel, 24

*Daily Mirror*, 75
Dalgety, Arthur, MFH, 137
Dalgety, Hugh, MFH, 137
Dalmeny, Lord (aft. 6th Earl of Rosebery), 127–128
Dangar, Capt. Richard (16th/5th Lancers), 83, 85, 155
Daresbury, Lord, MFH, 180
Darley, Capt. Mark (RHG), 41
Darling, Gen. Sir Kenneth, 77
David Davies Hunt, 150
Davis, Frank, author, 100, 104
Davies, Lord, MFH, 150
Dawnay, Major-Gen. David, 52
Dayan, Gen. Moshe, 65
Dear, William (Police Special Branch), EOKA victim, 71
De Burgh and North Essex Bassets, 172
de Klee, Capt. Murray (Scots Gds), 65, 67
Derwent Hunt, 156

d'Harcourt, Marquise (France), 200, 201
Diamond Horseshoe, The, 34
Dillon, Major Viscount (RHG), 53
Dog fighting, 113
Dolbey, Robert (LG), 51
Dormer, Baron Charles (Belgium), 205
Dormer, Baron de Fierlant (Belgium), 205, 206
Dormer, Baron Thierry (Belgium), 205
Douglas-Home, Charles, (*The Times*), 208
Douglas-Home, Hon. George, 23
Douglas-Home, Hon. William, 23–24
Douro, Marquess of, (RHG) (aft. Duke of Wellington), 44, 62, 80
Downside school, 28
Doyle, Capt. Patrick (Middlesex Yeo), 13
Drag hunting, 109
Drakos, Markos (EOKA), 68
Drysdale, Andrew, MH, 139
Duke of Beaufort's Hunt, 125–126
Duke of Buccleuch's Hunt, 160–61
Dumfriesshire hunt, 54–55, 160, 202
Dummer Beagles, 167–68
Dunne, Martin, MFH, 130
Dunne, Capt. Thomas (RHG), MFH, 74, 132–33
d'Ursel, Comte Raphael (Belgium), 205–206

Eames, Col. Richard, MFH, 143–44
Earle, Lady (Quorn), 50
Early hounds (USA), 188–189
East African Wildlife Society, 110
East Down Hunt, 174
Easton Harriers, 140
Eberle, Admiral Sir James, MH, 170
Eden, Rt Hon. Sir Anthony, MP, 62, 66
Edinburgh, HRH, Prince Philip, Duke of, 20, 87, 94, 95, 208, 209, 212
Edwards, Jimmy, comedian, 135
Edwards, Lionel, artist, 24, 121, 125
Edwards, Piper (Irish Gds), 66
Eglinton Hunt, 161
Egremont, Lord, 94
Eisenhower, Gen. Dwight, 28, 66
Elizabeth II, HM Queen, 21, 82, 87, 95
Elizabeth, HM Queen (Queen Mother), 13, 35, 45
Elliott, Claude (Eton Headmaster) 18, 27, 29
Elliott, Philip (polo player), 210
El Morocco, The, 34
Embiricos, Anthony, polo player, 211
EOKA, 59, 60–65, 68–79
Equipagem de Santo Huberto (Portugal), 183–185
Eskdale and Ennerdale Hunt, 159

Essex Hunt, 140–141
Essex Union Hunt, 141
Eton College, 18–29, 39
Eton College Hunt, 18, 26, 29, 136, 165
Eton OTC, 27
Eton Shooting VIII, 26, 95
Evans, Mrs Brian, MFH, 146
Everard, Mrs (Quorn), 50

Fairbairn, George, MFH, 54, 159
Fanshawe, Major-General Evelyn, 50
Farquhar, Ian, MFH, 118, 125
Farquhar, Sir Peter, MFH, 118, 125, 177
Farrin, Michael (Quorn), 119
Fell Hunting, 158–159
Ferguson, Major Ronald, 52, 95
Fergusson, Brig. Sir Bernard, 38
Festival of Britain, 52–53
Feversham, Anne, Countess of, MFH, 155
Field, The, 107
Field sports controversy, 106–109
Fiennes, Sir Ranulph (Scots Greys), 90
Fife Hunt, 160
Filgate, William, MFH, 180
Firr, Tom (Quorn), 121
Firth, Capt. (QM) Charles (RHG), 42, 43
Fitzalan-Howard, Alexander, MH, 136, 169
Fitzpatrick, Sir Percy, author, 9
Fitzwilliam Hunt, 124
Fitzwilliam, Thomas, Earl, MFH, 124
Fleming, Peter, author, 24
Flint and Denbigh Hunt, 150–151
Floor, Jacqueline, 48, 49
Foley, Charles, journalist and author
    (quoted), 73
Foot, Sir Hugh (Lord Caradon), 70–71
Foot, Paul, 74
Foot Guards, The, 30, 41, 56, 58–59, 82, 94,
    96
Forestry Commission, 108
Foster, Edward, MFH, 168
Foster, Col Neil, MFH, 128
Four Burrow Hunt, 104, 146
400, The, 48
Fox destruction societies (Wales), 147
Foxhunting, social trends, 115–117
Fox-Strangways, Hon. John, 103
Fox-Strangways, Hon. Stephen (RHG),
    EOKA victim, 73, 76
Foxley Wood, Hants, 219
Franco, Gen. Francisco, 87
Freeman, Frank (Pytchley), 120–121, 130
French, Arthur, 128, 160
French hunting, 196–204

Game Fair (CLA), 104

Gannet: The Story of a Terrier (novel), 217
Garth and South Berks Hunt, 138
Gascon-Saintongeois hounds (France), 202
George VI, HM King, 13, 35, 45
Gibbs's school, 12
Gibraltar, 82–88
Gibson, Col. Leonard, MH, 163
Gibson, Mrs George, MFH, 120
Gillson, George (Warwickshire), 130
Gingell, Betty, MH, 140
Girouard, Mark, author, 100
Glamorgan Hunt, 148
Glubb, Sir John ('Glubb Pasha'), 59
Glue, Martin, polo player, 210
Godfrey-Cass, Corporal-of-Horse (RHG), 70,
    72
Gogerddan Hunt, 147
Gold Stick, 45, 47, 62
Gontard, Jacques (France), 202, 203
Gonzalez, Roberto, polo player, 211
Goodson, Sir Alfred and Lady, 153–54, 176,
    188
Gordon, Lt-Col C.G.M., MFH, 41, 42, 43,
    104, 155, 156
Goschen, Ken, MFH, 138
Gracida, Carlos, polo player, 211–12
Graham, Robert, polo player, 210
Granada, Spain, 79–80, 86
Grant-Lawson, Lt-Col Sir Peter (RHG), 42
Greene, Jenny, Editor, Country Life, 101, 222
Gregson, Mrs Mollie, MFH, 135–36, 146
Griffon hounds (France), 202
Grivas, Col. George (EOKA), 59, 61–63,
    69–74
Guadiaro Hunt, 182
Guards Club, 102
Guards Independent Parachute Company,
    56, 61, 63, 68, 81–82
Guards Polo Club, 208
Guinness Book of Records, 104
Gundry, Major Gerald, MFH, 18, 157, 165
Gupwell, Brian (Duke of Beaufort's), 132
Gurney, Mrs Anthony, MH, 140
Gwynne, Edmund, 26

Hailsham, Lord, 103
Hale, Anne (Percy), 152
Halifax, Charles, 2nd Earl of, MFH, 18, 155,
    164–165, 169
Halifax, Edward, 1st Earl of, 104
Hall, Major and Mrs Peter, MFH (Spain),
    182
Hamburg, 36–38
Hamleys, 13
Hampshire Hunt, 137–38

Hanbury, James, MFH, 122
Hannum, Mrs John B., MFH (USA), 187
Harbour Club, Cyprus, 64
Hardaway, Ben H., III, MFH (USA), 194–96
Harding, Gilbert, journalist, 47
Harding, Field Marshal Sir John, 62, 63, 65, 68, 70
Harding, Lady, 62, 65
Hare hunting, 108, 109
Harmsworth, Thomas (RHG) 77
Harper, Lt-Col A. F. (Hurlingham Polo Association), 210
Harrods, 12
Hassan, Rt Hon. Joshua (Gibraltar), 85
Harvey, Anthony, MH, 140
Harvey, Terence, MH, 162
Harvey-Kelly, Col and Mrs William (Ireland), 178
Hawkins, Lady Margaret, Lady-in-Waiting, 86
Hawkins, Capt. Richard, MFH, 128, 167
Headdon, George (Curre), 149
Heber Percy, Col Cyril, MFH, 51
Hellyer, Mrs Diana, MFH, 120
Hemphill, Lord and Lady, MsFH (Galway Blazers), 178
Hennessy, Hon. Mary Lou, 53
Herbert, Hon. Henry (RHG) aft. Earl of Pembroke), 78
Heythrop Hunt, 126–27, 195
Hibbert-Foy, Mrs (Ashford Valley), 163
Hillsboro Hunt (USA), 193, 194
Hilton-Green, Major Chetwode, MFH, 120, 137
Hilton-Green, Lady Helena (aft. Lady Daresbury), 120
Hinckley, Col. Albert P., MFH (USA), 33–35, 187–88
Hinckley, Mrs Gilbert, MFH, 124
Hine, Andrew, polo player, 210
Hipwood, Howard, polo player, 210
Hipwood, Julian, polo player, 210
Hoare, Major Robert, MFH, 123
Hoare, Mrs Robert, 123
Holcombe Harriers, 160
Holland Hibbert, Hon. Michael, MH, 26, 165, 168
Holman, David, 42, 55
Hope, Lord John, (aft. Lord Glendevon), 92
Hope-Jones, Mr, Eton master, 25
Hornor, Col John L. Jr (MFH), 28, 29, 32, 185, 193, 195
Horrocks, Gen Sir Brian (quoted), 40
Horsbrugh Porter, Lt-Col Sir Andrew, polo correspondent, 208

Horsfall, Lady, MH, 160
Horswell, John, polo player, 210
Hook, Col Hilary, white hunter, 109
Hoskyns, John (Rifle Bde), 31–32
Household Brigade Saddle Club, 50, 82
Howard-Vyse, Gen. Sir Richard, 26
Hudson Bay Company, 112
Hudson, Edward, founder of Country Life, 100
Hudson, Lance-Corporal (RHG), 56
Hughes-Hallet, Michael, 21
Humfrey, Major Charles (Quorn), 119
Hunting dress, 116–17
Hurlingham Polo Association, 209, 212, 213
Huson, 'Nobby', Eton master, 22, 25
Hutchinson, Leslie ('Hutch'), singer, 23
Hyatt, George, MFH, 146
Hyde Park Barracks, 43–53, 93–94, 97

Irish hunting, 172–180

Jackson, Alastair, MFH, 145, 167
Jamison, David, polo player, 211
Janssen, Baron (Belgium), 204
Janssen, Eric (Belgium), 204
Jedforest Hunt, 160
Jotham, Neal, Canadian Humane Societies, 112
Jordan, HM Hussein, King of, 95
Jordan, HM Muna, Queen of, 95
Judy, a bull terrier, 214
July hounds (USA), 195
Junior Leaders Regiment RAC, 96

Karios, Andreas, EOKA terrorist, 72, 74
Keightley, Gen. Sir Charles, 83, 84, 85, 87, 88
Keith, David, MFH, 21
Keith, Robin (LG), 52–53
Kendrew, Maj.-Gen. J., 63, 76
Kennedy, John F., US President, 90
Kent, Alan, polo player, 210
Kenya, 109–111
Kenyatta, Jomo, President of Kenya, 109
Khrushchev, Nikita, Russian Premier, 90
Kidston, Archibald, 26, 27
Kilkenny Hunt, 179
King Edward VII's Hospital (Sister Agnes's), 92
King's Reach Tower (IPC Magazines), 100–101
King's Royal Rifle Corps (60th Rifles), 30
Kipling, Rudyard, author and poet, 10, 25
Knox, James, MH, 163
Knutsford, Viscount, MFH, 165

Kruger, Gene, MFH, 177
Kutchuk, Dr Fazil, Turkish Cypriot leader, 75

Lambert, Legge, Eton master, 27
Lambert, Sophia (Mrs Nigel Peel), 132
Lambert, Stephen, MFH, 126, 129, 167, 168
Lanarkshire and Renfrewshire hunt, 160
Lancaster, Osbert, cartoonist, 103
Lane-Fox, George, MFH, 156
Langdale, Oliver, MFH, 165
Langley, Tim (Berkeley), 132
Larrabee, Sterling, MFH (USA), 34, 188
Lawrence, Gertrude, 23
Leconfield, Lord, 13–15
Leconfield, Violet, Lady, 15
Ledbury Hunt, 132–33
Lee, Dr and Mrs Henry, 23
Leeds, Sir George (Gren. Gds), 48
Lees, Douglas Harcourt, MFH (USA), 191
Leigh, Col. W. H. Gerard, (LG), 44
Letts, Martin, MFH, 167
Lewis (Hendry), Eiluned, author, 100
Liddell, Alvar, 31
Life Guards, 39–40, 88, 90
Limerick Hunt, 180
Linlithgow and Stirlingshire Hunt, 160
Linnet, a terrier, 218
Lisney, Travers, MFH, 123
Llangibby Hunt, 150
Lloyd, Rt Hon. Selwyn, MP, 66, 70
Lockwood, Arthur, MFH, 131
Long, Thomas F., MFH, 177
Lonsdale, Norman, 21
Louth Hunt, 180
Loyd, Gen. Sir Charles, 82
Loyd, Major William (LG), 139
Lunesdale Hunt, 159
Lyster, Mr and Mrs Guy (East Essex), 140

Maiden, Chris (Berkeley), 132
Maitland, Col and Mrs, 11
Maitland-Carew, Hon. Gerald, MFH, 161
Makarios III, Mouskou, Archbishop of Cyprus, 62, 70, 78–79
Makellis, Antonis, EOKA terrorist, 78
Makins, Sir Paul, 88
Makins, Lady, 88
Malden, Viscount (Middlesex Yeo), 13
Mann, Alastair, MFH, 129, 164
Mann, Douglas, MFH, 129, 164
Mann, Jock, MFH, 129, 132, 164
Manners, Hon. Robert, MH, 18
Margaret, HRH Princess, 21, 45
Marlborough College Beagles, 166–167

Marten, Sir Henry, 21
Martyn, Mr and Mrs Anthony, MsFH, 148
Mary, HM Queen, 45
Mary HRH Princess (Princess Royal), 85–86, 140
Masters of Foxhounds Association, 107
Matterson, Capt. Robert (Percy), 152
Meads, Jim, hunting photographer, 123
Melbreak Hunt, 159
Mellon, Paul, MFH (USA), 190
Mells Hunt (USA), 193
Melton Hunt Club, 119
Melton Mowbray, 49–51
Menderes, Adnan, Turkish Premier, 75
Merlin, a Blues horse, 50
Merry, Davina, 48
Meynell Hunt, 124–125
Middlesex Yeomanry (Duke of Cambridge's Own Hussars), 13, 15
Middleton Hunt, 155–156
Midland Hunt (USA), 194–195
Milburn, Richard, MH, 165
Miller, Lt-Col Sir John, (Welsh Gds), 32–33, 128
Millington-Drake, Marie, 74
Milroy, The, 48
Mollet, M. Guy, French Premier, 66
Mond, Hon. Julian, MH, (Lord Melchett), 18
Monmouth, James Duke of, 121
Monspey, Comtesse de (France), 203
Montgarret, Lord, MFH, 156
Montgomery, William, MFH (Ulster), 178
Moore, Daphne, 125, 126
Mooreland Hunt (USA), 194
Moralee, Danny (Percy), 152
Morales, Luis, linguist, 88
Morgan, Tom and Elsie, MsFH, 176, 180
Morley, Earl and Countess of, 143
Mostyn, Mrs Timothy, 144
Motion, Robert, MFH, 166
Mountbatten, Admiral of the Fleet, Earl, of Burma, 86, 95
Murray, Trooper (RHG), 69
Murray Smith, Lt-Col. G. A., MFH, 104, 122–23
Murray Smith, Mrs G. A. (Sally), 122
Murray Smith, Mrs Ulrica, MFH, 119, 122
Muskerry Hunt, 179
Muthaiga Club, Kenya, 110
MacAndrew, Capt. Hon. Colin, 54, 154
Macdonald-Buchanan, Capt. John, polo player, 209
Mackenzie, Stuart, polo player, 211
MacMillan, Rt Hon. Harold, MP, 70, 72, 94
McCalmont, Major Victor, MFH, 177, 178–179

McCalmont, Mrs Victor, 177, 178–179
McCreery, Michael, 23
McCreery, General Sir Richard, 23
McEwan, Major Michael, MFH, 176
McKeever, Mrs Betty, MH, 163

NATO, 89
Nasser, Col. Gamal, President of Egypt, 59, 66
Nature Conservancy Council, 219
Nature reserves, 105
Naylor-Leyland, Capt. Michael (LG), 49
Naylor-Leyland, Sir Philip, MFH, 124
Newcastle and District Beagles, 163
New Forest buckhounds, 108
New Forest foxhounds, 137
Niall, Ian (John McNeillie), author, 100, 101, 104
Nicholas, Harry, MFH (USA), 186
Nix, Major Christopher (Royal Sussex), 16
Norfolk, Bernard, Duke of (Royal Sussex), 16
North Cotswold Hunt, 132
North Norfolk Harriers, 140
Northumberland, Hugh, 10th Duke of, 18, 151–53, 165, 169
Northumberland, Elizabeth, Duchess of, 152
Nuttall, Capt. Sir Nicholas (RHG), 78

Old Dominion Hunt (USA), 29, 32–34, 187–189
Old Surrey and Burstow Hunt, 135, 164
Operation Musketeer, 65–68
Orange County Hunt (USA), 33, 188, 190
Orchid Room, The, 48
Otter hunting, 109
Owen, Joan (Eton Dame), 23–24

Packer, Kerry, polo player, 211
Paddy, an Irish horse, 173
Palmer Milburn Beagles, 165
Palmer, Roger, MH, 165
Parachute Regt, 56, 59, 65
Paravicini, Nicholas (LG), 92
Parker, David, MFH, 133
Parker, Mrs Richard, MFH, 131
Parry, C. N. de Courcy, MFH, 55, 137
Payne-Gallwey, Lt-Col. Sir Peter (11th Hussars), 42
Pedersen, Trooper (Blues and Royals), 97, 98
Peel, Nigel, MFH, 132, 157
Pembroke, Col. Richard (Coldstream Gds), 99
Pembroke, Edward, author's great grandfather, 12

Pembrokeshire hunt, 146
Pendle Forest and Craven Harriers, 160
Penn-Marydel hounds (USA), 186–87, 193
Pentathlon, The British, 56, 92
Per Ardua Beagles, 167
Percy Hunt, 151–52
Peterborough Hound Show, 118, 130
Petworth, Sussex, 11, 12, 24, 214–15
Pickering Hunt (USA), 186
Piedmont Hunt (USA), 33, 189, 190
Pilkington, Ian (RHG) 69, 72, 73
Pirbright camp, 57–58
Poitou (Poitevin) hounds, (France), 202
Polo, 104–105, 208–213
Pony Club, 14, 116, 210
Poole, Willie, MFH, 165
Porter, Michael, MFH, 138
Portman, Davina, 48–49
Pratt's Club, 102–103
Proctor, Trooper (RHG), EOKA victim, 73, 76
Professional Hunters' Association (Kenya), 110
Pryse, Marjorie, Lady, MFH, 147
Purves, Peter, (Police Special Branch), 71
Pytchley Hunt, 120–121

Quaglino's Restaurant, 48
Quaker Church, Boston, 114
Queen Charlotte's Ball, 48
Quickswood, Lord, 21
Quorn Hunt, 21, 51, 118–119

Radbourne, James (Essex Hunt), 141
Radley College Beagles, 166
Radnorshire and West Herefordshire Hunt, 132
RAF Abingdon, 57, 81
Rallye Campine (Belgium), 204, 207–208
  Chapeau (France), 197, 203
  Les Amognes (France), 197, 202
  L'Aumance (France), 199–203
  La Folie (France), 202, 203
  Nomade (France), 197, 198–199
  Trois-Forêts (France), 197
  Vielsalm (Belgium), 204, 206
  Villers-Cotterets (France), 197, 198
  Vouzeron (France), 197, 199–202
Randolph, Mrs Archibald, MFH (USA), 189
Rappahannock Hunt (USA), 33
Reincke, Miles, 37
Rhett, Harry Moore Jr, MFH (USA), 194
Richthofen, Baronin Rosa von, 37–38
Rifle Brigade, 28, 30–32, 35–36
Rifle Depot, The, Winchester, 30

Roberts, Simon, MFH, 156, 166
Robinson, Mrs, EOKA victim, 76
Roch-Perks, Mrs (Ireland), 173
Rock 'n Roll, 65
Rodeo riding, 113
Roffe-Sylvester, Michael, MFH, 144
Rollin, Prof. Bernard (animal welfarist), 112
Rome Hunt, 182
Ronda, Spain, 99
Rook, Major Lawrence (RHG), 41
Routh, C. R. N. (Dick), Eton housemaster,
    21, 23, 24, 26, 28, 38
Rouse-Boughton, Mary, MFH, 133
Royal Agricultural College Beagles, 167
Royal Artillery, 25 Regt, 69, 76
Royal Artillery, 29 Regt, 69, 76
Royal Horse Guards (Blues), 38, 39–53,
    88–99
Royal Rock Beagles, 162
Royal Scots Greys, 90
Royal Sussex Regt, 15–16
Royal Ulster Rifles, 69, 74, 76
RSPCA, 103, 107
Rutland, Charles, Duke of, MFH, 121
Ryan, Thaddeus ('Thady'), MFH, 166,
    175–176
Rycroft, Sir Newton, MFH, 137, 167

Sabu, actor, 12
Sale, Col George (Middlesex Yeo.), 13, 38
Sale, Richard (RHG), 42
Sale, Col. Walter (RHG), 38, 42
Samaras, Christos (EOKA terrorist), 74
Samaras, Elias (EOKA terrorist), 74
Samworth, David, MFH, 120
Sassoon, Siegfried (quoted), 123
Scarteen Hunt (the 'Black and Tans'), 175
School of Infantry Beagles, 169
Scott Henderson committee on mammal
    control, 107
Scott, Peter, artist and conservationist, 24
Seal culling, 113
Sebastian, a terrier, 59
Sefton, Blues and Royals horse, 96–99, 114
Selby-Lowndes, Angela, 10
Selby-Lowndes, William, MFH, 127–28
Seymour-Williams, John, MH, 163
Shaw, George Bernard (quoted), 116
Shaw, Major John, (MFH), 104
Shipley village, Sussex, 215–21
Silver Stick, 45
Sinnington Hunt, 155
16th Parachute Brigade, 56, 57
67th (Armoured Car) Training Regt, 53–55
Skrine, Mrs Charles (Island Hunt), 173

Sloan, George, MFH (USA), 192
Smiley, Col. David (RHG), 42, 56
Smith, Mr, a cat, 10, 214
Smith Ryland, Sir Charles, polo player, 209
Smith's Lawn (Windsor Great Park), 82, 209
Somerleyton, Lord, MH, 140
Somerset and Cornwall Light Infantry, 83
Somerville, Edith, author, 175
South Devon Hunt, 146
South Dorset Hunt, 145
South Durham Hunt, 154
Southwell, Max, MH, 167
South Wold Hunt, 131–32
Spencer, Earl, 27, 121
Spencer, Countess, 121
Spoelberch, Vicomtesse de (France), 199
Spooner's and West Dartmoor Hunt, 143
St George, Col Ferris (LG), 46, 49, 52, 53
St James's Club, 102
St James's Palace, 46
St Michael's Cave (Gibraltar), 86
St Oswald, Lord, 87–88
Stacpoole, Capt. John (Parachute Regt), 64
Staghunting, 108
Stephenson, Brig. John, MFH, 133
Stevens, Christine, animal welfarist, 112
Stevens, John, MFH, 167
Stewart, Major Alastair, MFH, 155
Stirling, Charles, MFH, 154, 165
Stockwell, Gen. Sir Hugh, 66
Stoney, Cdr Oliver (Ballymacad), 178
Stowe Beagles, 167
Stourton, Major Michael (Gren. Gds), 76–77
Stringer, Major William, MH, 138
Surrey Union Hunt, 14, 137
Sutcliffe, Mrs, EOKA victim, 76
Sutherland, Capt Fergus, 180

Tanatside Hunt, 150
Tate, Sir Henry and Lady (Cottesmore),
    119–120
Taunton Vale Foxhounds, 145
Taunton Vale Harriers, 145
Telfer-Smollett, Michael, 37–38
Thomas, John, MFH, 146
Thynne, Lady Caroline, 48
Times, The, 9, 113, 208–209
Tonge, George (huntsman), 51
Tonson-Rye, Eudo and Rosemary, 79, 80
Towneley, Mr and Mrs Simon, 160
Trinity Foot Beagles, 163, 168
Tramontana, champion polo team, 211–212
Trollope-Bellew, Martin, MFH, 131, 132
Turner, Lt-Col V. B., VC (Rifle Bde), 35–36,
    38

Tweedmouth, Col Lord (RHG), 102
12th Lancers, 78
Tynedale Hunt, 54, 154

Ullswater Hunt, 158
University College, Oxford, 38
Unwin, Timothy, MFH, 118, 132
Ure, Sir John, diplomat, 184

Wales, HRH Prince of, 97, 111, 119, 126,
    128–29, 143, 148, 212
Wales, HRH Princess of, 27 97
Waldorf Astoria Hotel, 33–35
Walker, Mrs Diana Barnato, MFH, 135
Walker, Lance-Corporal (LG), 56
Walker hounds (USA), 192, 193
Wallace, Capt. R. E., MFH, 18, 118, 126,
    135, 142, 145, 165, 166
Wallace, William, polo player, 209
Wallis, Patience (Woodland Pytchley), 115
Walsh, John (WSPA), 112
Walter, Catherine ('Skittles'), 122
Walter Reed hospital (Washington), 33
Walters, Jeremy, MH, 167
Warburton Lee, Hetty (aft.
    Fetherstonhaugh), 104, 134
Warre, Anthony, MFH, 124
Warre, Edmond, 25
Warre, William, 25
Warrenton Hunt, USA, 33, 190–191
Warwickshire Hunt, 129–130
Waterford, Marquis of, 178
Watson, Arthur, author's grandfather, 13
Watson, Gerard, author's father, 9, 15–17,
    20–21, 214, 215–216
Watson, Jean (aft. Hornor, then Carlos-
    Clarke), author's mother, 15–17, 20, 28,
    38, 79, 99
Watson, Lavinia Marie, author's wife, 29,
    109, 111, 119, 131, 133, 135, 136–137, 140,
    153, 154, 161, 175, 184, 194, 195, 206,
    208–209, 215–223
Watson, Michael, author's brother, 19, 22,
    24, 27, 121
Watson, Moray, author's brother, 13, 17, 27,
    32, 33, 79
Waugh, Auberon (RHG), 73
Waugh, Evelyn (quoted), 116
Webster, Clarence (Warwickshire), 129
Webster, Jim (Belvoir), 121–22

Wedderburn, Alexander, QC, 103–104
Wedderburn, Major David (Gren. Gds), 74
Wellington Barracks, 94–95
Werve de Schilde, Roland and Anne van
    der, 204
Weser Vale Bloodhounds, 104, 138
Westmorland, Capt Earl of (RHG), 44, 49, 97
Westbury, Lord, MFH, 155, 157
West Carbery Hunt, 175
Western Hunt, 146
Wexford Hunt, 180
Whaddon Chase Hunt, 127
Whistler, Gen. Sir Lashmir, 15
White, Hon. Luke, MFH, 167
White's Club, 27, 103
Wick and District Beagles, 163
Wildlife conservation, 105, 111–112
Wilhelmina, Queen of the Netherlands, 43
Williams, Dorian, MFH, 128
WIlliams, John, MFH, 104, 146
Williams, Ian, MFH, 154
Williams Wynn, Sir Watkin's, Hunt, 104,
    133–34
Wilson, Hon. B. C. (RHG), Lord
    Nunburnholme, 51, 74
Wilson, Elsie, MFH, 123–24
Wilson, Rt Hon. Harold, MP, 95
Wilson, James (RHG), 77–78
Wilson, Lady, 32
Wilson, Mrs Tyler (USA), 190
Wilson of Libya, Field Marshal Lord, 32
Windsor, HRH Duke of, 86, 140
Windsor, Duchess of, 86,
Windsor Forest Bloodhounds, 139
Winston Churchill Memorial Trust, 111–114
Winterton, Earl, 15
Withers, Paul, polo player, 210
World Society for the Protection of Animals,
    112
Worsley, Gen. Sir Richard (Rifle Bde), 35
Worthington, Capt. Charles (RHG), 62
Wright, Peter (Cottesmore), 131
Wye College Beagles, 168

Yarborough, John, Earl of, MFH, 131
York and Ainsty (North) Hunt, 156
York and Ainsty (South) Hunt, 156–57
Younghusband, Anthony, MFH, 127

Zetland Hunt, 54, 154